D1565194

Democracy Unbound

Progressive Challenges to the Two Party System

David Reynolds

South End Press

Boston

Cover design by Beth Fortune
Text design and production in Garamond and Bernhard Modern typefaces
by the South End Press collective

Printed in the U.S.A.

Any properly footnoted quote of up to 500 sequential words may be used without permission, as long as the total number of words quoted does not exceed 2,000. For longer quotes or for a greater number of total words, please write for permission from South End Press.

Library of Congress Cataloging-in-Publication Data
Reynolds, David, 1963-
        Democracy unbound : progressive challenges to the two party system /David Reynolds.
            p.   cm.
        Includes bibliographical references and index.
        ISBN 0-89608-564-3 (cloth). -- ISBN 0-89608-563-5 (pbk.)
        1. Third parties (United States politics) 2. Progressivism
    (United States politics) 3. Democracy--United States.   I. Title.
    JK2265.R67   1997
    324.273--dc21   96-46276
                                                                  CIP

South End Press, 116 Saint Botolph Street, Boston, MA 02115
03 02 01 00 99 98 97   1 2 3 4 5 6 7

Democracy Unbound

Acknowledgments

There are those who struggle for a day and they are good. There are others who struggle for a year, and they are better. There are those who struggle many years, and they are better still. But, there are those who struggle all their lives: These are the indispensable ones.

— Bertolt Brecht

As this book has been a long time in the making, the contributions of many have helped to make it a reality. Much of the inspiration has come from the many informal discussions, debates, and real life activism in which I have been fortunate to participate for the past several years.

In addition, my dissertation committee at Cornell University provided the support and room to maneuver needed to write the precursor to this book: *Movement Politics: Grassroots Progressive Political Activism as Seen Through Jesse Jackson's 1988 Campaign.* My thanks to Michael Goldfield, Theodore Lowi, Elizabeth Sanders, and Pierre Clavel. Also while at Cornell, under the encouraging direction of Vivienne Shue, I undertook an independent study of the classics of socialist thought. This project provided me, early in my career, with the intellectual models of politically engaged scholarship that informs this current work. And at the Cornell Writing Center, I received enthusiastic tutoring from Keith Hjortshoj, who set me on the road to producing good prose.

My writing style was further enriched by my experience working for the UAW's national magazine *Solidarity.* Special thanks to Dave Elsila, Michael Funke, Nancy Brigham, and the other members of the publications department who taught me how to write from a human interest angle as well as offering me their wonderful friendship.

My life would not have taken the course it did had it not been for the political awakening I received in Gary Olson's political science classes at Moravian College. Thanks, Gary, for the wisdom and your friendship. The faculty of the history department also provided the kind of welcoming and open intellectual atmosphere that allowed a young undergraduate to grow in the world of thought and politics.

At South End Press, editor Steve Chase and intern Doug Watson combined excellent feedback with warm and friendly interaction. The same can be said of the South End Press collective generally—a professional, yet down-to-earth and welcoming bunch.

Years ago my parents, James and Mary Reynolds, set me on the road of concern for bettering the world. Their involvement has greatly influenced this book. Without their loving and unflagging material and moral support, I would not have been in a position to have researched and produced it in the first place. My mother not only raised me, but now has also become my proofreader. Thanks for all the hours spent wading through my first drafts. My companion, Susan Santone, also read early parts of this manuscript. Furthermore, her enthusiasm for the book and loving friendship helped me get through this rather long and involved project.

Finally, I can not thank enough the activists with whom I interacted and interviewed in preparing this book. They provided more than simple research data. They took time out of their busy schedules to meet with a stranger and share ideas. Their warm friendship, reflections on politics, and outright enthusiasm for what they are doing animate this book. In the words of Bertolt Brecht, "These are the indispensable ones." When I use such phrases as "our subject matter" or "our research," it is to this larger "we" I refer.

Breaking
the Two Party Monopoly

In November 1994, the Republican election victories were the big story on the evening news. While they didn't make it to the headlines, however, other groups also celebrated that Tuesday night.

In Vermont, independent progressive Bernie Sanders went on to his third term as the state's sole member of the US House of Representatives, defeating his Republican opponent in a hard-fought race. The Democrats had long ceased to be serious contenders in this contest. Also, that same day, in President Clinton's former town, Little Rock, Arkansas, activists from the local branch of the national New Party won a working majority on the school board while placing two New Party candidates on the city council and one New Party Democrat into the state legislature. The New Progressive Party (NPP) of Wisconsin, as the state's New Party chapter is named, celebrated its success in gaining enough votes for state treasurer to legally establish a place on the state ballot. Earlier that year, seven NPP candidates won election or re-election to the Dane County board which meets in Madison, the state capital and the county seat. In nearby Milwaukee, New Party Democrat incumbent Johnnie Morris-Tatum won a second term in the Wisconsin legislature.

Elsewhere, Green candidate Keiko Bonk-Abramson was re-elected to the county board of supervisors for the island of Hawaii, while the Green Party in New Mexico celebrated their legal major party status, with their candidate for governor receiving 11 percent of the vote and their state treasurer nominee 33 percent. While mainstream Democrats were going down to defeat that Tuesday, progressive Democrats, especially those with activist backgrounds, held their own or won elections. For example, activists involved with the Legislative Electoral Action Program (LEAP) in Connecticut saw twenty-five out of the thirty-five of their endorsed candidates win, including seven newcomers to the state legislature and their candidate for secretary of state, Miles Rappenport.

Many of those currently in power would like us to believe that these examples are unique and scattered cases that do not add up to anything.

This book is based on the opposite interpretation. These cases are but the tip of the iceberg. Today we can see the beginnings of a progressive movement to overthrow the two party monopoly and to decisively redirect the course of the nation.

The signs of this growing activism are everywhere. Early in 1995, the local branch of the New Party in Chicago won a stunning victory in their first electoral effort when Michael Chandler beat the fifteen-year-incumbent alderman in the city's twenty-fourth ward. By mid-1995, the still very young national New Party had built an electoral record of winning well over two-thirds of all the races that its candidates entered, with almost 100 officeholders throughout the nation. By the same time, the Green Party similarly could boast over seventy-five officeholders. In Burlington, Vermont, the Progressive Coalition retook the mayor's office in 1995 and won seven out of fourteen seats on the board of alderman, thus continuing their dominance of city politics for the past decade and a half. In 1994, progressive Mike Ferner ran an independent campaign for mayor of Toledo, Ohio, losing by a few hundred votes. In Pittsburgh, Pennsylvania, activists established the Independent Political Action Network, while in Houston, Texas, they set up the New Democracy Party. The summer of 1995 witnessed two gatherings of independent progressives and third party organizers—the National Independent Politics Summit in Pittsburgh and the Third Parties '96 gathering in Washington, DC. In June of 1996, after years of grassroots organizing, Labor Party Advocates launched a national Labor Party in Cleveland, Ohio.

While these efforts are promising, most Americans are unaware of this growing progressive activism. There are at least two reasons for this. First, the movement is locally based. Its activists aim to reshape US politics by rebuilding democracy from the grassroots on up, not by running some charismatic, but ultimately short-lived candidate for president, *a la* Ross Perot. Furthermore, the national media has largely ignored this story. Amid the thousands of words pronouncing the supposed move rightward of US politics in 1994, no mention was made of the fact that Vermonters re-elected a socialist as their sole federal representative.

The purpose of this book is to tell the story of this rich and growing movement. We want to inspire people to take the prospects of independent and third party organizing seriously. People have to begin "thinking the unthinkable." The two party system is vulnerable to being overthrown and there are many progressive groups out there organizing to do just that. We also want to provide would-be third party activists with a concrete sense of how one conducts electoral politics and builds a political organization. For this reason, we offer several case studies of progressive activism in enough detail so that people can get a sense of how to do this and what to avoid in their own communities. Finally, through our examples of several contrasting models, and our analysis of current opportunities and obstacles, we alert would-be activists to the strategic questions and trade-offs that the movement needs to think about as we move forward. With this in mind, let us turn to this growing experience...

What Makes Current Progressive Political Organizing Different

Often when we mention this book in casual conversation, people ask if it has anything to do with the Libertarians or Ross Perot—the kinds of independent political efforts that the media does expose people to.[1] Readers of this book will find few references to such efforts. The progressive activism that we discuss is a quite different animal.

The Ross Perot and Libertarian-type examples simply are not as significant as the groups we are studying. The corporate media provides them relatively greater coverage because they are more in line with official mainstream politics than progressive efforts. Yet, progressive organizing encompasses a much deeper and more developed level of grassroots organizing than do the Perot spin-offs or groups like the Libertarians. Progressives also advance an agenda that is truly independent of the major parties. Ross Perot, by contrast, simply offers another variation on the dominant corporate agenda.

Most importantly, Perot and the Libertarians are narrow electoral projects, while the groups we researched have broader social movement roots. This distinction is key. Mainstream political figures and groups that become disenchanted with the particular strategies and policies of their major parties have a long history of taking a plunge into independent politics—be they Theodore Roosevelt and his Progressive Party of 1912, John Anderson with Common Cause in 1980, or Ross Perot with United We Stand in 1992 and the Reform Party in 1996. While these efforts may get an impressive tally of votes in a specific election, they have not lasted very long. They run candidates and seek to win votes. When the election is over and they have not won, they typically fade. Unfortunately, these examples are what commonly passes for "third party politics" in official political debate.

By contrast, the groups that we examine are best described as currents of social movement activism that have adopted an electoral form. All of our progressive groups are based in local, grassroots, and social-movement-style activism. In fact, one of the central characteristics of progressive political organizing is its blurring of the distinction between electoral and non-electoral activity. Progressive political groups organize year round, regardless of whether they happen to be running for some office. As will become clear, if the progressive initiatives that we examine never ran another candidate, they would remain quite active.

This book examines political movements in the broadest sense of the term *political*. If we were to focus simply on election campaigns and vote-getting, we would, at best, describe only a small part of the story.

Because our official two party system operates within such narrow candidate- and electoral-centered terms, observers outside of progressive activism have had a difficult time appreciating or even realizing the existence of the growing progressive revolt.

Progressive groups can not be judged on the conventional basis of electoral results alone. While progressive groups have had growing success in electing their candidates to office, independent progressive politics operates within broader movement-building goals. Activists are using political organizing not just to win votes, but to develop a popular and comprehensive "people's" agenda, build broad coalitions among different progressive groups, reach out to and mobilize ordinary people who are currently apolitical, and build grassroots structures that allow people to actually participate in democracy. Progressive activists see their ultimate goal as rebuilding the US Left as a mass social movement. They thus have more in common with what we commonly call "social movements"—the Civil Rights movement, the labor movement, and the women's movement—than they do with Ross Perot, the Libertarians, or the Republican and Democratic Parties.

The Structure of the Book

Democracy Unbound divides into three main sections. Part One provides some background on where we are coming from and where we are heading. Within this section, Chapter One offers a brief history and analysis of progressive third party organizing in this country, focusing on the two most successful movements—the Populist and Socialist revolts of a century ago. As we will see, progressive attempts to challenge the two party system have been much stronger and had more of an impact on our nation than the official, mainstream historical memory would have us believe. Chapter Two examines the reasons for the defeat of populism and socialism, the failure of a national third party to develop out of the Great Depression, and the seeming disappearance of independent progressive politics during the 1950s, 1960s, and 1970s. In Chapter Three, we suggest how the more recent transformation of the nation's political economy has revived the prospects for progressive electoral activism—indeed, the opportunities for independent politics appear quite promising. We point to Jesse Jackson's two campaigns for the presidency as an important signpost for the growth in progressive activism. For Chapter Four, we dig deeper and use case studies from the grassroots mobilizations that surrounded Jackson's 1988 bid to illustrate the basic techniques that local activists used to organize volunteer-driven electoral campaigns.

The book's next section describes concrete examples of progressive activism today. As we will see, progressive activists are experimenting with a variety of approaches and strategies. Chapter Five examines the party-within-a-party model developed by the Legislative Electoral Action Program (LEAP) in Connecticut. The group was founded to bring together progressive organizations to run fellow activists for state offices as Democrats. As it has developed, the coalition has also fostered notable cooperation among progressive groups outside the campaign season. While remaining within the electoral confines of the Democratic Party, LEAP activists aim for the same goals as the other groups discussed in this book, namely finding ways to expand progressive activism, generate a popular alternative agenda, and develop a broader, more unified progressive political movement.

Chapter Six describes the success of the Progressive Coalition in Vermont. Starting with Bernie Sanders' surprise 1981 win for mayor of Burlington, the state's largest city, Vermont progressives have elected the one and only independent member of the US Congress to their state's sole seat in the House of Representatives. The Coalition is today laying the ground work for a statewide political party. In the meantime, activists operate as a coalition of individuals who run candidates independent of either major party.

In Chapter Seven, we examine the New Party, an outright national third party effort. Using the detailed example of its most developed state chapter, the Wisconsin branch, we outline the New Party's basic bottom-up, long-range strategy. As we show at the end of the chapter, the New Party is a vibrant and rapidly growing organization.

In Chapter Eight, we compare the New Party experience to that of other national groups, including the Labor Party Advocates, the Campaign for a New Tomorrow, and the Greens. We also examine the strengths and weaknesses that come from progressive activism being divided among so many different organizations. We will point to possible models for establishing greater operational unity over time, including two current unity-building efforts.

In the final section of the book, we look toward the future. Chapter Nine takes a serious look at the practical obstacles and opportunities confronting the electoral efforts of the progressive political movement. While the ability of the national media to ignore and distort progressive activism may seem daunting, we suggest that grassroots organizing still has a quite powerful role to play in US politics, one that is commonly understated. We also argue that, in addition to building active local groups, progressives need to press for changes in the electoral system. We outline several current efforts by groups to enact real campaign finance reform, introduce proportional representation systems, ease ballot access, and lift laws banning fusion candidacies.

In Chapter Ten, we highlight the potential dangers that successfully winning office can present to a movement dedicated to progressive ideals and democratic empowerment. In other countries, as well as more local experiences in this country, there is a history of progressive governments that, in the eyes of many of their supporters, have failed to live up to their founding ideals. Specifically, we examine the controversial experience of European and Canadian Social Democracy to sort out the positive aspects from those practices that many US progressives do not want to repeat. We then offer suggestions for how to build a lasting and democratic party with a fresh programmatic vision.

We conclude the book with a short chapter pointing out the benefits that a political party can provide to progressive activists building a diverse, successful movement for fundamental change, including benefits quite apart from the issue of electing officeholders. The book ends with a call to "think the unthinkable" and actively encourages readers to become involved in independent political organizing in their communities.

To help readers further explore the topic of progressive politics, we have also included an annotated bibliography. In addition, we provide the names and addresses for all of the groups that we have studied in the hope that readers will contact them directly. This book is an unabashed attempt to build a strong alternative to the two party system and reinvigorate US democracy. Its ultimate value is as an organizing tool.

The Author's Personal Relation to the Material

This book began as a dissertation on the grassroots mobilizations that surrounded Jesse Jackson's 1988 campaign. In exploring these local experiences, I began to see an emerging political potential that most commentators had completely missed. As time went on, the progressive activism that revealed itself during Jackson's campaign both broadened and deepened into more long-term efforts aimed at generating an independent political movement. Yet, outside of a few articles in progressive publications, this emerging movement has gone unnoticed. To my knowledge, this work is the first book-length treatment of the subject.

This research has not been simply an academic undertaking. I have been personally involved in progressive political organizing for some years. While in graduate school in the late 1980s and early 1990s, I had the good fortune to live in Ithaca, New York at a time when progressives emerged to become the dominant force in that city's politics. I volunteered to "pound the pavement" and "hit the phones" for city council races. I also had the rewarding experience of helping re-elect socialist and community activist Ben Nichols as the city's mayor (Nichols and others ran using the Democratic Party ballot line—paralleling LEAP's strategy outlined in Chapter Five). During Nichols' first term in office, I served on a citizen commission to investigate and make recommendations concerning the troubled relations between the community and its dominant private institution, Cornell University.

In addition to interview and document-based research, I have tried, whenever possible, to attend the meetings of the groups studied and to join in their activities. Thus, for example, this research took me door-to-door on the streets of Milwaukee one summer to spread the word about the local Living Wage Campaign. I am also a member of many of the groups studied here, including the New Party, the Labor Party, and the National Committee for Independent Political Action.

The energy and enthusiasm of people involved in building progressive independent politics has made this research an enjoyable and rewarding experience. While it is difficult to convey the lived experience between the pages of a book, I hope that some fraction of the excitement level of these groups comes through. The emerging progressive movement to challenge "politics as usual" is a truly inspiring story.

Part One

The Rise, Fall, and Rebirth
of Independent Politics

Chapter One

Rediscovering Our Legacy
The Populist and Socialist Years

> You know, if you look at US history,
> you people have a really radical country.
>
> —anonymous Australian student of US history

How do you prevent people who are fed up with the way they are being treated from doing anything about it? It's simple: deprive them of any sense that people have ever fought back. Most important, under no circumstance let them know that their forebearers achieved anything by doing so.

This point shows up clearly in the area of independent politics. For example, when I talk to people about establishing a new party—one that will actually reflect their reality, needs, and hopes—I get few objections to the general concept. The catch, however, comes with the reply, "Yeah, but I don't think it's possible. After all, third parties have never worked in the past." In response, I often mention the Socialist government in Milwaukee, the Populist legislature of Kansas, and the Communist congressman from New York. I describe scenes of thousands of farmers and workers camped out for days at a time at Socialist and Populist summer encampments, the radical church meetings, the Socialist and Populist lecturers, the radical schools. I mention that one of the three founding organs establishing the modern mass circulation newspaper was the *Appeal to Reason*, an openly Populist and then Socialist publication. I point to the extreme and often violent measures that the Democrats and Republicans took to block these efforts and ask: "If these movements were marginal parties with no chance of success, why did they receive such opposition from the two major parties?" In response, people often look at me and say: "I never knew that."

It is not accidental that few Americans know the long history of political activism outside the two major parties. After all, this powerful story could inspire us to think dangerous, subversive thoughts. Who knows, we might try the "impossible" and challenge the two party system. In the cause of encouraging just such "subversion," this chapter offers a brief sample of that history.

The bulk of the chapter examines the two most powerful progressive political movements in our nation's history: the Populist and Socialist revolts of a century ago. By delving into these movements in some detail, we aim to provide readers with a realistic picture of how activists can organize a serious political challenge on US soil. The great Populist and Socialist revolts, however, had many precursors. The efforts of ordinary people to organize politically on their own behalf goes back to the earliest days of the colonial settlement of this country. It is to this story we turn first.

Political Organizing in Colonial America and the Young Republic

Contrary to the rosy image most of us were fed in school, early America was anything but a tranquil time in which unified communities worked together to build a society of freedom and equality. Those who ran the colonies firmly believed that the vast majority of the population should have no role in politics. In their opinion, women, African Americans, native peoples, and indentured servants were considered some combination of property, savage, or dependent, childlike creatures. The distribution of political and economic power was hardly ideal for most of the white male population, either. At the moment of the outbreak of the War for Independence in 1776, less than 10 percent of the population owned fully one-half of all the wealth in the colonies.

These sharp divisions in early America propelled continuous and varied forms of popular organizing. The "proper and dignified" elements in colonial society had a notable tendency to resort to violence in order to keep the "rabble" in line. This repression, coupled with the political exclusion of most ordinary people by laws requiring various levels of property ownership to vote, meant that popular organizing often took on an armed character. For example, in 1676, crass colonial exploitation by the English crown combined with open political corruption and blatantly unfair taxation to spark Bacon's Rebellion. Through an armed, popular uprising, small farmers, indentured servants, slaves, and even some planters took over the Virginia capital for several months. Not all political conflict in early America was violent, however. In New England, for example, town meetings provided a forum for popular democracy at a local level. At times, popular influence even spread into the higher reaches of colonial government. In 1740, for example, ordinary people in Massachusetts gained control of the provisional assembly and, much to the horror of the rich, proceeded to enact measures designed to ease the crushing burden of debt.

Popular organizing was much in evidence at the birth of the United States. By the outbreak of the War for Independence, workers, artisans, and small farmers had gained the political upper hand in Pennsylvania. In 1776, they proceeded to adopt a new state constitution that was radically more democratic than either any other state government or the future US Constitution. When the new nation's wealthy drew up a new Constitution in 1787, the trauma of Shays' Rebellion dominated discussions. Shay's Rebellion started in Massachusetts, when growing assemblies of small farmers proceeded to physically block the state courts from foreclosing on any more family farms. The governor sent in 600 militia, only to see them join the rebellion. "Law and order" was restored after several wealthy merchants in Boston put up the money to hire a mercenary army that physically crushed the rebels. Despite defeating the open revolt, the state government felt compelled to make concessions to the economic demands of the farmers. Furthermore, events like Shays' Rebellion helped convince the "founding fathers," most of whom were quite hostile to the concept of democratic government, to only have the House of Representatives elected by popular vote. The hope was that such a concession would give ordinary white men enough feeling of having some say in the new government to avert further armed actions. In case this failed, the founders also made sure that the new Constitution created a centralized, federal army.

As the country moved through the nineteenth century, popular political organizing continued. With the birth of industrial capitalism and the extension of the right to vote to most white men organizing developed among a growing working class. Their political efforts became so strong that it helped compel the two elite parties (the Democrats and the Whigs) to develop a mass, grassroots apparatus early in the nineteenth century to counter and co-opt the popular threat.

Popular organizing played a key role in our nation's one example of an outright victory of a third party. By mid-nineteenth century, the division over slavery eventually split the two major parties. Following the flight of many free-soil, anti-slavery members from their party, the bulk of the remaining Democrats became the bulwark of pro-slavery sentiment. The other major party, the Whigs, never fully resolved its internal tensions, but remained divided over the question of whether to allow slavery into the new Western states. Into this crisis stepped a new third party. Calling themselves the Republicans, this group denounced slavery as immoral and insisted on halting its further spread westward. (The Republicans did not, however, call for its abolition in the South.) The new party's candidate for president, Abraham Lincoln, won the election of 1860—thereby signaling the rise of a new political force and the death of the Whigs. The Republican Party was certainly, at one level, an elite party—with a healthy degree of participation by wealthy merchants and manufacturers. The party, however, also had a grassroots abolitionist base that included small farmers, shopkeepers, and skilled urban workers. After the Civil War, the party also became a vehicle for black political empowerment. During the brief period of Reconstruction, before the black vote was purged, newly freed African Americans used the Republican Party line to run and elect hundreds of candidates.

Grassroots organizing also secured the right to vote for half the population. Beginning in the mid-nineteenth century, with launching events such as the Seneca Falls convention of 1848, women began their seven-decade-long battle to win this basic democratic right. Political discrimination against women also tied into a much broader system of oppression and second-class status. The laws of the day denied women such basic rights as ownership of property (literally including the clothes on their backs). Often women who married ceased to be separate human beings in the eyes of the law. In the end, the suffrage campaign became a mass movement complete with parades of ten of thousands of women dressed in white who defied society's efforts to relegate them solely to the home. Women who first won the vote, particularly in the Western states, used this electoral power to vote against the reigning national party if it did not support women's suffrage. In the end, the Nineteenth Amendment was ratified in 1920 amidst scenes of civil disobedience and hunger strikes.

Examples of early labor-related independent political efforts came out of the Knights of Labor. At its peak in 1886, the Noble Order of the Knights of Labor had over 700,000 members. Although its base lay in skilled white male workers, the Knights were open to all working people, including skilled and unskilled; men and women; white and black; and even farmers. Steeped in the nation's republican ideals, the Knights stretched this ideological tradition to its most radical limits. The republicanism that inspired the Knights firmly linked economic salvation with political organizing. Politics represented the noble public meeting place upon which civic virtue was built and a vision of the good society realized. More concretely, politics also controlled the sheriff, police, and courts, which were routinely used as weapons against organized workers. Therefore, wherever the Knights of Labor organized in the mid-1880s, contests over power and rights in the workplace soon became political struggles over the future of the community.

Between 1885 and 1888, the labor movement fielded its own political slates in some 200 towns and cities. Their activities stretched in urban areas across the country, from Rutland, Vermont to Richmond, Virginia; from Milwaukee, Wisconsin to Kansas City, Kansas; from San Francisco, California to East Portland, Oregon. They used various names—"Workingmen's," "United Labor," "Union Labor," "Independent"—for their tickets. Sometimes they took over the local apparatus of one of the two standing parties. Even where they never took office, these political efforts thrust people's concerns into the nation's politics—be it the establishment of an income tax, the abolition of child labor, workers' compensation, payment of wages every week and in legal money, a shorter workday, or public ownership of the railroads and utilities. Where the Knights were active, ordinary people had a space to get together and discuss their vision for their communities and the nation. After 1886, government and business opposition combined with the competition of the rival and more conservative American Federation of Labor to push the Knights, and, with it, labor's independent political activity, into decline.

Political revolt also came out of the nation's rural heartland. By the 1870s, the Republican Party had clearly betrayed the radical potential and ideals that came out of the struggle over the Civil War. In response, farmers organized the Greenback Party on a national level in 1875. The party's name pointed to its demand that the government expand the money supply by issuing paper "green" currency. The essential question boiled down to a basic struggle between ordinary people and the wealthy over who was going to enjoy the fruits of the nation's prosperity. A paper currency favored the majority of the population—who were debtors—at the expense of a currently privileged minority of creditors. In 1882, the party ran a surprisingly close, but ultimately losing, campaign for the governor in Texas. Generally, however, it did well only in isolated congressional districts. By 1886, the Greenbackers had seemingly little to show for their efforts. The two party system remained firmly in control. Yet a decade of third party organizing had left behind an important network of agrarian radicals whose presence would soon be felt as the country neared a new decade.

With the defeat of the Knights of Labor and Greenbackers, the nation's corporate class entered the late 1880s confident in the strength of their two party system. Little did they know that the nation was poised on the brink of the greatest political revolt by ordinary people in our country's history.

The Great Populist and Socialist Wave

The great agrarian revolt started modestly enough. In September 1877, a group of poor farmers met in Lampasas County, Texas, at the farm of J. R. Allen to discuss their impoverished economic condition. Although a small group from a frontier county, these farmers' concerns reached to the heart of the nation's politics. As one participant later explained: "The day is rapidly approaching when all the balance of labor's products will become concentrated into the hands of the few, there to constitute a power that would enslave prosperity."[1] The group's purpose, he explained, was to "educate ourselves in the science of free government." To this end, those assembled formed the Farmers Alliance.

Ironically, the original Lampasas Alliance chapter collapsed in 1880, following an abortive foray into third party politics. However, the agrarian movement, known as populism, remained alive and well in the statewide Grand State Farmers Alliance. By the late 1880s, the Farmers Alliance had grown into a powerful wave that swept the nation's agricultural South and Midwest. In 1892, this movement launched the People's Party, which for four years threatened the very existence of the entrenched two party system. Although the People's Party died in the disastrous fusion campaign with Democrat William Jennings Bryan in 1896, the grassroots revolt against the two party system continued. Five years after the People's Party faded from the national scene, the Socialist Party held its founding convention. For the next two decades, the Socialists led a renewed and powerful revolt against the two party system and the concentrated wealth that it served.

The Economic Question

While their radicalism could often stretch to a wide array of issues, both populism and socialism grew out of one basic problem facing the country's working people: the economic question. Put bluntly, the nation's economy was not serving the interests of the majority of the population. This problem became particularly clear during economic downturns, such as the depression of the 1890s. The economic violence experienced by working Americans, however, went beyond the question of ups and downs in the business cycle. Much like today, the nation was experiencing a fundamental economic transformation. The question was, would the country have an economy that benefited the few or the many?

By the 1880s, it had become clear that without ordinary people's intervention the nation's economy would serve only the few. Following the Civil War, the country's transition from an agrarian to an industrial society proceeded at an ever accelerating rate. Industrialization, however, was being organized to produce wealth for the few by exploiting the many. A growing corporate capitalism was gradually swallowing up the nation's economy. As one Populist wrote:

> *The army begging work is every year increasing, the small capitalist is being crowded down into the ranks of the wage earners by bigger, richer business rivals, and capital is concentrating and drawing to itself all power... All land which the poor can make a living on is taken.*[2]

This was the age in which the Rockefellers, the Carnegies, and the Du Ponts made their corporate fortunes. They did so on the backs of the country's working people. This process was clear to many of the nation's farmers.

The family farm is a core part of the nation's mythos. Ordinary people take the nation's abundant natural wealth and use it to raise healthy families and to create decent, vibrant communities. The family farm revolves around an image of rugged individualism. All a family needs is a plot of land and hard work and dedication to enjoy a slice of the American dream. The problem with this image is that throughout the nation's history family farmers have never been in control of their economic livelihood. Even when they have owned the land, they have had to rely on the services of others to produce the tools and inputs needed to raise the crops, and the transportation and marketing infrastructures to sell their crops once the harvest was in. As a result, merchants, bankers, and railroads controlled the lives of millions of family farms and they used this dependency to steal the wealth. The merchants controlled the price and availability of goods, the interest rates of loans, and the price of the farmers' crops. They virtually enslaved farmers in the cycle of exploitation known as the crop-lien system. As Lawrence Goodwyn has eloquently described:

> *Acted out at a thousand merchant encounters in the South after the Civil War, these scenes were so ubiquitous that to describe one is to convey a sense of them all. The farmer, his eyes downcast and his hat sometimes literally in his hand, approached the merchant with a list of his needs. The man behind the counter consulted a ledger, and after a mumbled exchange, moved to his shelves to select the goods that would satisfy at least a part of his customer's wants. Rarely did the farmer receive the range of items or even the quantity of one item he had requested. No money changed hands; the merchant merely made brief notations in his ledger… From early spring to late fall, the little ritual would be enacted until, at "settlin'-up" time, the farmer and the merchant would meet at the local cotton gin, where the fruits of a year's toil would be ginned, bagged, tied, weighed, and sold. At that moment, the farmer would learn what his cotton had brought. The merchant, who had possessed title to the crop even before the farmer had planted it, then consulted his ledger for a final time. The accumulated debt for the year, he informed the farmer, exceeded the income received from the cotton crop. The farmer had failed in his efforts to "pay out"… [The merchant] would then announce his intention to carry the farmer through the winter on a new account, the latter merely having to sign a note mortgaging to the merchant the next year's crop.*[3]

Corporate exploitation was not simply an issue of material well-being, but basic human dignity and development. As one Populist eloquently wrote:

> *Take a man, for instance, who labors hard from fourteen to sixteen hours a day to obtain the bare necessaries of life… He is brutalized both morally and physically. He has no ideas, only propensities. He has no beliefs, only instincts. He does not, often cannot, read. His contact with other people is only the relation of servant to master, of a machine to its director… Humanity must rise to its own needs, or the soul of man will flee, and the sense be left alone to reign.*[4]

While millions of working people struggled to survive the ravages of corporate capitalism, the Democratic and Republican parties went on with business as usual. The chasm between the dignified gentlemen who filled the halls of Congress and state capitals and ordinary working people is clearly revealed in a comparison of the political platforms of the age. The 1912 Republican and Democratic platforms are quite representative of the period. The Republican statement began with these pious words:

> *The Republican party... declares its unchanging faith in government of the people, by the people, and for the people. We renew our allegiance to the principles of the Republican party and our devotion to the cause of Republican institutions established by the fathers... It is appropriate that we should now recall with a sense of veneration and gratitude the name of our first great leader... Abraham Lincoln.*[5]

The platform proceeded to extol the achievements of past Republican administrations. That same year, the Democrats similarly invoked the legacy of the past. As they opened their platform: "We... reaffirm our devotion to the principles of Democratic government formulated by Thomas Jefferson and enforced by a long and illustrious line of Democratic Presidents."[6] This statement is followed by a lengthy section that focuses on the main topic of the platform—high Republican tariff policies. The platform attempts to link rising inequality and social hardship to the tariff policies of the Republican administration. A reading of both 1912 platforms reveals that the tariff was, indeed, the major issue of contention between the two parties, as it had been for quite some years.

By contrast, the Socialist Party's 1912 platform declared that "the capitalist system has outgrown its historical function, and now has become utterly incapable of meeting the problems now confronting society." Having denounced this system as "incompetent and corrupt and the source of unspeakable misery and suffering," the Socialists listed its specific crimes:

> *Under this system the industrial equipment of the nation has passed into the absolute control of plutocracy, which extracts an annual tribute of hundreds of millions of dollars from the producers...*
>
> *In spite of the multiplication of labor-saving machines and improved methods in industry, which cheapen the costs of production, the share of the producers grows ever less, and the prosperity of this nation is for the owning class alone... Millions of wage-workers have seen the purchasing power of their wages decrease until life has become a desperate battle for mere existence.*
>
> *Multitudes of unemployed walk the streets of our cities or trudge from state to state awaiting the will of the masters to move the wheels of industry.*
>
> *The farmers in every state are plundered by the increasing prices exacted for tools and machinery and by extortionate rent, freight rates and storage charges...*[7]

Or sample the following burning words from the opening lines of the People's Party's 1892 platform:

> *The conditions which surround us best justify our co-operation; we meet in the midst of a nation brought to the verge of moral, political, and material ruin. Corruption dominates the ballot-box, the Legislatures, the Congress, and touches even the ermine of the bench. The people are demoralized...*
>
> *We charge that the controlling influences dominating the old political parties have allowed the existing dreadful conditions to develop without serious effort to restrain or prevent them. They have agreed together to ignore in the coming campaign every issue but one. They propose to drown cries of plundered people with the uproar of a sham battle over the tariff...*[8]

In short, the nation's two major parties simply refused to publicly address the fundamental economic question of the day. The contentless character of their public political agenda was not accidental. Both parties had already decided their answer: the corporate development of the country would continue without opposition. The task of government, according to this logic, was to aid this development and keep "the rabble" from organizing effective opposition or alternatives. The worldview of the people who made up the leadership of both parties and the leadership of corporate America was identical—indeed, politicians and businesspeople were typically drawn from the same class. Republicans and Democrats waved the "bloody shirt" and denounced each other's tariff policies because they had nothing else to disagree over.

With the two major parties refusing to confront the economic transformation that was injuring the lives of millions, it was only a matter of time before people began to organize a political alternative.

The Populist Crusade

The Populists' strategy was straightforward. By cooperating together, they developed their own collective buying and selling enterprises that provided an alternative to the wealth-hungry merchants. Through their cooperatives, farmers bought their supplies directly from industry, overstepping the middle-merchants' prices and credit rates. The farmers also sold their crops en masse—using their collective power to have greater control over crop prices. More generally, the farmers attempted to use self-organization to fight the economic giants that constantly threatened their lives. This cooperation included such actions as boycotting railroads that charged unreasonable rates for shipping goods and pressuring state governments that did not respect the needs of the majority. By 1886, members of the Farmers Alliance were already demanding major changes in government policy. At their convention that same year in Cleburne, Texas, farmers issued thirteen demands, including a call for a federally administered banking system that would embrace flexible currency, the legal recognition of trade unions and cooperative stores, legislation to more tightly regulate the railroads, and several planks concerning taxation and land use.

The "cooperative crusade" of the Farmers Alliance soon began to spill over state boundaries. Between 1887 and 1891, the now National Farmers Alliance sent hundreds of lecturers throughout the South and Midwest to spread the gospel of cooperation. Ordinary farmers took to the crusade in droves. In the South, Alliances sprouted up not only in every state of the old Confederacy, but in almost every county. The Georgia Alliance, for example, grew quickly to over 100,000 members; in Tennessee, 125,000 farmers joined over 3,600 local chapters. The crusade spread like a fire across the plains of Kansas and then moved up into the Dakotas. Across the nation, ordinary working people got a taste of their own power and creativity as they worked together in thousands of local cooperative experiments. By 1890, over one million white farmers had joined the Alliance, while by the same year the companion Colored Farmers Alliance had enrolled over 250,000 black members.

Not everyone greeted this discovery of the power of human solidarity with open arms. Merchants, bankers, railroad barons, and the great monopolies generally saw it as a threat to their very existence. Not only did the farmers organize to counter these people's economic power and privileges, but the Alliance's cooperation put into question, by concrete, practical demonstration, the very notion that society could only prosper if its economic resources were privately owned and controlled by the wealthy few. Not surprisingly, the wealthy set out to sabotage this subversive crusade. At the same time, the Alliance movement ran up against an obstacle: where to get the capital needed for their cooperative enterprises. To provide its members with goods, the cooperatives themselves needed credit. Pooling the resources of poor people did not produce the capital needed to establish the cooperative exchanges on a stable basis. Needless to say, the wealthy who controlled the financial institutions were not about to cooperate.

This search for financial resources helped move populism further down the road of independent politics. Discussions of outright independent politics had been heard in Alliance circles since its founding. What pushed the Populists to a final break with the two party system was a novel idea for a national sub-treasury system. While the details of the plan are too involved to discuss here, the basic idea was straightforward: mobilize the monetary authority of the nation to work on behalf of ordinary people by having the government underwrite the cooperative crusade. Since neither major party was about to advocate the sub-treasury plan, the road to independent politics was clear. To save the cooperative crusade, the people themselves would have to take control of government.

In 1892, a general conference of radical reformers in St. Louis, Missouri, voted to found the People's Party. In his opening address to the convention, Leonidas Lafayette Polk announced that "the time has arrived for the great West, the great South, and the great Northwest, to link their hands and hearts together and march to the ballot box and take possession of the government, restore it to the principles of our fathers, and run it in the interests of the people."[9] The battle lines were drawn. Ordinary people would have to use democracy to counter the power of wealth, before wealth destroyed democracy in order to exploit the people.

Five months later, the People's Party held its first presidential nominating convention on July 4, 1892. The platforms that came out of this and subsequent conventions revealed a mass movement desiring fundamental change. Some of the specific Populist reforms seem today so much a natural part of US society that we risk forgetting that they first came out of a radical mass movement. Take, for example, such a basic democratic notion as the direct election of the Senate. In the 1890s, US senators were selected by votes from the state legislatures. Or how about having free and fair voting procedures that ensure an honest count, a national post office run by the government, a graduated income tax, public highways, pensions for disabled soldiers, or a national monetary system independent of the gold standard? These were all Populist demands.

The People's Party also fought for reforms that many people would consider a good idea today. For example, the Populists sought to enhance the direct participation of people in the government through a national system of initiative and referendum. They felt that basic economic assets such as the railroads and the emerging communication system, in their day the telegraph, were too important to be left in private, profit-seeking hands, and should be run in the interests of everyone. Staunch anti-monopolists, they felt that the government needed to break-up any large concentration of economic power. The Populists were also firm believers that everyone who was willing and able to work should have an opportunity to earn a living. To this end, they demanded that the government provide public jobs during times when the private economy did not offer work. Four decades later, the Great Depression forced the government to do just that by putting millions to work building roads, bridges, schools, libraries, hospitals, and even producing popular forms of culture and art.

These specific reforms, however, were only one part of populism. At its core, populism offered a vision of a new and better society. The Cooperative Commonwealth, as it was often called, was a vision based on a fundamental rejection of the competitive and exploitative values of corporate society. As one Kansas farmer asserted, "There never was, nor can there be, a more brutal, utterly selfish, and despicable doctrine than the Darwinian 'struggle for existence' when applied to the social relations of man."[10]

In the minds of these farmers, human beings were naturally social animals who improved their lives through mutual cooperation and collective advancement. Needless to say, these values made Populists extremely suspicious of concentrated wealth. In their experience, lying beneath the hoard of every rich person were the broken bodies of millions of impoverished working people who had created that wealth. How far the Populists were willing to take their critique of wealth varied within the movement. Some contemplated the full-scale abolition of capitalism and, with it, all private ownership of large economic resources. For these Populists, the Cooperative Commonwealth meant an economy run directly and collectively by the people. Many others did not go so far, hoping instead to simply restrain and subordinate the corporate economy to the needs of the vast majority.

What most Populists agreed on, however, was a basic faith in republican values of democratic self-government—values that the country had supposedly been founded on, but which were certainly not being practiced. Living today, in an age when attacks on "big government" are prevalent and popular "empowerment" is translated as "getting government off the backs of the people," we could do well to take note that there was a time when an active, expanding government run in the interests of the people was the main hope for millions of Americans. The Populists demonstrated an unbridled faith in the power of democratic government in their 1892 People's Party platform. It stated:

> We believe the powers of the government—in other words, of the
> people—should be expanded as rapidly and as far as the good sense of an
> intelligent people and the teaching of experience shall justify, to the end that
> oppression, injustice, and poverty shall eventually cease in the land.[11]

The Populists' foray into third party politics met with initial success. In the 1892 election, the Populist presidential candidate gained over one million votes, carrying the electoral vote in five states. The Populists also elected five senators, ten congressmen, three governors, and over 1,500 local and state officials. In areas where the cooperative movement had been well-developed and grassroots debate and activity flourished, so did the People's Party. In Kansas, for example, the over 100,000-member-strong Alliance predated the People's Party, even running an Alliance ticket in the 1890 election. Although the Alliance candidate for governor lost by a narrow margin, few others did. In the state legislature, ninety-six out of 125 seats fell to Alliance-elected candidates. In 1892, by fusing with the Democratic Party on Populist terms, the movement took complete control of the state government.

The real test, and true potential, of the People's Party lay in the nation's South. For years, third party efforts had broken against the wall of the one party, Democratic Solid South. Built on the mantels of white supremacy and sectional loyalties, the South provided the Democratic Party with its strongest base. The ability to defeat the Democrats in their home area would not only have demonstrate the power of the Populists, but also would have, in all likelihood, destroyed the Democratic Party.

The People's Party had the potential for doing just that. In states such as Texas, Georgia, and Alabama, the Farmers Alliance had sunk deep roots. In these areas, the Democratic Party found itself in a battle for its very life. Not able to stem the Populist tide, the party of the old Confederacy saved itself only through a combination of violence, intimidation, and stolen elections. Communities that were especially vulnerable to intimidation, such as blacks and Mexican Americans, were informed about who to vote for by their Democratic landlords, backed by armed thugs. Furthermore, since the people who controlled the polling stations and ballot counts were also Democratic partisans, it is not surprising that many Populist votes were "lost" while the number of votes cast in heavily Democratic areas could often exceed the total possible number of eligible voters! Repeatedly, the People's Party ran a strong race only to discover that its candidate had "surprisingly" been narrowly defeated. Repression and fraud were so blatant that in Louisiana in 1894, well-organized Populist campaigns ended with armed farmers marching on polling stations to seize control of the ballot boxes before they were stuffed with "extra" Democratic votes. "Order" was restored at the hands of the state militia as the "re-elected" Democratic legislature met in a state capital ringed with rifles.

The Populists also had strong showings elsewhere. Farmer-labor coalitions produced strong third place showings for the People's Party in California, Oregon, Washington, and Montana. Nationally, in 1892, General James Weaver, the People's Party's candidate for president, polled over one million votes. However, the Populist success and strong showings did not develop everywhere. In many areas where the grassroots movement of the Alliance had been partial or non-existent, the People's Party did not fair well. The People's Party had only a minor presence in the Northeast. In the entire Great Lakes region, where the Northwest Alliance had proven to be an inept and pale imitation of populism, the People's Party made little impact.

Even more ominous for the long-term future of populism were the dangerous trends emerging in areas not touched by the cooperative crusade, but in which the People's Party met with seeming electoral success. Here, organizations and political figures who had come late to the Populist crusade developed a distorted, one-dimensional version of populism—a tendency that Lawrence Goodwyn has termed the Shadow Movement. In the core areas of the Farmers Alliance, populism developed first as a grassroots movement and was then politically radicalized through its experience in mass organizing. In states like Colorado, Nebraska, and Illinois, however, "populism" developed as a much more one-dimensional electoral movement. This Shadow Movement enjoyed some success, not by building on grassroots radicalism, but through a combination of "single-issue" populism and fusion politics. In the Western mining areas, "populism" was stripped down to the specific demand for the free coinage of silver—reflecting the direct economic interests of the mining communities rather than a broader radical critique of the nation's monetary system. Through fusion, the third party movement joined with one of the major parties, most typically the Democrats, to run either common candidates or agree not to challenge each other in specific districts. Fusion had a practical appeal. Even if the People's Party was strong, that strength might not be strong enough to bring victory. In certain cases, fusing with one of the old parties could be the key to victory. The often brutally repressive and fraudulent efforts of a state's ruling party also helped encourage the tactic of fusing with the other opposition party.

Fusion politics, however, was a tricky business. If not done on activists' own terms, fusing with a mainstream party could result in the watering down or loss of the movement's ideals and demands. Building upon a solid grassroots cooperative crusade, Kansas Populists were able to hold true to the People's Party platform despite fusing with the Democrats. By doing so, they won outright control of the state government. Even here, however, the tactic met with controversy. In other states, fusion politics—as used by the Shadow Movement—led to the abandonment of populism for a modified version of two party politics.

The danger of the Shadow Movement for populism as a whole was that, although it had little to do with the mass democratic crusade that was at the heart of the revolt, "single-issue populism" and fusion politics did deliver electoral success. Shadow Populists won in states like Nebraska, Colorado, and North Carolina, while genuine Populists had victories stolen from them in state after state. As a result, while the rank-and file-base of the movement remained in the core areas of the cooperative crusade, the national leadership body of the People's Party became more and more composed of the elected officials who came out of Shadow Populism.

This dangerous organizational trend set the stage for the People's Party's destruction in 1896. The Party's eventual fate had already been foreshadowed by events in South Carolina between 1891 and 1892. There, Democratic Governor "Pitchfork Ben" Tillman found himself faced with the powerful South Carolina Farmers Alliance and their popular sub-treasury plan. When his early strategy of branding the plan "socialistic" failed, Tillman resorted to the novel strategy of publicly embracing the plan. At the Democratic Party's state convention, Tillman prevailed in having the entire Populist platform officially endorsed! With the governor pretending to be their friend, the state Alliance was thrown into so much confusion that it eventually collapsed.

The same scenario happened with the People's Party nationally. Four years of electoral organizing had put the Party at a strategic crossroads. Those leaders who came out of the cooperative crusade interpreted the prior four years as a validation of their strategy. Despite setbacks and powerful opposition, the People's Party had polled between 25 and 45 percent of the vote in at least twenty different states. Moreover, in spite of being deprived of outright victory, the Populists had clearly shaken the Solid South. A Democratic Party that had to use fraud and violence to stay in office was a party in deep trouble. In fact, so the argument went, years of agrarian revolt had dealt the Party a fatal blow. The People's Party only needed to keep fighting true to its founding principles to destroy this bastion of privilege and take over as one of the country's two major parties.

Members of the Shadow Movement, however, argued for further fusion with the major parties and a watering down of populism's radicalism to win more votes. Their fusion strategy came to national importance when William Jennings Bryan received the nomination as the Democratic Party's presidential standard-bearer for 1896. To refurbish a party damaged by years of Populist onslaught, the Democrats opted to steal the silver issue. Not only was free silver one component of the People's Party platform, but the silverite cause had significant support among non-Populists, including certain business elements such as the mining companies. In addition to championing this single Populist plank, William Jennings Bryan made ample use of Populist-sounding rhetoric. Shadow Populists, for whom the silver cause had assumed a disproportionate weight, saw an incredible opportunity. Their cause, free silver, had prevailed among the Democrats. The People's Party only needed to fuse with the Democrats, nominate Bryan as their standard-bearer, and move on to victory. In reality, however, William Jennings Bryan was not a Populist and did not share the movement's commitment to grassroots empowerment and democracy. Many rank-and-file Populists thought fusion with Bryan would betray the movement and destroy the Party.

Thus began populism's last crusade. While activists of the Cooperative Crusade included much of the Farmers Alliance's rank-and-file base, the fusionists held sway in the national party apparatus. They used this control to tip the balance in their favor by stacking the People's Party 1896 national convention with silverites. Then, at the stormy convention where shouting matches and heated exchanges threatened to degenerate into a riot, the fusionists used open deception and the suppression of key information to win a Bryan nomination. In all probability, many of those who voted for Bryan did not realize the full ramification of what they were doing.

The dire warnings of the grassroots Populists proved true. With Bryan as the Populist standard-bearer, the People's Party lost its identity. Why should people support a third party if it merely endorsed Democrats? The splits and disillusionment caused by the Bryan nomination drove thousands out of the movement. Furthermore, fusion did not even deliver victory on its own terms. A few months later, the Republican Party ushered in a new brand of corporate politics by spending an unprecedented amount of money in a mass advertising campaign that soundly defeated Bryan. The election of 1896 divided the nation's politics into essentially two one-party systems: a Democratic Solid South and a nationally dominant Republican majority. In the meantime, populism as a national force had collapsed.

The Socialist Party of America's Electoral Success

As the country neared the twentieth century, the "powers that be" could congratulate themselves on having defeated the most serious third party challenge to their political rule since the nation's founding. Little did they know that while populism was sounding its death knell, other radical groupings were beginning to coalesce. Within only a few years of the People's Party's decline, these currents launched a third party movement that ideologically represented an even more fundamental challenge to the system of wealth and privilege in the United States: the Socialist Party of America.

The Economic Question Revisited

The nation's farmers were not the only group of ordinary Americans preoccupied with the economic question. Just as the railroads, merchants, and bankers were enriching themselves on the backs of family farmers, corporate industrialists were building huge economic empires through the hard work and toil of a growing working class. The antagonism between workers and owners comes built into the capitalist system. Although workers do the actual labor to produce a product, the owners control the organization of work and, most importantly, the distribution of the wealth generated by this work. Owners grow and advance their business endeavors by obtaining an ever greater share of this wealth. Capitalism thus produces a strong tendency to erode the well-being of workers, as the power and wealth of the owning class grows and expands.

The exploitation of workers was readily apparent at the turn of the century. The conditions of the satanic mills and the desperate poverty of the English working class so eloquently described in the famous works of Charles Dickens, applied equally well in the United States. At the end of a workweek, which could easily exceed sixty hours, workers found that their paychecks could not feed their families. Obsessed with the bottom line, companies often found even basic safety precautions an unnecessary expense. Instead, management would "crack the whip" to speed up already backbreaking work even further. Not only did workers find their lives ruled over by the company at work, but many found that the tyranny of the boss followed them home as well. Companies often owned or controlled the houses that workers lived in, the stores where they bought their goods, the churches where they worshipped, and the politicians who ran the local government. Some owners didn't even pay workers in real money, but gave them company script usable only at company-owned establishments!

One sign of the mass misery caused by turn-of-the-century capitalism was the prevalent use of child labor. Owners felt little moral hesitancy in forcing ten-, eleven-, and twelve-year-old children to work fulltime in the factories when they could get away with paying them only a fraction of an adult's wage. The very existence of this pool of workers reveals how desperately working class families needed money to buy food and clothing, even after both parents had worked fifty- or sixty-hour weeks.

The Socialist Party's Ideals

The Socialist Party of America was founded in 1901 explicitly to overthrow the capitalist system that had thrown millions into lives of misery. The Socialists were quite up-front about their ultimate goal. For example, the preamble to their 1912 national platform declares that for the conditions of human misery and exploitation "there will be and can be no remedy and no substantial relief except through socialism, under which industry will be carried on for the common good and every worker receive the full social value of the wealth he creates."[12] They also wanted to foster the full humanity of working people. The Socialists, like their Populist predecessors, were true believers in the creativity, intellectual and cultural abilities, and essential goodness of ordinary people. As the Party's five-time presidential candidate, Eugene V. Debs, once put it:

> When the bread-and-butter problem is settled and all men and women and children the world around are rendered secure from dread of war and fear of want, then the mind and soul will be free to develop as they never were before. We shall have a literature and an art such as the troubled heart and brain of man never before conceived. We shall have beautiful houses and happy homes such as want could never foster or drudgery secure. We shall have beautiful thoughts and sentiments, and a divinity in religion, such as man weighted down by the machine could never imagine.[13]

Toward this end, the Socialists projected a society in which the wealth of the nation was shared among and controlled by those who produce it; a society in which human interaction was based upon cooperation, not competition; and a society in which decisions were made democratically among an informed and active citizenry. A leaflet issued by the National Party Office defined socialism as follows:

> Socialism stands for a new civilization... Broadly speaking, it means: First. That the means of production and distribution of wealth which are social and

public in nature be publicly owned... Second. That all social utilities, being
collectively owned, shall be under democratic control for the benefit of all who
work... Third. That all who are able shall be given opportunity to labor in the
collectively owned industries and each shall receive the full product of his toil.
Fourth. That each shall have for his own private property all that his labor
earns of food and clothing, shelter, house and home—books, music,
education, recreation, and culture. Fifth. That the government... shall be
made truly democratic, so that the will and wish of the people may be the law
of the land. This will be accomplished by means of the initiative, referendum,
recall, proportional representation, and other measures making for popular
government.[14]

The Socialists wanted to radically democratize America. In doing so, they saw themselves as simply carrying through many of the ideals upon which America was supposedly founded, but which capitalism hardly encouraged. A 1900 article in *The People* argued that "society should be so organized, in its economic foundation and political forms as to promote liberty, equality, and fraternity, to secure to the greatest possible number of people the greatest possible amount of leisure, the greatest possible share of material well-being, and the greatest possible enjoyment of the pleasures of civilization."[15]

The Cooperative Commonwealth, a basic vision shared with the Populists, was the long-term goal. In the meantime, the Socialists sought to educate the public in the ideals of socialism and put their values into immediate practice through concrete reforms. The Party advocated such measures to mitigate industrial exploitation as minimum wage scales and shortened workdays. Socialists also supported the efforts of workers to form unions. In particular, Socialist municipal administrations neutralized the power of the police and courts, the traditional allies of the owners. Such measures aimed to provide immediate improvements in the lives of workers while, at the same time, helping to prepare them to seize "the whole power of government in order that they may thereby lay hold of the whole system of socialized industry."[16] Similarly, the Socialist demand for women's suffrage fit into their overall democratic vision. Even for the more Victorian among them, true democracy could only exist if all citizens possessed equal and full political rights.

Internal Diversity

The Socialist Party of America was formally launched in the summer of 1901 at a convention in St. Louis. This convention officially joined the Social Democratic Party with elements of the Socialist Labor Party and various independent socialist groups. Reflective of its decentralized character, the new party was actually born the year before when, at the local level, socialist activists from all three groupings began operating as a single group, despite the official opposition of the Social Democratic Party's executive board to a merger plan. Ultimately, the rank and file pushed through the merger.

The new Socialist Party of America was notable for its internal democracy, decentralized structure, and ideological diversity. In part, this reflected the desire of different groups not to have a rival faction dominate the national apparatus. This structure also grew out of socialism's ideals. The Party's constitution gave a large degree of autonomy to local and state organizations. The state chapters had sole control over their organization, financial affairs, popular education strategy, and ideology. The national organization suggested direction more than it issued firm commands. Indeed, all actions of the National Committee were subject to referendum by the general membership.

Because of its decentralized and democratic organization, the Socialist Party was able to become home to a wide array of American radicals. The ideological mix embodied by the Party included such diverse currents as Social Democrats, Christian Socialists, labor radicals, various Marxists, radical Populists, utopians, and syndicalists. All were united by the common rejection of the capitalist system and their desire to build a Cooperative Commonwealth. Additionally, in one way or another, all saw electoral politics as a key part of the struggle. They also shared a strong defense of the independence of their Party—drawing from populism's demise the lesson that alliances with less radical reform movements were dangerous undertakings.

Although they all believed in socialism, the Socialists developed major disagreements over how the Cooperative Commonwealth would come to America. Historians have generally divided the Socialist Party leadership into three major currents: Left, Right, and Center. These divisions are worth explaining as they point to strategic dilemmas that progressives undertaking independent politics today will likely encounter.

The Socialist Left, of whom the long-time presidential candidate Eugene Debs was an example, saw socialism coming through a peaceful revolution. Capitalism could not be replaced piecemeal. The central components of the nation's economy had to be seized en masse by an organized working population that had grown and developed to the point where they could democratically run the economy. For the Left, the role of the Party was to use political work to educate and mobilize working people around the principles of socialism until a majority of the population supported revolutionary change. Then the people would vote in a revolutionary government and the new era would begin.

The Left placed great emphasis on class struggle. The interests of workers and owners were fundamentally at odds, they claimed. The goal was to help the working class organize in its own independent interests. To this end, the Left were strong supporters of unionizing unskilled industrial workers.

Although the major national labor organization of this era, the American Federation of Labor (AFL), did include some industrial unions, its core and overall perspective lay with the more traditional craft unions of skilled workers. Socialists of all persuasions criticized the AFL, typified by the leadership of Samuel Gompers, as too narrowly focused on skilled workers, too cooperative with employers, and too politically conservative. What was distinct about the Left Socialists was their conclusion that the AFL was a lost cause. In 1905, when labor radicals launched the Industrial Workers of the World (IWW), the Left openly embraced the new organization for its militancy and its commitment to unite all workers, regardless of skill, race, gender, or creed. In fact, all of the officials and most of the delegates to the IWW's founding convention were members of the Socialist Party.

In contrast to the Left's revolutionary vision, the Socialist Right promoted an evolutionary or "constructive" version of socialism. For the Right, developments such as state-run operations— like the post office—and the growth of corporate stock companies indicated that capitalism was already evolving toward a cooperative economy. Socialism would not come in one major breakthrough, but through the gradual accumulation of small, yet important reforms. The municipal experience of the highly successful Milwaukee Socialist branch and the ideology of its leader, Victor Berger, typified this "constructive socialism." In Milwaukee, the Socialist city administration proceeded to enact a series of reforms designed to provide immediate aid to working people. At the same time, calls for municipal ownership of public utilities were seen as first steps in the transition to socialism. In contrast, the Left, while not rejecting measures that provided concrete relief to working families, saw such incremental reforms as merely reforming capitalism, not creating socialism. Since the Right placed their hopes on incremental reforms, they also put great emphasis on winning office. For the Left, the main goal of campaigning was political education. Local Socialist votes simply registered the more important transformation of people's understanding and class consciousness. For the Right, however, such votes became an end in themselves. It was through electoral pluralities that Socialist city officials and state representatives were elected, thus allowing them to enact the reforms that would gradually build socialism.

The drive to win elections led the Socialist Right to downplay class conflict. In many areas, the mobilized working class vote was not numerous enough to prove the margin of local victory. The Left often criticized the Right for winning office by appealing to middle-class constituencies with calls for honest government and progressive reform. These appeals to the more prosperous went so far that Victor Berger once stated with pride that Milwaukee's Socialist administration had decreased the number of labor strikes. Such appeals produced the rather incredible phenomenon in which at least two millionaires, J. G. Phelps Stokes and William Bross Lloyd, became Party members, declaring that the Party was not really hostile to capitalism!

The Right also had a different position on the question of organized labor. While generally supportive of efforts to organize industrial workers, the Right placed more hope in influencing the AFL, and felt that strikes and other forms of direct confrontation were usually counter-productive since they often prompted violent state repression. For years, the Right lobbied the AFL to support socialism. Although it never achieved this ultimate aim, in 1912, Socialist Max Hayes did receive almost one-third of the votes for president of the federation in a campaign against Gompers. Several major AFL unions were Socialist-led, including the Brewery Workers, the Western Federation of Miners, and, in 1914, the newly formed Amalgamated Clothing Workers.

In the middle of the Left/Right divide, and key to the dominant direction of the Party, lay the Center Socialists, typified by Morris Hillquit. Hillquit became the most prominent of a number of workers turned lawyers who defended the rights of workers in the courts. Although opposed to Berger and the Right on such questions as restricting immigration and courageously opposed to World War I, Hillquit increasingly sided with the Right on such major issues as hostility toward the IWW and the overall evolutionary road to socialism.

Although at different times different coalitions of Left, Right, and Center would predominate in national Party decision-making, the Party's decentralized structure allowed these tendencies to coexist, though not always harmoniously, and contribute to building the movement. Indeed, as different factions reflected different local experiences, internal diversity was critical to providing the flexibility necessary to organize a national movement in a heterogeneous country. For over two decades, this internal diversity helped foster a vibrant and growing movement.

Decentralization and ideological diversity did not come without a price, however. Richard Judd, in his detailed study of local Socialist experiences, *Socialist Cities*, has argued that the weak national structure left many local Party chapters without adequate direction. By avoiding taking a decisive stance on the questions that split Left and Right, the national Party apparatus largely limited itself to supplying locals with technical advise on "nuts-and-bolts" organizing. According to Judd:

> *Facing situations for which neither the pragmatic Right nor the doctrinaire Left prepared them, rank-and-file Socialists likely as not had no definite idea of what they were to accomplish in politics, who they were to help, or why. Independently, each local had to resolve the grand theoretical and strategic problems over which the party as a whole was agonizing... The local inevitably entered the realm of theory through concrete administrative decisions they made, and for this they were woefully unprepared. The loss of*

*revolutionary integrity among various locals, the contradictory programs, the
shocking number of expulsions and blunders and the ideological fighting
suggests fundamental organizational weaknesses emerging as the party shifted
from an agitational orientation to practical politics. Entering office, the
Socialists confronted the delicate task of balancing ideological commitment
and practical politics, or in class terms, balancing their appeals to workers
and businessmen. The two goals were not irreconcilable, but they involved
choices for which the practical advice from the National Office had not
prepared them.*[17]

Growth and Peak

In 1900, the Socialist Party launched its first presidential campaign with
Eugene V. Debs as its nominee. The 96,981 votes Debs received was a
promising start, especially given the smaller population in the country at the
turn of the century and that women were still denied the vote. For the next
decade and a half, the Socialist vote would steadily grow, making the
prospects of an electoral road to socialism appear more than a mere pipe
dream. Starting in the East and spreading steadily throughout the Midwest
and West, the Socialist vote grew every election season. In 1904, Debs polled
408,230 votes; in 1908, his vote tally climbed to 424,488; and, in 1912, it
spectacularly doubled to over 900,000 (6 percent of the total vote)! The
mushrooming strength of socialism was not lost on those in power.
Republican Party leader Mark Hanna had predicted that by 1912 socialism
would be the most significant issue in America. Indeed, between 1908 and
1912, Party membership tripled to almost 120,000—no small achievement
given the increasing personal risk that members faced due to repression and
intimidation. Between its founding and 1912, the Party succeeded in electing
sixty of its candidates to various state legislatures. These officeholders
introduced some 520 bills and succeeded in getting 147 of them enacted
into law. This legislation included laws concerning shorter work hours,
higher wages, child labor, employer liability, municipal home rule, easing
restrictions on municipal ownership of utilities, and referendum and recall
mechanisms.

In his detailed study of the Party's rank-and-file activists, James Green
documented the Party's solid working-class base. In 1912, this Socialist
support had taken on several distinct characteristics. Most notable was the
Socialist strength in small cities and large towns. Here, the working-class
movement was able to build alliances with professional and middle-class
populations who also felt squeezed by the economic power of the wealthy.
This connection proved more difficult in the nation's larger cities. The Party's
native-born character also limited Socialist strength in the big cities. The
Socialists only made significant inroads among the large immigrant working
class after World War I.

In 1912, the Party's largest state organization was in Oklahoma. Indeed, the Socialists represented a vibrant political force throughout the Southwest. In part, the Party inherited the spirit of populism. Yet most Southwest Socialists were too young to have been active at the height of the Populist crusade. Furthermore, with the defeat of populism, the forces of corporate capitalism had been able to proceed unchecked, driving more and more farmers into tenancy. The Socialists' genius was to build a unique base that combined workers with tenant farmers. The Party's decentralized and diverse character proved an asset here. Southwest organizers largely ignored the national Party's official calls for collectivized agriculture. Instead, they took up the tenant farmers' own demands for a return to the family farm.

Socialists greeted their 1912 victories and expanding membership with visions of impending triumph. This, however, was not to be. In the 1914 off-year elections, the Socialist vote dipped significantly downward. Then, in 1916, with Debs refusing to run as the presidential nominee, the Socialists polled a disappointing 585,000 votes. Even worse, dues-paying membership had dropped considerably. The Party's steady growth had been stymied. Still, it remained a significant force in US politics. Between 1912 and 1918, the Party elected over eighty Socialists to various state legislatures. Approximately 62 percent of these were either workers at the time of their election or had been workers most of their lives. Ten percent were farmers. Disillusionment had set in, however, and led the *Appeal to Reason* to lament: "to find that after... seventeen years of organizing activity on the part of the Socialist Party that our numbers have diminished and our common influence has lessened is to find SOMETHING RADICALLY WRONG..."[18]

Part of the Party's difficulty was factionalism. By 1912, the Right dominated the national leadership and removed IWW union leader William D. Haywood from the national executive committee. This showdown had been coming for some time. The IWW was a revolutionary organization that sought to unite workers throughout the country to destroy the wage system. It also placed much less emphasis on the electoral road to power. Instead, the IWW sought to organize workers into one big union that could launch a general strike through which the workers would directly take over the nation's factories and workplaces. The IWW also challenged the AFL and officially endorsed industrial sabotage among its weapons in the class struggle.

Besides expelling Haywood, the Right won a further victory against the IWW in 1912 when it succeeded in amending the Party constitution to expel any member "who opposed political action or advocates crime, sabotage, or other methods of violence as a weapon of the working class." The recall of Haywood and the change in the constitution compelled many thousand IWW supporters to leave the party.

World War I also had an enormous impact on the Socialist Party. For all of the major countries involved, the war confronted the socialist movement with a serious dilemma. According to the Socialists' class analysis, the war represented nothing more than a squabble between different national capitalist classes that used the blood of the working class as cannon fodder. The Socialists' opposition to the war, however, threatened to jeopardize their electoral gains and left them open to massive repression. In Europe, most socialist parties caved into war-time chauvinism. They placed themselves firmly behind their respective national war efforts. The Socialist Party of America became notable for its consistent official opposition to the war.

The Party paid an enormous price for its principles. Its opposition gave the US government an official pretext to try to destroy the movement as a traitorous organization. State authorities banned Socialist publications, arrested Party leaders, broke into the organization's offices, and generally harassed the movement. The fact that over 1,500 Party locals were destroyed during the war testifies to the scale of this repression.

The Party survived the war, however, in part because its opposition brought not only governmental repression, but also newfound support among those who shared the Party's indictment of the war. Indeed, the Socialist Party represented the one major, national organization to speak out against it. In doing so, it led an anti-war movement of hundreds of thousands. In the 1917 municipal races, and again in the 1918 mid-term elections, the Socialists made notable gains. In 1920, Eugene Debs ran for the presidency from a prison cell and received 919,000 votes.[19]

The war years transformed the Socialist Party. Much of the Party's strength moved from small and mid-sized towns and cities to larger cities. In part, this reflected governmental repression, which was most effective on locals in smaller communities. It also reflected an increasing immigrant presence within the Party. In 1912, the Party leadership reluctantly agreed to charter foreign-language groups into associative federations. Between 1912 and 1916, the Party's percentage of foreign-born members more than doubled, from 15 percent to 35 percent. By 1917, over half of the Party's now growing membership was foreign-born. The war years also saw the Party for the first time attracting significant numbers of African Americans, mostly in northern cities. These internal changes altered the Party's political dynamics as the Left grew in influence.

In 1917, the Russian Revolution shook the world and split the socialist movement worldwide. For the first time in history, a revolutionary socialist movement had come to power. This triumph placed the question of imminent revolution in Europe and elsewhere firmly on the table. Should US and European socialists push for a revolutionary outbreak or continue their evolutionary strategy? This issue came to the forefront in Europe against a background of sharp divisions over the war and the Left Socialists' accusation that the Right Socialists had sold out the revolutionary ideals of the movement. Once the war ended, revolution did, indeed, break out in Germany, only to be defeated at the hands of a Social Democratic government. Revolutionaries in the new Soviet Union called on Left Socialists to break with their Right counterparts to form Communist parties united into a "Third International."

This worldwide split eventually came to the United States, although in a different form. Unlike in Europe, all major factions of the US Socialist Party had, at least officially, opposed the war. The Right and Left, for the most part, both had supportive positions on the October Revolution. Left/Right tensions did exist, however. Although in practical activities they were often quite similar, the two sides split over whether or not the Party should adopt a more revolutionary or more reformist image. Right-leaning members, who were mostly native born or from older immigrant stock, were also increasingly worried about the Party's changing internal demographics and the growing influence of the foreign-language federations. Ultimately, Right-wing maneuvers prompted the Left to leave the Party in two waves, first to form the Communist Party and then the Communist Labor Party. The split occurred amid renewed waves of government repression and proved disastrous. From a membership of nearly 110,000 at the beginning of 1919, the combined membership of all three socialist fragments dwindled to some 36,000 by the end of the year.

The Socialist Party did not disappear. During the Great Depression, it had a larger membership than the Communist Party, and played a significant role in the protests and organizing of that period. Some of its municipal chapters remained strong well after the national Party had declined. In the early 1930s, the Party experienced a brief revival under the leadership of Norman Thomas, who gained over 880,000 votes in his 1932 presidential race. In 1934, socialist author Upton Sinclair garnered nearly 900,000 votes in his unsuccessful bid for governor of California on the Democratic ticket. Yet, by 1930, the Party had an aging membership, with the majority of young radicals joining the Communists. In 1936, the Party suffered the beginning of a new round of splits that only ensured its ever shrinking status, although officially, it still exists today.

Municipal Socialism's Successes

In looking at the history of the Socialist Party, we should avoid falling into the common trap in which politics is seen as what goes on in the White House and on Capitol Hill. Scholars who aim to discredit or downplay the history of third parties in this country often point to the rather modest totals such movements won within national races. For example, at its peak, the Socialist Party never received more than 6 percent of the vote for president—

that's less than a third of the proportion that Ross Perot won in 1994. Yet national vote totals do not provide a good measure of a grassroots-based movement like the Socialist Party. Most people who went to the polls may have cast their presidential and congressional choices for a member of the two major parties. Many of these same people, however, were pulling the Socialist Party lever for their local councilperson, county representative, or mayor. Indeed, the most visible signs of Socialist vitality came not at the national level, but in state and local politics across the country.

The most famous and largest urban area to embody municipal socialism was the brewery city of Milwaukee, Wisconsin. In the early part of this century, Milwaukee was particularly open to Socialist initiatives. A large German immigrant population brought to the city an established socialist tradition, a strong community structure, and a vibrant German-language press. This leading German population coupled with an influx of "new" immigrants, such as the Poles, made Milwaukee one of the most "foreign" of the nation's large cities. Also key to Milwaukee socialism was the firm support of organized labor. Early on, the local Federated Trades Council saw the local Socialist chapter as its political vehicle. The relationship between the two proved mutually beneficial. The local Party played a significant role in helping labor win public acceptance much earlier than in other major cities. Local Socialist administrations also delivered concrete and valuable government support. In turn, the local unions provided the Socialist candidates and media with key endorsements, volunteers, and financial resources.

While somewhat unique in its ethnic make up, Milwaukee shared with most other major cities the conditions of desperate want and neglect of its working-class neighborhoods. These common issues involved very basic needs: sewers, public transportation, affordable utilities, streetlights, and schools. Living without adequate municipal services in neighborhoods saturated with industrial pollution, working families fell victim to Republican and Democratic politicians who offered the rich lower taxes by avoiding costly municipal improvements. In contrast, the Socialists pledged to place the needs of working families first and use local government as a tool for building decent communities.

The Milwaukee movement started modestly enough. In 1900, the Socialist candidate for mayor received only 5 percent of the vote. This small percentage signified a growing grassroots force. In 1902, the Socialist vote for mayor climbed to 14 percent; in 1904, it reached 25 percent. That same year, the Socialists sent five members to the Wisconsin state assembly and one to the state senate. In 1910, the movement made national news when Milwaukee Socialists delivered the largest local victory in the country. Gaining nearly half of the total vote, Socialist Emil Seidel was elected mayor by a large plurality. He also entered city hall with a Socialist-dominated administration. Voters had gone to the polls and voted Socialist across the ballot. That year, the city attorney, city treasurer, comptroller, twenty-five of thirty-five alderpeople, and one-fourth of the school board were Socialists. The Socialists also won a majority on the county board, and sent twelve members to the statehouse and two to the state senate. At the same time, Socialist Victor Berger was elected to the US Congress.

The new Socialist government faced a number of obstacles. As with any municipal administration, many of the economic forces and powerholders lay outside its control. No matter what local Socialists hoped to achieve, the basic structures and conditions of the capitalist system would remain in operation. To make matters worse, the city of Milwaukee could not even control its own destiny. The state legislature had reserved for itself the power to interfere in local government, especially over financial matters. For example, the state legislature was able to rebuff the Milwaukee Socialists' initiatives to establish a municipal icehouse and slaughterhouse, as well as lodging houses and municipal markets.

Despite these limitations, Milwaukee Socialists achieved some notable changes. Today, when touring the city, one is struck by the ample tree-lined boulevards and public parks throughout the city's working-class neighborhoods. These serve as a living reminder of the years when city hall sought to provide Milwaukee's working people the same public life as the wealthy enjoyed. After taking office in 1910, the new administration pushed for factory and building inspections, increased public supervision of long-term utility franchises, and won a major rate reduction from the Milwaukee Electric Railway and Light Company. For labor, the Socialists instituted union wages and an eight-hour workday for city employees, provided a free unemployment office, offered to arbitrate major strikes, encouraged companies to unionize, and forced the police to respect strikers' rights. The administration was active in promoting decent housing and health services, preserving open space, and regulating private development. Working-class culture was encouraged through new recreation programs, free concerts, and a reorganized public library.

While such reforms brought direct benefits to Milwaukee's working class, the administration also appealed to middle-class voters. In an age when big city administrations were known for corruption, Socialists ran on anti-graft platforms. Not only were they consistently honest, but Milwaukee Socialists proved instrumental in developing modern, efficient local government. They streamlined the city administration, improved the city's credit rating, and ended deficit financing. The Socialists also fostered public debate by sponsoring free lectures and publishing a weekly newspaper to inform residents about government. Within the state legislature, Socialists succeeded in securing passage of notable legislation, such as a comprehensive workers' compensation act, safety legislation, regulation of women's hours, and child labor laws.

At their best, however, these reforms only made Milwaukee capitalism more humane. They did not challenge capitalism itself. Indeed, by proving to be more honest and efficient than either major party, the Milwaukee Socialists even gained tentative support from some of the city's capitalists. Reformist in nature and cultivating middle-class voters, the Milwaukee movement drew fire from Left Socialists. They saw such "sewer-socialism" as differing little from non-socialist reformers. In the eyes of the Left, Milwaukee Socialists were simply helping capitalism modernize itself. In appealing to middle-class voters, Milwaukee Socialists were accused of moderating their platform and actions in ways detrimental to the working class.

Although some of their reforms seem quite similar to those enacted by the "Progressive" reformers of that age, Milwaukee Socialists did differ in important ways from the pro-business Progressive movement. Progressive reformers sought to rationalize local government in such a way as to take control away from the public and place it in the hands of professional managers and centralized administrations. In contrast, the Socialists consistently opposed any measure that sought to limit working-class democracy, including a strong mayor's office, at-large council elections, and manager and commission forms of government. The Socialists also always linked, at least officially, their local reforms to a broader critique of the capitalist system. Finally, unlike Progressives, Socialists openly embraced working people— not just their needs and demands, but their culture and traditions. The Socialists were part of the working class. Progressives were part of the nation's elite.

Regardless of the Left's criticism of Milwaukee socialism, it proved to be the strongest, most lasting chapter of the Party. After the 1910 sweep, opponents in the state legislature passed a measure transforming the city's elections into non-partisan races. This meant that no party, including the Socialists, appeared on the ballot line. The measure was clearly intended to break up the Socialist voting block. At the same time, the Republicans and Democrats demonstrated their similarities by running common fusion candidates. This anti-Socialist mobilization produced major Socialist losses in 1912. Mayor Seidel failed in his re-election bid despite winning 3,000 more votes than in 1910. All seven Socialist county administrators were defeated, the Socialist state delegation was cut in half, and Victor Berger was defeated in the race for Milwaukee's seat in the US House of Representatives.

Such a setback, however, did not signify an end or even a decline of the local movement. The 1912 defeat was more a sign of the business community's local strength and control of the state legislature. Indeed, despite the varied tactics used to undermine them, the Socialists' support continued to grow. In 1914, they regained the mayor's office. Except for a brief period in the 1940s, a Socialist mayor would remain in city hall until

1960. Socialists regained other lost offices. Victor Berger, for example, returned for two more terms in the House of Representatives.

The years between 1910 and 1912 did mark the golden era. The Socialists never regained the same level of municipal control that they had enjoyed during these years. From 1914 onward, Milwaukee's Socialist mayors had to work with city councils and county boards in which the Socialists did not have a majority. With the national party split in 1919, Milwaukee Socialists found themselves more and more on their own. Reflecting this changed atmosphere, their local platforms increasingly emphasized immediate social reforms rather than the replacement of capitalism.

Socialist administrations did continue to deliver very tangible gains. In his long tenure between 1916 and 1940, Mayor Dan Hoan succeeded in establishing or implementing a municipal stone quarry, a streetlighting system, sewage disposal and water purification plants, and the first low-cost cooperative housing project to be built by any municipality in the country. He further refined city finances, encouraged health and safety measures, and promoted city planning, zoning, and community recreation. Frank Zeidler, first elected mayor in 1948, continued this reform tradition until he stepped down in 1960.

Some other cities also had long years of Socialist governments. For example, the textile city of Reading, Pennsylvania defied the conservative stereotype associated with its Pennsylvania Dutch heritage to boast a strong Socialist movement. While Socialists were first elected to city council between 1910 and 1916, it was not until after the national party had already peaked that Reading socialism really came into its own. In 1927, the Socialists won the mayor's office, winning almost half the vote, as well as two city council seats, two school board directors, and the city controller. Between 1927 and 1935, the Socialist Party was the major party in city politics. Socialists continued to be a powerful force in local politics well into the late 1940s. The Reading Socialists also influenced state politics by repeatedly sending Socialists to the Pennsylvania legislature.

Historian William Pratt identified several factors that accounted for the Socialists' success.[20] They concerned themselves with local issues, while not forgetting they were Socialists; ran full slates for both local and state offices; gained the active support of organized labor; and spoke to the general public in the "common sense" language of the community. Most importantly, the Socialists built a strong grassroots organization. Socialism became part of the daily life of the community. Socialist activists lived and died, celebrated and mourned, and worked and played with other Socialist comrades. This community spirit helped propel Socialists into elected office. In turn, political success helped to reinforce and expand the social network.

While Milwaukee, Reading, and other cases represent lasting success stories, other Socialist experiences with local political power proved short-lived. For example, in 1911, Ohio Socialists celebrated electoral victories in thirty of the state's ninety-three towns and cities. Voters selected a Socialist as mayor in seventeen municipalities. Yet although the Socialist vote continued to grow in many of these strongholds, the level of these officeholding gains were not repeated. Indeed, in 1913, all but two of the Socialist mayors were defeated. In four cases, factional fights produced the defeats by leading to the expulsion of the mayor from the party. In the others, however, the major parties combined their efforts to get rid of Socialists who had been elected in three- and four-way races.[21] The typical Socialist gains came in working-class towns with modest- sized populations of around 10,000. In Martins Ferry, for example, the Socialist slate swept local office in 1911. Bitter suppression of union activity by the town's steel companies had given workers a common bond that translated into Socialist votes. The craft-unionism of skilled workers, with its complicated, yet at times narrow, sense of solidarity clashed with the immigrant diversity of the town. Divisions between ethnic groups as well as between union supporters and those who crossed picket lines eventually broke up the Socialist electoral coalition— although the Socialist mayor did go on to win a second term.

The experience of another small industrial city, St. Mary's, was even more typical. In 1911, Socialists gained what one observer termed the "most sweeping victory by the Socialists in the country." The Party won every race that it entered. While St. Mary's population was much less divided ethnicly, the local Socialists proved ill-prepared to face the vicious business counter-attack that their sweeping victory provoked. Soon after the election, local politicians and the town newspaper began pressing businesses to withdraw advertising from the St. Mary's Socialist. When the newly elected mayor invited organizers from the Industrial Workers of the World into the city, the business community hired thugs to harass union meetings. The city admini-stration was also unable to counter the threat that if the Socialists were re-elected in 1913, the city would loose several of its largest manufacturing plants. To save their jobs, workers voted for the fusion Democrat-Republican ticket. Because of solid union support, however, the Socialists did not disappear. Instead, they fell into a stable second-party status—serving as a kind of official opposition party.

Despite the defeats, 1913 also brought fresh victories for Socialists statewide. In Toledo, for example, the Socialists elected two city councilors. In Akron, the Socialists' mayoral candidate came in a close second in a four-way race, while two Socialist city councilors were re-elected and two more added.

Successful elections do not tell the whole story. At times, the Socialist experience of governing worked out differently from what Party activists hoped. The most famous example of the pressures and tensions produced by officeholding is the open battle that erupted between the Socialist Party membership in Schenectady, New York and their charismatic mayor, George Lunn. A rapidly growing industrial city of over 72,000, Schenectady boasted a higher average wage than most industrial cities its size and a relatively strong labor movement. In 1911, a Socialist administration swept into power, winning the mayor's office and electing eight of thirteen alderpeople, several district supervisors, and sending one of their own to the New York state assembly.

The city's future looked promising. The alliance between the new mayor, George Lunn, and the Socialist Party had been a relatively recent marriage of convenience, however. A pastor and Christian Socialist, Lunn had become a powerful political force in his own right. Before he became mayor, Lunn had first attracted public attention when he led a crusade from his pulpit against fare increases by the city's street railway company. Following this initial fame, Lunn founded his own newspaper, *The Citizen*, to fulfill the need for a "fearless weekly newspaper whose primary purpose is to stand for the great silent majority."[22] By 1911, Lunn was looking to expand his public activities and needed an electoral vehicle. At the same time, the growing local Socialist movement needed a charismatic public figure to lead the charge in contesting for power. Lunn, now a Socialist Party member, ran as their candidate for mayor.

Initially, the alliance between Lunn and the Socialist Party worked well. The new mayor took power prepared to make some major changes, but the local establishment proved a powerful opponent. When Lunn announced his intentions to have the city sell residents ice at cost, the local ice dealers secured a court injunction to block the city from either giving away or selling ice. Although Lunn and his supporters got around the injunction by acting officially as private individuals, the operation only lasted a year due to financial losses. A similar effort to make cheap coal available to city residents also failed. Programs to establish a municipal grocery store, a city lodging house, and a Socialist "school of social science," while not encountering legal opposition, also failed in the long run. Lunn and the Socialists did, however, bring efficient, honest government to the city, increase public wages, improve sanitation, expand the number of parks, and successfully mediate a labor dispute. In 1913, the Socialists increased their votes, but a combined fusion campaign by the Democratic and Republican parties forced Lunn out of office.

Despite their notable success, tensions between Lunn and the leadership of the Socialist Party began to escalate. Lunn's popularity had brought many new recruits into the Socialist local organization. Serious debates broke out between long-time Party members and Lunn's new allies. Independent to begin with, Lunn tried successfully, in 1914, to change the Socialists' state constitution to take away the power of the local chapters to dictate the political appointments made by their officeholders. Lunn also made efforts to try to centralize the local organization and place his followers into the dominant positions. The Left Socialists mounted a counter-attack, and the balance of power between the two sides drifted back and forth. Despite these internal tensions, Lunn was able to pull together a strong election campaign in 1915 that put him back into the mayor's office. Unlike 1911, however, this win was not accompanied by Socialist victories in other layers of government. When, after taking power, Lunn tried to appoint several Republicans and Democrats to city offices, the internal dispute in the local erupted anew. The conflict became so severe that the Socialists' state executive committee revoked the local's charter and reestablished the party without Lunn and his backers. Although this created a unified party, the Socialists began to fade away without Lunn. In 1919 and 1921, Lunn won re-election, but no longer as a Socialist. He had comfortably made the transition to the Democratic Party.

The stories of Socialist municipal administrations could go on. In 1911, by conservative estimates, the Party elected some 1,141 Socialists to office in thirty-six states and in 324 municipalities. At that time, the Socialists had majority control of at least twenty-three communities, from the larger cities like Milwaukee, Wisconsin, Butte, Montana, and Berkeley, California, to smaller communities like Star City, West Virginia, with a population of 318.[23] Notably missing from this success list were the nation's largest industrial areas. While Socialists did have viable movements in such cities as Cleveland, Chicago, and New York, their electoral victories here were largely in terms of individual council seats, rather than majority power. The nation's large cities proved hostile environments.

As Ira Katznelson argues in his often-cited book, *City Trenches*, the major parties used big city politics to aggravate racial and ethnic differences and divide the working class.[24] While workers could develop a strong sense of their class interests at work, they often practiced a different identity in their community when they were home. Both parties built up powerful urban machines that drew loyalties based on patronage spoils intertwined with ethnic identity. In contrast, smaller cities and towns were either more ethnically homogeneous or of a size that the outside pressures impacting the community could generate a sense of common interest and solidarity. A similar dynamic differentiated the role of the middle class. In smaller cities, the fate of middle class was often tied directly to their working-class neighbors. A strike or shutdown at one of the town's major employers could impact the livelihood of professionals and storekeepers who relied on working-class customers. In contrast, in the nation's larger cities, the working and middle classes lived much more separate lives.

The experiments in Socialist local government left behind a lasting legacy. Some of the changes may not seem terribly revolutionary today, but, at the time, made major differences in people's lives. For example, Socialists made improving sanitary conditions in working-class districts a high priority. Under Socialist administrations, sanitary and health commissions received better funding and support, factory inspections were expanded, and streets, sidewalks and alleys were paved, repaired, and kept clean. Socialists set up hygienic demonstrations, pure-milk stations, pediatric care, quarantine programs, and launched campaigns against infant mortality. They expanded park development—a common demand in working-class neighborhoods. Socialists politicized unemployment, connecting joblessness to the actions of employers rather than the "inadequacies" or "laziness" of those without work. Socialist administrations often proved quite critical in providing support to striking workers. While mainstream politicians often protected the companies by sending police to club workers, Socialist administrations refused to do the same. In Schenectady, Mayor Lunn even had the police arrest Pinkerton Detectives, the employers' common "thugs" of choice, for carrying concealed weapons. He also enforced a local hotel ordinance to prevent the American Locomotive Company from housing scab labor in the plant. At the same time, he gave many striking workers temporary jobs in the municipal ice works. More intangibly, Socialist governments gave their working-class supporters a sense of dignity. Through Socialist electoral victories, ordinary factory workers, miners, and street cleaners were holding public office while their working-class supporters discussed the central political issues of the day to decide what their government should do.

Populist and Socialist Educational Strategies

The emphasis on building a grassroots democratic political culture, shared by both Populists and Socialists, is quite important for activists today. While the Democrats and Republicans viewed, and continue to view, politics as a question of winning votes and electing candidates, the Populists and the Socialists saw their tasks in much broader terms. To overcome media hostility and to follow their democratic and revolutionary values, Populists and Socialists spent considerable time and energy developing mass political education and grassroots movement-building activity.

Progressive activists must do the same today. We cannot simply copy the narrow, candidate-centered example offered by the major parties. Since an educational, movement-building politics is so different from the dominant practices surrounding us at present, it is worth spending a brief moment to examine in detail how the Populists and Socialists engaged in their grassroots work. Their educational strategies can be placed in two major categories: printed matter and community activities. Let's look at each in turn.

Printed Matter

Populists and Socialists relied heavily on the power of the written word. In a 1908 survey of 6,300 Socialist Party members, 52 percent of respondents claimed that they had been converted to socialism through reading socialist literature.[25] In his major work on the agrarian revolt, Lawrence Goodwyn considered the reform press one of the core experiences of the Populist movement. He wrote:

> Very close to the heart of the matter was the relationship of corporate wealth and the public press. It was a crucial imbalance, and Populists made massive allocations of time, energy, and sheer physical and financial effort to correct it. Out of this effort came the foremost internal achievement of the People's Party: the National Reform Press Association.
>
> Had Populism been nothing else, the Reform Press Association could stand as a monument to the moral intensity of the agrarian crusade.[26]

Radical daily, weekly, and monthly papers and periodicals formed the basis for Socialist and Populist educational outreach. At the height of each movement, the scale of such publications reached truly impressive numbers. For example, when formed in 1890, the Populists' National Reform Press Association encompassed over 1,000 papers.[27] In 1912, the Socialist Party claimed some 323 papers and periodicals—five English and eight foreign-language dailies, 298 weeklies, and twelve monthlies.[28] The most famous radical publication of this era was J. A. Wayland's *Appeal to Reason*. Begun in 1895, the editor's "One Hoss" philosophy, low subscription price, and shrewd, if not unproblematic, use of modern promotional and business techniques made the *Appeal* not only the most successful radical paper, but also one of the most widely read weekly publications of its day. In 1913, the *Appeal* reached a paid circulation of 760,000. Special editions could sell as many as three million copies.[29]

In addition to the *Appeal,* other major papers included such Populist organs as the *National Economist,* the *American Non-Conformist,* the *Advocate,* and the *People's Party Paper,* and such Socialist publications as the *National Rip Saw,* the *Jewish Daily Forward,* and the *International Socialist Review.* While these papers enjoyed a relatively large circulation, the task of fanning the flames of discontent involved thousands of small-scale operations. Like many of their more mainstream counterparts, these radical editors and publishers devoted considerable time and sacrifice to establishing modest community papers. Usually working alone or with one other person, local editors typically produced a weekly product printed in a four- to eight-page format. The Populist and Socialist press combined often sensational exposés of the establishment with movement news and ample material extolling and explaining the virtues of the Cooperative Commonwealth.[30] While larger publications could sometimes afford paid reporters, most radical papers depended upon volunteer writing supplemented by reprints of stories from other publications and national sources. Socialist publications also provided popular translations of European socialist thinkers. Much of the printed material came directly from the pen and philosophy of the newspaper's editor.

As major vehicles of Socialist and Populist education, both parties directly and indirectly supported and fostered their radical press. Originating out of the Farmers Alliance, the National Reform Press Association provided Populist editors with a national organization. Among its services, the Association gave members weekly two-page "ready prints." These often became the interior of many four-page local Populist papers. Partly as a result of the negative experience of the authoritarian use of the party press in Daniel De Leon's Socialist Labor Party, members of the Socialist Party of America deliberately avoided sponsoring an official national party newspaper until 1914. Instead, many Party locals established their own papers. For example, in Ohio, Socialist activists established the Cooperative Publishing Corporation of Findely. Each week, the chain produced local publications with a front and back page of common press items and four pages of specialized local news.

Both parties also provided the radical press with crucial financial support. Turn-of-the-century publishing was a risky business. Although some papers did print commercial advertising, most alternative publications had to rely upon subscription revenues. Yet as the primary readership often came from poor farmers and workers, radical editors tried to keep their prices low. Indeed, as spreading the movement's ideals was more important than business success, local Populist and Socialist papers often delivered each edition regardless of whether or not a subscriber had paid up.[31] With a typically perilous financial situation, many papers operated at a deficit—kept afloat by party locals who raised funds among their membership.

In addition to financial help, People's and Socialist Party activists provided the radical press with its main source of promotion. Ignored by the major corporate-controlled distribution channels, too poor to afford postage to each subscriber, and occasionally barred from the mail, the alternative press had to rely on the door-to-door subscription hustling and distribution efforts of thousands of local members. The most famous and elaborate of these operations was the "Salesmen- Soldier Army" of the *Appeal to Reason*. By 1913, the paper's army had grown to about 80,000 individuals who combed the nation's communities selling subscriptions, distributing papers, organizing study groups, and founding Socialist Party locals.

In short, while the Populist and Socialist movements could not have spread without the radical press, the alternative press could equally not have existed without the two movements. As the above discussion has tried to demonstrate, the movements did not simply offer a general atmosphere of rebellion that provided the radical press's readership. Rather, both movements self-consciously promoted the radical press as the primary vehicle for achieving their all-important task of educating the public toward new ways of thinking. Even those many publications that had no formal or legal ties to a party organization owed their livelihood to the deliberate support they received from the broader movement.[32]

In addition to the radical press, the Populist and Socialist movements also supported other forms of written education. For example, each movement sustained both private and cooperative publishing houses. Through advertisements in the alternative newspapers and promotion by party activists and lecturers, Populist books—such as Henry D. Lloyd's *Wealth Against Commonwealth*, Milford W. Howard's *If Christ Came To Congress*, and Cyclone Davis' *A Political Revelation*—and Socialist titles—such as Oscar Ameringer's *Life and Deeds of Uncle Sam*, A. M. Simon's *Wasting Human Life*, and Allan L. Benson's *The Truth About Socialism*—reached thousands, possibly millions, of readers. Those unable to purchase such works could often borrow them from radical libraries run by local party activists.

Local activists also promoted written arguments for populism or socialism by distributing leaflets and flyers. Many in the Socialist Party were especially fond of mass literature distribution. As *The Party Builder* advised in an article intended to be read aloud at local Party meetings:

> *Comrades: Pay dues. Distribute leaflets. And again, pay dues that there may be leaflets to distribute. And again, distribute leaflets that there may be Socialists to pay dues.*[33]

The same issue advised that "the systematic house to house distribution of leaflets, repeated at regular intervals, has been found most effective."[34]

The volume of literature that the Socialist Party put into circulation was truly impressive. In 1917, the national office sent locals thirty-seven different leaflets and pamphlets totaling almost five million pieces. In addition, it printed 800,000 copies of Victor Berger's congressional speech on tariffs.[35] Ads in *The Party Builder* requested orders of at least 5,000 for any single piece of literature.

To a significant degree, Populist and Socialist efforts to promote printed educational material represented community efforts in and of themselves. Both parties also fostered a range of additional activities that not only furthered the process of direct political education, but helped to establish the local Party as a part of community life and culture.

Community Activities

One key strategy involved extensive public speaking. Through the Farmers Alliance, the Populists developed an elaborate internal lecturing system. Along with the reform press, this system provided a good method for informing farmers of such complex topics as national monetary policy or the sub-treasury system. The lecturing efforts also fostered a democratic atmosphere of debate and discussion. Lecturers generally did not present a one-way transmission of knowledge. In his study of political education in the Southern Farmers Alliance, Theodore Mitchell found that lectures often took the form of debates in which "ideas were presented by speakers, countered by others, discussed by those in attendance during the meals and games, and refined or altered by still more speakers in the afternoon... It was a format that encouraged participation which in turn directed the outcome of the educational process."[36]

In addition to fostering popular education, roving lecturers also organized local chapters of the movement. Indeed, in the Southern Farmers Alliance, most lecturers lived off the fees received from new local organizations. According to C. Vann Woodward's research, in 1891 the Alliance was reported to have had 35,000 official lecturers in the field, variously classified as national, state, district, county, and sub-alliance lecturers. The first three categories were paid positions. In the summer of 1893, ex-congressional representative Tom Watson toured thirty-five Georgia counties speaking to crowds of no less than 2,000 and as many as 5,000 people. He claimed to have reached as many as 150,000 individuals.[37] This lecturing activity was key to the Populists' strength. According to Lawrence Goodwyn, "in states where Alliance leaders, for whatever reason, did not implement a massive lecturing campaign on the sub-treasury in 1891-92, the People's Party had only a shadow presence."[38]

The Socialist movement also fostered its share of public speaking. Such activity occurred before, during, and after the electoral campaign season. In addition to the wide-ranging "stump oratory" of local activists, the national office supported professional lecturer-organizers who participated in more formally organized assemblies. The Party kept a list of roughly fifty such speakers. In 1911, the national office initiated a Socialist Lyceum Bureau that provided subscribing locals a course of five lectures. In its first year of operation, the Bureau sponsored 1,500 lectures with an average reported attendance of 300 people.[39] One such national lecturer-organizer, Oscar Ameringer, described his methods in Oklahoma as using protracted meetings patterned after those of religious congregations: "They were held in country schoolhouses, village churches, and more rarely in the courtrooms of county courthouses, and usually lasted a week or two, according to the attendance and the results obtained."[40]

In addition to local and national speaking events, both movements sponsored a good deal of continuing education though small local schools and study groups. In 1905, the Socialist Party established the Rand School of Social Science. It offered courses on a wide range of subjects, including socialism, psychology, popular science, literature, music, foreign languages, and drama.[41] This modest national project was supplemented by numerous local study groups and schools that sought both to explain socialist ideas as well as provide working-class people with avenues for their intellectual development.

Such outreach efforts were often enhanced by their blending of educational and social components. At local Socialist headquarters, according to Richard Judd:

> *Members could read, converse, play cards, and discuss politics informally. The halls were common ground where "an iron molder... could rub shoulders on an equal footing with a lawyer from the other end of town."*[42]

Populist meetings were daylong family events. Scott McNall captures a sense of the festivity in his description of the parades leading up to local meetings in Kansas:

> *Those gathered at a town's picnic area would first see clouds of dust on the horizon, and then catch a glimpse of the colored banners fluttering in the breeze. Winding into town on wagons loaded with food for a day of celebration, with as many people as could be squeezed on, the farmers came. Those waiting in Augusta, Kansas, saw wagons roll by with banners bearing these mottoes: "United We Stand, Divided We Fall," "In Union, Strength,"... and "Truth Is Our Anchor"... The parades were elaborately structured events, and drew crowds of thousands.*[43]

The most elaborate fusion of education and social activity occurred during the Populist and Socialist encampments. Drawing upon the tradition of religious revival meetings, Populists and Socialists turned encampments into vast movement experiences. In his autobiography, Oscar Ameringer described his experience of such encampments in Oklahoma:

> *As the movement developed, we added summer encampments to schoolhouse meetings. These encampments were lineal descendants of the religious and Populist camp meetings of former days. They usually lasted a full week. The audience came in covered wagons from as far away as seventy miles. The pilgrims brought their own commissary, cooked, ate, and slept on the ground of their covered wagons...*
>
> *These encampments were attended by an average of five thousand people...*
>
> *On the morning of the first day a mixed chorus was organized and rehearsed in Socialist songs, usually of Populist origin, sung to familiar melodies. After singing school we conducted economic and historical mass lessons. They were exceedingly informal. The instructor planted himself in the chair or store box on a raised platform, then urged the audience on the ground or pine planks to ask questions...*
>
> *Dinner over, and dishes washed, the two o'clock meeting started under the big tent with singing and instrumental music... The instrumental music was*

supplied by myself and three sons, and we played only the best, so far as the best can be played by a brass quartet augmented by piano. Before our instrumental concert, I usually gave a short lecture on classical music...

At night we held another meeting with singing and music. After the night meetings, discussions around the glowing campfire continued on into the small hours. For to these people radicalism was not an intellectual plaything. Pressure was upon them. Many of their homesteads were already under mortgage. Some had actually been lost by foreclosure. They were looking for delivery from the eastern monster whose lair they saw in Wall Street. They took their socialism like a new religion. And they fought and sacrificed for the spreading of the new faith like the martyrs of other faiths.[44]

As Ameringer's account suggests, the encampments were impressive events. A 1913 advertisement for the tenth annual Socialist encampment in Grand Saline, Texas demonstrated the combination of education with family entertainment. While much of the ad was devoted to listing scheduled speakers, it also mentions a ferris wheel and the "picturesque" location.[45] In Texas, Populist camp meetings of 15,000 were not unknown. These events did not just occur in the Southwest. One 1913 edition of *The Party Builder* mentioned yearly summer encampments near Schenectady.[46]

In addition to these week-long crusades, Populist and Socialist activists commonly organized such community events as parades, barbecues, and dances. Describing Socialist activities in Ohio, Richard Judd writes:

In August 1915, for instance, the Cleveland Socialist News *announced a speaking contest at the city park, tryouts for the Socialist brass band, a continuing Socialist Sunday school, a petition drive for municipal ownership of the Cleveland street railway, a nature hike led by Charles Ruthenberg, evening lectures on labor-related topics, and a picnic at which the prize for the largest family in attendance was Engels'* Origin of the Family, Private Property, and the State. *The local was selling tickets to an upcoming Debs lecture and the Sixth Ward branch was peddling stock in a cooperative store.*

As the Cleveland agenda indicates, Socialist locals were more than propaganda units; they were outlets for working-class culture. Advertising their upcoming winter carnival, Martin Ferry Socialists promised there would be "no speechifying, just good fun." Lorain's 1909 masquerade ball attracted over a thousand merrymakers; their 1911 picnic, between 1,200 and 1,500. The Ohio state Socialist picnic drew crowds of 20,000, while the 1912 tri-state Socialist picnic at East Liverpool catered to as many as 30,000.[47]

In comparison to today, the Populists and Socialists may seem to have operated on relatively favorable terrain. When viewed from the context of the modern suburb, the turn of the century may appear as a bygone era of active community spirit and strong local institutions. Populists and Socialists, however, did not just build from existing community structures. They were instrumental in developing a sense of community.[48] This accomplishment can most clearly be seen in the Southwest, where geographical dispersion, recent arrival, and rapid economic transformation combined to produce a farm life that could be particularly isolating. In 1889, for example, the president of the Beaver Valley Alliance in Kansas described that they were "allied together to render the lives of farmers and laborers more attractive, country life less lonely and more social, and to better our financial condition."[49] As daylong family events, sub-alliance meetings were instrumental in providing farmers with a social existence. In establishing a sense of community, the political and social goals of the movements became inseparable.

In addition to blending educational work with local culture and community life, both parties developed ongoing local ties to the non-electoral social movements of their day. Indeed, the People's Party grew out of the cooperative organizing efforts of the Farmers Alliance. In effect, the party represented the ultimate political expression of the Alliance. In addition, agrarian Populists developed close sympathies with the cause of organized labor, especially the Knights of Labor. Similarly, the Socialist Party developed substantial ties among organized labor, the unemployed, agrarian radicals, suffragists, and, during World War I, pacifists and anti-war activists.

These connections to other social movements grew out of shared ideological orientations and mutual goals. Yet the ties went deeper. Both parties could solicit active support from social movement activists because they could offer concrete benefits. On the one hand, both parties provided an electoral vehicle for putting social movement sympathizers and members into office. On the other hand, the substantial and ongoing educational activity promoted by the parties not only provided the electoral movement channels into the popular consciousness, but it also provided a forum for the cause of unionists, blacks, women, and farmers. In this sense, the Populist and Socialist press, their social events, their schools and study groups, and their youth programs represented collective resources open to all who sought to challenge the status quo. Thus, local activists whose primary focus may have gone into specifically non-electoral concerns, nevertheless could still promote these concerns by aiding the educational work of the Populist and Socialist organizations. In essence, overcoming the influence of mainstream media and education represented a shared task.

The Combined Experience

When added together, Populist and Socialist printed matter and community activities represented a serious long-term political project. Henry Stetler's 1943 dissertation on the Socialist Party of Reading, Pennsylvania provides a comprehensive sense of this project. In a city with a population of just over 100,000, the Reading Socialist local represented a substantial political force for over thirty years during the period spanning the two world wars. They repeatedly elected Socialists to the state assembly, city council, and the mayor's office. With the local labor unions, the Reading Socialist Party developed a local radical newspaper: the *Reading Labor Advocate*. In addition, a group of Party workers called "The Flying Squadron" distributed a four-page local leaflet, called the *Pioneer*, to homes throughout the county. The local's library housed several thousand volumes. Its Young People's Socialist League reached out to youth, while the Socialist-supported Reading Labor College helped to further working-class education.

Reading Socialists also owned several cooperative enterprises, including a publishing house. They established a Socialist park, and inspired several vocal and instrumental groups. In addition, the local's repeated gaining of city, county, and state offices provided the Party opportunities to use government administration to demonstrate socialist ideals. Key to its success, the Reading Socialist Party enjoyed substantial ties of mutual support with the area's labor movement, including overlapping leadership. Through such activities, the Reading Socialist local established a physical presence in the life of the community—one that spread the ideals of the movement and enmeshed local residents in a socialist culture.

Theodore Mitchell's study of political education in the Southern Farmers Alliance provides an informative case study about how different educational components can intertwine and evolve. In focusing upon the pedagogical methods of such key figures as Charles Macune, Mitchell identifies a distinct evolution in Populist educational strategies. The movement began with an extensive lecturing system and network of local meetings. Although lecturing could win people to the cause and begin to develop a sense of class consciousness, it proved limited in its ability to provide the extensive training and individual intellectual skills necessary for the kind of active citizenship that the Alliance sought. Thus, in 1888, Alliance leaders launched the *National Economist*, with Macune as editor, as a vehicle for stimulating more extensive education. Through this journal and other smaller papers, Populists sought not only to debate national issues and spread Alliance ideas, but more generally to provide basic texts for the development of intellectual skills within the sub-alliances.

To overcome the problems of poverty and illiteracy, as well as to promote more active, participatory forms of learning, Macune further developed the *National Economist* into an explicit primer for use in sub-alliance meetings. He aimed to literally turn the sub-alliances into classrooms in which farmers would not only discuss the political issues of the day, but learn basic skills in reading, writing, and arithmetic. He also placed emphasis on promoting an extensive understanding of history from the viewpoint of the downtrodden.

In January 1892, Macune began publishing a series of Educational Exercises that laid out a sample curriculum for the sub-alliances. The

Exercises emphasized a participatory pedagogy. All members of the family were encouraged to become involved. For example, the curriculum asked children to aid their parents with basic math and reading as well as develop short skits of their own. Urging lots of music and dialogue, Macune saw educational and social interactions as reinforcing each other. The connection between technical skills and politics was often quite overt. One exercise had the class divide the entire gross wealth of the country by the current population. While this activity taught students how to manipulate large numbers, it could also easily lead into a political discussion, given that the result of the equation was far more money than most farmers had ever seen.[50]

Conclusion

Although many of these details have direct parallels for activists today, the overall focus of Populist and Socialist strategy is far more important than any of their specific tactics. Neither movement conceived of its educational efforts as momentary phenomenon restricted to periods of electoral campaigning. Rather, both Parties aimed to educate the largest possible audience in their ideals regardless of whether or not the Party happened to have someone running for office. As Gail McDermott wrote in a *Party Builder* article titled "The Unceasing Campaign":

> *This living example drove home to his listeners the thrust of our statement that the Socialist campaign is carried on 365 days in every year, with no rest, and no end except the Co-operative Commonwealth.*[51]

The living example that she referred to was the continuing "campaign" activities of Seymour Steadman, newly elected Illinois state legislator, who kept "campaigning" weeks after election day had past.

While both parties defined outreach as their primary and ongoing task, the manner in which individual Populists or Socialists interpreted this educational project varied within the ranks of both movements. For some, such work represented the election campaign writ large. Having encountered the difficulties of existing partisan loyalties and hostile press coverage, these Populists and Socialists sought to use ongoing educational work to achieve what they saw as the ultimate goal: election to office.

In contrast, many in both movements attached a deeper significance to educational work. Their ultimate goal was transforming the public's understanding of itself and society. For them, only changing people's perceptions and heightening their ability to mobilize themselves collectively could bring about the new society. In a personal letter, Schenectady Socialist Walter Lippman offered an excellent example of this way of thinking that is worth quoting at length. Having strongly objected to appeals and campaign techniques that sought to gain political office on the votes of non-socialist voters, Lippman argued:

> *The work we are engaged in lies a great deal deeper than politics can ever go. Politics is very near the surface of life; it expresses rather clumsily forces that are much more important. For the currents that move the world do not start in legislatures; occasionally they reach the legislature. Revolutions are not made by statute, or Socialist congresses. All that politics can do is to clarify and put a sort of concluding stamp on revolutions that have worked themselves out in the lives of people. I need hardly say to you that we are concerned with the revolution, and interested in politics only because it can aid it.*
>
> *Our great task to which politics is entirely subordinate is the organization of labor so that it understands its position, realizes its possibilities, and learns how to apply the power it possesses. Winning elections or fighting the subway issue are utterly trivial compared to the creation of this power among the working classes. Politics is only one small factor in this much more comprehensive work. Politics will be useful to labor only when labor has trained itself to self-government, has built its unions into centers of power, and saturated its daily life with a concrete and imaginative vision. That is the first work of the Socialist movement. If it is well done, our political action will reflect it. If it is neglected, no amount of fuss over the size of our vote will cover it up.*[52]

Although a necessary component of the struggle, the election of their Party to government office was insufficient to bring about revolutionary change. The Cooperative Commonwealth could not be legislated. Only the population as a whole, through its collective organization and daily activity, had the ability to transform fundamental social, political, and economic relationships.

Left populist Charles Macune clearly saw a difference between winning people's support for an organization's agenda and educating them to think for themselves. The Alliance's aim should be "first to educate the people," he wrote in 1891, "and when that is done, [to] have an abiding faith in… the integrity of the people in living up to the full measure of the light as they see it."[53]

Because of such an educational commitment, Macune and other like-minded populists greeted the Alliance's launching of the People's Party with mixed feelings. They clearly saw populism and the Alliance as a political movement. They sought to develop people's political abilities so that they, "the people," could govern in a truly democratic society. Many feared that the People's Party had a dangerous obsession with electoralism. D. D. Langford, an organizer and lecturer in Kentucky, argued after the elections of 1892 that "we have let partyism, in many instances, get the better of our judgment by making a great effort to get our demands before we have gotten the people educated up to the point that principle is above parties and men."[54]

For a person who defined the achievement of the Cooperative Commonwealth in terms of a mass process in which ordinary people liberated themselves, the task of popular education could never imply a one-way transmission of knowledge. Although they critiqued the status quo and offered a vision of a better society, populist and socialist activists did not define their educational work as attempting to implant in the passive minds of followers a predefined truth. Rather, they sought to aid a process in which people developed their own critical understanding through individual and collective experience.[55] As Goodwyn has written of populism:

> it was, first and most centrally, a cooperative movement that imparted a
> sense of self-worth to individual people and provided them with the
> instruments of self-education about the world they lived in. The movement
> gave them hope—a shared hope—that they were not impersonal victims of a
> gigantic industrial engine ruled by others but that they were, instead, people
> who could perform specific political acts of self-determination... Populism was,
> at bottom, a movement of ordinary Americans to gain control over their own
> lives and futures, a massive democratic effort to gain that most central
> component of human freedom—dignity.[56]

Activists joined the movement not simply to promote specific reforms, but to help build the Cooperative Commonwealth. With such a grand goal, the tasks of spreading the critique of the status quo, fostering people's intellectual development, and raising their cooperative capacities could easily eclipse the individual electoral campaign. This was the Populists' and Socialists' greatest success.

Chapter Two

Insignificant Movements?
The Historic Defeat
of Third Parties

One of the ongoing differences between the United States and most of our European counterparts is the absence of an institutionalized party of the Left here. Compared to European standards, where some manner of Social Democratic, Socialist, or Labor party exists as a seemingly natural political force in most countries, political debates in the United States take place in a very narrow spectrum. In most European countries, the major political fault lines lie between the Left parties (Social Democrat, Socialist, Labor, Green, and Communist) and parties on the Right (Christian Democrat, Tory, Conservative, and Liberal). From a European perspective, we have a political system in which two parties on the Right battle it out against each other.

A great deal of ink has been spilt trying to explain why the United States is so different. Despite notable gains and momentum, neither the People's Party nor the Socialist Party succeeded in establishing itself as a lasting institutional part of US politics. This failure has led many, including many progressives, to simply write off this history as an insignificant blip that only confirms the strength and permanence of the two party system. We believe that such a conclusion is both unfair and far too politically convenient for those who hope to maintain the two party monopoly. We need to dig deeper to draw useful lessons from this all too often neglected history.

These movements were not insignificant. Although neither third party succeeded in its ultimate aim, this does not mean that these movements had no impact on US politics. Quite to the contrary, even a casual glance at Populist and Socialist reform proposals will demonstrate how much we are indebted to their trailblazing. Notice how familiar and taken for granted these concepts are today:

- the election of the Senate by a direct vote of the population rather than selection by state legislatures, as originally designed in the Constitution;
- the right of all adults to vote regardless of race, ethnic background, gender, or class;
- the graduated income tax;
- laws to reduce corruption in local, state, and national government;
- the prohibition of child labor;
- the two-day weekend;
- enhancing direct democracy through initiative and referendum laws;
- the establishment of the Department of Labor;
- the free administration of justice;
- municipal ownership of utilities;
- the expansion of public education; and
- an expanded money supply no longer tied to the gold standard.

The two major parties defeated Populists and Socialists, in part, by adopting and co-opting all of these specific reform ideas. Even for reforms not directly taken up by the two party system at the time, Populists and Socialists paved the way for future popular victories by helping to place issues into the national debate. Even in defeat, these organizations were hardly insignificant.

The actual reasons for the decline of the Populists and Socialists hardly paint a picture of an indestructible two party system, either. The question of why these movements ultimately failed is highly contested. Many historians, especially those who have firm allegiances to the two party system, argue that the two movements failed to appeal to a significant number of Americans. This basic argument has several variations. Some say that both parties were too radical and marginal in their thinking. One wing of the scholarship on populism has devoted itself to portraying the Populists as simply a bunch of backward-looking, racist, prejudiced, and ignorant country hicks. Similar scholars have assumed that socialism has nothing to do with America, but came as a foreign ideology brought over from Europe. Other historians focus on the supposed triumph of a so-called American creed: our nation's dream of individual liberty, free market capitalism, and a two party system. Another variation on this theme is the notion that most people did not support populism or socialism because America is a success story. We have the great middle-class society. America is the land of opportunity. We don't have strong class divisions or inequalities. Therefore, such "radicalism" has no home on our shores.

All of these explanations fit in well with a great deal of mythology that the rich and powerful like to use in defining America. The reality is quite different, of course. The very existence of the Populists and Socialists speaks to the huge inequalities endemic to US society. As labor historians point out, class struggle is nothing new to this country. Indeed, the US working class has been known for its militancy and labor battles. We must not forget that May 1, the international holiday of the labor movement celebrated world-wide, actually began in the United States in 1886 when half a million workers laid down their tools to demand the eight-hour day.

This country also has a long and proud tradition of homegrown radicalism. The American Revolution witnessed various brands of working-class and agrarian radicalism that defined liberty, freedom, and democracy in ways quite different from the elitist conceptions of the "founding fathers." Such key revolutionary figures as Thomas Paine and Samuel Adams have been de-emphasized in the official historical memory precisely because their notions of popular self-government were deemed subversive in the eyes of the official founders. Even such a supposedly conservative force as Christianity has had a radical form. Today, we call it liberation theology. At the time of the Populists and Socialists, many people saw their religious beliefs as radical tools for fostering fundamental social change. As one Christian radical wrote in his rewording of a popular hymn:

> *I have seen the healthy fading for the lack of food and care,*
> *And the city toiler sicken for the want of rest and air;*
> *I have seen the gorgeous follies of the pampered millionaire—*
> *But our God is marching on.*[1]

Those who claim that populism and socialism simply did not have mass appeal also ignore the substantial numbers of people involved in the movements. There is a good dose of elitism going on here, as the radicalism of millions of farmers and workers is written off. The assumption seems to be that only the reform ideas of middle-class professionals and "enlightened" rich people merit serious consideration.

We suggest a different way of looking at the decline of populism and socialism. Their demise came not as a failure to appeal, but as a defeat at the hands of powerful opponents. In other words, the Populists and Socialists failed to become a permanent part of our political landscape not because large numbers of Americans would not have supported them, but because the powerful and privileged were able to mobilize successful efforts to destroy them. Indeed, as we go through the drastic measures that the established authorities used to defeat these challengers, we might keep in mind an important question: Why, if these movements were so marginal and unappealing to a majority of Americans, did the defenders of the two party monopoly have to resort to such extreme and blatantly undemocratic practices to defeat them?

Why the Defeat of Populism and Socialism

The defenders of the two party system used seven major methods to fight off the Populists and Socialists. Many of these methods will likely be used against third party efforts today. They deserve to be better understood.

1. Major Party Fusion and Cooperation

Historically, the Republican and Democratic parties confirmed the Populists' and Socialists' accusations that they were simply two sides of the same coin by teaming up together to defeat their challengers. This occurred quite blatantly through the process of fusion, in which the two parties would endorse the same candidate. It could also happen more informally by having the weaker of the two candidates step out of a particular race in order to avoid dividing the non-Populist or non-Socialist vote. Through such coop-eration, the two parties upped the political threshold, forcing the third party to win an absolute majority of the vote instead of simply the single largest block. Populists and Socialists were frequently elected one year only to find themselves driven out of office the next election, when Republicans and Democrats combined their votes.

This cooperation came to national fruition with the election of 1896. The two major parties reduced their competition with each other to such an extent that the United States became essentially two one-party systems. The Republicans and Democrats basically divided the nation into distinct geo-graphic areas. Each party had overwhelming power and superiority in its area. In his classic work on US electoral evolution, E. E. Schattschneider described this new political order as follows:

> The 1896 party cleavage resulted from the tremendous reaction of conservatives in both major parties to the Populist movement, a radical agrarian agitation that alarmed people of substance all over the country... Southern conservatives reacted so strongly that they were willing to revive the tensions and animosities of the Civil War and the Reconstruction in order to set up a one-party sectional southern political monopoly in which nearly all Negroes [sic] and many poor whites were disenfranchised. One of the most important consequences of the creation of the Solid South was that it severed permanently the connection between the western and the southern wings of the Populist movement... The conservative reaction in the North was almost as spectacular as the conservative reaction to Populism in the South... the Republican party consolidated its supremacy in all of the most populous areas of the country. The resulting party line-up was one of the sharply sectional political divisions in American history. In effect, the new party divisions turned the country over to two powerful sectional minorities: (1) the northern business-Republican minority and (2) its southern conservative Democratic counterpart.[2]

In these one party monopolies, meaningful elections often ceased to exist. The dominant party chose its candidate and the electorate merely reconfirmed the predominance of that party by rubber-stamping that person into office.

2. Legal "Reforms"

With the legislatures and courts solidly in Democratic and Republican hands, the two major parties enacted a series of reforms that rearranged electoral competition to the detriment of challenger movements. Much of these changes are still part of the political landscape today.

For example, by selectively redrawing electoral boundary lines, Democrats and Republicans could either isolate heavily Populist and Socialist areas or dilute such votes by splitting them up and combining them with Republican- and Democratic-controlled areas. Although technically illegal, this process, known as "gerrymandering," is still an issue today. A look at district boundaries reveals that they do not always conform to any straightforward geographic or demographic characteristics.

Another legal tactic used to block political insurgency at a municipal level was to change the forms of representation in ways least favorable to a small, but growing movement. For example, defenders of the status quo in Milwaukee changed the city's government from a ward system to an at-large body selected by a citywide vote. The old ward system favored groups like the Socialists, which attracted heavy support in very specific areas of the city. In contrast, the at-large system favored both those already in the majority and candidates whose support spread throughout the city. When it worked, the at-large system meant that the anti-Socialist vote in middle- and upper-class areas could swamp the Socialist support in working-class wards. In Milwaukee, however, the Socialists were able to expand their appeal to attract enough middle-class support to continue growing. Following the Socialist 1910 sweep of local races, the state legislature tried yet another tactic to undercut Socialist strength by removing all party labels from local elections, making them non-partisan. Forced to run as individuals rather than as a party ticket, the Socialists never regained the total dominance they had achieved in 1910.

At-large systems and non-partisan races were soon introduced in local governments across the country. They became common tools for defeating radical political activism. In Dayton, Ohio, for instance, local Socialists had been looking forward to eventually controlling the city council. However, as they explained in a letter following the 1913 election season, "The reason the Socialists failed to re-elect councilmen and assessors was because there aren't no such animal anymore in Dayton!"[3] The city had abolished ward-based elections, replacing them with a new at-large system that swamped the Socialist vote.

Another anti-democratic "reform" was the commission-manager form of local government. Such systems move from larger representative bodies to much smaller, more centralized councils in which commissioners directly head governmental departments. The mayor, or manager, is often selected by these same people. The commission-manager model is founded on the view that government is a technical, administrative matter best handled by competent professionals. The system serves to insulate local government from public debate and pressure. Combined with non-partisan races and at-large elections, such a system moved local politics away from contests of differing ideologies and political platforms toward questions of an individual's competency. Such reforms steered local politics in a direction opposite from radical priorities. Both Populists and Socialists emphasized ideological differences, partisan politics, and popular participation.

3. Repression

Neither of the major parties were above the tried and true method of using the state apparatus to repress dissent and thwart one's opponents. The most blatant and shameless repression began during World War I. In June 1917, Congress passed the Espionage Act and, in May 1918, the Sedition Act. Both laws render it essentially illegal to speak out against a US war effort. Even before these federal laws, many state governments had taken similar measures to outlaw "subversion." The two main targets of these measures were the IWW and the Socialist Party. Armed with such repressive legislation, police busted up Socialist Party and anti-war meetings, arrested radicals, broke into offices, destroyed Party chapters, and banned publications. The post office played a major role by confiscating materials deemed subversive and banning radical publications from the mail altogether. Immigration laws were also used to deport hundreds and eventually thousands of "radical foreign elements." Officials forced 2,300 German-Americans deemed "dangerous" into concentration camps. Such official government repression also gave a green light to private vigilantism, in which "true patriots" proceeded to attack, beat up, ban, and murder "subversives."

After the end of the war, the nation's elite launched another round of political repression, known as the Red Scare, between 1919 and 1920. This campaign brought more arrests, banned publications, deportations, raids on offices, vigilantism, and destroyed careers. Morris Hillquit, a Socialist elected and re-elected to the House of Representatives, was repeatedly denied his seat in Congress. Because of this repression, Socialist Party presidential candidate Eugene Debs had to campaign from a prison cell in 1920. The Red Scare climaxed with the infamous Palmer Raids, in which a vastly expanded Bureau of Investigation ran roughshod over due process and other legal formalities to arrest over 10,000 persons.

The wave of repression during the war era is notable mainly for its blatantness. Throughout the Populist and Socialist revolts, the powers-that-be used the strong arm of the state to silence opposition. The post office continuously betrayed its political loyalties as did many local and state police and judicial systems. In 1890, amid a growing Populist movement in Kansas, the state's senior senator gave a startlingly frank justification for the use of intimidation, corruption, and repression. When a reporter from a New York paper asked him if the "ends justified the means," he replied:

> *The purification of politics is an iridescent dream. Government is force. Politics is the battle for supremacy. Parties are the armies... [The two major parties] use the ballots instead of guns, but the struggle is the same [as in the battles of the Civil War]. In war, it is lawful to deceive the adversary, to hire hessians, to purchase mercenaries, to mutilate, to destroy. The commander who lost a battle through the activity of his moral nature would be the derision and jest of history. This modern cant about the corruption of politics is fatiguing in the extreme...*[4]

With attitudes like these floating around in "respectable circles," it is no wonder that when the first Populist-majority legislature met in Kansas, they did so fully armed!

Political repression was not limited to governmental authorities. To the contrary, their actions simply encouraged and bolstered widespread private efforts to stamp out radicalism. The wealthy used their economic power as a tool against political opposition. Populist and Socialist activists and sympathizers were fired from their jobs, expelled from their tenant farms, and evicted from their homes. Employers and landlords kept "blacklists" of known "troublemakers" so that they could drive these Populists and Socialists out of the area. When all else failed, the "respectable" in society would simply turn to violence. The Ku Klux Klan, for example, experienced a major revival during the Populist and Socialist years. Founded in 1866 by the Southern economic elite, the Klan served as a primary weapon to fight black organizing during Reconstruction and to terrorize African Americans generally. During the Populist and Socialist eras, the Klan continued this role, hunting down black Populists and Socialists. They also revealed their class mission when they went after white radicals as well, beating them up, burning their houses, killing their livestock, and even engaging in murder.

The mainstream party and business press of this country also kept up a steady war of misinformation and ridicule against the mass movements. Today, living among all the high-tech communication methods, it may seem as though corporate media domination and control is a new challenge. It isn't.

A century ago, local and regional newspapers were either affiliated with the Republican or Democratic Party, or owned by the local business elite committed to the status quo. Also during this era, figures such as Joseph Pulitzer, William Randolph Hearst, and Edward Willis Scripps began carving out huge empires that virtually monopolized certain aspects of the nation's media, especially the press wire and cable services. Additionally, newspapers of all kinds found themselves becoming increasingly reliant on revenues from business advertising. Even such radical publications as the *Appeal to Reason* were forced to display announcements as a way of staying in business.

All of these forces combined to make the media of the day an instrument for the repression of radical movements and ideas. Since modern norms advocating at least the appearance of objectivity (many question the reality) had not yet decisively influenced writing styles, this repression was often quite visceral and blatant. For example, *The New York Times* evaluated the Farmers Alliance's sub-treasury plan in 1893 as "one of the wildest and most fantastic projects ever seriously proposed by a sober man."[5] The Nebraska *State Journal* described Populist leaders as representing "the shiftless, lazy, and improvident" among the homesteaders "whose sole object in availing themselves of Uncle Sam's gift of farms... appears to be to mortgage their property and live off the loans until they are foreclosed." It continued on to lament that "it is a sin and a shame that these pests are permitted to beslime the state..."[6]

The establishment press of a hundred years ago also largely ignored the issues raised by progressive activists, preferring instead to undermine them through ugly association and inference. Evaluating the typical performance of the metropolitan dailies, Lawrence Goodwyn wrote:

> By and large... the nation's metropolitan dailies did not press discussions of economic issues as defined by the Populists, especially during the heat of election campaigns. The patent all-season remedy for the third party was the politics of sectionalism... Eastern Republicans decided the only rational explanation for Western discontent was that the plains states were laying proper ground for seceding from the Union![7]

The Socialists fared no better than their Populist predecessors. When the press opposed the movement it did so by substituting ridicule in place of the real issues. For example, one Oklahoma paper attacked J. A. Wayland, editor of what the paper called the "*Appeal to Treason*," for publishing "more rot per square inch in his paper than any other." It continued by arguing that "he calculated to poison and influence the minds of the vicious and ignorant class of people more than any other person alive—with the possible exception of Eugene V. Debbs [sic]."[8] Accusations of advocating such things as "free love" and the complete abolition of all personal property (farms, houses, clothes, tools, and so on) were common enough that the Socialists felt they had to reply to such notions in their campaign literature. J. A. Wayland evaluated the influence of the party and corporate press in the following characteristically blunt terms:

> There were wise men when there were no papers and books cost a fortune...
> The ignorance of today is the creation of the newspapers more than anything

else... *Every base idea, every false impression you have is traceable to the vileness and villainousness of the daily press in the pay of the monopolies of this country... stop reading the vile press of America and you will be wiser.*[9]

4. Race-Baiting

In a country founded on white supremacy, opponents of populism and socialism made ample use of race-baiting. By doing so, the "respectable elements" in society tried to deflect the political debate away from movements that were essentially class-based. While by modern standards both movements suffered serious limitations in their anti-racism, Populists and Socialists did make genuine efforts to unite black and white. The Populists, especially, challenged white supremacy head on in its southern home by having whites and blacks in the same meeting hall or running multiracial tickets.

In response, elites heaped the crassest forms of racial attacks and white supremacy appeals upon both movements. For example, when the Arkansas Alliance overwhelmingly voted in favor of the sub-treasury plan, the *Dallas Herald* congratulated the Alliance for standing "shoulder to shoulder" with "the niggers of Arkansas."[10] Such white supremacy attacks attempted to turn the economic issues raised by the Populists into a question of "racial" loyalty. An Oklahoma paper denounced Socialist publicist Oscar Ameringer, stating that "the nigger-loving Dutchman is the chief attraction at the socialist encampment in Hollis... It is the first opportunity many of our people have ever had of seeing this freak who has been imported to tell the people of Oklahoma that the negro is their equal."[11]

With racism so deeply entrenched in popular culture, appeals to white loyalty had a serious impact. In addition to the rhetoric used by politicians and the media, racism also took on a physical form through the reinvigorating of white supremacist violence. As mentioned before, groups like the Ku Klux Klan not only attempted to terrorize the African-American population away from radical politics, but attacked and killed white Populists and Socialists as well.

While the open use of racism came most crassly and violently in the South, race-baiting was used by both Republicans and Democrats throughout the country. In addition to playing up the "black menace," the establishment utilized attacks on other communities of color, such as Chinese and Mexican Americans, as well as blaming immigrants for people's economic troubles. Those in power also used the nation's ethnic diversity as another substitute for class-based politics. Both parties built up cultural and patronage loyalties to certain ethnic groups while playing them off against others. At the same time, they raised the flag of "patriotism" by appealing to nativist sentiment as a compliment to white supremacy.

5. The Purge of the Electorate

While major party cooperation, repression, race-baiting, and structural reforms were used as immediate responses to the popular challenges, the defenders of the status quo also sought more long-term solutions to protect the two party system. Defeating the Populists and Socialists was not enough if the same social forces continued producing mass unrest. Since neither major party was willing to address the economic question underlying this protest, they latched on instead to a nakedly undemocratic alternative. If the poor and working class were going to support radical challenges, then the solution was to simply remove these people from the ranks of active voters. Thus began a massive purge of the American electorate—one whose legacy is still with us today in our continued low rates of voter turnout.

The purge occurred most openly in the South. Following the Populist wave, southern states enacted or further strengthened laws and procedures intended to keep "undesirables" away from the polls. Poll taxes, literacy tests, and rigid residency requirements all served as legal mechanisms for reducing the electorate. Klan terror added further disincentives toward voting. Politicians justified the voter purge using the banner of white supremacy. White folk's "democracy" needed to be protected from the "civilization-destroying" impulses of black Americans. This effort worked. African-American electoral participation was practically eliminated. In Louisiana, for example, the black vote fell from 130,334 in 1896 to 1,342 by 1904. While those in power went about decrying the racial threat, when the smoke had cleared the majority of whites found that they, too, had been blocked from voting. While the black vote dropped by 90 percent in Louisiana, white participation also fell by 60 percent.[12] Speaking of the South overall, political scientist Walter Dean Burnham noted that "by the mid-1920s presidential turnout had declined to about 18 percent of the potential electorate, while in the off-year congressional election of 1926 only 8.5 percent of the South's potential voters actually went to the polls."[13]

This disenfranchisement of the southern electorate was clearly aimed at populism's electoral base. Having narrowly escaped electoral destruction at the hands of the People's Party, southern Democrats ensured their survival and continued hegemony by purging the electorate of Populist voters. In his book length study of suffrage restrictions in the South, J. Morgan Kousser writes:

> The new political structure was not the product of accident or other
> impersonal forces, nor the decisions demanded by the masses, nor even the
> white masses. The system which insured the absolute control of predominantly
> black counties by upper-class whites, the elimination in most areas of parties
> as a means of organized competition between politicians, and, in general, the
> nonrepresentation of lower-class interests in political decision-making was
> shaped by those who stood to benefit most from it—Democrats, usually from

the black belt and always socioeconomically privileged... the disfranchisers
articulated consciously elitist theories about suffrage and wrote these theories
into law in a successful effort to reform the polity.[14]

While not as blatant as in the South, the major parties presided over a
similar process of voter decline throughout the country. For example, the
percentage of the eligible population that actually voted in the presidential
elections fell from 87 percent in 1880 to 40 percent by 1926. Between 1880
and 1924, the percentage of eligible voters voting in congressional races fell
from 87 percent to 52 percent.[15]

The reduction of the electorate came through a number of channels.
Paralleling the southern experience, in form if not in degree, state governments throughout the country adopted various legal "reforms" that discour-
aged voter participation. These measures included registration laws, literacy
tests, and the elimination of alien voting. Some of these measures had merit.
For example, before the introduction of voter registration, Democratic and
Republican maneuvering could produce turn-outs of over 100 percent as
party loyalists traveled from poll to poll. While many other countries took
on responsibility for registering voters, the United States did not. As if the
class bias of such systems was not clear enough, local registration offices
would routinely open only during certain days of the week and always at
times when most people had to be at work.

An exact evaluation of the impact of these legal changes upon voter
turn-out remains a matter of some scholarly dispute. Where implemented,
however, these changes clearly had an effect. Conservative estimates
attribute roughly one-third of the decline in voter participation during the
turn of the century to rule changes.[16]

Reduced electoral participation also involved a much more subtle
process. Over time, both major parties simply de-emphasized their traditional
efforts to get out the vote. The new campaign methods that emerged toward
the end of the nineteenth century aimed more at persuading those who did
vote to choose a given candidate, rather than getting more supporters to the
polls. Political campaigns became less and less community events and more
and more exercises in advertising. As the country entered the new century,
popular interest in electoral politics showed signs of decline. As Robert
Dinkin has commented:

> *the upper classes who in the past had encouraged mass participation in the*
> *political sphere were not as inclined to do so, believing that reduced*
> *involvement might help bring about a less corrupt system and one less likely to*
> *become radicalized. Given little encouragement to remain politically involved,*
> *the mass of people began to find alternative outlets in the new leisure-time*
> *activities available.*[17]

Both major parties, having largely eliminated competition between themselves, welcomed this shrunken electorate. As Walter Dean Burnham has described:

> Essentially, a political system which was congruent with the hegemony of laissez-faire corporate capitalism over the society as a whole had come into being. The era of "normalcy" was one of two noncompetitive party hegemonies: the Democrats in the South and the Republicans throughout much of the North and West. Both implicitly rested on a huge mass of non-voters.[18]

Proponents of restricted suffrage often made the connections quite clear. In 1918 two Yale historians surveying attitudes on voting found that "the theory that every man has a natural right to vote no longer commands the support of students of political science." They pointed out that "if the state gives the vote to the ignorant, they will fall into anarchy today and into despotism tomorrow."[19]

6. Progressive Reformism

Another strategy used by both parties was to steal many of the specific demands raised by the insurgent movements. As mentioned before, many specific reforms that we enjoy today were originally raised by Populists and Socialists. Where possible, the nation's wealthy would defuse a radical challenge by adopting those reforms that did not cost too much or that helped to modernize the country's evolving capitalist system. As a 1912 Socialist campaign flyer asked voters: "All 'reform parties' are trying to steal some of our planks—why?"

This shadow reformism coalesced into a coherent movement that historians have termed the Progressive Era. Not to be confused with activists who today call themselves progressives, these turn-of-the-century reformers came from the more privileged sectors of the population. Their overriding goals were modernizing the nation's economy and undermining more radical alternatives. Much of their agenda had elements of popular appeal. For example, the Progressives' call to end corruption in the halls of government did address a reality of party machine favoritism and incompetence. Their attacks on large corporate monopolies also paralleled popular hostility to the nation's concentrated wealth.

The Progressives' alternative to populism and socialism was also profoundly elitist. Rather than reducing public corruption by increasing direct mass participation in government, the Progressives replaced elected representatives with non-elected, professional technocrats. Rather than building democratic parties controlled from below, the Progressive alternative to the corrupt old-style party machines was to eliminate political parties altogether. Through mechanisms such as the direct primary, Progressives sought to make the party system no more than a label used by individual candidates who basically controlled their own destiny. This across-the-board anti-party effort was not accidental. Strong party organizations not only favored old-style machine bosses, but, in the hands of Populists and Socialists, were vehicles of mass democracy. Strong parties that are democratically organized provide a way for their members to develop a political agenda and hold their elected officials accountable to that program. In contrast, the candidate-centered, individualistic politics successfully fostered by Progressive reformers moved the nation's elections into personality contests in which the best-funded candidates predominated.

The ability of "progressive" reforms to undercut genuine popular organizing is well illustrated in the rise and fall of the Socialist Party in Flint, Michigan.[20] Early in this century, Flint was an industrial boomtown. Flint's expanding automobile industry, with its promise of high-paying jobs (relative to other working-class occupations), drew a steady migration of laborers. Not only did the influx of people put a strain on city services and housing, but the local business and political establishment demonstrated little concern for working-class neighborhoods or labor conditions in the emerging auto industry. Politics as usual, however, came to an abrupt end on April 4, 1911, when the people of Flint elected John Menton, a Socialist, as mayor. They also elected several Socialists to the city council, school board, and as the justice of the peace.

Menton immediately got to work fulfilling his campaign promises. Some measures, such as stiffer building and health codes, greater efforts to expand public parks and boulevards, investigation of corruption at the Flint Water Works, and crackdowns on unlicensed drinking establishments, were relatively uncontroversial. However, the well-organized business community successfully mobilized to block Menton's plans for a night school for dayshift workers, a local labor temple for union meetings, a citywide eight-hour workday, improved workplace safety inspection, and municipal ownership of all utilities, including a free public hospital. The business class was also quite alarmed at Menton's efforts to redefine the role of the police department, especially his bold action in appointing a black carpenter as police commissioner.

In the short run, the local establishment was able to counter the Socialist upsurge with their usual combination of repression and ridicule. The pro-business majority on the city council blocked most of Menton's reforms, while local management blacklisted prominent Socialists. One Socialist council member found himself without a day job soon after he won election. Similarly, the local financial authorities tried to push Menton in a more conservative direction by taking hold of his mortgage. The local press wasted no opportunity to ridicule the Socialist administration for supposedly being "unpatriotic," "atheistic," against "individual freedom," and out to "destroy the family."

Reformism was key to the business community's ability to recapture political power. Led by millionaire industrialist C. S. Mott, the Republican and Democratic parties ran a fusion slate that promised to champion the "factory men of Flint." During the campaign, Mott personally raised the wages at Weston-Mott, the city's second-largest employer. Despite a furious class-based counter-attack by the Socialists, Mott won. Voter rejection in Menton's working-class strongholds proved crucial to his defeat. Although Menton was on the side of working-class voters, he could not deliver on many needed reforms. In contrast, Mott had the full backing of the economic and political establishment. He could press forward rapidly with his own version of reforms. For example, Mott paved miles of streets, expanded sewers and water lines, cracked down on local vice, built a new YMCA, passed a child welfare ordinance, and set up new regulatory laws. More generally, Flint's business elite discovered the virtues of civic responsibility. With the auto industry booming, the wealthy were willing to use a modest amount of their profits to establish a system of corporate paternalism. For instance, workers at General Motors (GM), the center of Flint's economic life, could enjoy relatively high wages; live in company-built housing or buy their own house through GM-provided mortgages; deposit their money in the company's savings and loan bank; receive health insurance, sick pay, and low-cost life insurance from their employer; and spend a good amount of their recreation time at GM-sponsored bowling alleys, card rooms, dance halls, and sports teams. Especially for those fleeing rural poverty, life in Flint's auto industry, at least materially, seemed pretty good by the 1920s.

Of course, all these benefits came at a cost. Auto workers had to endure strenuous and degrading conditions at work. And, as workers found out during the Great Depression, what employers gave they could also take away. In the meantime, Flint's system of corporate paternalism helped to destroy third party politics in the city by wedding a clear block of working-class voters to business-driven "progressive" reform.

7. Fraud

We should also note again the major parties' tactic of last resort. When all else failed, partisans of the status quo were not above illegally stealing elections. The Democratic Party maintained its Solid South against the Populists by stealing the statewide elections in Alabama, Georgia, and Texas. Many other examples could be cited.

The Problem of Internal Weaknesses

Combining the above fight-back tactics with greater financial resources, the defenders of the status quo succeeded in blocking the growth of both the Populists and Socialists. In addition, the two movements suffered from several internal weakness that placed a brake on their further growth and expansion. Two are worth mentioning here as they are issues that continue to confront progressive activists today.

The first weakness concerns the internal diversity of these movements. While their decentralized, democratic structures opened them to wide participation, these movements clearly did not bring together all of the potential protest groups of their age. For example, the Populists defined themselves as working people and made significant appeals to industrial workers. Yet, the Populists remained, at their base, an agrarian movement. Partly, this is explained by the fact that the Populists developed at a time when their natural ally among industrial workers, the Knights of Labor, had entered a period of serious decline. Yet the Populists also formulated their critique of society in ways that appealed more to farmers than urban workers. While they tried hard to connect their attacks on the nation's financial system and corporate monopolies to the struggles of industrial workers, they ultimately spoke the language of the small producer battling crushing market forces, not the working class fighting the plant boss.

Similarly, the Socialists never fully reached beyond their base of skilled workers, who were largely native-born or old-stock immigrants. Much of the party's overall culture and rhetoric was built on native-born radical republicanism, rather than the reality of the growing mass of unskilled, mostly new immigrant, working class. Indeed, members of the movement's Right often got pulled onto the anti-immigrant bandwagon. Not until 1912 did the party leadership reluctantly agree to officially charter the growing foreign-language socialist groups into associated federations. By 1916, 40 percent of the diminished Party came from the foreign-language sections. However, the skilled/unskilled, native/foreign-born tensions were never resolved. Indeed, the 1919 split would occur, in part, along these lines. The Socialist Party also had a complex relationship to agrarian radicalism. The Party's national call for collectivized agriculture failed to appeal to the mass of poor farmers. Indeed, the movement's notable success among tenant farmers in the Southwest was due to local organizers dropping their national farm policy program plank. Instead, they took up the old Populist call to restore the family farm.

Both parties also had a complex experience confronting racism. We mentioned earlier the notable efforts of both movements to challenge flagrant white supremacy and racial separation. Neither movement, however, went very far beyond the limitations of their age. While some Populists and Socialists clearly struggled to overcome the barriers of race, others openly embraced racist rhetoric and ideas. For example, after the movements' defeat, Georgia Populist Tom Watson turned into a rabid and reactionary racist, blaming African Americans, many of whom had been terrorized by the white landlords and authorities into supporting the establishment, for the Populists' decline. Even many white Populists and Socialists who actively sought to ally with their black comrades suffered from the racist limitations of their times. For example, while many Populists realized their shared economic struggle with black sharecroppers, most did not embrace social equality and integration between the races. While the People's Party brought black and white farmers together, the National Farmers Alliance was not a multiracial organization, but worked in alliance with the separate Colored Farmers Alliance.

Similarly, while the Socialist Party did have a small but notable component of black socialists, the organization remained a largely white movement. Part of the problem was ideological. Officially, the party subsumed the racial question within the overall class struggle. Most Socialists believed that a working-class revolution would solve racial divisions—divisions they saw as nothing more than a false issue used by employers to distract workers from their common class interests. The Socialists never developed a full understanding of racism, especially how it could operate within the movement and privilege white farmers and workers over their black comrades. Not until the Communist Party of the 1920s and 30s would a predominately white radical movement recognize the centrality of the anti-racist struggle.

Furthermore, neither movement completely embraced the struggle for women's equality. As Mari Jo Buhle has described in her excellent study, *Women and American Socialism 1890-1920*, there was a genuine, largely native-born, Socialist women's movement. Engaging in struggles around women's right to labor, suffrage, birth control, and against prostitution, these Socialist women developed their own distinct vision of socialism and a truly emancipated society. Nevertheless, despite notable examples of some outstanding radical women who became recognized leaders, the Socialist Party remained a male-dominated movement steeped in the Victorian ideals of its age.

The second major limitation that afflicted both movements was ideological splits and sectarianism. The diversity of political outlook that both movements embraced clearly provided a source of strength by permitting flexibility in the way in which the organizations appealed to different groups. Yet both the People's Party and the Socialist Party died in major factional battles. On the Right, both movements attracted opportunistic leaders who clearly did not share the central tenants of the movements, especially a commitment to grassroots democracy. The Left, in turn, contained many ultrarevolutionaries, who held to uncompromising stances in the face of practical reality. At times, neither group showed much respect for open, democratic procedures.

The problem of sectarianism went beyond the limitations of specific individuals or tendencies, however. In part, the division between Left and Right factions reflected the complex dilemmas facing a radical movement confronting serious opposition. Indeed, as the efforts of those in power began to significantly block the movements' growth, both the Populists and the Socialists confronted a serious strategic question: Should the movement moderate its program to build alliances with sections of the middle class and major party reformers, or should it stick to its working-class base and emphasize the fundamental divisions in society?

Such debates helped split both movements, particularly under the pressures of counter-attack. The lesson for activists today seems to be that, although one has to make clear strategic decisions, the dilemmas facing a radical political movement defy simplistic, one-dimensional answers. We should also never forget that political differences are inherent to any democratic movement seeking to challenge the status quo. We, thus, need to creatively work on internal structures and organizational cultures that can best negotiate these differences and avoid unnecessary splits.

The Grass is Not Always Greener

One of the burdens that US activists have to bear today is the historical precedent that in Europe the Left succeeded in establishing institutionalized parties, while in the United States these movements were ultimately defeated. The fact that third party politics seems natural across the Atlantic makes activists only that much more cynical here.

Scholars have advanced a wide range of explanations for what makes the United States unique.[21] Some of the particular obstacles found in the United States, such as the absence of proportional representation, still operate today. Many other difficulties are no longer valid. In order to dispel an undue sense that the grass is always greener in Europe, we will briefly examine two major differences that were active a century ago, but today seem much less significant.

First, mass suffrage came quite early in this country relative to Europe. In the "old country," mass political movements, while initially undermined by the smaller electorate, also benefited enormously from being able to lead the battle for the right to vote. By contrast, because of the early suffrage given to white men, in the United States elite parties had to face mass politics almost 100 years before their European counterparts. As a result, long before the great Populist and Socialist wave, the two major US parties had figured out how to capture the votes of ordinary people. Populists and Socialists had to confront fully developed, long-entrenched grassroots party structures that had ample experience in using patronage and racial, ethnic, and other identities to ensure popular loyalties. Yet today, these entrenched structures are now a thing of the past. Partisan loyalties have declined noticeably within the electorate during the past half century, and local Republican and Democratic party structures, to the extent that they exist as mass institutions at all, are at best pale imitations of the old-style machines.

Second, the United States became the first mass consumer society. US industrialists pioneered the transition from old craft-based industrial work to mass production. Because it lowered the cost of industrial goods relative to people's wages, US mass production created a mass market for industrial goods. By contrast, differing economic conditions helped to hold Europe well behind the United States until after World War II. Even today, while only 6 percent of the world's population, Americans own one-half of all automobiles.[22] This fundamental social and economic transformation helped employers destroy the existing, craft-based US labor movement—part of which had fed into third party organizing. Furthermore, the advent of the mass consumer society transformed people's aspirations by offering them an alternative to collective organizing. For important sections of the working class, if they put up with often hard and tedious jobs, they could earn enough money and leisure time to enjoy a life of relatively high material prosperity outside of work. While the world's premier consumer society, the United States today is clearly not alone. In their own way, Europeans also enjoy the "American consumer dream."

We should also note that the traditional line of questioning that compares a "progressive," multiparty Europe to an "elite-dominated," two party United States, risks overstating even the historical differences between the two. The contrast between Europe and the United States revolves around a variation of outcome, not a fundamental difference in kind. Socialism as a revolutionary force, for example, also failed in Europe. As we will examine in Chapter Ten, the movements that went on to form the social-democratic-type parties of Europe became major institutional players in their nation's politics only by abandoning their commitment to a more fundamental transformation of their societies. In the eyes of many activists on the Left, these parties are part of the establishment. US activists in some ways actually have an advantage since their task is to build, where none currently exists, a genuine party of the Left, while in Europe activists have to confront entrenched party organizations that come out of a radical history.

Independent Politics Between the World Wars

While the Populists and Socialists were both defeated, political revolts against the two party system did not disappear entirely. With the economic question still unresolved, the potential for a new wave of independent politics on a national scale remained high. Yet a lack of unity between different groups in the 1920s, and the eventual co-optation of the industrial labor movement of the 1930s into the Democratic Party, prevented this prospect from being realized on the same scale as the turn-of-the-century movements.

After World War I, and into the 1920s, a renewed crisis in agriculture and the continuing struggles of urban workers helped to produce several currents of independent politics. For example, the Non-Partisan League, formed by agrarian radicals in 1915, picked up steam in the Midwest. In 1916, its candidate for governor, Lynn Frazier, was elected in North Dakota. Within four years the League had effectively taken over the state's legislature. When the opponents of the League forced a successful recall election in 1921, however, it fell into decline.

In 1920, the Farmer-Labor Party (FLP) was launched by Socialists, Communists, and many non-Marxist radicals in Chicago under the leadership of that city's Federation of Labor. That year, despite the famous campaign of Eugene Debs from his prison cell, the FLP's candidate for president gained over a quarter of a million votes. While some of the more militant labor unions flirted with the idea of independent politics, most unions never fully committed themselves to any specific effort. The Farmer-Labor Party was undermined by strategic disagreements within its own ranks. Despite a hopeful beginning, the organization faded after 1923.

Independent politics was still very much in the air, however, and sentiments in favor of such a revolt were alive among many farmers and workers. In 1924, the FLP and other radical groups joined together to support the independent presidential bid of Wisconsin reformer and US Senator Robert La Follette. The unhappiness of workers and farmers with the two party system was clear as La Follette garnered over five million votes, compared to eight million for Democrat John Davis and fifteen million for Republican Calvin Coolidge. A year before, the Minnesota Farmer-Laborites elected their own people to the state's two US Senate seats. In other states, similar state-based third parties demonstrated considerable energy and potential. Yet these efforts and clear third party sympathies never cohered into a strong and unified national movement.

The resurgence of union organizing in the 1930s fostered a vibrant movement for independent politics at the local level, however.[23] The list of towns where such groups fielded their own candidates included: Cambridge, New Bedford, and Springfield, Massachusetts; Berlin and Lincoln, New Hampshire; Danbury and Hartford, Connecticut; Buffalo and New York, New York; Allentown and Philadelphia, Pennsylvania; Akron, Canton, and Toledo, Ohio; Detroit, Hamtranck, and Port Huron, Michigan; Chicago and Hillsboro, Illinois; Sioux Falls, South Dakota; Everett and Goldbar, Washington; and San Francisco, California. By the mid-1930s, the prospects for this grassroots activism to cohere into a national movement seemed promising. At the American Federation of Labor's 1935 convention, for example, a resolution to support an independent labor party narrowly lost. Ultimately, the fateful decision of the nation's new industrial unions and the rising Congress of Industrial Organizations to join President Roosevelt's New Deal Coalition killed the potential for a labor-based party.

In New York, radical currents, led by the Communist Party, came together in the American Labor Party (ALP). Key to the Party's strategy was the tactic of having more than one party endorse the same candidate. Indeed, the ALP was formed to provide radicals a way of comfortably supporting Democrat Franklin Roosevelt. Using New York State's electoral law, the Party allowed people to vote for Roosevelt, yet express their radical sympathies by doing so on the ALP ballot line. In a similar way, the ALP provided crucial margins of victory for New York's mayor Fiorello LaGuardia. In 1937, 21 percent of LaGuardia's vote came on the ALP line. By presenting black and Latino candidates, the ALP also forced the issue of minority representation. With the majority of his votes coming on the ALP line, Oscar Garcia Rivera became the first Puerto Rican officeholder in the continental United States when he won election to the state assembly. When the ALP ran African-American candidates for local offices, they compelled the Democratic Party to do the same. The ALP also played a central role in electing Adam Clayton Powell to Congress in 1942.

In addition to cross endorsements, the Party ran its own candidates. For example, before the abolition of proportional representation in 1947, the ALP had members on the New York city council as well as the state legislature. In a special election in 1948, the Party elected Leo Issacson to Congress from the South Bronx.

The most famous public figure associated with the ALP, however, was Congressman Vito Marcantonio. For over a decade and a half the primarily Italian and Puerto Rican residents of East Harlem elected Vito Marcantonio, a radical politician with close ties to the Communist Party, as their representative to Congress. Marcantonio ran on the ALP line, but also entered and usually won one or both of the major party primaries as well. To get rid of him, Marcantonio's opponents tried redrawing his district's boundaries, and even reformed the state's election laws to ban candidates from registering with one party and then entering the primary of another. Only in 1950, however, did these legal stratagems, plus the combined opposition of the Republican, Democratic, and Liberal parties, force him out of office.

The New Deal marked a major historical change in the nation's economy and politics as the federal government took on major responsibilities for regulating the economy and protecting citizens from the worst excesses of the capitalist system. Although popular protest did often criticize the limitations of the New Deal, reforms, such as legalizing unions and establishing federal unemployment and social security, wed many working-class voters solidly to the Democratic Party. Indeed, within the New Deal coalition, the Democrats pushed significant reforms advocated by popular groups. It would be wrong to view the New Deal realignment as simply a question of liberals co-opting popular unrest. President Roosevelt stayed in office only because he fulfilled his popular mandate. Furthermore, workers used the Democratic Party as a genuine tool for their political empowerment. Organized labor became the grassroots base of the Party and pro-labor New Deal Democratic candidacies provided the mechanism for working-class voters to overthrow the political dominance of local businesses in their communities.

The last significant effort at national independent politics before our current era came in 1948 with the presidential campaign of Henry Wallace. With both major parties embracing the anti-labor, anti-communist, and repressive policies of the Cold War, the Communist Party, labor activists, and other radicals and progressives founded the Progressive Party in 1948 and nominated former Vice President Henry Wallace, a left-wing New Dealer, as their standard-bearer. Organizers hoped to draw millions of working-class and minority voters away from the Democratic Party by offering a program that remained true to the left-leaning aspects of the New Deal. Initial polls showed a promising potential as estimates for Wallace ran as high as eight million votes. Harry Truman, however, skillfully downplayed his party's embrace of the Cold War, and instead offered several strong civil rights planks and called for national health insurance, protection for small farmers, and repeal of the anti-labor Taft-Hartley Act. Truman's temporary leaning to the left combined with massive bipartisan red-baiting against the Progressive Party doomed the Wallace campaign.

The Seeming Death of Independent Politics During the Post-War Boom

After 1948, the anti-communist, anti-left hysteria and persecutions of the Cold War helped to render further national progressive independent politics impossible. Even after McCarthyism had calmed down, progressive efforts to challenge the two party system remained ineffective. In contrast to earlier periods, mass unrest did not produce serious independent political challenges. In spite of the major social movement upheavals of the 1950s, 1960s, and 1970s, independent politics and third party organizing remained largely absent from the political scene.

Realizing the unique and time-limited nature of the conditions of the 1950s through 1970s is a crucial ingredient for building a progressive political movement into the next century. The decline of third party movements, particularly these past three decades, have informed the activism of many progressives today. While some have greeted recent developments in progressive political organizing with a high level of enthusiasm, others remain quite skeptical. This caution is understandable. For most progressives who grew up during the post-war period, the experience of building an independent political party was an exercise in futility. Many activists and scholars look at the experiences of the decades of the boom years and conclude that the prospects for a viable progressive political movement is a hopeless fantasy.

During the 1950s, 1960s, and 1970s many factors helped to prevent the post-war Left from mounting a serious independent political challenge. Three internal characteristics stand out in particular: the Left's relative isolation from a large number of "mainstream" Americans;[24] a tendency toward fragmentation; and an inclination to utilize protest strategies at the expense of electoral forms of struggle. These patterns grew, in turn, out of two central aspects of life in America during those years: the post-war economic boom and the political dominance of New Deal liberalism.

The Political Impact
of the Post-War Economic Boom

The Great Depression and World War II had been periods of significant unrest within broad sections of the US population. Social disillusionment and frustration translated into a series of mobilizations, including the unemployed workers' movements, the labor movement, and sporadic independent political action. The post-war boom, however, fundamentally altered the dynamic of protest in the United States by helping to demobilize large sections of the working class. To the surprise of many observers who feared a renewed slip into depression, the US economy emerged from World War II with energy and vigor. The 1950s and 1960s represented decades of unprecedented prosperity for both US business and many ordinary Americans. For example, during these two decades the rate of return on investments soared to an average of 10.2 percent.[25] The GNP growth rate averaged 3.8 percent between 1948 and 1966.[26] At the same time, between 1947 and 1966, wages in the core industries climbed 20 percent on average and unemployment averaged only 4.5 percent.[27] While the United States quickly became the world's economic and military leader, millions of Americans experienced upward mobility, or at least the prospect of a better future.

Sociologist Richard Flacks provides a helpful framework for understanding this change. As Flacks argues, most people's political actions are based upon a commitment to their everyday lives. When channels for the individual construction of a fulfilling private life become available, people will pursue them. In such a situation, individuals expend their time and energy on personal and apolitical pursuits rather than collective social and political action. Individuals only become receptive to collective mobilization when such personal space is not available, threatened by outside forces, not adequately fulfilling, or when a superior alternative becomes a realistic possibility.[28]

In Flacks' framework, post-war capitalism provided many Americans with the option to individually pursue a fulfilling everyday life. The advent of mass production created the material conditions for a mass consumer society. Through the New Deal's mechanisms of collective bargaining, unions won steady increases in wages and benefits. These gains spilled over into unorganized sectors of the working population. Many working Americans began to enjoy a level of material prosperity unknown to previous generations. For those who participated in the post-war prosperity, growing incomes, job security, and the availability of leisure time enabled a fulfilling private life in the hours between work. In response, a large number of workers now tolerated a dull job and management rule in return for the freedom and ability to enjoy life outside of the workplace.

Not everyone participated in this prosperity, of course. Those left out included a disproportionate number of minorities and women. In addition, some among those born into material prosperity found the rampant consumerism and suburban lifestyle unfulfilling, if not outright stultifying. These contradictions of the new "middle class" society produced major social movements among African Americans, Latinos, women, youth, and poor whites. During the boom years, however, these movements did not succeed in mobilizing the large blocks of white "mainstream" Americans enjoying the benefits of increasing material prosperity.

For many progressives, as well as many students of social movements, the evolution of US capitalism had proven Marx wrong. The working class as a whole would not serve as the gravedigger of capitalism. Theories of social movements in general, as well as of the socialist movement in particular, seemed in need of major revision. Too many ordinary Americans had been simply "bought off" by the post-war prosperity for the old scenarios to remain viable. Social struggles would take place either within the ranks of those "minority" groups left outside the prosperity or over the new "post-material" issues of the affluent young. The title of Andre Gorz's book *Farewell to the Working Class* expressed the opinion of many post-war observers.[29] The dream, if not the reality, of a better life through one's own personal efforts guided a large number of Americans into "conservative" and apolitical behavior.

The Rise of Interest-Group Liberalism

Mainstream Democrats also used the New Deal coalition to capture the political loyalties of many of the Left's traditional constituencies. The economics of post-war capitalism had its political dimension in what is best called "interest-group liberalism."[30] Interest-group liberalism grew out of the major transformation of the capitalist state brought about by the New Deal. Breaking with the old laissez-faire, minimal government norms of the nineteenth century, the Democratic Party under Franklin Roosevelt significantly expanded the size and role of the national government. Under the New Deal system, the state took responsibility for regulating the behavior of the "free" market to ensure a minimal level of rationality. State regulation and spending also protected the population from the worst excesses of capitalist exploitation. This political economy established a politics in which individuals were expected to form interest groups to mobilize around their specific issues. Through lobbying and pressure tactics, these groups could win government programs and regulations that met some of their specific needs. This had several effects on progressive activism, including movement fragmentation and the decline of electoral strategies.

Fragmentation

The basis of interest-group liberalism lies in single-issue politics. The post-war boom presented different sections of the population with very different material realities. New Deal liberalism encouraged these groups to focus on their particular realities and, in return, the state would respond with special actions and programs.

While the post-war political economy guided the currents of US social protest in many separate directions, three broad trajectories stand out. First, the New Deal system of labor relations helped to steer the trajectory of a majority of the nation's unions away from a broad identity as organizations of working people generally, and toward a more narrow self-conception as service organizations for their membership. The New Deal channeled labor conflicts into increasingly bureaucratic and state-mediated procedures. Unions no longer had to rely upon the militancy and participation of their rank and file. Instead, a bureaucratic-oriented leadership could win, and enforce, materially beneficial contracts through the mechanisms of collective bargaining.[31] Labor became a demobilized movement.

Those left outside of the post-war boom followed a different path. The selective nature of the post-war prosperity produced many of the major social mobilizations of the post-war period, including the Civil Rights and Welfare Rights movements. While involving a diverse array of groups and political orientations, these movements shared several common characteristics. They aimed for an equal share in the "American dream." They also all focused their attention, to a significant degree, upon the state. While unions used collective bargaining within the firm, the movements of African Americans, Latinos, and other people of color resorted to such tactics as civil disobedience and mass protest to force the state to respond to their concerns.

Activists in what could be termed the "post-material" movements followed a third trajectory. This category encompasses a very heterogeneous collection of movements, including the peace movement, the environmental movement, important aspects of the women's movement, the student New Left, and consumer advocacy groups. Unlike the other two trajectories, these post-material currents pursued agendas that did not revolve around bread and butter issues. The dominant participants in these movements also came from the ranks of the so-called "middle class" for whom the post-war boom had delivered material security and well-being.[32] In pursuing such post-material agendas, these movements often pursued goals and used strategies that differed from the other two trajectories as well as from each other.[33] Common ground among the three types of movements was often illusive.

While this brief overview risks simplifying a complex array of post-war social movements, the post-war economy and its interest-group politics did foster separate movements with separate sets of concerns.[34] Even among groups and organizations that were sympathetic and sensitive to each other, the issues that mobilized various sections of the progressive community often differed. While the post-war movements all shared a common aim for a just and more democratic society in a general sense, this did not translate into a common concrete agenda. Instead, New Deal liberalism encouraged each group to pursue its own set of issues in relative isolation. Though the post-war period experienced numerous individual instances of cross-movement coalitions and united activities, the political economy did not provide the framework necessary to maintain such coalitions on an ongoing and national basis.

Decline of Electoral Strategies

The post-war Left's relative fragmentation and insulation from "mainstream" America also helped create a legacy of distrust for electoral forms of struggle as social activists found protest strategies far more effective than electoral campaigns. Many activist groups learned to view support for mainstream political candidates as a waste of effort and independent progressive electoral campaigns seemed like exercises in futility.

Such a legacy was not accidental. The nation's corporate class eventually, and reluctantly, agreed to the New Deal, in part, to ward off renewed and powerful mass challenges to the two party system of the kind that had developed repeatedly ever since the nation's founding. Under interest-group liberalism, the state held out to progressive activists ample channels for making changes without having to resort to electoral politics.

During the height of New Deal politics, the 1950s, 1960s, and early 1970s, protest strategies—civil disobedience, lobbying, mass protests, urban uprisings, and demonstrations—were all able to force some form of state response. While activists may have often quite rightly criticized state actions as partial, problematic, and even repressive, nevertheless, protest strategies could and did deliver real benefits for many ordinary people. This dynamic was made possible because the economic conditions of the boom period permitted the state to support capital accumulation while being able to respond, at least in part, to social demands. In other words, post-war economic conditions allowed for the relative avoidance of a zero-sum game between the needs of capital and the demands of popular protest. In some instances the requirements of capital accumulation and social need could even prove complementary.

For example, while the New Deal represented a partial state response to the protest movements of the 1930s and 1940s, it also aided US-based capitalists. While the state had to drag many corporate leaders into the new era, the New Deal's limited redistribution of wealth aided US capitalism by helping to solve its "demand-side" crisis. At the same time, the New Deal provided many Americans a minimum social security and a rising standard of living.[35] Similarly, by legalizing unions, the New Deal represented a major victory for the labor movement. State mediated labor relations also helped employers bring peace to the workplace.

Similarly, during the 1950s and 1960s the state could at least partially respond to the protest strategies of the Civil Rights movement, while at the same time maintain capital accumulation. Clearly, the Civil Rights movement's social mobilization placed serious pressure on the national government to intervene against a US form of apartheid in the South. Yet, to an important degree, southern segregation had become economically counterproductive. This is not to argue that federal intervention would have occurred without popular protest. By the post-war period, however, US-based capitalism had evolved to a point where the protest strategies of southern blacks could yield a partially positive state response without having to face the full-fledged opposition of corporate America. When the Civil Rights movement began to move northward as well as address broad economic questions, the potential conflict between it and corporate capitalism become more severe. Nevertheless, the post-war New Deal regime permitted political and economic space in which protest activities could win substantial (although not entirely unproblematic) expansions in the safety net.[36]

A similarly favorable dynamic aided the protest strategies of many of the post-material movements. Because of the New Deal framework and relative economic boom, popular protest mobilizations and advocacy work could win a range of new government regulations and interventions in such areas as affirmative action, environmental protection, and consumer safety—in effect, broadening and expanding the New Deal state. Social activists could thus afford the luxury of approaching the political system from the outside because the post-war political economy allowed for at least a partially positive reaction from the state.

For those activists still attracted to electoral politics, the Democratic Party seemed the most practical alternative. Although both parties operated within the context of the New Deal system, the Democratic Party emerged from the Depression as the party of the New Deal coalition. It also became the party of the civil rights laws and the Great Society programs.

As long as it could serve as the party of New Deal liberalism, the Democrats proved an obstacle to independent political action. On the one hand, many activists could view the election efforts of the Democratic Party in some kind of positive light—either as an ally or at least the "lesser of two evils." For many of these people, the Democratic Party possessed a strong enough "left-wing" and sufficient electoral dominance to merit some form of active or passive support. On the other hand, for those who saw less progressive potential within the Democratic Party, its relatively successful ability to pose as the liberal champion of ordinary citizens gave it enough of a claim to loyalties among the Left's potential constituencies that independent political action seemed futile.

Progressive independent politics thus disappeared during the boom years. To most activists of the day, the dominant two party structure seemed unchangeable. By the late 1970s, however, our nation's political economy had begun to shift in ways that would make a political revolt not only possible, but, to a growing number of progressives, a necessity. The last ten to fifteen years has witnessed a rebirth of independent party initiatives. These will become even more significant in the years ahead.

Chapter Three

Our Time Has Come

Corporate Restructuring
and New Political Possibilities

While the 1950s, 1960s, and 1970s confronted progressive activists with severe obstacles to third party organizing, the 1990s (and beyond) provide opportunities reminiscent of the Populist and Socialist eras. The election and re-elections of socialist Bernie Sanders to the US Congress; the strong showings by Greens in New Mexico, Alaska, and Hawaii; the steady growth of the New Party; and the Labor Party's founding convention in 1996—these and many other examples are signs of a growing movement toward a progressive alternative to the two major parties.

Key to this change of progressive fortunes has been the transformation of the US economy and the nation's politics. Most progressive economists argue that by the late 1960s, US capitalism had entered a serious and prolonged crisis. By the late 1970s, many corporate and political leaders had concluded that the days of New Deal liberalism were over. Although begun in the late years of the Carter administration, the election of Ronald Reagan signaled the open ascendance of a right-wing solution to the economic problems of US capitalism.[1] This new agenda signified a shift in state and corporate policies arguably of a historical magnitude similar to the rise of New Deal liberalism in the 1930s and 1940s.

The right-wing program involved two major dynamics. First, corporate America and the US government attempted to redistribute resources and power upward. This included taxation and spending policies that directly transferred wealth to those who already had it, an extensive state and corporate offensive against organized labor, and similar right-wing efforts to rollback the material gains of a wide range of US social movements as well as to discredit them ideologically. Second, US capital engaged in an intensified restructuring of its own operations. Through deregulation, the right-wing agenda sought to reduce government controls over corporate behavior—promoting the supposed virtues of the free market. Deindustrialization noticeably accelerated as corporate investment moved overseas and into low-paying sectors of the economy. In search of lower labor costs, capital made increasing use of part-time work as well as exploiting the most disadvantaged sectors of the working population—women, immigrants, minorities, and youth. Internationally, US capital attempted to bolster its position by reasserting the US government's role as world policeman through an extensive military buildup.

The US political economy of the 1980s looked quite different from the post-war boom period. The New Deal regime had fostered a series of compromises between management and labor, producers and consumers, the state and minorities, and businesses and citizens. The right-wing agenda, however, sought to dismantle these compromises. Norms that the post-war generations had taken for granted were now shattered. Whereas the post-war boom had produced the "prosperous society," the crisis and right-wing solution to the changing economy initiated a period of renewed class warfare and social polarization. The evolution of US capitalism had established a transformed social reality—one with important political implications and opportunities for progressive activists. This transformation warrants a closer look.

From Crisis To Right-Wing Response

Internationally, US capitalism emerged from World War II with global predominance. From this powerful position, US capital reconstructed the world economy. The United States played the dominant role in establishing such post-war international economic institutions as the Bretton Woods monetary system (which established the dollar as the international currency), the World Bank and International Monetary Fund, and the General Agreement on Tariffs and Trade (GATT). In addition, the war's destruction of the European and Japanese economies had temporarily eliminated corporate America's major rivals. In the developing world, post-war decolonization permitted US capital to extend its unrivaled dominance to the "third world" as well. Through private corporate activities and the US state's economic and military power, US capitalism enjoyed relatively free access to cheap raw materials and favorable markets throughout the world.

After two decades of growth, expansion, and prosperity, the basis of the post-war boom began to sow the seeds of crisis.[2] Internationally, United States power began to face significant challenges on several fronts. By the mid-1960s, Japanese and European firms had recovered from the war and entered US-controlled markets. In such encounters, the enormous economic resources that US capital had channeled into military spending placed the US economy at a distinct disadvantage in relation to emerging rivals not similarly burdened. The 1960s also witnessed a growing challenge to corporate freedom of action in the developing world. Nationalist and revolutionary movements repeatedly challenged Western, particularly US, dominance of their economies. The inability of the US government to defeat the independence movement in Vietnam marked a major blow for US international "police" powers, while the 1973 OPEC oil price increase challenged the United States' ability to maintain access to cheap raw materials.[3]

As corporate America experienced increasing competition abroad, the post-war boom and New Deal anti-trust activities opened up inter-capitalist competition domestically.[4] In addition, a wide variety of social groups used the New Deal's expanded role of national government to make increasing demands on the corporate economy. On the one hand, those excluded from the post-war prosperity forced further expansion of New Deal policies. The civil rights struggles, the inner-city explosions, and the welfare rights movements of the 1960s represented major mobilizations of the nation's poor. While state authorities could and often did use the repressive apparatuses at their disposal, the quelling of these challenges also required major increases in social spending—such as contained in the Great Society programs.[5] On the other hand, various citizens movements forced the expansion of the national government's regulation of business. By the early 1970s, popular movements had won major victories in such areas as environmental regulation, consumer protection, and nuclear power.[6]

While government regulation and redistribution placed new burdens on US capital from the outside, corporate managers experienced renewed unrest within their own firms. Corporate leaders had never fully accepted a social contract with labor. When pressures to increase the rate of profit began to mount, such as during the 1958 recession, corporate America moved against labor. While not completely breaking with the New Deal system of labor relations, as it would later, management did attempt to gain greater power and performance on the shop floor. This sparked greater resistance from the rank and file. For increasing numbers of workers, the low unemployment rates fostered by the boom made the prospect of finding a new job relatively easy. This, along with the ability of the government safety net to offset the worst dangers of unemployment, helped increase worker resistance to management authority. Within the workplace, worker demands increasingly moved beyond immediate bread and butter issues to such concerns as health and safety, influence over workplace decisions, and job satisfaction.[7]

With the erosion of its foundations, the post-war prosperity gave way to long-term crisis, as real growth rates and after-tax profits fell. Internationally, the US share of world manufacturing exports dropped from 25 percent in 1965 to 18 percent in 1973. Imports, on the other hand, rose from 4.7 percent of the US market in 1960 to 10.3 percent in 1970 to 20.1 percent in 1979.

The economic crisis caused by increasing international competition and activist resistance is not some form of temporary economic downturn or recession. It signals the end of an old order. When initial responses to the crisis either failed or only prevented further erosion, US capital began to move toward a more complete and comprehensive break with the past. The New Deal mechanisms and compromises that had once helped establish renewed capitalist expansion had become obstacles. To combat international and domestic pressures, more and more corporate and political leaders concluded that the years of liberal policies had to go. By the late 1970s, the new right-wing corporate program was in place.

For starters, corporate leaders aggressively sought to redistribute resources and power away from ordinary Americans. First, the right-wing program directly redistributed wealth toward those who already had it through a complete restructuring of the nation's tax system—"reverse Robin Hood," as Jesse Jackson called it. By 1987, the top personal income tax bracket had dropped from a 70 percent to 28 percent rate—in a mere seven years. The capital gains tax fell from 49 to 28 percent in 1978, and then to 20 percent under Reagan. Although proponents wrapped their tax restructuring in populist-sounding rhetoric, the majority of Americans actually ended up paying higher taxes as a result of the Reagan era policies.[8]

Corporate America also sought to regain unchallenged control over the workplace.[9] In industry after industry, corporate negotiators demanded increasingly severe wage and benefit cuts from its workforce while at the same time channeling greater resources toward the development of more sophisticated methods of managerial control and more effective anti-union techniques.[10] The rise in union decertification elections from 239 in 1968 to 902 in 1980 reflected the corporate decision to dismantle organized labor.[11] In conjunction, right-wing-oriented governmental policy provided support for the corporate offensive against labor. Many laws protecting workers from their employers were either reduced or rendered ineffective. The Reagan administration altered the composition of the National Labor Relations Board in ways that made it far more favorable to business than to labor. Federal Reserve Board policies helped create higher levels of unemployment, which, in turn, undercut worker resistance as management's power to fire carried increasing weight.[12] At the same time, the government enhanced the danger of unemployment by severely cutting unemployment assistance.[13]

The right-wing program also targeted both the gains of past US social movements as well as the movements themselves.[14] This occurred at both a material and ideological level. Materially, the right-wing agenda cut relative spending in such areas as welfare, aid to towns and cities, housing, childcare, education, health care, job training, and environmental protection.[15] In total, spending on human resources (including Medicare and Social Security) fell from roughly 28 percent of the federal budget in 1980 to 22 percent by 1987.[16] Moreover, the material component of the right-wing agenda entailed greater recourse to repressive solutions to social problems. As Clarence Lusane has argued, the major target of the "war on drugs" has been neither the social and economic problems fostering drug use nor the upper echelons of the trafficking network, but, rather, poor people of color.[17] Today, the United States has a far higher proportion of its residents behind bars than any other industrialized nation.[18] Anticipating the need to "handle" growing social resistance, the Reagan administration also expanded the FBI's and CIA's ability to investigate and repress left-leaning groups.[19]

Ideologically, the right-wing agenda attempted to discredit the actions and values of past and current social movements. Right-wing explanations for economic problems frequently attributed declining US productivity and international competitiveness to lazy and overpaid unionized workers. Right-wing policymakers blamed growing incidents of poverty and federal budget deficits on the Great Society and other "liberal" social programs, arguing that such government spending had created an unproductive population (often implied to be black) dependent on government hand-outs.[20] Similarly, the right-wing logic argued that the "liberal" values promoted during the 1960s had created the crisis of the family by eroding "traditional moral values." Indeed, according to right-wing theorists, women today suffered from too much feminism.[21] In each case, right-wing explanations sought to divide people by portraying the enemy as some kind of "other"—blacks, women, foreigners, radicals, Latinos, Asians, or the elderly.[22] In both its physical and ideological components, the right-wing program sought to dismantle the claims made by social movements upon the nation's economic resources, to undermine the opponents of deregulation, and to pit social groups against each other. When successful, the results helped free state and private power to shift wealth upward.

In addition to redistributing social power and resources, US capital sought to restructure its own operations.[23] This occurred at three different levels. First, capital redefined its relation to the state. Through deregulation, the right-wing agenda reduced governmental controls over corporate actions and promoted the "virtues" of the free market. As the 1988 Republican platform put it: "from freedom comes opportunity; from opportunity comes growth; and from growth comes prosperity." Right-wing policies achieved deregulation by cutting the budgets of regulatory agencies and staffing them with officers sympathetic to the free market and hostile to "government interference." The right-wing agenda also opposed new governmental protections, in such areas as race and sex discrimination and environmental protection, while attempting to undermine old ones.[24]

Second, the right-wing agenda sought to further a major restructuring of the US economy away from high wage industries and toward low wage sectors. This included significant deindustrialization as US manufacturing firms, US industrial investment, and sources of manufacturing inputs shifted either into anti-union, "right to work" states or overseas.[25] In its place, US capital offered low paid, mostly service sector jobs. In 1968, manufacturing's share of total employment was 29 percent. This fell to 22 percent by 1984.[26] Capital also sought to move what manufacturing remained in the United States into the lower wage sectors of the economy. This included increasing use of both female labor and unorganized, unprotected immigrant labor. Federal policies have facilitated such exploitation by eroding affirmative action and undermining immigrant rights.[27] Right-wing economic restructuring has also promoted an explosion of speculation, mergers, and other forms of unproductive, yet, in the short-term sense, profitable financial activity.[28]

Finally, US capital attempted to reassert its dominance internationally by expanding the US state's "big-stick diplomacy" and reasserting the US's role as world policeman. While the Reagan era witnessed drastic cuts in domestic spending, military outlays increased at almost the same rate.[29] Between 1980 and 1987, the defense budget increased by approximately 50 percent.[30] This shift in resources translated into expanded US troop presence abroad, a new generation of weapon systems, an enhanced counterinsurgency capability, and an unfettered and expanded Central Intelligence Agency. The US military buildup served three major purposes. First, it permitted a powerful counteroffensive against the latest wave of revolutionary and nationalist movements threatening corporate interests in the "third word."[31] Second, the right-wing solution sought to use US military power as a counterweight to the growing economic power of such chief rivals as Japan and Germany.[32] Third, increased military spending helped foster a further transfer of public wealth into the corporate economy through a kind of military Keynesianism.

The Political Implications
of the Transformation of US Capitalism

For all of the suffering it caused, the right-wing transformation of US capitalism has begun to dismantle and reverse the causes of the disappearance of independent politics during the boom era. Progressive activism of the 1950s through 1970s was characterized by a relative separation from "mainstream" America, fragmentation into different movements and causes, and distance from electoral activism. In contrast, the new political and economic conditions today favor an expanded progressive political base, greater operational unity among different social movement currents, and a renewed interest in electoral politics.

The End of the American Dream and the Expansion of the Left's Potential Political Base

Post-war prosperity provided the material basis for the kind of mass consumption life-style that helped steer millions of ordinary working people into the individual pursuit of "happiness," rather than collective political action. Now, the post-war dream has come to an end. The crisis of US capitalism and rise of the right-wing solution has spelled an end to material prosperity for millions of "mainstream" Americans.[33] The signs of spreading crisis can be seen across the social landscape. The corporate offensive against organized labor has succeeded in lowering the standard of living for unionized and non-unionized workers alike. The industry-wide pattern of bargaining that once gave prosperity to millions of workers, today, exists only as a memory of past good times. Overall, between 1977 and 1989, hourly wages eroded 10.5 percent. Between 1989 and 1991, the median family experienced an income loss of 4.4 percent.[34] Conditions within the workplace have also deteriorated as corporate strategies of "down-sizing" their workforce and speeding up the work pace have produced unemployment for many, and more working hours, greater work stress, and exploding rates of work-related accidents for the rest.

Corporate restructuring has similarly altered the economic outlook for millions of Americans. Communities that relied upon a single or a few companies have experienced extreme social and economic devastation when those firms either went bankrupt or moved elsewhere. Those displaced by the economic restructuring found that, if they could find work, they often had to settle for jobs that paid lower wages and required far less skill than their past experience. According to statistics compiled by Lawrence Mishel and David Frankel, two-thirds of an almost 10 percent drop in average hourly compensation between 1980 and 1989 was due to shifts toward jobs in low paying industries.[35] Despite an increase in two-income households, real weekly family income had fallen 19 percent below the 1973 level by the 1990s. In 1991, one out of every four households had experienced at least one person out of work during the previous twelve months.[36] At the same time, the percentage of unemployed who received some form of unemployment insurance payments had dropped from 43 percent in 1967 to 34 percent by 1989.[37] Involuntary part-time employment had increased from 2.6 percent of the workforce in 1969 to 4.7 percent by 1988.[38] Many young people entering the job market found that they would not be able to maintain the kind of lifestyle enjoyed by their parents. In 1987, for example, a male high school graduate with one to five years of work experience earned 18 percent less than his counterpart in 1979.[39] In the 1980s, 80 percent of families who depended almost exclusively on wage earnings saw their real income fall while their taxes increased.[40]

For those who had not experienced the post-war prosperity or had to fight for their share of it, the transformation of US capitalism took an especially hard toll. The downward shift was pronounced among minorities, particularly Latinos. For example, while the percentage of white and black children in poverty jumped 7 to 8 percentage points, the percentage of impoverished hispanic children jumped from 29 percent to 45 percent between 1979 and 1987.[41]

Many of the same conditions that had fostered the ghetto riots in the 1960s had only become worse by the 1980s. Today, a black male resident of Harlem or the South Bronx has a lower life expectancy than if he lived in Bangladesh. Three percent of the black male population lives behind bars. African Americans make up 44 percent of the US prison population—a reflection of desperate social conditions and a racist judicial system.[42] The poor have gotten poorer. Black urban poverty grew from 21 percent in 1969 to 34 percent by 1992. In 1979, 32.9 percent of those below the poverty level lived at less than one-half the poverty income threshold. By 1988, this number had increased to 38 percent. While the ratio of male to female income has actually narrowed since the 1960s, declining male wages, rather than an increase in female wages, have been the major cause of the shift.[43] According to official government statistics, 33.6 percent of persons in female-headed families lived below the poverty level in 1987. Some analysts have placed the actual number as high as 49.8 percent.[44]

The decline of material well-being among the majority of Americans has translated into general social deterioration. While different sectors may have experienced the growing hardships to different degrees, the signs of social crisis have spread to communities throughout the country. As wages fell, households tried to maintain their standard of living by sending more members into the workforce or by having individuals work more hours. By 1989, Americans spent 149 more hours in the public workforce on average than in 1969.[45] In 1989, over seven million Americans held more than one job. This shift meant not only less leisure time, but also a general degradation of domestic life.[46] The average yearly time spent on childcare, housework, and hobbies in a two-parent, two-child family fell 165 hours between 1969 and 1987.[47] Since women were the ones that most often increased their wage earning work while also being held responsible for most of the housework and childrearing, they have had to bear the heaviest burden. The social strain and insecurity produced by declining material well-being has become apparent in other areas as well. The rising ranks of the homeless included families across the social spectrum, from upper-middle class to underclass. When Jesse Jackson ran for office in 1988, thirty-seven million Americans had no health insurance, and twenty-five million more had such inadequate health insurance that a major illness could bankrupt them.[48]

The transformation of US capitalism has torn apart the very fabric of daily life. Its victims lay across the US social spectrum. Most significantly, in addition to a downturn in their immediate material well-being, many in "mainstream" America have lost hope as well. The post-war American dream has come to an end. In a newspaper interview during the 1988 primary campaign, a grandmother of four explained her support for Jesse Jackson with a concise summary of this transformation of expectations. She argued, "in the 1950's you went to high school, graduated from college, and got a job. Now you graduate and you have no choices."[49]

This women's perspective is not an isolated case. In a variety of polls and interviews, Americans expressed their belief that their children would not experience the same quality of life that they had enjoyed. In a 1987 *Wall Street Journal* survey, 65 percent of respondents felt that it was more difficult for "middle-class" Americans to maintain their standard of living than it had been five years earlier. According to a January 1988 *USA Today*/CNN poll, 72 percent believed that the rich were better off than in 1981, while the poor had lost ground.[50] These trends in pubic opinion have only intensified. In a November 18, 1991 CBS News/*New York Times* poll, 39 percent (including 45 percent of those earning under $30,000 a year) replied that they were financially worse off than they had expected to be by their age. Only 16 percent said they were better off. In the experience of the majority of Americans, the status quo no longer worked. According to an April 4, 1992 ABC poll, 81 percent of the respondents felt that the United States was not on the right track. An October 1991 CBS/*New York Times* poll asked the question: "Do you feel things in this country are generally going in the right direction, or do you feel things have pretty seriously gotten off onto the wrong track?" Sixty percent answered that the country was on the wrong track.

The political implications are clear. By the 1980s, people were becoming open to change. The options for a private pursuit of a decent life had narrowed considerably. The corporate agenda had helped to dismantle the political complacency that a previous generation of activists had found so frustrating. Polls also showed that the vast majority of Americans saw government as run by a few big interests and did not trust it to do what was right.[51] An October 1991 CBS/*New York Times* poll found that only 29 percent approved of the way Congress was "doing its job." An April 14, 1992 ABC poll found that that number had dropped to only 17 percent of respondents. A 1995 CNN/*USA Today*/Gallop poll, which found that only 32 percent of the public was satisfied with a Clinton/Dole matchup, is simply one example of a long-term trend in public opinion. Almost two-thirds of those polled wanted to see a third party alternative, though election results suggest they were not sufficiently impressed with Ross Perot's Reform Party.

Falling standards of living and lowered expectations do not necessarily push people in a progressive direction, of course. Anti-establishment sentiment can be organized in many directions. This country has a complex cultural legacy. We have a rich tradition of social movements and collective organizing tied to a national mythos born of a revolution and continued struggles for freedom. This country also contains a long tradition of selfish individualism that can breed a culture of isolation, cynicism, and passivity. Narrow individualism can be coupled with the nation's deep traditions of classism, patriarchy, religious conservatism, and, above all, racism to undergird very reactionary movements.

Groups and individuals as diverse as the Christian Coalition, the militia movement, David Duke, and Pat Buchanan demonstrate the reactionary potential of ordinary people's falling living standards. Progressives would do well, however, to look beyond the rather repulsive ideologies of these movements. We need to understand how they work and how we can best organize an alternative. By scapegoating people of color and government regulation for people's falling standard of living rather than corporate economic restructuring, these movements have made some inroads into the white working-class suburbs. We can ill afford not to mobilize these communities in a more progressive direction. The right-wing's techniques of community-building and grassroots leadership development are not tied to one ideology, and may prove useful for us as well.

The existence of growing right-wing grassroots organizing should underline the battle that we have before us, but it should not leave us demoralized. Because the media publicizes right-wing activity much more readily than our own, we could get the false impression that the conservative drift is the only thing happening. The Republican upset of 1994 was built on a very narrow margin of voters, with the majority of the population staying home. Furthermore, the Republican win also signified the bankruptcy of so-called moderate and liberal Democrats who refused to attack the corporate agenda. In 1994, Democrats who stuck to more populist messages did far better, and a host of progressive organizing both inside and outside the Party continued to pick up steam.

More progressive-minded independents were elected to local, state, and national offices in 1994 than at any time in decades. While arguably overstated in the media, the fact that segments of ordinary working people are attracted to the Republican's government bashing does not necessarily mean that people are moving to the Right. Indeed, from a progressive perspective, people are correct to conclude that governmental authorities are not on their side. The difference between the Right and the progressives is in their solutions. The Right seeks to dismantle government to give free reign to private economic power, while progressives try to democratize the state as a positive force to offset and counter private power.

The transformed political economy establishes a political potential that we have to organize before the Right does. Tony Mazzocchi of the Labor Party put the matter quite clearly when he argued:

My own feeling is that there will be another party. The question is: whose
party is it going to be? Is it going to be a party of working people? Or a party of
the right wing? There's a vacuum out there.[52]

There is reason to believe that progressives could fill this vacuum. This
will take initiative and new thinking, however. The old patterns of political
behavior will not suffice. Not only has the evolving political economy
brought hard times, it has also restructured the issues and political dynamics
facing social movement activists. The right-wing agenda seeks to return to
the nineteenth century era of minimal government by dismantling much of
the New Deal state, and, with it, interest-group liberalism. As a result,
grassroots activists are finding that playing politics in the old interest-group
way is no longer a viable option.

Progressive Opportunities

While the post-war boom tended to divide the progressive community,
the crisis of post-war capitalism and the right-wing solution has helped to
push groups closer together. This can be seen in a number of ways. The
evolution of US capitalism has not simply caused increasing pain and misery.
Its negative effects have reached broad sections of the US population—blue
collar and white collar, professional and unskilled, white, black, and brown,
male and female, young and old. During the mass mobilizations of the 1950s
and 1960s, for example, when the African-American community raised issues
of poverty, homelessness, quality education, adequate wages, unemployment, affordable health care, and hunger, such concerns could be characterized, at least in the minds of many who were experiencing the post-war
prosperity, as "minority issues" or "poor people's issues." By the 1980s, many
of these same issues had become, in kind if not in degree, the concerns and
demands of "mainstream" Americans as well.

The right-wing budget program, for instance, has highlighted the
trade-off between domestic and military spending. Groups concerned with
either US intervention abroad or the prospect of nuclear annihilation share
increasingly common ground with those suffering from the transfer of state
resources away from domestic spending and into the military buildup. These
groups are potentially joined by increasing numbers of US workers effected
by the US government's protection of a favorable investment climate
overseas, aiding capital flight at home.

Right-wing deregulation has also increased the potential for bringing
groups together. Workers who find it increasingly difficult to protect
themselves against unsafe and unhealthy working conditions due to a lack
of governmental protection can find potential common ground with environmental groups concerned with the effect that the same or related
corporate practices have upon the environment. These people are joined by
minority groups who suffer the effects of environmental pollution and

government deregulation disproportionately—a phenomenon that is often referred to as "environmental racism."

Similarly, changes in the US workforce offer new organizing possibilities. One of the major changes in the US economy over the past few decades has been the accelerating entrance of women into the workforce. By increasingly relying on female labor, US corporations have created the objective conditions for mobilizing individuals whose life experience cuts across dimensions of class and gender—thus offering the possibility of combining traditional concerns of the labor and women's movements. A similar dynamic is occurring around race, as the workforce, and the population generally, is increasingly made up of people of color.[53]

Ultimately, the right-wing attack has placed groups that simply pursue single-issue politics in a very weak and vulnerable position. For example, merely defending welfare spending places activists on the defensive. We are left protecting programs that are inadequate and perceived by much of the public as only benefiting minorities. In the long run, the only way to throw back the right-wing, welfare-bashing agenda is to take the offensive by countering the Right with a comprehensive agenda of our own. More and more activists realize this. Yet simply getting together and drawing up a laundry list of our single-issue concerns is not adequate. An organizing process is needed to produce a more integrated and holistic agenda. Electoral politics, with its focus on comprehensive programs, is an arena that allows activists to gather and develop just such a compelling alternative vision.

The decline of interest-group liberalism has also rendered protest strategies more difficult as the demands of social movements conflict head on with the dominant state and corporate agenda. Today, mainstream politicians have much less room to maneuver. The right-wing solution involves a reduction of social movement gains, not further accommodation. It seeks to move in the direction of dismantling the New Deal, not expanding upon it. The state is no longer simply a defender of the status quo, but an overt and active agent for implementing an agenda that undermines the social welfare of its citizens and the movements that represent them.[54]

This is not to say that protest tactics are no longer effective; nor that they no longer serve as a primary method of social mobilization. The right-wing climate encourages activists to also move toward the conclusion that making government officials responsive to social movement activity increasingly requires getting people from within progressive activist ranks elected to office.

This move toward electoral strategies has been increasingly focused on independent politics. The transformation of US capitalism has placed the Democratic Party's liberal image in jeopardy. While the Republican Party carried the banner of the right-wing solution, both parties have realigned around the new agenda. Indeed, the dominant forces in the Democratic Party have also abandoned New Deal liberalism.[55] Clinton's signing of the "welfare reform" bill is only one example. Many of the policies associated with Reaganism actually began in the later years of the Carter administration. In addition, Reagan's policy initiatives were enacted by a Democratic Congress.

The Democratic Party's rightward lurch influenced progressive activists in two ways. For those activists who had viewed the Party in some kind of positive light, it seemed less and less an effective vehicle for liberal reform. The 1994 Republican victory has only further underlined the inability of centrist Democrats to appeal to people's frustrations or stave off reactionary anti-establishmentism. Furthermore, even when Democrats have won office, as in 1996, they often have not spoken or acted differently than their Republican opponents. In the experience of many local activists, the Democrats proved just as unresponsive, if not hostile, to social movement concerns as did the party of Reagan. Thus, many activists have concluded that the Democratic Party no longer serves their interests, even partially. In response, local activists who had previously looked toward Democratic victories increasingly viewed running and supporting their own candidates as the only political option. In their eyes, only genuinely progressive candidates could both win mass support and respond to the concerns and demands of the activist community once in office.

For activists who had never placed much faith in the Democratic Party, its rightward shift signaled not so much a need as an opportunity. While both parties had realigned around the right-wing agenda, the public had not. As Thomas Ferguson and Joel Rogers have documented, the poll data show that the majority of Americans still favored specific New Deal programs.[56] By surrendering the terrain of populism, the dominant forces in the Democratic Party had left the electoral playing field open for an unrivaled progressive critique of the status quo. With voter alienation and frustration climbing, the possibilities for a progressive political challenge seemed credible.

The Movement Toward Independent Politics

Today there is a rich growth of grassroots groups and organizations pursuing a variety of strategies. Their existence testifies to the fact that the United States now reflects political, economic, and social dynamics different from those found two decades ago. The political economy of the prosperous "middle-class," "liberal" society has evaporated into social, economic, and political crisis. Although the new conditions have brought pain and frustration, they have also brought new opportunities. This process continues to develop. During interviews conducted across the country in 1995, activists all commented on the growing interest by both the general population and the activist community in independent politics. Bill Clinton's continuation, and active promotion, of most elements of the right-wing agenda, coupled with his ready retreat away from the few progressive elements of his campaign platform, has simply heightened people's sense of the Democratic Party's bankruptcy.

The 1994 Republican victory has done even more to further the cause of progressive third parties. The "Contract With America" has underlined the weakness of single-issue politics and the neglect of electoral strategies. After over a decade of Reaganism, we now face a political situation in which those in power are not simply maintaining the policies of the 1980s, but furthering the right-wing agenda in a manner that is even more blatant, sweeping, and reactionary.

The Republican Congress has also shown the inadequacy of the strategy of voting for the lesser evil. In 1994, supporting mainstream Democrats only ensured Republican victories as the Democrats continued to refuse to raise a populist attack on the right-wing agenda. In 1996, the Democrats moved further to the Right. In more and more areas, running independent progressive candidates and engaging in third party organizing represents the most effective way of countering the Republican momentum. Progressive organizing has a growing potential to displace the Democrats as the effective force balancing the corporations and the right-wing.

Hints from the Rainbow Coalition

The new political potential of progressive electoral politics became clearer at the national level when Jesse Jackson decided to run for the presidency in the 1980s. Although Jackson chose to mount his political challenge within the Democratic Party, he and his supporters proved keen observers of the new political opportunities developing for progressives.

Jackson ran because he perceived a growing electoral base for progressive politics. As one local activist commented, "In this country there is a need. Someone has to rise to the occasion." In 1988, Jackson's Rainbow Coalition did just that. Jackson received seven million primary votes, including 20 percent of the total white vote. He did so by placing the economic question at the center of his agenda. As he routinely emphasized:

> *Economic violence is the critical issue of our day. When plants close on workers without notice—that's economic violence. When merger maniacs make windfall profits and top management is given excessive bonuses—that's economic violence. When two to three million Americans are on the street and homeless—that's economic violence. When children are victimized by poor health care, poor education, poor housing, poor diets and more—that's economic violence against our children and it must stop.*[57]

While the Jackson campaign encompassed a wide range of progressive concerns, the basis of his appeal lay in his ability to speak to people's sense that their material well-being and standard of living were becoming increasingly insecure and under attack.

We noted a similar pattern in our study of the 1988 Jackson campaign in several local communities in upstate New York.[58] In terms of their sheer scale, the local campaigns reached out to, and included, people from "mainstream" society. For example, in many ways local activists in nearly all-white Binghamton, New York, confronted the dilemma faced by the US Left generally throughout the post-war period—namely, of being surrounded by a large mass of complacent, if not seemingly conservative, people. A majority of the population of Broome County is registered as Republican. The area is not known as a hotbed of progressive activity. In 1988, however, Jackson received 20 to 25 percent of this "mainstream" vote in the county. For local activists, this represented a significant inroad into a population that, in their experience, had proven quite resistant to progressive activism. As one local Jackson activist described, "The mobilization that came was unreal—unbelievable for this conservative community."

The true potential revealed by Jackson's two campaigns was not visible in the places where most political observers were focused (the candidate's campaign trail or in national media coverage), but in the diverse experience of the nation's local communities. Jackson gained over seven million votes in 1988 not just as a result of his program or the media attention that he succeeded in gaining, but also due to the intense efforts of literally tens of thousands of volunteers. The Jackson campaign witnessed a level of grassroots mobilization unprecedented in recent national elections.

These grassroots mobilizations had several noteworthy characteristics. First, they were large. For example, in the nearly all-white, relatively conservative, small- to medium-sized urban area of Binghamton, Jackson organizers succeeded in mobilizing over 400 volunteers by election day. In contrast, the Dukakis campaign produced only a few dozen. Second, the grassroots mobilizations encompassed a genuine diversity.[59] Jackson activists repeatedly and consistently raised the breadth and diversity of the campaign as an important accomplishment. A Jackson organizer in Binghamton remembered that:

> *A whole lot of people were interested in our campaign. They came out of the woodwork…all walks of life. People in public office, workers, unemployed people, welfare recipients, housewives, elderly; everybody was interested in the Jackson campaign and was willing to volunteer.*

While Jackson's campaign was notable in its ability to cut across single issues, its diversity stood out in contrast to the relative lack of activist unity that existed prior to the campaign. Almost without exception, the individuals who made up the core leadership of the local campaigns had accumulated years of experience in grassroots activism. These activists came from the full spectrum of progressive movements, including labor, women, environmental, peace, gay, lesbian, bisexual, anti-racist, anti-poverty, and citizen action. Although individual members had often sympathized with the concerns of other movements, and most Jackson activists had been involved in a variety of causes, few had actively worked together before the Jackson campaigns despite having often lived in the same communities for a number of years. Jackson encapsulated this sense of progressive unity in his famous metaphor of a rainbow quilt:

> But don't despair. Be as wise as my grandmama. Pool the patches and the pieces together, bound by a common thread. When we form a great quilt of unity and common ground, we'll have the power to bring about health care and housing and jobs and education and hope to our nation.[60]

Although Jackson championed many progressive policy initiatives, most activists did not support him simply because of the details of his platform, but because he spoke with a comprehensive vision that provided an alternative to politics as usual. Unlike moderate and even liberal Democrats, Jackson unabashedly defended the positive role of government when it is in the hands of the people. Fundamentally, Jackson saw the political debate as a question of basic morality. Countering the Right's claim to moral virtue, Jackson attacked the right-wing agenda for being spiritually bankrupt and morally hypocritical. Jackson called for values that placed identification with the oppressed above the interests of the wealthy, social justice above political expediency, and embracing diversity over fears and suspicion. By basing his campaign on a moral logic, Jackson was able to appeal to a diverse pool of activists. Despite their individual differences in social and political analysis, and their contrasting visions of an alternative politics, activists involved in Jackson's campaign could all agree on the fundamental values that he articulated.

Jackson was also able to pull together his National Rainbow Coalition because of his deliberate and extensive efforts to personally experience and participate in a diverse array of progressive struggles. In 1983, he had witnessed Harold Washington's construction of a rainbow coalition strong enough to defeat the Democratic Party machine and win the mayoral office.[61] He learned this lesson well. Even before the 1988 campaign, Jackson had stood outside plant gates with striking workers. He had talked with members of inner-city gangs. He had visited the "rustbelt," the "farmbelt," and the "sunbelt." He had met the nation's younger generation in schools across the country. He had spoken at rallies for reproductive choice, for civil rights, for gay and lesbian rights, and for "jobs, peace, and justice." He had been inside the nation's homeless shelters, health care clinics, welfare offices, and prisons.

These personal experiences, coupled with his extensive contacts with progressive activists and organizations, provided Jackson the breadth necessary to conceive and implement a political challenge based upon a diverse "rainbow coalition" of social activists. In doing so, his campaign momentarily revealed the human building blocks of further left/progressive political movements. The contemporary Left appears weak nationally, but it maintains an active local presence—one that, if brought together, could produce considerable energy.

Jackson's campaigns also involved a large number of political newcomers. The majority of volunteers we studied had had little electoral experience. Indeed, many viewed the electoral process with a great degree of distrust and suspicion. Despite this history, these people joined Jackson's campaign. A staff person for the local Citizen Action group in Binghamton echoed the sentiments of many activists when she argued:

> *What we found is that for years we would work on just issues and try to influence policy-makers with grassroots people... But our elected officials were unresponsive. We found out that we actually stayed home the most important day of the year. We did voter registration and voter education, but we never worked in political campaigns. It became frustrating to us. [We concluded that] what we needed to start doing is promoting progressive candidates who have the interests of the "common man" at heart. We need to start developing our own candidates at the local level as well as promoting and working for real candidates because we need effective leadership which we currently don't see. Probably about 1986 we actually formed a PAC and started involving ourselves in political races figuring that this was one of the most effective ways to move our whole issue agenda.*

In supporting his campaign, activists were not simply joining electoral politics as usual. Rather they were transforming the electoral process so that it was a vehicle of popular protest against the right-wing agenda. Many grassroots organizers and volunteers had the sense that this campaign was part of a larger political development that signified history in the making.

While remarkable in so many ways, Jackson's campaign failed to steer the Democratic Party in a progressive direction. His bids occurred at a time when the debates within the Party over how to respond to Reaganism were not yet over. Yet Jackson's defeat in 1988, the way in which his supporters were dismissively treated at the national convention, and the nomination of Bill Clinton in 1992 all signified a resolution to that struggle. The mainstream of the Party adopted Reaganism, trying to win over Republicans voters rather than mobilize the vast half of the electorate that doesn't vote at all.

Many grassroots Jackson activists with whom we spoke had little illusions about the ultimate direction of the Party. They joined Jackson's campaign because it existed outside the Democratic Party in everything but their candidate's party label. Many hoped that the Rainbow Coalition would turn into a third party, or some form of autonomous grassroots political organization. Locally, the Jackson campaigns had little to do with activists from the mainstream of the Party. In some places they were able to get along with liberal Democratic activists, in others open hostility existed between the two camps. Many Jackson activists were already moving toward independent politics, or at least a grassroots-based political organization within the Democratic Party.

Unfortunately, Jackson chose not to take the political potential revealed and mobilized by his campaigns and establish an ongoing grassroots-driven progressive political movement. Having inspired hundreds of grassroots coalitions across the country and fired up thousands of activists, Jackson let his supporters languish. Groups who set up local Rainbow Coalition chapters found they received little support or even contact from the national leadership. Jackson, and the national Rainbow leadership, remained wedded to the Democrats. In the end, the future of the Rainbow was decided through a centralization of the organization that placed Jackson and the national leadership in firm control and let the grassroots structure wither away.

Whatever the campaign's failures, it offers many lessons in progressive political movement-building that should not be lost. Progressives organize election campaigns in ways that differ from the media- and money-driven politics of their mainstream rivals. Jackson's campaigns illustrate these basic grassroots campaign techniques, as well as point to some of the limitations that separate, one-shot candidacies pose for progressive organizers. Looking closely at this experience, as we do in the next chapter, allows us to rethink electoral politics in the years ahead.

Beating
Big Money and Media

Lessons from
Jesse Jackson's 1988 Campaign

The "powers-that-be" would like us all to believe that elections have undergone a single, inevitable, and irrevocable evolution. The typical scenario goes as follows: During the nineteenth century, electoral competition witnessed the struggle between strong party organizations that used extensive grassroots participation to mobilize the electorate for their cause. By the early twentieth century, these old labor-intensive campaigns began to give way to new high-tech strategies. Dominant today, these new methods emphasized individual candidates over party, capital-driven media blitzes over grassroots crusades, and professional polling over local knowledge. Thus, elections have become candidate-centered advertising exercises where the most important political resource is money rather than people. According to this mainstream wisdom, progressive activists face a hopeless barrier. Unless their candidates can amass a considerable campaign chest, one assumed to come from big money donors, they do not stand a chance of winning.

While winning favorable media coverage for progressive campaigns does present a real challenge, progressives do not have to run campaigns that merely copy the money-driven techniques used by mainstream politicians. Indeed, progressives can distinguish themselves by bringing supposedly obsolete grassroots methods back into national politics. To better understand this possibility, we turn to the lens of history to see how money- and media-driven politics first began.

There is no doubt that elections in this country moved from battles between opposing grassroots armies to expensive exercises in corporate advertising. The question is, why did this transformation take place and why did it produce the electoral system we have now? Mainstream academics and politicians offer us two possible explanations. Most argue that techno-logical innovations made the old methods obsolete. The rise of television, for example, provided a communication medium so powerful that political campaigns had to restructure themselves or risk defeat. Television is said to favor candidate-centered, rather than party-centered, campaigns. Further-more, candidates are forced to use superficial image appeal since network television confines political messages to sound-bites and two-minute news reports. According to official wisdom, other technology, such as modern polling techniques, is also supposed to have inevitably transformed elec-tioneering.

Other mainstream scholars point to an erosion of party structure. New technology did not create decisively superior campaign methods. Instead, the parties lost their ability to maintain party unity and mobilize local volunteers. During the nineteenth century, both internal discipline and grassroots Republican and Democratic volunteers came from one political resource in particular: patronage. Residents worked for the local party organization in the hope of obtaining a politically-controlled job or similar spoils of office. By the turn of the century, however, political reform movements began to whittle away at this patronage base. As a result, the parties gradually lost the ability to maintain their internal unity and their ranks of local activists. Today, therefore, the parties have to rely upon their policy programs or the personal satisfaction some individuals may get from political participation to inspire volunteers—mechanisms that appear weak, indeed.

While wrapped in the cloak of "value-free" research, both explanations are highly biased. They imply that the transformation of electioneering was determined by forces beyond the realm of self-consciousness. Even more importantly, both explanations imply that there is nothing that current political participants can do about it. To compete in the electoral arena, one has to play by the predetermined rules or be relegated to the sidelines. Such a perspective tells progressives that we must suffer severe disadvantages because current elections are structured entirely around a money-driven process that is beyond the bounds of human intervention. The grassroots resources that progressives rely on have become relics of a past era.

The Jackson campaigns suggest that these conclusions are highly misleading. The problem with mainstream explanations is that they treat the practices of the two dominant parties as the universal experience. Thus, they miss the way in which the particular political interests of the Democrats and Republicans have determined how these parties conduct elections. Indeed, upon closer examination, both the technological and patronage explanations reveal major weaknesses. For example, the two major parties began shifting to the advertising style of campaigning at the turn of the century, well in advance of such supposedly decisive new technologies as television. Mainstream scholars fail to appreciate the degree to which a reliance upon candidate personality, superficiality, avoidance of comprehensive policy concerns, and resort to advertising are not simply modern phenomenon, but often go back to the earliest days of Republican and Democratic political campaigning.

Furthermore, new technologies such as television do not simply require one predetermined way that they have to be used. If the Republicans and Democrats were really concerned about campaigning on the details of the issues and their platforms, for example, they could pass laws to change the way television is used. In many other countries, the government provides all parties free television airtime—airtime that could be assigned in half-hour or hour-long blocks to encourage far more substance than the thirty second sound-bites typical now.

Similarly, while declining patronage certainly produced an erosion of grassroots activism and party unity, scholars who point to this factor fail to ask a very important question: why were the major parties unable or unwilling to use motivations other than the patronage system to maintain their internal organization? There must have been ways other than appealing to material rewards to inspire people to join one's campaign. One hundred years ago, when the Republicans and Democrats were still relying on patronage, the Populists and Socialists did not, and usually could not, offer their volunteers and organizers individual material gain. People campaigned for the Populists and Socialists because of the ideals and programs for which the parties stood. These challenger parties saw themselves as part of a broad movement of humanity for a better world.

The Republicans and Democrats could not, and can not, mobilize grassroots energy in this way. If they campaign on their platforms and the substance of the issues, they would only highlight for voters just how little they differ from each other. Furthermore, an honest discussion of what they intended to do while in office would also open both major parties to accusations that they favor the rich and powerful. Therefore, both parties have generally avoided campaigning on substance. They focus instead on electing individual candidates to political office rather than on raising a broader political discussion. Historically, even in their patronage-driven grassroots days, both major parties appealed to voters not over comprehensive policy questions, but often on regional, ethnic, religious, and racial identities. While, in the "good old days," the two parties used their considerable grassroots energy to develop elaborate spectacles during the campaign season—torchlight parades, community barbecues, and door-to-door canvasses—all of these activities were intended to mobilize supporters and demoralize opponents without ever having to touch too deeply on the real issues. Between elections, these Democratic and Republican electoral machines tried to maintain and extend voter loyalty by use of personal favors and patronage, not by standing for any higher agenda.

Understanding this history places today's situation in a different light. The money-driven, high-tech model of electioneering is dominant now mainly because both major parties want elections organized this way. When the Republicans and Democrats defeated the Populist and Socialist challenges they became free to transform the nation's elections without opposition.

Their gravitation to new high-tech methods can be seen at three different levels. First, with the decline of patronage, neither Democrats nor Republicans were willing to utilize alternative methods for mobilizing grassroots support. Second, as a result of the Populist and Socialist threats, neither major party had much incentive to maintain grassroots participation. Indeed, the Republican and Democratic parties defeated the Populists and Socialists, in part, by purging the electoral system of "undesirable" elements through various "electoral reforms" that reduced voter participation. Finally, the major parties' close alliance with corporate America provided them a viable political alternative.

The emerging forms of modern corporate advertising fit quite well with past Republican and Democratic desires for spectacle, image appeal, and general avoidance of comprehensive policy questions. The growing concentration of corporate wealth also provided the massive financial resources needed to abandon grassroots activists and develop the new advertising campaign on a mass basis.

The lesson of this history is that the electoral process is not fixed, but is highly malleable. The major political actors can and do structure the process to fit their own interests and resources. Progressives, therefore, must follow the examples of their predecessors by defining their political activities in terms of the logic of their struggle, rather than conforming to the dominant practices. This means that we should take supposedly "obsolete" grassroots methods seriously.

The Nuts and Bolts of Grassroots Electioneering

Jesse Jackson's 1988 race for the Democratic presidential nomination is a good example of this "back to the future" process. Presidential races are the most capital-intensive of all elections in this country. Even when local mainstream organizers want to develop grassroots campaigns, they usually simply cannot find the volunteers. As a Michael Dukakis campaign organizer in Binghamton, New York commented: "we would sit in the phone banks each night hoping and praying that some volunteers would show up." His experience was not unique. Mainstream presidential campaigns generally do not invoke much volunteer energy. The small group of local party activists generally focus on local races, where the spoils of victory are much more tangible. As one long-time Democratic organizer described:

> *You work for a presidential election for the fun of it. You work for a county executive or a gubernatorial election hoping there is a pot of gold at the end of the rainbow.*

Jesse Jackson's campaign shattered this apathetic picture. While in Binghamton, New York, the Dukakis campaign struggled to maintain any local presence with the few dozen volunteers at its disposal, local Jackson organizers placed several hundred people out in the community on election day. In the neighboring cities of Ithaca and Syracuse a similar picture emerged as hundreds of enthusiastic Jackson volunteers combed their neighborhoods, while the other Democratic and Republican candidates failed to establish any real presence in the community.

What kinds of communities did Jackson organizers and volunteers come from? Ithaca is a small city situated in the middle of rural Tompkins County. The city's 29,541 residents constitute a third of the county's 94,097 inhabitants. The county is overwhelmingly white. The African-American population numbers 1,916—just 6 percent of the city's total population. Home to Cornell University, Ithaca is very much a progressive college town.

In contrast, the greater metropolitan areas of Syracuse and Binghamton offer more "mainstream" and comparatively conservative communities. Syracuse has the largest population of the three cases: 163,860 residents in the city and 468,873 for all of Onondaga County. While the county is overwhelmingly white, Syracuse does have a substantial African-American population and a small Latino community that, respectively, constitute 20 percent and 3 percent of the city's inhabitants. Both Binghamton and Broome County are almost all white. The 2,584 African Americans who live in Binghamton make up only 0.5 percent of the 53,008 residents. The contrast is even starker in the neighboring cities and towns. Of Broome County's population of 202,949, African Americans constitute less than one-fifth of 1 percent.

Both cities are located within staunchly Republican counties. In 1988, Onondaga County Republicans outnumbered their Democratic neighbors by 92,729 to 37,014. In Broome County, the margin was closer—47,943 Republicans to 34,874 Democrats. In both cities, however, the Democrats held a small margin of predominance. In the 1980s, Democratic registration in both cities exceeded Republican by margins of 5 percent or less. Each city has a history of predominantly Democratic administrations.

All three cases were located in upstate New York which, in 1988, offered a particularly pivotal moment in the primary season. Following a stunning victory in Michigan, Jackson held the serious prospect, midway through the season, of winning the nomination. The local Jackson campaign divided into three major phases: early preparation, the main campaign, and, finally, election day. These are key phases in any grassroots electoral campaign.

Phase One: The Preparation Stage

During the early stages of a presidential campaign, organizers need to use their initial pool of volunteers to deal with two aspects of elections imposed by US law: getting on the ballot and registering voters. If all goes well, this period should provide the campaign some visibility and momentum to bring in new volunteers.

Getting on the Ballot

Under the election laws, candidates and parties must meet certain qualifications to place their name on the ballot. Typically this requires collecting a certain number of petition signatures from fellow citizens. The exact requirements are set by state laws and vary by the office sought.

For Jesse Jackson's campaign in New York, he needed to get roughly one thousand signatures in each congressional district. Since New York has a history of candidates using lawyers to challenge their opponents' qualifying signatures, often for quite trivial reasons, Jackson organizers in each district set out to make sure that they collected at least twice the required number. In addition to getting Jackson's name on the ballot, these petitions were also helpful in developing a list of potential Jackson voters. While a person who signs a petition is officially only saying that they would like to see the candidate's name as a choice on the ballot, obviously people who sign are more likely to support the candidate.

In Syracuse, Ithaca, and Binghamton, Jackson organizers put a fair number of volunteers on the street—at least a few dozen in each city. Yet a small group of committed organizers who sacrifice a few week's evenings and weekends can collect enough signatures. In Ithaca, for example, most of the petitioning work to get several hundred signatures for Michael Dukakis was almost entirely carried out by two campaign organizers. In all three cities, Jackson organizers held training sessions to launch their petition drives. While not terribly complex, the petition process can be formal and, therefore, Jackson volunteers needed to know precisely how to fill out the forms and gather signatures. Jackson organizers also took the opportunity to discuss his candidacy with the volunteers and to provide them with some literature to hand out while at people's doors.

Voter Registration

Elections in the United States are notable for the high proportion of citizens who do not vote. Part of the reason for this is undemocratic registration laws. While some states allow people to register at the polls, most require registration well before an election. To vote for Jesse Jackson in New York state, would-be voters needed to register up to a full two months before the primary election. These deadlines came well before most people even began thinking about the election. In addition, finding a place to register and actually getting there is not always a convenient process. All these factors, coupled with many people's general lack of enthusiasm for the political process, mean that many US citizens are not registered to vote.

Jackson activists were well aware of this problem. Some of Jackson's core constituencies were among low-income people who tend to move around a good deal and have the lowest rates of registration. To help ensure that Jackson supporters were on the official registration rolls come election day, activists organized major volunteer efforts to register voters. They used a variety of methods. Some volunteers went into community colleges and set up tables. Others distributed registration materials through local churches and other organizations. In Syracuse, the campaign got service agencies to either provide voter registration cards in their offices or actually allow Jackson volunteers to set up registration tables at the location. In all three cities, Jackson organizers developed major door-to-door drives.

In practice, one-on-one contact has proven the most effective way for overcoming people's alienation. In many cases, Jackson volunteers were encountering residents who had not voted in years, if ever. Such people saw the political system as incapable of making any positive difference in their lives. Their alienation was an accurate reaction to the attitude of most politicians toward people like themselves. In short, Jackson activists knew they were going into neighborhoods long neglected by the political establishment.

As with petitioning, Jackson organizers kicked off their registration drive with volunteer training sessions. The registration process involves some technicalities that volunteers need to know about when helping people to fill out their forms. State law can also regulate who can do voter registration. In Wisconsin, for example, volunteers must be officially sworn in by local registration authorities. During the training sessions, Jackson organizers talked with volunteers about how to deal with people's apathy. Volunteers needed to have effective answers to questions like, "Why should I bother voting? It doesn't make any difference."

Generally, local Jackson campaigns organized the door-to-door efforts as group events. Volunteers would show up at a set location and then break down into teams assigned to specific areas. By doing registration in groups, campaign organizers could carefully target volunteer efforts at specific populations as well as keep better track of the results. The local Jackson campaigns also organized some follow-up work to help ensure that newly registered voters came out on election day. As one Syracuse activists explained:

> *For people for whom it is their first time voting, it takes persistence. The voting booth and the voting process is something that we take for granted, but*

for someone who has never voted before it's intimidating. It is intimidating for a number of different reasons. [For example], for someone who has never voted, it's a little embarrassing to go in there and not know how to do it. And so it takes a little voter education and cajoling to get that person to vote. The most difficult component of drawing new people into the process is getting them to the polls. Voter registration is much easier. My guess is that the Jackson campaign was able to get a higher participation rate out of newly registered voters than we have seen in the past twenty years... Jackson had the potential to get unregistered voters registered and to the polls whereas for the traditional campaign by Governor Mario Cuomo, Michael Dukakis, or whoever, the problem that they have is that you go knock on someone's door and it's nothing for the person to sign the form. The problem is transforming that into the education process of getting people interested enough and educated enough to go to the polling place.

Once having registered people, Jackson volunteers sent out cards explaining the date of the primary, the location of the polling place, and the importance of their vote. Some campaigns also set up phone banks to contact newly registered people to explain the voting process and to see if they had any questions or concerns. In Syracuse, Jackson activists in the Latino community ensured that the primary day ballot was accurately printed in Spanish in addition to English. They also set up a practice voting machine at the offices of the community's Spanish Action League so that residents could drop by and directly experience the voting process.

Building the Volunteer Base

Volunteer-run petitioning and registration drives will hopefully provide a local campaign with some public visibility—if nothing else, by word of mouth. Along with the volunteer work during this initial period, organizers should be developing and implementing plans to recruit more people.

A good number of volunteers will always come through the grapevine: people who are already involved talk to people they know, who then talk to people they know. Using modest phone banks and mailings can also bring in new volunteers. Lists that point to potentially sympathetic people are like gold for local campaign organizers. Jackson activists sought out the membership and mailing lists of local progressive organizations. They also tracked down records from past mobilizations, such as marches on the nation's capital, previous progressive election campaigns, or local Take-Back-the-Night marches. In Binghamton, Jackson organizers raised enough money early on so that they were able to open a campaign headquarters downtown. This gave people a clear and available place to drop by to volunteer some time. Always bustling with activity, the local Jackson headquarters also attracted local reporters who wanted to write an upbeat story on citizen election activity.

All three campaigns were very successful in attracting volunteers. The Ithaca campaign developed an active volunteer list of over 150 people. The

Binghamton and Syracuse efforts were even larger with between 300 and 450 volunteers.

Phase Two: The Main Campaign

With the primary election in early April, Jackson organizers spent January and February setting up their campaign and running petition and registration drives. By early March, however, with the election one month away, the campaign began mobilizing volunteers to create a major presence within the community. The most obvious task facing any election campaign is to ensure that voters know about and support your candidate. An equally important task, in the United States, where even for the most popular of elections—that of president—almost half the public stays home, is making sure that people who support you actually go to the polls. Indeed, with Jesse Jackson already making national headlines, local organizers saw the task of getting out the vote as all the more central.

Getting Out the Vote—Identifying Supporters

The basic get-out-the-vote techniques are as old as campaigning in this country. The organizer's goal is to identify, among registered voters, those who support your candidate so that on election day you can make sure these people actually vote.

For the Jackson campaigns in Ithaca and Binghamton, identifying supporters meant organizing large-scale volunteer efforts to phone every registered Democrat to determine their candidate preference. The county election offices provided or sold the campaigns a complete list of registered voters. Today, such authorities can often provide computerized lists.

In Ithaca, the phone efforts were mainly organized by providing volunteers with a section of the registration lists that they could then call at their leisure. While this offered volunteers flexibility, this method involved a good deal of organizer energy to keep track of who had which list and to make sure the work was actually done and handed back. In Binghamton, activists set up phone banks in offices that volunteered their facilities. For example, a local business might donate four phone lines, a local attorney three, and a community organization four more.

Regardless of how they were organized, phone volunteers did the same task. Working from a script, they asked residents: "If the election were held today, which candidate would you vote for?" These calls could also be used to ask people about their concerns and to recruit those who seemed obviously enthusiastic about Jesse Jackson. In doing this kind of phone work, organizers are faced with a minor dilemma: do volunteers identify themselves as part of the campaign? If so, they risk biasing the results. For example, some residents may say that they are for your candidate just to get you to hang up. For this reason, local election campaigns will sometimes identify themselves with a more neutral-sounding polling name. Jackson organizers had ethical problems with such an approach. Therefore, their phone script had people identifying themselves as from Jackson's campaign.

Voter Education and Further Motivation

In Syracuse, organizers did not need such an identification effort as the city's political geography provided entire neighborhoods of high Jackson support. Instead, organizers used their volunteer energy to encourage people in these areas to vote. A wide variety of techniques exist to help make residents familiar with one's candidate and to gain their support. These same methods can also serve as additional get-out-the-vote efforts. As a result, Jackson literature emphasized the seriousness of his candidacy and the importance of being part of this historic effort by going to the polls. In Syracuse, Jackson organizers did large-scale literature drops.

In races for local offices, the grassroots campaign develops and mails out literature. Because Jackson's effort was national in scope, state organizers often provided the campaign with leaflets and mailings. Local Jackson volunteers, however, did organize some literature drops in order to substitute people power for money power. Mailing campaign brochures can be an expensive business. For example, in a small-sized city like Ithaca, a mailing just to registered Democrats involves over 10,000 pieces. That's several thousand dollars in postage alone!

Jackson activists tried to get out the message in other ways. In Binghamton, they set up a speakers bureau of volunteers trained to talk on behalf of the campaign. They sent any extra volunteers door-to-door to speak directly with their fellow citizens about Jackson's candidacy. All three Jackson campaigns also utilized the local media. While the national media generally set out to undermine Jackson's effort, local organizers often found they had the upper hand. Some local reporters were even sympathetic to the grassroots Jackson people. Certainly the local campaign's media volunteers tried to cultivate friendly relations with town reporters.

Furthermore, editors and reporters who wanted to give a community angle to the national primary race really did not have much of a choice on what to cover. The other candidates simply did not have much newsworthy activity at the local level. In contrast, when reporters showed up to Jackson campaign meetings at the local headquarters they found a continuous bustle of energized and inspiring activism. As a result of their efforts, Jackson campaigners in Ithaca, Binghamton, and Syracuse all succeeded in gaining favorable stories on their efforts in community media. Ironically, the same papers that ran such favorable local stories were also filled with hostile material from the national press wires. The helpful local coverage, however, continued almost up to election day, though some editors began switching over to the official line developed by the national media—that Jackson could not win and was not a desirable candidate.

The enthusiasm and persistent organizing of the local campaigns combined with Jackson's own charisma to grab the local headlines when the candidate, himself, entered town. The contrast between Jackson's grassroots crusade and the lackluster local campaigns of his opponents could not have been more clearly illustrated. When Jackson came to Binghamton, despite airplane problems that delayed him for over two hours, he spoke to a packed auditorium of 3,700 to 4,500 people. When Dukakis rolled in to town a few days later, he spoke to a crowd of 500—a total that local organizers seemed grateful to get. In Syracuse, at least 6,500 came to hear Jackson speak, while both Dukakis and Gore got no more than 200. Even then Vice President George Bush could barely draw 300 people when he came to the city.

Grassroots Fundraising

Jackson organizers also found creative ways to translate their volunteer strength into money for the campaign. The ability of mainstream candidates to bring in millions of dollars to support their bids can leave progressive activists demoralized. While a Dukakis may get the big campaign contributions, the $5, $10, and $20 contributions given by ordinary citizens, when multiplied by thousands upon thousands of people, can add up to some pretty big money.

Mainstream candidates usually do not go after this grassroots money because they do not have the necessary volunteers or the need. As one local Dukakis chair explained:

> *Local fundraising just was not worth it... We had a lawyer locally who volunteered to make sure we did not do anything illegal. The only way you can get in trouble with a federal election is by money raising. It's just too easy to violate one of those rules. So we didn't bother. We didn't need to do that. The little money that we spent we got right from Dukakis headquarters—less than $1,000. We used it to copy and to rent phones—that was it.*

Overall, almost two-thirds of Dukakis' national campaign contributions came in amounts over $500. In contrast, Jackson received almost no corporate money and nine out of ten of his contributions were under $500.[1]

While the national Jackson effort did do some fundraising of its own, Jackson's campaign clearly relied on locally raised money. Throughout the campaign season, Jackson volunteers in Ithaca, Binghamton, and Syracuse brought in the cash a few dollars at a time—through bake sales, bowling nights, cocktail parties, raffles, dinners, and house parties. In most cases, the events were affordably priced as organizers wanted them to be open to people of modest income. In Binghamton, the local Jackson campaign sent over $14,000 to the state campaign. In Syracuse, activists raised even more. Of course, when combined with grassroots organization and preparation, Jackson proved to be his own fundraising machine. When he came to

Syracuse, for example, he raised over $30,000 by "passing the hat" at his public rally.

Phase Three: Election Day

From March, the volunteer momentum grew until election day, when campaign organizers launched a truly massive grassroots effort. The goal was simple: to make sure registered voters who support Jackson got to the polls.

Because of their phone work, Jackson volunteers in Binghamton and Ithaca entered election day with long lists of identified supporters. On election day, volunteers waited in the phone banks for the first reports to come in from Jackson people stationed at the polls. In both cities, campaign organizers placed at least one, and usually several, volunteers at each polling station. While some people handed out campaign literature, legally at least 100 feet from the polls, other volunteers kept track of who had voted. With a list of identified Jackson supporters in hand, each poll watcher stood near the voter check-in table. Each time an identified supporter voted, the poll watchers crossed that person off their lists. Legally, authorities have to let volunteers see the names of those who vote, although obviously how they vote is secret.

At prearranged points in the day, campaign organizers had copies of each poll watcher's marked up lists sent to the phone banks. Volunteers then called supporters who had not voted to ask them to do so, and to offer assistance, if needed. Volunteer drivers were ready to chauffeur anyone who asked for help to and from the polls. As anyone who has done this kind of election day phone work will testify, the experience can be both immensely rewarding and frustrating. Some people will clearly appreciate your concern. Others, especially those who have absolutely no intention of showing up at their polling place, can get quite disagreeable, especially after the third or fourth phone call. Nevertheless, despite the occasional ugly comment, this get-out-the-vote work does pay off.

While using the basic poll watcher/phone bank strategy, local Jackson efforts did show some variations. In Binghamton, at polling places that had more than one volunteer, the extra people went door-to-door in the neighborhood to locations, such as public housing complexes, where Jackson support was expected to be high. In addition to encouraging those registered to go vote, volunteers also carried voter registration cards for future use by unregistered residents fired up by Jackson's campaign.

In Syracuse, organizers did not develop lists of supporters, but instead targeted entire sections of the city where they knew that people would most likely pull the lever for Jesse Jackson. In such neighborhoods, hundreds of Jackson activists combed the streets on election day trying to get people to the polls. Jackson organizers even drove a truck through the community playing prerecorded messages from prominent community leaders and such celebrities as Bill Cosby and Spike Lee. By the end of the day, the get-out-the-vote drive became more focused as poll watcher data showed which registered Democrats had voted and which had not.

The local Jackson campaigns also began election day prepared to handle any legal difficulties that might arise. Poll watchers could report if people were turned away or if problems developed with voting machines. Several progressive lawyers volunteered their time to counter any problems. Irregularities did occur. In two of the three cites, voting machines, which normally are fairly reliable, malfunctioned. In such cases, the polls were shut down, for up to several hours, when paper ballots were either not available or in short supply. Coincidentally, all of these poll problems happened in areas that heavily favored Jackson. As one Jackson activist described: "It was hard to put your finger on, but a number of strange circumstances did seem to effect the Jackson vote." However, not even Jackson organizers felt that such events lowered their final vote totals in a decisive way.

The Celebration

By nine o'clock the polls closed. In each community, Jackson volunteers began to gather at local meeting halls. After four months of intense campaigning, they had reason to both celebrate and mourn. Thanks to their hard work, Jackson won both the city of Syracuse and Ithaca. In Binghamton, Jackson lost to Dukakis, 22 to 60 percent. Yet even there he tripled his vote from 1984—something that local organizers in this conservative community considered quite an accomplishment.

Despite these gains, the New York primary has gone down in the history books as a key defeat for Jesse Jackson. In the end, large-scale Dukakis returns in other parts of upstate New York overwhelmed the healthy totals Jackson gained in New York City. Race also played an important factor as only 15 percent of whites voted for Jackson. Even in places such as Syracuse, Jackson's win in the city was outnumbered by the Dukakis sweep of the surrounding suburbs. The Jackson vote points to the problem confronting progressives of mobilizing support in suburbia.

Variations on Local Campaigning

The Jackson grassroots campaigns were part of a broader national effort. Their activity was, in part, shaped by this reality. Most of the electoral activism that we will examine in the chapters ahead does not aim for national office, however, but involves candidacies for state legislatures, city councils, school boards, and mayoral offices.

The basic techniques used for these more local races are generally the same as for campaigns such as Jesse Jackson's. There are some differences, of course. For local offices, there is no national media coverage or high-powered media strategy. Instead, local organizers have to get out the candidate's message just as much as they need to get out the vote. Campaign materials, such as flyers and local radio ads, take on even greater weight when one is running for local office.

In more local contests, personal contact also becomes more important, both by volunteers and by the candidates themselves. In cases where the size of the potential electorate is below a couple thousand, such as in a city council race, a committed candidate can literally attempt to personally talk to every voter in the district. Such direct contact requires a candidate to sacrifice a good amount of personal time. For example, to get himself elected to city council in Ithaca, progressive activist John Efroymson spent every weekend and many weekday nights for almost two months canvassing. Similarly, in Vermont, Progressive Coalition candidates for the state legislature, such as Dean Corren and Terry Bouricius, also used their off-work hours to personally talk one-on-one with voters. In all of these cases, the candidates were campaigning among roughly two thousand potential voters. Veteran local campaigners stress that such door-to-door contact can make a big difference. Personal contact helps a candidate become "flesh and blood." Furthermore, due to their real commitment to ordinary people, progressive candidates can come across as especially sincere and genuine. Meeting one's constituency one-on-one can also help once in office. As Connecticut state legislator, Chris Donavan, explains:

> By doing such things as going door to door, I have been able to translate progressive ideas into terms which common people understand. They have then given back to me their input and support. While the political establishment might consider my politics way out, I know that I am not considered that way in my district. I have found that the general public is much more predisposed toward progressive politics than I expected. People really welcomed and appreciated my efforts. Therefore, I can take a strong principled policy position in the state house knowing that I am doing what people really want.

Can Volunteers Make A Difference?

Ordinary people can do a lot of work for an election campaign, but does it have any effect? A whirlwind of grassroots activism only matters if it really does have an impact on election day. The local Jackson campaigns had influence in three major areas: voter turn-out, campaign finances, and voter education.

Voter Turn-out

> To win New York we need to massively raise turn-out as well as
> our percentage in each community.
>
> —From "New Yorkers for Jackson '88"
> election day manual

Ever since the Republicans and Democrats drove down voter turn-out to defeat the Populists and Socialists, relatively few Americans actually participate in our supposedly democratic process. Even at the best of times, during an election for president, only slightly more than half the possible electorate turns out to the polls. In off years and more local races, as few as 20 percent, 15 percent, or even 10 percent of citizens actually vote. Those who do not vote are the very people potentially most receptive to a progressive message. People who are lower down the social-economic ladder, racial minorities, and young people all vote in lower rates than those who are better off, white, and older.

The largest "party" in this country is not the Republicans or Democrats, but the party of people who stay home—voting for "none of the above." Since so many people don't vote, getting them to the polls can be a potentially decisive political asset. As political scientist E. E. Schattschneider wrote over three decades ago: "Anyone who finds out how to involve the forty million [non-voters] in American politics will run the country for a generation."[2]

Schattschneider believed that the struggle to expand people's participation in elections involved not only efforts to eliminate the remaining legal barriers, but, more importantly, a significant expansion in the range of political options well beyond the two major parties so that current non-voters felt represented. As Jackson's campaign illustrated, however, merely offering voters a real alternative, especially just a single candidacy, is not, by itself, going to lead to large increases in voting. The level of alienation from the political system that people have developed over many years is not likely to be dispelled simply by the momentary existence of a single candidate. Thus, the grassroots door-to-door work done by Jackson activists was the critical ingredient to raise voter turn-out.

The election returns in Syracuse illustrate these points. Unlike the other cases we examined, the Syracuse effort focused almost entirely upon raising voter registration and turn-out in the central-city wards. The local campaign's get-out-the-vote activities had a clear effect. In 1984, only 39 percent of eligible voters in Jackson's core wards voted. By 1988, the percentage of people voting rose to 54 percent. In 1992, in the absense of a Jackson campaign, the voting percentage in his core wards dropped down to only

25 percent. Get-out-the-vote efforts work, but they do not lead to lasting change as one shot efforts.

Measuring the impact of voter turn-out in Ithaca and Binghamton is more involved because the local campaigns identified and mobilized supporters throughout both cities. By comparing areas where the local campaigns identified a relatively large number of Jackson supporters with areas with fewer identified supporters, a pattern similar to Syracuse becomes clear. In both cities, voting districts that had a relatively high Jackson vote in 1988 were areas that historically displayed low turn-out rates relative to other parts of the community. In 1988, in most of those areas, turn-out increased to equal to, if not better than, the community's higher turn-out areas.

The voting patterns in the county surrounding Ithaca provide further evidence that it was local volunteer efforts, not just Jackson's candidacy, that got people to the polls. Ithaca activists did not develop a full countywide get-out-the-vote drive. Therefore, registered Jackson supporters in some areas received a good amount of phone calling while in other areas they were left on their own. Countywide, those wards that Jackson phone volunteers targeted had the highest turn-out rates. Areas that brought in a high Jackson vote, but that did not receive get-out-the-vote efforts, had noticeably lower turn-outs than those strong Jackson areas where volunteers were active.[3] Since Jackson won the city of Ithaca by a margin of 102 votes, out of over 25,000 cast, it is fair to say that the local campaign's ability to raise turn-out among his supporters accounts for this victory.

Although providing the margin of victory in two out of three cases, the Jackson get-out-the-vote experience did reveal several limitations. First, despite even such impressive gains in turn-out rates as found in Syracuse, a large number of eligible voters still did not vote. In Ward Eighteen, the heart of Syracuse's African-American community, 46 percent of those registered did not vote, even though turn-out increased a full twenty-one points over 1984.

Here again, the increased participation encouraged by the Jackson get-out-the-vote campaigns did not translate into a long-term pattern. As the Syracuse figures suggest, without subsequent grassroots mobilizations, the heightened participation developed in 1988 did not last in 1992. When local activists mounted subsequent grassroots campaigns in support of local progressive candidates, the turn-out experience of the 1988 primary could be duplicated. Yet, when no such projects presented themselves, the Jackson areas tended to lapse back into their previous levels of apathy. Philip Thompson found a similar pattern of momentary increases that lapsed back into the normal patterns of low turn-out in his study of the Jackson campaign in Atlanta, New York City, and Oakland.[4]

Most importantly, increasing voter participation raises the effectiveness of an existing base of support, but it does not create or expand it. In Syracuse and Ithaca, the inherent progressive voting population was large enough that local activists could push it into majority status by raising turn-out. In Binghamton, however, this base represented only a fifth of registered Democrats. Although the get-out-the-vote activities of the local campaign could increase the relative weight of this base, activists had to find a way of penetrating further into "mainstream" neighborhoods to win the city.

In examining voter turn-out, we have only looked at what happened on election day among registered voters. But what about the people who a few months before the election may not have been registered? Jackson activists made serious efforts to register these people to vote. Unfortunately, because the county election boards only total the registration figures once a year, measuring the influence of the local registration drives is difficult. In Syracuse, Jackson activists claimed to have registered 5,000 people during the course of the 1988 election season—with roughly a quarter of that amount coming during the primary season, and the rest from their efforts up to the general election. By comparing the April 1988 figures with registration numbers a year later, it is clear that 3,056 people registered during that time in the center-city wards. This was more than double the average registration increase found in the city's outlying areas, where Jackson organizers had little activity.

As with voter turn-out, the impact on registration did not continue over time. By 1992, with no Jackson campaign and little local electoral activism, registration figures in the central city had fallen back to their historic low rates. "Registering voters is a time consuming effort," explained one Syracuse advocate of same-day registration, adding, "A lot more positive energy could be spent if we did not have to chase people around to get them registered." Clearly, progressives need to push for legal changes to increase access to voting. Organizers also need to develop political movements that can translate the excitement of a single election campaign into a lasting commitment by people to participate in the political system.

Despite these limitations, for any given election effort, a volunteer-intensive campaign's ability to get supporters registered and to the polls is a clear advantage. It may not deliver such dramatic returns as doubling a candidate's vote, but it can increase a campaign's voting returns by several percentage points. While this may not seem like much, we have to keep in mind that most seriously contested races are won by relatively narrow margins. Eight of the twelve US presidential elections between 1944 and 1988 have been decided by a difference of under ten percentage points: four of these elections by four percentage points or less (1948, 1960, 1968, and 1976). The losers in these four races, Thomas Dewey, Richard Nixon, Hubert Humphrey, and Gerald Ford, may well have wished that they could have inspired a volunteer crusade like the one that supported Jesse Jackson. In 1994, the Republican's won the upper-hand in Congress, in part, because Republican turn-out went up in every region of the country, while Democratic turn-out fell except in the Mid-Atlantic states and on the West Coast. In comparing 1990 to 1994, Curtis Gans found a 21 percent drop in voting by people with incomes under $15,000, while the share of the vote cast by those who earned over $50,000 went up by a third.[5] The New Right has realized the importance of voter turn-out. As Guy Rogers, then National Director of the Christian Coalition, once stated:

> *We don't have to worry about convincing a majority of Americans to agree with us. Most of them are staying home on election day and watching Falcon Crest.*[6]

Campaign Finances

In looking at the primary season as a whole, the corporate-driven Dukakis machine not surprisingly outspent Jesse Jackson. For the primary season, Dukakis raised $29 million. Jackson's campaign chest was not tiny, however. Thanks to grassroots fundraising efforts, his campaign exceeded $18 million by the end of the primary. This cash supply meant that, for the critical New York state primary, Jackson's campaign was able to spend $825,000—almost as much as Dukakis' $937,200.[7] This money enabled Jackson to buy television and radio time—mostly in the New York City area. While not providing an advantage, or even parity, locally raised money did allow Jackson a minimum presence in the paid media. While corporate backers can provide mainstream candidates with significant financial resources, the Jackson campaign suggests that high-tech campaign methods do not have to serve as the exclusive tools of business-supported candidates.

Indeed, strong progressive campaigns can effectively translate volunteer energy into cash, so much so that progressive candidates may outspend their opponents. During the 1988 primary, the local financial contrast between the Jackson effort and his opponents was ironically the opposite of the national picture. Mainstream campaigns not only raised their money at a higher level, they also let little of it trickle down to the grassroots. In contrast, the Jackson campaign in Binghamton was able to do pretty much what it wanted within the scope of a local effort, while local Dukakis organizers could not even open a campaign office due to insufficient funds. With neither money nor volunteers, it is not surprising that the other candidates' primary campaigns had little community presence.

Voter Education

While increasing turn-out can have an impact, and may even win an election, progressives mount an election campaign not simply to win votes for a candidate, but also to talk with the public about politics and progressive alternatives. Although paid media ads can accomplish this somewhat, progressive organizers would ideally like to use grassroots volunteers to directly interact with their neighbors.

Short of a massive research study that included repeated opinion polls of targeted communities, evaluating the educational impact of local volunteer work is difficult to do. The limitations of local Jackson education efforts, however, is clear from the activities themselves.

Although in all three cases campaign volunteers went door-to-door, much of this activity revolved around voter registration and petition signature collection—purposes not specifically aimed at influencing voter preferences. The door-to-door activity that was deliberately aimed at educating voters had significant utility. One Binghamton activist who went door-to-door on election day described the value of such activities:

> *I came to believe in direct access to people. It is very easy to throw away a pamphlet, it's a little less easy to ask someone to go away. When you can talk back and forth to someone, you can answer a lot of their questions and concerns a lot better.*   -

Door-to-door contact involves slow, time-consuming work. These difficulties can be illustrated by the uniquely detailed records kept by the Ithaca petition drive.[8] Of the twenty people who braved the cold weather to walk door-to-door in this small city, 60 percent spent one day, 15 percent two days, and 25 percent three or more. One densely Democratic block required up to a half hour or more, so most petitioners covered less than half a dozen blocks. The volunteers' success rates also varied enormously. One core member and her husband managed to single-handedly collected 103 signatures over the course of three weekends. Most petitioners turned in signature results ranging in the teens or lower twenties. Of the city's twenty election districts, only three were canvassed completely (meaning that the addresses of petition signatures covered the entire geographical area); two received half-coverage; seven had more than a couple blocks covered; and eight were not canvassed at all, including one entire ward. In short, to have directly contacted anywhere near the majority of registered Democrats in Ithaca, the campaign would have needed a considerably greater number of volunteers and/or more time than the one-month petition period.

Door-to-door volunteers are limited by what they can accomplish in one conversation, of course. Volunteers remember most residents as at least polite and commonly quite interested, yet found that people would not engage in a long conversation with someone who simply knocks at their door. As one Binghamton volunteer commented on her canvass of a white working-class neighborhood:

> *People were very receptive to [Jackson]. I was very surprised. I think because the economy was really starting to go bad, people were seeing the results of Reaganomics at this point, so people were very receptive to what you had to tell them. You would talk to them about his social policies, his economic policies,*

> *his views on labor, his history with the civil rights movement... They would ask*
> *why I was working for the campaign and I would tell them: "This is the first*
> *political candidate that I have worked for because he represents*
> *Americans—us, the people on the street, not the rich and the powerful... "*

Even short conversations can help address people's concerns on specific policy issues. In addition, the mere physical presence of a volunteer at a person's door may help convince them that a genuine alternative to mainstream politics actually exists. A New York volunteers' manual summarized the relative importance of door-to-door canvassing as follows:

> *Door-to-door canvassing is the highest quality and most labor intensive*
> *form of voter contact. It is very effective for persuasion—nothing is more*
> *convincing than an honest, friendly face—and not effective for identifying*
> *voters—people do not like to be negative face-to-face, phone-banking gets more*
> *honest answers.*

Local volunteers also distributed campaign literature, a key part of the Jackson educational strategy. As with most political campaigns, the Jackson literature was brief. Unlike many other candidate's materials, however, the Jackson literature stressed specific policy proposals. For example, a newspaper-sized, four-page piece produced by the Jackson state office devoted the center pages to a comprehensive summary of Jackson's policy proposals. In Binghamton, door-to-door volunteers handed out Jackson "issue briefs," one- or two-page sheets that summarized his analysis and proposals on such issues as AIDS, education, hunger, national security, international policy, and health care. The campaigns also distributed material targeted to specific constituencies. A "Students for Jesse Jackson '88" flyer stressed his advocacy of lower tuition, recruitment and retention of people of color, accessibility for the disabled, childcare, expanded federal financial aid, the Civil Rights Restoration Act, and support for community colleges. A pamphlet produced by the New York state office aimed at union members listed examples of Jackson's personal interventions on behalf of striking workers as well as a letter of endorsement from the executive director of District Council 37, AFSCME.

This literature, with its specific stands on the issues, and linking the candidate with social struggles, must have had some effect on voter preference. As used by the campaigns, however, the literature had several limitations. First, in Syracuse, which had the largest effort, organizers distributed literature primarily in high Jackson constituency areas. Its purpose was to convince people to vote as much as who to vote for. A New York state campaign manual summarized the importance of literature drops in terms of raising turn-out, not voter education. It stated:

> *Target literature distribution into communities with very high Jackson*
> *percentages and low and then high turnout. Massive literature distribution is*

a blind pull. It should be done in communities in which raising turnout across the board will help us.

Second, the brief, advertising format of the literature lent itself far more to influencing a person's candidate preference than their broader political perspective. Jackson's issue concerns and solutions could be summarized in short sentences and phrases. A detailed critique of the status quo or a broader sense of the political possibilities would have required a longer text.

Jackson organizers did try to utilize forums where a more detailed discussion of politics was possible. The Binghamton campaign's speaker's bureau was the most developed of these efforts, although the most readily available audiences were groups of already progressive-leaning constituencies. Indeed, the Binghamton campaign used the speakers' bureau as much to recruit volunteers and raise money as to convince people to vote for Jackson. Since the audiences tended to sympathize with Jackson's broad agenda, speakers did not so much need to challenge entire political perspectives, as convince the audience of the seriousness of Jackson's candidacy and respond to specific issue concerns.

Jackson activists also worked hard to get favorable stories in the local media. Since local reporters proved willing to accurately convey the energy level and agenda of the local campaigns, this media effort clearly helped put progressive politics in people's minds. The gains in this local coverage have to be compared with the power of the national media to shape people's perceptions. Indeed, even in the local media, home-grown stories were often outnumbered by nationally produced material. In examining the coverage found in the daily local papers of our three communities, we found that stories of the primary campaign from national press wire services and syndicated columnists outnumbered those written by local reporters by a two to one margin.

These figures point to a larger problem. No matter how much volunteers knock on their neighbors' doors, drop literature, and contact local reporters, people are going to come home, pick up their newspaper, or turn on the evening news, and be bombarded by images and arguments made by the corporate-owned national media. Needless to say, these sources of political information are not going to be sympathetic to progressive politics.

The national media's typical response to progressive electoral activism is to ignore it altogether. This is how it treated Ron Daniels' 1992 independent presidential bid. It seems that only independent candidates who are billionaires can be considered "legitimate" news. The national press also helped kill Larry Agran's Democratic presidential primary bid that same year. At one point, *The New York Times* even went so far as to alter a photograph that showed all of the Democratic Party contenders at a campaign function. It removed Larry Agran from the picture!

Jesse Jackson deserves the honor of being one of the few progressive candidates to run for a national office and actually win coverage on the

evening news. The media did not do this out of the goodness of its heart or
out of a commitment to "objectivity." It tried ignoring him in 1984, but his
campaign picked up so much momentum, due to large-scale grassroots
activity, that the story could not be suppressed. This national coverage did
help legitimize Jackson as a candidate. While the national media had to
show him as part of the process, it did not have to portray him as a good
potential president. In fact, the national media set out to convince voters
that Jesse Jackson was the last person they would want to sit in the oval
office. Since the patterns of this coverage are representative of the kinds of
attacks that most progressives will face at the hands of any kind of hostile
media, we will go over it in some detail.

The National Media's Attack on Jesse Jackson

Many political commentators, both inside and outside the media, did
not view the national media's treatment of Jackson as opposition. Some
argued that the media attention had helped legitimize Jackson's campaign
and expose him to a national audience.[9] That Jackson's candidacy did
provide one of the central stories of the campaign season, by itself, does
seem to support such a conclusion.

The quality of this coverage was overwhelmingly negative, however.
We examined 126 articles published in the *Press & Sun-Bulletin* (Binghamton), *Ithaca Journal,* and *The Post Standard* (Syracuse) from national
press wires or syndicated columnists during the one-month period leading
up to the New York state primary. Other newspapers across the country
used these same national sources. Thus, our findings from these three papers
have a far broader significance.

Each news article was given an overall assessment based on which
points it made. Articles rated as unfavorable discussed Jackson using entirely
negative points. Those that made any positive references were rated as
"mixed." Articles in which the dominant number of points were positive
have been labeled favorable. All syndicated columns took a clear political
stance—either attacking one candidate or supporting another. Their most
common activity was in explaining why people should not support Jesse
Jackson.

Although Jackson received continual national attention, the coverage
proved overwhelmingly negative. Among the three papers, 60 percent of all
nationally produced news articles and 75 percent of all opinion columns
directly portrayed Jackson's candidacy in a negative light. In contrast, less
than 10 percent of the coverage could even partially have left the reader
with positive information or perspectives.

By picking apart the details of this coverage, we can see that the national
press wires and syndicated columnists followed a very clear common

strategy. In criticizing Jackson, they largely ignored issues of his concrete program. Instead, national sources focused on two major messages: Jackson's "unelectability" and his "unappealing" personality.

The negative personality theme revolved around a number of components. The notion that Jackson's personality made him unqualified to hold presidential office figured predominantly. For example, while polls have shown that the public supports specific New-Deal-type policies similar to Jackson's own proposals, the national press repeatedly asserted, without offering elaboration, that he was "too liberal."[10] Similarly, although national sources frequently reported that Americans distrusted politicians and political insiders, they also continually criticized Jackson for not having held political office. The national sources often described Jackson narrowly as a black phenomenon, and characterized Jackson as egocentric and big-mouthed. They also routinely claimed that he had no substantive policy positions!

In addition to disqualifying Jackson as an individual, the media held one of Jackson's greatest personal assets against him. As all sources admitted, Jackson is an eloquent and inspiring speaker. The national media hinted that his charisma had sinister and demagogic overtones. In an opinion piece, syndicated columnist Ellen Goodman specified this image quite explicitly. She wrote:

> *There has rarely been a starker contrast between candidates and I do not mean skin color. Jackson pitches to the heart, Dukakis to the head... Jackson plays on the impulse buyer, Dukakis to the cautious, unit-price reading, comparison shopper... Is it an imperative, as Jackson suggests, for a leader to physically connect with citizens, for candidates to attract voters into their circle of believers? Is the powerful emotional surge—including the one that comes from watching a black man breaking through barriers of racism—a compelling plus? Or is there also something to be wary of in a mass chanting of rhymes and slogans?... We have seen it work both ways. The energy and passion that impels a movement. The loss of individuality, the giving up of reason that empowers a demagogue.*[11]

According to the media, people who supported Jackson had simply been caught up in an emotional fervor, rather than really thinking things through. A comparison never explicitly stated, but strongly hinted at, was to Hitler and Mussolini, both of whom had supposedly swayed the masses into blind obedience with their powerful personalities.

Finally, since up to one quarter of New York's Democratic voters were Jewish Americans, the national media sources dredged up the dirt from Jackson's 1984 campaign, when his disastrous anti-Semitic "Hymie town" remark combined with his meeting with Yasser Arafat and unsolicited support from Louis Farrakhan had caused major controversies. Ignoring the complexities of the issue, and the significant number of Jackson activists who were Jewish, the media instead gave front-page headlines to New York's

Mayor Koch, who publicly declared that Jews would "be crazy" to vote for Jackson.

The other major theme found in the national coverage revolved around Jackson's presumed "unelectability." While constant reference to Jackson's supposed personality flaws gave people an unfavorable impression of the candidate, the unelectability theme seemed directed at people who may have still found Jackson appealing. For these people, the national press and opinion sources declared that, although people may support Jackson, a vote for him would be wasted and even counterproductive.

The unelectability theme took on two major aspects. First, the national sources suggested that Jackson had no chance of winning the primary. While writers often simply asserted the impossibility of a Jackson nomination without evidence, polls carried out in New York state provided an additional and steady supply of ammunition. For example, the day before the primary, *The Post Standard* ran an article titled "Dukakis Solidifies His Lead in New York." The subheading read "Jackson's Not Doing as Well Among Whites as in Past States." The article placed the victory at 48 percent for Dukakis and 25 percent for Jackson. This poll, however, exaggerated the distance between the two. The actual election day totals ran much closer: 51 to 37 percent. While the article estimated Jackson's white support at 8 percent, the actual count ran over 15 percent in the state, and between 12 and 34 percent in the primarily white neighborhoods and suburbs of Syracuse.[12]

Second, and even more frequently, the unelectability theme involved speculation on the supposed harm a Jackson nomination would bring to the Democratic Party. For instance, all of the writers who chose to offer an opinion on the general election assumed that Jackson could not defeat George Bush. Syndicated columnist George Will was quite explicit. The headline of one of his columns read "Democrats Can Not Win With Jackson." David Yepsen of the Gannett News Service combined the unelectability attack with the demagogue that appeals-to-emotion-not-reason theme. He reported that:

> For many, it may come down to voting with their hearts for Jackson whose rhetoric they love, or for Dukakis, who they believe can beat George Bush in November.[13]

Reinforcing the assumption that Jackson could not possibly win the general election, national writers continually speculated on how the Democratic Party would "handle" him.

Incredibly, given the predominantly negative material found in the national coverage, several national sources stated quite explicitly that Jackson had been immune from criticism because he was black. Both politicians and several national writers claimed that no one could criticize Jackson for fear of being labeled racist, then went on to offer ample evidence of why people should not support him. Having assumed that Jackson's program and qualifications were weak, writers used this theme to argue that if politicians and the media had not been so intimidated, Jackson would not have gotten as far as he did.

While throwing a great deal of mud, the national news and opinion sources also chose to leave a great deal out of the news. Chief among these were Jackson's victories. The media initially downplayed his landslide win in Michigan, while giving big headlines to Dukakis' subsequent victory in Wisconsin. Even worse for a campaign run on substance, the national media sources largely ignored Jackson's issue concerns and specific policy proposals. Only two of the 126 articles surveyed mentioned "economic violence"— the central issue of Jackson's campaign. Furthermore, while Jackson and his campaign focused most of their criticism on Reaganism and the right-wing agenda, and not on the other Democratic contenders, only one article out of the 126 placed Jackson in the context of a critic of the current policies and administration. In contrast, the criticism made by the other candidates of the Reagan administration received far more print.

Nor did Jackson receive many openly supportive political commentaries. Of the forty-nine articles by syndicated columnists, only two writers openly endorsed Jackson in terms of his having the best program to meet the needs of the country. One of these, Courtland Milloy of *The Washington Post* devoted a large portion of his article to critiquing the national media. Since he offered an accurate and concise summary, he is worth quoting at length. He wrote:

> *Front page news stories too often take on the tone of editorials trying to type Jackson out of the race by stating as unsubstantiated but generally agreed-upon fact that Jackson is "unelectable."*
>
> *In the face of support that cuts across race and class lines, Jackson continues to be portrayed as appealing to "blacks and liberals." The way the word "blacks" is used deliberately plays down the diversity of black America. Blacks, we are told, vote for Jackson only because he is black. His message somehow has nothing to do with it.*
>
> *To call white midwestern farmers "liberals" is plain old wrong. Yet the brush-offs and inaccuracies about Jackson persist... What Jackson has been doing for the past four years explains a lot about why he is winning. He has been building bridges and mending fences. He has been bringing new voters to the party. He has been appealing to unemployed people across the board. He has spent more of his time getting to know people and their problems, and that's why other candidates are now trying to steal his platform.[14]*

The last paragraph is the only instance in all 126 articles surveyed that mentioned, let alone stressed, Jackson's efforts toward building a rainbow coalition of ordinary Americans.

The pattern of hostility found in most press wire and syndicated columnist articles reflects the stance of the national media generally toward

Jackson. In his extensive study of television news coverage of Jackson's 1984 bid, C. Anthony Broh concluded:

> *Television news coverage of the 1984 Democratic nominating campaign helped Jesse Jackson and it hurt him. It helped him by legitimating his candidacy; it hurt him by giving him different treatment from the treatment it gave the other potential nominees. What is more, the differences were generally not to Jackson's advantage.*[15]

On the latter point, Broh explains that:

> *Being a significant candidate is not the same as being a potential nominee. And because television news assumed that Jackson was not a potential nominee, it set him apart.*[16]

Charles Henry echoes Broh when he concludes, in his study of both the 1984 and 1988 campaigns:

> *The media did help to legitimate [Jackson's] candidacy by accepting his right to be in the race. He was shown as a full participant in all the activities of the electoral process… At the same time, the media helped to limit Jackson's candidacy by treating him as unelectable. His very participation in the process was regarded as a victory. The question "What does Jesse Jackson want?" became a constant refrain. By giving him a racial identity rather than a cross-cutting image, the media portrayed him as a candidate with a narrow base.*[17]

Poll data provides some indication that the national media's message was influential. In 1988, Jackson clearly had potential. A March Gallop poll found voters wanting candidates to discuss more frequently the very issues that Jackson routinely raised in his campaign—education, drugs, health care, AIDS, foreign competition, and homelessness.[18] The national media successfully kept Jackson's policy proposals and general agenda out of the debate. With little substantive content at their disposal, the national media's audience was left to judge Jackson based upon image, conjecture, and association. As the media argued, Jackson was a colorful, yet marginal, unqualified, and potentially dangerous candidate.

The media's negative messages showed up in surveys of voter opinion. A second March Gallop poll found that 53 percent of those interviewed saw Jackson in a very favorable or most favorable light—with 60 percent considering him a champion of social justice. Yet only 34 percent felt that he could manage the federal government and only 37 percent felt that he could deal with the complex issues facing a president.[19] An ABC News exit poll in New York state found that one in three Dukakis voters cast their ballot against someone else, probably Jackson.[20]

To argue for the influence of the national media is not to assert that people are complete captives of the corporate media. People make decisions based on their life experience and the information available to them. For

Jackson, despite the national media's continual barrage of negative information, his campaign did have some success in getting out an alternative point of view. People could watch Jackson in the debates and many could see him personally in their communities. In their local papers, they could read about the energetic activities of his visible local supporters. Many had direct contact with the campaign, either through conversations with local volunteers or through Jackson literature distributed by those same volunteers. Obviously these efforts had some effect. Despite media opposition in 1988, seven million people, including 20 percent of Democratic white voters, selected Jesse Jackson as their party's nominee.

Local Progressives and the Corporate Media

By entering more local races, progressives will largely avoid attacks from the national media, but they may still face media opposition. Politically, local media does offer a potentially greater spectrum of opinion and access. Local reporters provided Jackson activists with some favorable coverage. Similarly, many of the groups that we will discuss in the chapters ahead have also won some favorable media coverage—most of it tending to be in more local rather than national sources. Local media, however, presents a complex picture. Many local newspapers are owned by large corporations, such as Gannett or Knight-Ridder. Even locally owned media is still a private business and could be hostile to progressive change. As we will see in Chapter Six, progressive activists in Burlington, Vermont have continuously been attacked and/or ignored by the local media, even as they have become more and more electorally successful.

Local media may also give some positive coverage to activists when they are part of a much broader and distant effort, yet may change their tune when the matter hits closer to home. In Ithaca, activists supporting Jackson got several favorable stories during the primary campaign from the local daily paper and the two weeklies. A year and a half later, however, when a similar group ran Democratic Socialists of America member Ben Nichols in the Democratic mayoral primary and, upon winning this, the general election, the daily and one of the weeklies openly red-baited him and predicted dire consequences if he were elected. Two years later, they again endorsed Nichols' Republican opponent.

What can progressives do about this media hostility? Is a mass electoral movement even possible today, when the media plays such an important role in shaping people's political knowledge? How can progressives get around the media obstacle?

Using Grassroots Strength
To Get Out Your Message

The problem posed by the private media is nothing new to progressives. The Populists and Socialists also faced staunch opposition from the media of their age. These historical movements also point the way toward a response. The Populists and Socialists devoted considerable grassroots energy to developing an alternative press, speaking to people directly, setting up schools, and sponsoring community events. They made themselves part of the culture, politics, and social life of their communities. What enabled them to translate their grassroots energy into these broad forms of community outreach was their rejection of "politics as usual."

Both then and today, the two major parties largely focus on winning votes for individual candidates. Democratic and Republican activists are expected to campaign hard during an election, but then go home and wait till the next race. In contrast, Populists and Socialists defined their outreach efforts in much broader terms. They wanted to change people's basic political outlook, not just get them to vote for Jane Doe or John Smith on election day. They saw themselves as building a new society, with new values, and new understandings of how the world works. With such a perspective, Populist and Socialist organizers designed grassroots activities that extended well beyond the election cycle. They used tactics that required years, not months to come to full fruition.

Today, progressive activists must do the same. If our goal is to change our country's basic political culture and debate, then election campaigns for specific candidates must become part of a much broader strategy. Only by embarking on long-term strategies can progressives hope to translate their grassroots energy into a force that can offset the corporate media.

The problem in pursing such strategies is that they look very different from what the major parties do today. On entering electoral politics, it may seem only natural to many activists to simply get behind a candidate and campaign hard for that person. That many activists today often place their political hopes in a high-profile progressive presidential bid reflects the candidate-centered definition of politics that we have all been taught to believe is normal. Such activity, by itself, is not going to establish a lasting progressive political effort capable of seriously transforming the country.

Long-term outreach efforts require a level of organization that continues irrespective of the election cycle. Unfortunately, candidate campaigns, by themselves, do not produce such lasting organizations. The aftermath of the 1988 Jackson campaign illustrates this point quite well. In Ithaca, Binghamton, and Syracuse, Jackson activists tried to translate the momentum of his campaign into an ongoing local movement. Unfortunately, when embarking on this task, they were not helped by the national organization.

Even if grassroots activists had received better support and direction from the national office, they would still have faced major problems.

In all three cases, local organizers tried to continue their movement by following the pattern of the two major parties. In other words, they recruited candidates, ran them for office, and then went home after election day. Activists in Ithaca have been the most successful electorally. Jackson's supporters joined with other progressives to place long-time community activist Ben Nichols into the mayor's office in 1989 as a Democrat. Since then, he has been re-elected three times in a row while progressives have established themselves as the strongest force on city council. Overall, Ithaca politics has clearly moved to the left as city government has pursued an agenda somewhat similar to that found in Burlington, Vermont.

Yet Ithaca progressives utterly failed to establish a permanent political organization or a broader and systematic outreach effort. Instead, informal networks, past lists, and personal relationships help to pull together activists for each given election campaign. These local progressive election efforts have generated considerable volunteer energy. In 1991, for example, Ben Nichols faced off against Democrat-turned-Republican Mark Finkelstein. A wealthy landlord, Finkelstein spent a considerable sum of money—over $37,000 before the last week of the campaign—to send out slick flyers, hire a professional polling firm, and purchase media time. Nichols, however, proved the victor, in part because several hundred volunteers helped educate the public and, most crucially, got people to the polls on election day. Yet, as typically happens in any hard-fought race, by election day the main Nichols' campaign organizers were clearly burned out. Most spent the next few months rebuilding other parts of their lives and catching up on sleep and relaxation. None were in a position to maintain a progressive organization. Thus, the volunteers went home to await the next campaign season.

In Ithaca, years of continued progressive electoral success has not translated into ongoing outreach efforts. After Nichols' first election, organizers did try to establish a local coalition, called the Progressive Forum, that would establish a broader progressive political strategy. This effort failed, however, because most activists were already involved in various other social movement activity. The coalition did not produce a new and clear vision of what it would bring to local activism. As one Ithaca activist commented:

> *The Progressive Forum didn't fail because people disagreed on fundamental issues of what was important. It is just that you can't take people who are leaders in these constituencies and ask them to attend another set of meetings.*

Participation in a formal coalition requires local activists to make a serious sacrifice of scarce time and energy. To sustain itself, an umbrella organization has to either gain the participation of activists not tied to other concerns, or provide local activists with important benefits or opportunities that they could not obtain through existing channels. The Progressive Forum went the road of many such coalitions by not developing a concrete mission beyond a desire for greater general coordination and communication between progressive groups. Clearly, activists have to develop a grassroots movement that is an organizing project in its own right, separate from any specific election bid.

This lack of an active grassroots political structure clearly handicapped progressive officeholders, who, at times, found themselves without the power to overcome opposition to new policies. For example, Ben Nichols established a citizen commission to investigate relations between the city and Cornell University, the area's largest employer. Residents had expressed a series of grievances against the university's administration, including the polluting of nearby streams, paying poverty wages, and driving up city rental rates by not housing sufficient numbers of students on-campus. After public hearings, the commission presented its findings and recommendations for Cornell policy changes to the mayor and the university. The city soon found itself in a David versus Goliath struggle. With a budget ten times the size of the city's and an ability to play different municipalities against each other, Cornell was able to ignore the recommendations that it did not support. Grassroots pressure could have helped compel the very image-conscious university to pursue a more cooperative direction. Yet no political structure existed to mobilize community residents or to pull together the different groups that had obvious grievances with Cornell.

The difference between running candidates and building a broader political movement is even clearer in the cases of Binghamton and Syracuse, where activists never succeeded in taking control of local government. In Syracuse, Jackson organizers set up an active local branch of the Rainbow Coalition following his 1984 bid. At its peak, the organization had roughly 150 members. By 1992, however, the local Rainbow was clearly in decline, with organizers suspending regular meetings. In many ways, the Rainbow's eventual outcome was foreordained in the conceptualization of the project. The group mainly focused on recruiting candidates and running them for office.

Activists and volunteers worked hard during the election season and then dispersed after it was over. As a result, the local Rainbow developed along the same lines as the two major parties. Local Republican and Democratic party chapters have become mainly informal networks that supply a few volunteers for election campaigns. They provide little in terms of sustained grassroots energy with activities outside of electoral contests. Had the local Rainbow succeeded in coming to local power, rather than winning isolated races, it may have been able to use this position to maintain some sense of identity and purpose. Without such a victory, the local group gradually faded as those candidates available who could win office did so, leaving a shrinking number of new election bids available to mobilize people.

The same story happened in Binghamton, where a significant block of local Jackson supporters, disillusioned with the direction of the national Rainbow, decided to establish their own organization after the 1988 campaign. Called "Southern Tier for Jobs, Peace, and Justice," the group did mount several serious, although ultimately unsuccessful, election campaigns. The progressive voting base in and around Binghamton, while up to a fifth of Democratic-registered voters, was not concentrated enough in any given area to provide a majority. On the other hand, the steady economic decline hitting much of the area did provide a large number of people potentially open to a progressive message. But, to take political office, progressive organizers need to find ways of interacting with voters in a much more sustained way than individual candidate campaigns. They need an ongoing community-based movement to expose people to progressive politics. Unfortunately, single-candidate campaigns, by themselves, were not enough and the group soon faded.

Reflecting on the limitations of candidate-centered politics, one Rainbow activist in Syracuse commented:

> *It's a shame when you form a political organization that it's formed around elections because then you have those down periods and sometimes it's hard to recultivate those people.*

An Ithaca union activist who had participated in several progressive electoral efforts explained the same basic problem in a slightly different manner. He argued that:

> *Elections don't build an organization. It's a big contrast to union organizing. When you organize a union you are building toward a vote, but also an organization which will continue afterwards is built into what you are doing. With elections, once you have the vote it's all over.*

Do these experiences mean that establishing a sustained grassroots effort is impossible? No. While not easy, activists who set out to build such a structure, rather than running a few people for office, can succeed. In the next four chapters, we will compare several successful examples of local organizing that suggest contrasting models for achieving just this goal. We will begin with the Legislative and Electoral Action Program established in Connecticut, which uses a coalition-of-organizations approach and a party-within-a-party strategy. We will then turn to the coalition-of-individuals model developed by progressive organizers engaged in the growing independent political movement in Vermont. Finally, we consider strategies that aim to build, from the outset, outright third party organizations by looking in depth at the New Party and then more briefly at other party-organizing groups, such as the Labor Party Advocates, the Campaign for a New Tomorrow, and the Greens.

Part Two

Independent Politics Today

Chapter Five

Building a Party
Within a Party

Connecticut's
Legislative Electoral Action Program

Back in 1980, the regional office of the United Auto Workers (UAW) got together with the Connecticut Citizen Action Group (CCAG), as well as other organizations, to launch the Legislative Electoral Action Program (LEAP). Since then, LEAP has developed as a distinct and highly successful model of an electoral coalition. Today, LEAP-type groups have spread throughout New England and to other areas of the country. While not an independent party, their experience is worth looking at carefully.

The LEAP Model

LEAP formed in reaction to the general rightward drift of this country's electoral politics. In the words of the Lynne Ide, the current director:

> *LEAP was formed by progressive groups sick of being ignored by legislators. The attitude of those in power was kind of like: "If you don't support me, what else are you going to do?" We needed to come up with a reply so that we would be taken more seriously.*

The reply, given structure by LEAP, was to build a coalition of activist groups that would reach into their ranks and find progressives willing to run for office. The coalition would then mobilize its member groups to help propel these people to victory. At a minimum, mainstream legislators who did not respond to progressive concerns would have to face the possibility of confronting a LEAP-backed challenger in a primary. Ideally, however, LEAP sought to get its own into office and thereby directly transform the course of state politics.

LEAP has had notable electoral success. Today, the coalition consists of almost thirty progressive organizations. With their support, LEAP has established a modest staff and office. By combining these collective resources with those of member organizations, the coalition provides concrete support to progressives who want to run for election. Through numerous workshops, seminars, and other programs, LEAP encourages activists from within the progressive community to enter electoral politics and to build up basic electoral skills. LEAP has also gotten behind progressively minded politicians who seek its support. The process requires prospective candidates to provide definite answers concerning specific upcoming legislative issues as well as their more general political philosophy. Once the coalition has developed its own candidates, or endorsed those seeking its support, LEAP then organizes behind them. The LEAP staff provides candidate training, technical assistance, and grassroots activists from its member organizations.

LEAP's electoral strategy is to work primarily within the Democratic Party. The coalition seeks to pressure and displace centrist Democrats by using the primary system. Due to Connecticut's electoral laws, this strategy has not always been easy. Despite progressive efforts to change the system, the state does not have a direct primary. Instead, a prospective challenger must get 15 percent of the delegates to a party's state convention in order to petition for a primary election.

Despite these difficulties, an ever growing number of "LEAP Democrats" have won state office. In its first year, LEAP elected all four of its candidates. By 1989, LEAP had achieved the most remarkable success record of any progressive electoral coalition in the country. In the 1988 Connecticut general assembly election, thirty-five of the forty-two LEAP-endorsed candidates won seats in the state legislature, including fourteen of the fifteen "targeted" candidates who received LEAP technical help. As a result, the halls of the Connecticut legislature now include former officers, staff, and members of such groups as the Health and Hospital Workers Union, the National Organization of Women, the nuclear freeze campaign, and a variety of community organizations.

State Senator Tom Colapietro is representative of what LEAP has achieved. A retired auto worker and president of the UAW's state political action council, Colapietro originally saw running for office as "a quick way to leave you high and dry and broke." LEAP's assistance in recruiting volunteers, developing brochures, and providing training for him and his staff proved key in convincing him to run. Colapietro decisively beat out a four-term Republican mayor for his district's senate seat. Now in his second term, Colapietro sees himself as a populist voice in a legislature that often has "very little sympathy for the lives of ordinary working people."

Many of LEAP's victories demonstrate the ability of grassroots organizing to defeat the money and official endorsements of the establishment. The classic LEAP campaign is volunteer intensive, using strong get-out-the-vote drives and community fundraising to defeat party regulars. In 1994, the coalition achieved a major upset for the opposition when one of its founders, State Comptroller William Curry, beat out John Larson to become the Democratic Party's candidate for governor. Larson had been the Party establishment's candidate until LEAP activism forced a primary and pro-pelled Curry to victory. Outspent five to one in television ads from Larson's $1.4 million war chest, Curry's win came from a massive grassroots drive to get his supporters to the polls.

Later that November, Connecticut followed the national pattern set by the Republican upsurge as Curry narrowly lost to Republican John Rowland in a three-way race. Grassroots campaigning and progressive politics carried the day in many other Connecticut races that November. Twenty-five of LEAP's thirty-five endorsed candidates won, including seven newcomers to the state legislature. Campaigning on a strong call for fundamental campaign finance reform, Miles Rappenport, former director of the Connecticut Citizen Action Group, won the office of the secretary of state, while another LEAP candidate, Nancy Wyman, became the new comptroller. These gains are all the more remarkable when compared to the performance of the estab-lishment Democrats, who, following the national pattern, took a beating with several incumbents losing to Republicans. Not one LEAP incumbent lost. For several years since, LEAP has maintained a strength of roughly twenty-five to thirty officeholders among the 187 members of the state legislature.

While election tallies and LEAP legislators are the most readily visible signs of the coalition's success, over time LEAP's mission has broadened beyond its founding purpose of running progressive candidates. As with the country as a whole, Connecticut's progressive community is fragmented into organizations formed around single issues and specialized concerns. Thus, unions have traditionally worked on labor issues, women's organizations on gender issues, and environmentalists on ecological issues. The rightward drift of US politics can potentially make this division and fragmentation even worse as groups who feel under attack respond defensively by further protecting their particular turf.

In contrast to this separation, LEAP's electoral work has brought together a wide variety of progressive groups around a practical set of activities. Electoral politics are inherently a coalition-builder because, within the comprehensive policies of government, all groups can find their issues and concerns. Therefore, when LEAP mobilized groups within electoral politics, it found that it had accomplished something regardless of whether its candidates won or lost. Through the coalition-building process, union leaders interacted with environmentalists, who met welfare rights groups, who joined with women's organizations, who worked with members of the Puerto Rican community. People began talking to each other, learning each other's concerns, and building relationships.

Such concrete interactions produce learning. Lynne Ide, who originally came from the Connecticut Citizen Action Group, explained how her own view of labor unions changed dramatically as a result of LEAP:

> *I used to think that unions were obsolete relics that were not in touch with what was important, broadly speaking, to everyday working families today. I thought they just narrowly focused on the terms of the contract. Now I realize that they are a part of the progressive history of this country. They will be part of the progressive struggle for the future of this country.*

Senator Tom Colapietro put it this way: "You get a whole bunch of different people into a room and you're going to really learn a lot." Through personal interactions, LEAP's electoral coalition produces those individual contacts and networks that, while not often visible to the outside, prove critical to pulling together a more unified political movement. When people in different organizations confront an issue, they now know other like-minded groups and individuals they can call on.

As LEAP has grown, this coalition-building process has moved from a by-product of the electoral work to a central focus of its activities. Marc Caplan, former LEAP director, argues: "The most important thing is to build up trust between different groups so that people will really become committed to each other's issues." LEAP now believes that helping transform the state's collection of progressive interest groups into a united progressive movement is central to its mission.

LEAP continues to recruit and promote progressive candidates, yet its activities extend well beyond the election season. Today, LEAP is as much a lobbying coalition as an electoral one. "LEAP tries to get groups to fight for issues outside their main focus, but which are important to other members of the coalition," explains Director Lynne Ide. "That way legislators don't just get the same old suspects, but a broad coalition."

LEAP promotes coalition lobbying in a variety of ways. Through meetings, shared information, and joint election efforts, different members of the coalition learn about each other's issues. The LEAP staff then organizes concrete cooperative lobbying efforts among the coalition's member organizations. LEAP has set up joint lobbying days where, for example, a member of a union may team up with a lobbyist from a women's organization and an environmentalist to go as a group to meet with legislators. Thus, during state hearings on a global warming bill, legislators were surprised to find themselves not just hearing testimony from the usual environmental activists, but from groups such as the UAW as well. LEAP has also tried to get its coalition to mobilize their membership to lobby, demonstrate, and picket on each other's behalf. For example, LEAP mobilized a diverse array of organizations to send members to the state capital to join gay and lesbian groups fighting for civil rights legislation.

Once different groups learn about each other, and begin fighting for each other's concerns, such cooperation can extend well beyond the halls of government. When the 1,000 members of UAW Local 376 went out on a long strike against Colt Firearms, the previous coalition work of LEAP and related efforts had paved the way for an effective community support effort. The workers on the picket lines were joined by lawyers, residents, women, and gays and lesbians who were members of LEAP organizations. Through participation in LEAP, the union had learned the value of reaching out to the broader community and the broader progressive community had learned the value of supporting labor struggles.

LEAP has also carried its coalition process into the legislature. Due to the weak internal structure of the major parties and the candidate-centered focus of US elections, the law-making process can seem like the work of collections of individuals rather than a clear party agenda. To provide some internal coherence to the work of the people it helped to elect, LEAP actively seeks to get progressive legislators together to both talk with each other and with member organizations. Until recently, this legislator coalition-building had been formalized as an official progressive caucus within the state legislature. Today, LEAP sponsors weekly meetings of its endorsed state officeholders to discuss and coordinate progressive politics.

Through joint lobbying and coalition-building within the government, LEAP has been able to achieve some notable legislative victories in areas such as pay equity, electoral reforms, and gay and lesbian civil rights. The most notable success came in the summer of 1991 with the passage of a state income tax. Up until that time, Connecticut government had funded itself through a series of regressive taxes, such as a high sales tax. For years, various progressive groups had worked unsuccessfully to equalize the burden, making the rich pay a greater share, through a progressive income tax. By the 1990s, several conditions came together to make an income tax a potential reality. Connecticut enjoyed budget surpluses throughout the 1980s, but deindustrialization and federal budget cuts had combined to give the state a one billion dollar budget deficit by 1991. This made taxes a key issue at a particularly useful time. In 1990, Connecticut voters elected Lowell Weicker, an ex-Republican turned independent, as governor. Not tied to either party, and having committed himself to only one term in office, Weicker had little incentive to tow the official political line. Weicker proved to be a maverick in his support for a state income tax.

Seizing this window of opportunity, LEAP helped form the Taxpayers Alliance to Serve Connecticut (TASC). In classic LEAP style, TASC brought together members of the LEAP coalition with other progressive groups to mobilize behind an income tax. The measure eventually won, but only after a painful and dramatic process. During the spring and summer of 1991, the

Connecticut legislature passed three different budgets, only to have them vetoed by Governor Weicker because they relied on regressive budget-balancing measures. This impasse between the legislator and the governor went on for fifty-three days after the end of the fiscal year, during which Connecticut had no budget.

Faced with the looming prospect of having to shut down the government, several key legislators broke ranks to pass an income tax by the narrow margin of seventy-five to seventy-three in the House and an eighteen to eighteen tie, broken by the vote of the lieutenant governor, in the Senate. Given this close margin, LEAP's coalition-building efforts clearly played a role. The actual tax structure certainly reflects the progressive ideal of redistributing wealth. Under the income tax law, families earning $20,000 a year or less paid no taxes, those with $40,000 paid just over 1 percent of their income, while those who made over $100,000 paid the full 4.5 percent.

More recently, LEAP's coalition-building contributed to the passage of two landmark pieces of legislation that attempt to establish greater community control over the private decisions of corporations. The first, An Act Concerning Economic Development Program Accountability, makes companies receiving public economic development funds accountable for job creation. In 1991 and 1992, the state spent $350 million in tax dollars on direct economic assistance to Connecticut companies, yet a survey of the businesses showed a net increase of only 621 jobs! It was also determined that companies had used public funds to set up non-union shops and even to move jobs from union to non-union facilities. The new legislation requires companies applying for public assistance to list concretely the number of jobs to be created and/or retained. Each year, companies receiving assistance must submit a report on their progress in expanding or retaining jobs. More importantly, the bill requires worker and community participation in the initial granting process as well as the annual evaluations. Companies that misuse public funds must repay the assistance and may be subject to further penalties.

The second law, An Act Concerning Defense Diversification, requires any company receiving over $1 million in defense contracts per year to establish an alternative use committee that includes worker representatives and encourages community participation. The committee must prepare a plan to reduce or eliminate the dependence of the company on defense contracts by suggesting alternative products and markets. This legislation grows out of LEAP's work as part of a regionwide coalition, called A Call to Action, that joins unions with community groups and LEAP-style electoral coalitions. This regional coalition was formed in 1992 to develop a proactive, progressive economic conversion agenda to respond to defense cuts. Together, both bills provide workers and communities with new avenues to fight for greater control over the companies whose decisions dominate their lives.

Lessons from LEAP

LEAP's fifteen-year record illustrates what progressive organizations can accomplish by working together politically. Its rich history also points to some of the potential obstacles such undertakings might encounter. These difficulties involve complex issues that, in many cases, have no easy solutions. Would-be coalitions would do well to strategize around these problems before the potential tensions flare into major issues. Success depends, in large measure, on how groups address the difficulties of building broad coalitions, balancing influence within the coalition, accountability of officeholders, and the vulnerability of local government.

Building Broad Coalitions

The task of broadening LEAP's coalition is an ongoing effort. LEAP has achieved notable success in bringing together a diverse array of groups. Labor, one of the key founding components, is well represented through the participation of such unions as the United Auto Workers, the Health Care Workers District 1199, and several city labor councils and state employees unions. LEAP also includes the Lesbian and Gay Rights Coalition PAC, the Women's Issues Network PAC, Bridgeport ACORN, the Congress of Connecticut Community Colleges, Connecticut Citizen Action Group, the Environmentalists to Elect Legislators in Connecticut, the National Organization for Women, and the National Abortion Rights Action League. Connecticut has many other progressive groups that are not part of LEAP, however.

As with other progressive efforts throughout the country, the racial divide has proven a significant stumbling block to coalition-building. LEAP's current composition reflects the long-standing separation between suburban white progressives and inner city communities of color. LEAP has been largely unsuccessful in including African-American groups as part of the coalition. African-American communities across the country have historically experienced tensions and problems when working with white suburban progressives who do not share their reality. These difficulties have ranged from subtle forms of racism to simply not feeling like equal partners in the coalition.

One of the truisms of grassroots organizing is that, from the outset, you have to include all of the social groups that you want to be involved in your mobilization. One's organizing committee must look like those it is trying to organize. Having been founded as a coalition of unions and primarily white progressive groups, LEAP faces the task of having to go into minority communities and convince them that, despite its legacy of past divisions, participation in a new coalition can work for them.

It is possible to cross the racial divide. LEAP's difficulties in reaching the African-American community contrast sharply with its success in the Puerto Rican community. The Puerto Rican Political Action Committee is a member of LEAP. Relative to African Americans, the Puerto Rican community has been less organized into formal structures. Thus, it has fewer institutional ties to the mainstream of the Democratic Party. LEAP had the opportunity to build ties with the community by offering its resources to Puerto Rican candidates and organizers. The result has been a mutually beneficial relationship that bodes well for the future.

The Northeast Citizen Action Resource Center (NECARC), which provides support to LEAP-type coalitions throughout New England and New York, recently established a training and internship program that seeks to build further ties between white activists and communities of color. Over a three-month period, new and less experienced organizers of color get a chance to improve their activist skills through training sessions, peer group meetings, and one-on-one mentoring with experienced progressive leaders.

NECARC organizers see building bridges across racial lines as critical to building an effective progressive movement. "Race is certainly being used by the Right as a way of splitting our communities," stressed Marc Caplan, NECARC's director. "Coalition-building between whites and people of color and between different communities of color is critical. Progressives can never be doing too much work to make this happen."

Balancing Influence Within the Coalition

LEAP's decade and a half of coalition-building points to related tension areas. In any broad coalition, the various member organizations vary enormously in their size and resources. How to balance the need to fully utilize the resources of all the groups while at the same time ensuring a decision-making process in which everyone has an equal voice can be tricky. During the income tax fight, for example, the Taxpayers Alliance to Serve Connecticut received a large proportion of its financial support from several major unions as well as the state AFL-CIO. Because of their dues-paying membership base, unions tend to be financially stronger than other progressive organizations. They are natural sources of funding. With some members of the coalition assuming a greater share of the financial burden, TASC faced tensions between its coalition partners. The funders felt that, because of their financial commitment, they should have a greater say in decisions than other groups that did not have the same resources. These other groups, in turn, felt they had an equal stake in the cause and should have an equal say in decision-making.

Finances are just one area of conflict. Writing about the experience of coalition-building between labor and community groups in Hartford, local activist and academic Louise Simmons outlines several potential tension areas between members of a coalition. Unions and neighborhood groups have very different internal structures. Unions have a fulltime paid leadership and parliamentary methods of group decision-making, while many community groups rely on a combination of staff and elected volunteer leadership and use a more consensus-oriented decision-making process. Unions also tend to rely much more on the legal process than neighborhood organizations, which often mobilize outside and even in opposition to such channels.[1]

Despite bringing together a broad diversity of progressive groups, LEAP has had notable success in avoiding major interorganizational disputes. Part of this achievement has been the coalition's commitment to taking on only those projects that are agreeable to all participants and to working with commonly defined and agreed upon goals.

Accountability of Officeholders

Once a fair number of LEAP candidates began winning office, the coalition experienced a new set of issues. The US electoral system, with its weak party structure, does not encourage a very high degree of accountability between officeholders and the people who voted for them. LEAP officeholders operate within a political milieu that is decidedly to the right of the progressive community. As some LEAP Democrats have progressed into successful political careers, moving into positions of greater power and authority within the state government and the Democratic Party, they have come closer to their centrist colleagues. This moderating potential of holding office is enhanced by LEAP's strategy of working within, rather than outside, the Democratic Party. LEAP candidates always have a dual identity as members of the coalition and as Democrats.

With two to three dozen legislators in the halls of the House and Senate, progressives have a voice in state policy. Yet that voice has always been a minority force. To get any piece of legislation passed, the LEAP Democrats have to work with their more centrist colleagues and moderate Republicans. This often means compromising on issues in order to achieve the main goals. For example, although the new state income tax was a progressive system, it also included such regressive components as cuts in the corporate tax rate, the elimination of separate levies on unearned income, and the extension of a sales tax to twenty-one new goods and services.

LEAP officeholders have also voted well on issues of central concern to some members of the coalition, but against the interests of other members. This problem has led the coalition to rethink and revise its candidate endorsement process to include an evaluation of a person's general political philosophy in addition to their stance on a "laundry list" of specific issues.

These difficulties also point to a limitation of LEAP's current structure. LEAP has neither a fully developed political platform to hold its officeholders to, nor a grassroots base of its own to mobilize in their support. This becomes particularly obvious on the local level.

The Vulnerability of Local Government

LEAP's primary focus is on statewide activity. Yet the coalition has, at times, ventured forth into municipal politics. The experience often yielded initial success, followed by disappointment. This was true in the coalition's major foray into municipal politics, centered on the state's capital of Hartford. With its labyrinth of patronage networks and individual debts, big-city politics can prove a source of division and frustration for an outside group. In 1987, a group of Hartford community activists allied with LEAP sought to outflank these networks by moving outside of the Democratic Party. Hartford is a solidly Democratic city—with Democratic registrations outnumbering Republican by a seven to one margin. The coalition hoped to take advantage of a state law that requires minority party representation in city government. Hartford city council is elected by an at-large system in which voters may select up to six council candidates. The top vote-getters are elected to council. According to state law, three of the nine members of council cannot be from the majority party. Thus, Hartford city elections split between the selection of a six-member Democratic majority and three minority party positions. LEAP endorsed the formation of a "People for a Change" independent slate that sought to challenge the Republican Party's three minority seats. The new coalition included key area unions, neighborhood organizations, and the Puerto Rican political action committee. Different groups joined for different reasons. Some activists saw People for a Change as a way of pressuring the local Democratic Party. Other groups hoped that the coalition would become a more permanent independent voice for those locked out by major party politics.

With the help of training and technical support from LEAP, People for a Change ran three candidates for city council in 1987. Two won: African American Marie Kirkley-Bey and Puerto Rican community activist Eugenio Caro. The coalition repeated its success in 1989 by re-electing Eugenio Caro and replacing Kirkley-Bey, who had switched to the Democratic Party, with Sandra Little, an African-American school social worker. While its third candidate lost again, John Bonelii made history as the city's first openly gay candidate.

Although only a two-seat minority voice, People for a Change clearly helped to redefine the local political atmosphere. In early 1989, the group launched a neighborhood empowerment campaign several months before the city budget process. The goal was to develop a community-driven alternative budget. The twenty-four specific budget resolutions encapsulated many long-standing concerns, such as exacting new taxes and fees from downtown development and supporting local labor struggles. Although most were rejected by the city council, their introduction helped to publicize a progressive agenda and place the incumbent city council on the spot by having to vote down community-driven policies.

People for a Change's agenda and coalition-building helped contribute to a major change in city politics in 1991. That year, all three of the coalition's candidates won office. Even more dramatic, the election saw a major shift within the city's Democratic majority. With the previous election of former social worker and state representative Carrie Saxon Perry as mayor, Hartford had the first African-American woman to head a major city government. After two terms of escalating tensions between her and the mainstream of the Democratic Party, Perry broke with the Party's establishment in 1991 by backing a slate of challengers who forced the six incumbent Democrats on the council into a primary. All six challengers won. Perry and her reform slate, with the support of People for a Change, then went on to victory in November's general election. The triumph of the left-liberal wing of the Democratic Party, along with the sweep by People for a Change, gave Hartford a decidedly progressive city government.

What the electoral victory really began, however, was a two-year lesson in the frustrations of city government. The 1991 electoral victory reflected the dire needs of many of Hartford's residents. The city had become symptomatic of the pain caused by the corporate restructuring of the 1980s and 1990s. The signs are all too familiar: corporate abandonment and down-sizing, white and middle-class flight, boarded-up housing, deteriorating schools, and rising expenditures for public assistance. By 1990, 17,000 manufacturing jobs had left the city, while the growing insurance industry provided only low wage service sector jobs for the city's poor residents. While capital of a state with the highest per capita income in the country, Hartford ranked the fourth poorest city in the country throughout the 1980s, when measured by percentage of population in poverty.[2]

During the campaign season, the new city council members had attacked the old council for kowtowing far too much to the designs of the business community. They pledged to reverse the budget-slashing priorities of former administrations, place the needs of ordinary residents first, work more cooperatively with the city's unions, and open up the process of city government to greater citizen participation.

This is much easier said than done, however. Once in power, the new administration found itself powerless to implement much of its agenda. They took hold of a local governing structure that was highly fragmented. Hartford has a strong city manager, who serves as the top administrative officer. The mayor has clear visibility, but lacks authority. In addition, numerous commissions and authorities, such as the redevelopment authority and the zoning board of appeals, exert significant power and influence beyond the control of the city council. The city council was also internally weak. The victorious reform slate had not been forged in the kind of broad and long-running community effort that might foster a strong sense of unity, discipline, and common mission. Indeed, very quickly, the fledgling council coalition fell apart and split in the face of mounting pressures.

The new governing coalition did not have to wait long for the outside pressures to hit. Thanks to major cuts in state aid to cities, the council found that the $20 million budget shortfall it had inherited soon doubled to $41.9 million. The council's hands were tied. They had been elected on a pledge not to increase city taxes. Thus, instead of fulfilling their calls to restore spending and expand much needed programs, the mayor and the council quickly found themselves fighting defensive battles around which areas not to cut further. Even so, the business community greeted the progressive city government with hostility. *Fortune* magazine placed Hartford at the bottom of a list of fifty "pro-business" urban markets. Several major area employers made ominous rumblings of either leaving the city or at least taking any expansions elsewhere.

Despite achievements such as a city ordinance banning contracts with firms having ties to South Africa, endorsement of a statewide single-payer health care system, and numerous public hearings and workshops to increase citizen participation, the mayor and council were largely unable to make significant changes. Instead, the economic situation of the city continued to deteriorate. The number of residents on public assistance reached an all-time high. The vacancy rate for downtown office space climbed to 19 percent and the city estimated that as many as 100 family housing units were being vacated per month.[3] The inability of the progressives to implement their vision provided the city's daily paper with an unending supply of ammunition to heap ridicule on the mayor and the council. The growing disunity within the council only provided further fuel to the opposition.

The end result was a crushing defeat in the city's next elections. Republican Michael Peters won election as mayor, while all three council members from People for a Change lost their re-election bids. The Hartford experience seems to underline the futility of engaging in isolated city politics. "Unless they are part of a larger plan, municipal races are useless," comments Lynne Ide. To achieve any significant change in Hartford, elected officials would have needed to be a part of a larger organized movement.

A political movement with a clear agenda could have helped produce a stronger, more unified candidate slate. Furthermore, real change requires an organized grassroots base prepared to mobilize on behalf of its agenda and to hold its elected officials accountable. A broader organized movement is crucial to helping progressive officeholders counter the enormous opposition and structural limitations that a government cannot overcome by itself.

LEAP at the Crossroads

The question of movement-building leads to our final and most important observation about the LEAP experience. LEAP has not been simply about winning elections and getting pieces of legislation passed. More fundamentally, it has sought to build a united progressive political movement by pulling together all the various strands of activism within the state. While LEAP has had notable success in this regard, its achievements and disappointments point toward the need for major transformation if the movement is to develop and grow.

This transformation reaches to the core of LEAP's strategy. The basis of LEAP lays in a coalition of organizations. This strategy of pooling the resources of separate groups has allowed LEAP to accomplish much with very modest resources of its own. With both a small staff and budget, LEAP has built a solid progressive voice in the state legislature and executive branch, and in 1994 almost succeeded in getting one of its own elected as governor. It has built lasting relationships among progressive organizations that previously had little knowledge of and connection with each other. While much of this coalition-building does not make for flashy news, over time it does change the dynamics of progressive activism as groups learn to cooperate. Such cooperation opens the door for levels of progressive action that would have seemed beyond the horizon of separate groups.

As a coalition of organizations, LEAP relies upon the staff and leadership of its member groups. LEAP does not have individual members. It is a formal alliance of existing progressive organizations. "LEAP is probably best described as a coalition of PACs because that was the way to quickly get a lot of people and a lot of resources," describes LEAP President George Springer.[4] Yet, by organizing in this way, LEAP has based its activities around people who by their very position are already quite busy and committed to the individual needs of their own groups. LEAP work adds on another round of meetings and organizing for people who already have busy schedules. Because it has no grassroots membership base of its own, LEAP must rely on its member organizations to mobilize their rank and file around an election or lobbying campaign.

While the membership rolls of the progressive groups who are part of LEAP add up to hundreds of thousands of people, activating them requires organizations to commit scarce and often overtaxed energy and resources. Some of the organizations simply may not have the ability to mobilize their members in any large number. Furthermore, while it has achieved valuable gains in breaking down barriers between the staff and leaders of progressive organizations, this process has not extended as completely to the grassroots level. Even in large-scale mobilizations, the rank-and-file members of each organization may still only work within their existing groups. There is relatively little direct membership-to-membership interaction.

While building a coalition of progressive organizations gives LEAP at least potential access to hundreds of thousands of rank-and-file members, it provides only indirect contact with the vast number of ordinary Connecticut residents who are not part of any progressive group. LEAP's strategy relies upon existing progressive energy. It does not produce significantly new resources of its own—be it financial or people power. Yet for the progressive movement to go forward, it has to find ways of reaching into these communities and getting more ordinary people involved. These people are a major source of new resources and energy. A majority-seeking progressive movement needs to develop the potential leadership and political consciousness that remains unmobilized in communities across the state.

Finally, despite its successful coalition-building, LEAP is still within the boundaries of liberal interest-group politics. Indeed, it is a coalition of groups organized around such politics. And while different groups may cooperative with each other, they are still by and large promoting their own specific issue concerns. For example, when LEAP is able to get unions and other groups to testify on behalf of clean air legislation sponsored by environmental groups it has achieved something new. Yet this greater cooperation has still occurred around a single issue.

What is missing from LEAP's coalition is a more comprehensive progressive political agenda that transcends a laundry list of each member organization's issue areas. The Right has an agenda that links different groups' specific concerns to a comprehensive view of politics and a broad political agenda. Stuck in interest-group politics, the Left has been thrown on the defensive—fighting battles to fend off the Right's attack on specific areas, but unable to offer a comprehensive alternative.

Because of these limitations, LEAP's very success has now brought it to a major transition. To expand its influence in the halls of government, and, more importantly, to expand the political movement, LEAP must evolve beyond a coalition of existing organizations. Specifically, LEAP activists speak of moving in two interrelated directions. The first is to develop ways of directly involving more ordinary people. The second is to move beyond interest-group politics by generating a cohesive progressive political platform that can serve as a clear alternative to the Right.

The first move could even involve LEAP building its own grassroots base by becoming an individual membership organization. This would allow the organization to have direct access to the rank and file. It would also provide the basis for reaching out and involving all those people who are not members of any progressive group. Such a membership base could provide greater financial and volunteer resources, allowing LEAP to expand the scope of its activities. In this way, LEAP would be generating its own sources of energy.

Developing a cohesive agenda would allow LEAP to move onto the offensive as well. Beginning a process that will produce such a program is critical for broadening the membership base of the movement. This process can serve as a way of reaching ordinary people on a mass scale as well as including some constituencies, such as African-American groups, that currently are not part of the coalition. Progressives can not hope to win a majority of ordinary people until they have answers to such basic questions as: how can we create decent jobs, how can we rebuild our cities, what can we do about education, crime, or deficits? Progressives have to be clear about what makes them different from politics as usual, not just making a critique of the status quo, but by offering a real alternative.

Developing such a platform would permit greater accountability between officeholders and the movement. Candidates could be required to sign onto a much more highly defined project. They would no longer be individuals tied to a loose network, but agents of an organized movement capable of holding its officeholders accountable to the broader movement while providing mobilized support. Building a membership organization that generates a political agenda that reflects the reality and desires of its rank-and-file members would indeed represent the democratic ideal of ordinary people deciding how to run their government.

As many LEAP activists acknowledge, these next steps point toward becoming more like a political party. "The coalition has to do what, in a healthy political culture, parties would normally do, namely build our own agenda, recruit and run candidates, and establish our own grassroots," explains Marc Caplan. "We need to rebuild our democracy—the major parties have not done so."

The transition from a coalition of organizations to a more party-type structure is a difficult one. Interest-group politics generates forces that perpetuate itself. For example, an independent membership could be seen as a potential threat to the authority and control of existing issue organizations. The progressive community has been locked into single-issue politics for so many years that the concept of a comprehensive, united political project requires significant changes in existing activist cultures and ways of thinking. Moving beyond interest-group politics at a time when right-wing successes have forced progressive groups to increasingly fight for their very survival seems risky. Right-wing attacks are happening now. In contrast, producing a comprehensive progressive alternative involves a long-term process that may not have benefits for years.

Despite these potential obstacles, LEAP is taking steps to transform its mode of operation. In early 1994, the coalition sponsored a broad meeting, called the Congress for Connecticut's Future, attended by over 300 activists from across the progressive community who discussed policy alternatives for use in the upcoming fall elections.

Three months after the 1994 elections, LEAP pulled together a similar meeting with equal success. Out of that meeting, LEAP launched the Progress and Equity Partnership (PEP). PEP's short-term goal was to counter the budgetary attack of newly elected Republican Governor John Rowland. Under the much hailed populist guise of reducing taxes and promoting "sound fiscal management," Rowland's agenda cut taxes for the wealthy while increasing hidden taxes for most other people. It also slashed social spending and created a huge budget deficit. PEP hoped to bring together progressive groups to work out a coordinated strategy to fight the governor's agenda by developing a priority list on which areas of the budget to place their energy. In the long-term, however, the Progress and Equity Partnership aimed to develop a more cohesive progressive budget alternative to the Right's cynical anti-government crusade.

LEAP established PEP as a separate coalition as a way of reaching out to groups that are not part of LEAP. PEP organizers were quite successful in this regard. Five months after its founding, the Progress and Equity Partnership had a membership list of over eighty organizations. Furthermore, PEP brought in new kinds of groups, including religious groups, social service organizations, and institutions within the African-American community, such as the NAACP. During the summer of 1995, PEP's staff person devoted a great deal of time to traveling around the state talking with local progressive groups to build up personal contacts and hear their concerns and ideas. Such is the time-consuming but crucial work of building a broad coalition. By encouraging coordination and vision around the specific budget battles, PEP hoped to lay the ground work for developing a more comprehensive progressive platform.

The Progress and Equity Partnership was replaced at the end of the 1995 session of the legislature by a new initiative, called the Jobs and Economic Security Campaign. Like its forerunner, the campaign seeks to unite LEAP member groups with a broader coalition. Campaign organizers have concluded that corporate restructuring and rising economic insecurity is an issue that impacts a broad array of groups and is a top concern of the general public. The ultimate aim of the Jobs and Economic Security Campaign is to develop a bottom-up progressive economic alternative to the current right-wing agenda. Through a series of hearings around the state, organizers hope to build a comprehensive platform around such elements as a living wage, corporate accountability, alternatives to down-sizing, and environmentally responsible economic activity.

LEAP has also participated in launching a regionwide Money and Power Project to build progressive action for campaign finance reform. The current money-driven electoral system offers a potential coalition-building tool. It is an issue that lies outside the work of existing progressive organizations, but that clearly impacts them all.

Having conducted and publicized several studies exposing who is funding Connecticut politics, LEAP is building support for legislation aimed at serious reform. LEAP is currently pushing a reform bill to establish public financing of the state's gubernatorial races. Candidates who accept a $1.6 million spending limit would have almost all of the costs of their convention, primary, and general election race paid for out of public funds. Candidates would only have to raise the first $100,000. Those who face opponents who reject the spending limit and rely on private contributions would receive additional amounts of public funds to ensure greater equality of spending. As with the budget battle, campaign finance reform represents a step away from interest-group politics, and places the progressive community on the offensive with an agenda that cuts across single-issue concerns.

Independence from the Democratic Party?

The task of expanding the progressive political movement by enhancing grassroots participation and building a comprehensive agenda also raises questions concerning LEAP's strategy of working within the Democratic Party. The benefits of operating formally within the Party are clear. In building a coalition of organizations, especially with those that may have extensive prior ties to the Democrats, it is far easier to ask them to adopt a strategy that tries to transform the Party rather than break with it. The leadership of the United Auto Workers, for example, is clearly unwilling to support third party politics, yet it offers major technical resources for LEAP's activism within the Democratic Party.

Even developing an autonomous progressive voice within the Democratic Party has caused controversy. Some leaders of the Connecticut AFL-CIO tried to block LEAP's formation by pressing the national AFL-CIO to bar local labor councils from taking part in the coalition. When local council presidents refused to succumb to this pressure, the national AFL-CIO leadership dropped the issue. Yet the ties of organized labor to the Democratic Party remain strong.

Working within the Democratic Party has other attractions as well. Although its national and state leadership has clearly moved to the Right, this drift has left behind many local Party activists who remain committed to progressive ideals. The Party's weak internal structure permits progressives to build a kind of party-within-a-party in opposition to the leadership. Potentially, progressives could even take over the Party at the local level. Even in Connecticut, which does not have a direct primary, progressive activists have been able to use the existing nomination system to displace mainstream Democrats. As one LEAP state legislator commented: "Inside the Democratic Party is an empty shell. There is ample opportunity for progressive influence and even a take over."

Running under a major party label helps progressives win office. Voters have been conditioned to see third parties as hopeless. Using the Democratic label also makes it much more difficult for the media to ignore a campaign or reject it out of hand. LEAP President George Springer summarizes the party-within-a-party strategy as follows:

> We see a lot of people who are natural allies within the Democratic Party. We see a lot of people who are candidates who are running with that party that we can support. We don't for a minute believe that the Democratic Party is led by progressives... Very often we get in trouble with the regular party because we recruit and run candidates who challenge people in the Party who we believe are not representing the interests of the people of this country and the people of this area. Our goal has been to create a generally independent political force that articulates a message that touches the lives of low- and middle-income citizens by providing candidates within the Democratic Party who offer a clear progressive vision. LEAP has shown that it is possible to elect strong progressive Democrats who end up making a real difference.[5]

NECARC Director Marc Caplan sees the issue of third party versus Democratic Party politics in movement-building terms:

> We are building independent political forces that choose to run candidates within the Democratic Party. The issue is not running people as Democrats or as independents. The real task is developing a progressive program. The major thing holding us back is not having a comprehensive agenda. To get people involved we have to provide a believable alternative to the current right-wing politics. Once we have that, the institutional forces will follow.

The question, according to Caplan, is not what label progressives choose for their candidates, but how to produce a bottom-up agenda that reflects the real needs and aspirations of ordinary Americans. LEAP hopes to use the opportunities available within an amorphous Democratic Party as tools for building a movement that has its own identity and membership. Once progressives have developed a process and institutions for producing such an agenda, the question of the formal route to power becomes more appropriate. Some within the LEAP coalition clearly have third party sympathies, while others are committed to transforming the Democrats.

Working within the Democratic Party as a way of building a movement that has its own agenda and grassroots base does present a contradiction, however. The Democrats embody the kind of liberal interest-group politics that the coalition hopes to move beyond. Rank-and-file membership in both major parties is nearly meaningless. During elections and within the halls of government, both parties avoid articulating a strong, comprehensive agenda. Institutionally, the Democratic Party revolves around the candidate-centered, money-driven politics that it helped create. LEAP thus confronts the contradiction of seeking to go beyond traditional politics while at the same time enmeshing itself in one of the major institutions designed to avoid movement politics.

If LEAP hopes to build a more party-like and movement-directed organization, might it not make more sense to build a new party? Notions such as a grassroots base and a progressive platform flow more directly, and become much more tangible, if one is building an independent political organization. And while such a step would place the movement outside the boundaries of what the media commonly consider newsworthy politics, what publicity a third party does achieve is entirely its own. In contrast, LEAP is continuously in danger of having its identity absorbed into mainstream, candidate-centered politics. During elections, the media typically identifies and covers LEAP-endorsed candidates as generic Democrats. Rarely is LEAP's name or identity mentioned in the media coverage. LEAP's current strategy thus forces it to navigate a tenuous path that continuously threatens to sidetrack its grassroots organizing and agenda development back into the interest-group norm.

LEAP's effort to generate a comprehensive response to the right-wing agenda also holds the potential for straining its insider/outsider strategy. If such an agenda is actively promoted, Democratic Party organizers, candidates, and elected officials are going to have to take a clear stance. The political difference between progressives who champion the alternative economic agenda and those who shy away from it is going to be highlighted. Interest-group politics may spotlight the differences between progressives and Democratic politicians on specific issues, but comprehensive programs push fundamental differences in philosophy and vision to the forefront.

Can progressives gain effective support for an alternative economic vision working within the Democratic Party? If so, they will have transformed the Party. If not, a new party provides the only other political channel for pushing an alternative economic platform. A century ago, the Populists did not set out to build a political party, yet, their economic agenda developed to the point where a political revolt became the only way of propelling the movement forward. This may well be true of LEAP.

LEAP's current direction is based upon the assumption that, despite these dilemmas, working within the Democratic Party is still more viable than the third party option. Third party advocates must demonstrate how their strategy can provide a better avenue for building a grassroots movement than LEAP's insider/outsider approach.

In the meantime, LEAP's efforts to rebuild the political balance of power using the Democratic Party offer immediate benefits. With a Republican governor and state senate, Connecticut government is in sorry shape. Using its basic strategy, LEAP has already identified several people from among the ranks of its member groups who are willing to challenge the freshman Republican senators.

LEAP's Model Spreads

With its solid record of electoral victories, legislative action, and coalition-building, LEAP's example has spread to almost a dozen other states. In 1992, the Massachusetts Commonwealth Coalition won eight out of nine state senate races, Rhode Island's Ocean State Action Network elected or re-elected five senators, and the Granite State Coalition in New Hampshire won ten out of twelve senate races. In Maine, the Dirigo Alliance elected thirty-three of its forty-four endorsed candidates, giving the state the largest group of progressive state legislators in the country.

The significance of these efforts go beyond the numbers. In 1996, for example, the Dirigo Alliance got behind the first openly gay man to run for the state legislature. Expanding beyond the LEAP model, Maine activists have begun targeting both local races where the Right is very active and national elections. In 1996, the Dirigo Alliance ran progressive state Senator Dale McCormick for US Congress. McCormick is representative of the way in which LEAP-style groups open politics to new people. She was the first female member of the local carpenters union, an out lesbian, and a founder of the Dirigo Alliance. She won her state senate seat campaign in a conservative district.

Working with state citizen action groups, these electoral coalitions have also pushed major initiatives around such issues as single-payer health care reform, economic conversion, and campaign finance reform. This progressive electoral and legislative action is supported by regional resources. Since 1984, the Northeast Citizen Action Resource Center has provided research, technical support, and training to member organizations. It also coordinated regional campaigns on such issues as parental leave, health care, solid and toxic waste, utility regulation, and voter registration. By sponsoring regular conferences, NECARC brings progressive activists and legislators together throughout the region. The group works closely with the Northeast Network of Progressive Elected Officials (NNPEO). In 1992, NECARC and NNPEO jointly produced a primer on progressive economic development alternatives, *Jobs and the Economy,* to provide legislators and activists with a practical set of progressive economic policy options and analysis.

The transition point reached by LEAP in its own evolution is also reflected in the region as a whole. Many progressives feel the need to develop a more coherent independent agenda and to enhance grassroots participation. The Massachusetts jobs coalition, for example, brings the Commonwealth Coalition together with a diverse array of unions, community organizations, and social justice groups to develop a progressive agenda on the economy.

As its first campaign, the coalition has chosen to focus on temporary and contingent work. On the legislative front, organizers hope to pull together concrete policy proposals that would remove some of the cost benefits that companies receive by replacing fulltime jobs with temporary and contingent work. For example, state policies could extend the reach of existing labor laws to all contingent workers. A corporate code of conduct applied, for example, to all companies that receive public money could end discriminatory practices against temporary workers by mandating equal pay and benefits for equal jobs, regardless of the employment status of the worker. In Boston, the coalition is also opening a center for temporary and contingent workers. Housed at a UAW local, the center provides a meeting place and focal point for a range of organizing activity around contingent work.

In Maine, the Dirigo Alliance hopes to prepare the groundwork for a membership organization. Unlike Connecticut, Maine activists have the advantage of a citizen initiative process. The Right has made ample use of this process in the state by running strong campaigns to roll back gay rights provisions and to try to ban same sex marriages. Maine activists are taking a page from the Right's strategy by realizing that referendum campaigns can be used not only to enact new policies, but to develop the kinds of grassroots mobilizations that build the broader movement.

Working in coalition with other groups, the Dirigo Alliance succeeded in getting a sweeping campaign finance reform initiative placed on the ballot in 1996. To do so, more than 1,000 volunteers collected over 65,000 signatures. In mobilizing to get the reforms passed, the Alliance hopes to draw in many more volunteers. After the election, the coalition plans to use the volunteer list from the ballot initiative campaign to further develop local and regional leadership that will continue to expand the grassroots base.

Other possible referendum campaigns include a living wage initiative that would raise the minimum wage; establishing a corporate code of conduct; and removing the cost benefits companies receive for replacing fulltime jobs with temporary and contingent work. Through such concrete efforts, progressive organizers hope to bring in large numbers of ordinary people who are currently not involved in any kind of activism. These campaigns also offer members of progressive organizations new and accessible channels for political participation. Mobilizing for the campaign helps organizations identify new volunteers and would-be activists and leaders within their own ranks. For the Dirigo Alliance, a growing volunteer list and a grassroots leadership structure lay the ground work for a more formal progressive political organization in the future.

New England also provides the most dramatic example of successful independent politics outside of the Democratic Party: the Vermont Progressive Coalition.

Chapter Six

Independent Politics in Vermont

The Progressive Coalition

For close to two decades, Vermont has made national headlines for its strong independent political movement symbolized in the remarkable career of long-time activist Bernie Sanders. Progressives elsewhere in the country first heard of Sanders in 1981 when he won a surprise victory to become the independent socialist mayor of Burlington, Vermont's largest city. Throughout most of the 1980s, Sanders continued to head this municipal "People's Republic." In 1990, he again made headlines by becoming the first independent, and the first socialist, elected to the US House of Representatives in decades. He is now in his third term.

An interesting phenomenon in and of himself, Bernie Sanders is just one part of a much broader and growing political movement. Today, this movement is heading toward becoming an outright political party that would be a serious player in statewide politics. In this chapter, we will explore this decade and a half evolution in progressive growth, starting with the "revolution" in Burlington and ending with progressive efforts to lay the foundations for a statewide party.

The Sanders Revolution

In March 1981, the Democratic Party of Burlington, along with the rest of the local establishment, was in a state of shock. For years Burlington had been such a solidly Democratic city that the Republicans had ceased to run challengers for many local offices. Democrats occupied eleven of the thirteen seats on the board of alders. Then in his fifth term, Mayor Gordon Paquette looked forward to another two years in office as he entered the 1981 campaign season with no Republican opponent. Yet, a few months later, the city's entire political landscape had been turned on its head. Seemingly coming from nowhere, independent Bernie Sanders defeated Paquette by the slim plurality of ten votes. Burlington has never been the same since.

Following Sander's victory, the local business and political establishment tried to console themselves by thinking that 1981 had simply been a fluke and that two years later things would return to normal. The political climate did not, on the surface, seem promising. Even Sanders and his supporters had been surprised by their outright victory. When Sanders took office he immediately ran into the uncompromising opposition of the Republican and Democratic majority on the city's board of alders and the continual ridicule of the local media. During his first year in office, the council rejected all of the new mayor's governmental appointments.

The tide of political change, however, swept on. The same election that put Sanders in the mayor's office also saw Terry Bouricius, a member of the short-lived Citizens Party, elected to the board of alders. Independent Sadie White also won a seat. Even worse for the defenders of the status quo, the stonewalling of Sanders had the opposite of its intended effect. In 1982, a voter backlash removed every Democratic alderperson who was up for election, save one. Sanders' supporters, who ran either as independents or under the Citizen Party label, grew to five, while the Republicans gained the other council victory.

The years following the 1982 vote have been a testament to how quickly a seemingly dominant political party can fall from power under the right conditions. In 1983, Sanders' re-election campaign resulted in the highest voter turn-out in years. Although the Democrats persuaded the leader of the Vermont state house, Judy Stephany, to run against Sanders, the socialist mayor crushed his opponents, winning a victory with 52 percent of the vote. That same year, progressives gained a sixth seat on the board of alders and, for two years after, even held the presidency. From their eleven-seat majority in 1980, the Democrats dropped to two seats by 1983. They have never recovered.

Today, the now formalized Progressive Coalition is the dominant political force in Burlington politics. Since 1981 they have held the mayor's office for every term except between 1993 and 1995. Although not achieving a majority on the board of alders until 1995, the Progressives have been the single largest bloc since 1983. They have achieved all this success despite active hostility from most of the local media and extensive cooperation between the Republicans and Democrats, who have commonly run only one candidate between them for many local offices. The city of Burlington clearly bears the beneficial stamp of a decade and a half of progressive policies. How have progressives done it?

The Building Blocks of Progressive Strength

Several factors account for Bernie Sanders' victory in 1981. Some are unique to that particular campaign and others to Vermont. Yet many are applicable to progressive activism in communities across the country.[1]

The 1981 campaign had several aspects distinct to that election. The local Democratic Party had clearly become a complacent organization. The incumbent mayor's serious overconfidence was reflected in his move to place a major property tax increase on the ballot for that same election. Paquette had also alienated some key supporters. In 1981, friction between the mayor and the police led the police union to endorse Sanders—an action that seriously added to the socialist's credibility.

Furthermore, the Republican's tacit support for Paquette meant that the race became a two-way battle between the Democrat and Sanders. This made Sanders the only alternative to the incumbent mayor, rather than a mere spoiler. People could go to the polls and vote their true conscience. The worst that could happen, if someone voted for Sanders, was that Paquette would remain.

Because of the two-way race in 1981, the local media also could not ignore the Sanders campaign, as it probably would have liked to have done. If they were going to cover the election at all, editors had to show Sanders as a serious contender and as the only legitimate challenger. While this helped the campaign, it did not usually win favorable commentary for the progressives. During Sanders' campaign, the local press missed no opportunity to red-bait him. This is hardly surprising. The city's one daily paper, the *Free Press*, is owned by corporate giant Gannett. One of the local television stations regularly makes campaign contributions to Republican coffers. Ever since the progressives have come to power, they have either been ignored or ridiculed by most of the local media.

Offsetting the negative coverage, Bernie Sanders brought to the race his own brand of charisma. His public speaking style has become legendary. Sanders has developed a powerful ability to talk to ordinary working people in a language that makes sense to them. Sanders' popular appeal is reflected in the fact that, despite his status as mayor and then as a congressperson, everyone from his core activists to the average person on the street continues to refer to him as "Bernie." Today, Bernie bumper stickers are a distinct feature of a noticeable number of cars that bear Vermont license plates. While Vermont is known for its pockets of progressive- and liberal-minded professionals who have moved to the Green Mountain state to pursue a different kind of life-style, Sanders has been able to reach out to a much broader constituency.

Progressive politics in Vermont also benefits from the state's small scale. The entire population is less than 600,000. Although Burlington is Vermont's largest city, its population is just over 38,000 for the city and 123,000 for the greater metropolitan area. Politics on this scale makes grassroots democracy relatively accessible. In a city of under 40,000 residents, door-to-door campaigning and literature drops can literally reach every resident. Individual voting districts usually encompass no more than several thousand people. In Burlington, progressive candidates, from the board of alders to the state assembly, have campaigned by literally visiting every home in their district.

Despite these particularly favorable characteristics, Vermont Progressives frequently stress that there is nothing so unique to their movement that it can not be done elsewhere. Indeed, the base of the Burlington revolution lies in four elements available to activists across the country. First, Sanders and the Progressive Coalition champion a basic progressive message. Although their agenda spans the spectrum of progressive concerns—from divestment from South Africa to environmentally friendly development to domestic partner benefits—the heart of their appeal lies in the economic question. Bernie Sanders, and the Progressive Coalition as a whole, speaks a language of class politics. They see themselves as representing the average working person who faces the greed and corruption of the powerful few. When he ran in 1981, Sanders tarred the major parties as closed old boy networks and pledged to open government to ordinary people. For example, for almost two decades the future of Burlington's waterfront along Lake Champlain had been a pivotal issue in local politics. Sander's 1981 campaign slogan, "Burlington is not for sale," encapsulated his opposition to development plans that would turn the waterfront into a playground for the rich.

This populist dimension shows clearly in the Progressive's voting base. Many outside commentators, especially those hostile to progressive politics, have interpreted the Burlington revolution and its spread statewide as simply reflecting the votes of "hippie-minded" professionals who have moved into the state. While certainly part of the progressive activist base does come from this element, its voting strength in Burlington reflects class politics. The city is divided into six wards with two representatives each on the board of alders (except Ward Four, which until recently has had three). The core of progressive dominance is in wards two and three, which lie in the heart of the city. These are the poorest sections of Burlington and the ones on which the Progressives have focused their agenda both during the campaign seasons and while in city hall.

The residents of these areas have returned the progressives' support. By 1983, Sanders was receiving at least 70 percent of the votes in wards two and three, while the Progressive Coalition has yet to be defeated in these ward races for the board of alders. Throughout the 1980s, in wards one and five, progressives typically won, with some fluctuation, one seat in each area. Ward One encompasses the University of Vermont and includes much of the student vote, while Ward Five is a mixed-income area that extends from downtown out toward the suburbs. Ward Six is very affluent and Ward

Four is very suburban. Both have developed as Republican strongholds. What has allowed the Progressive Coalition to knock out the Democratic Party as the dominant player in local politics has been the decisive move of the city's low-income voters away from the Democrats and toward the Progressives.

These victories have also come through the hard work of grassroots organizing. Progressive campaigns have involved large numbers of volunteers. Originally this helped to offset disadvantages in campaign funding by using door-to-door energy to gain the margins of victory. Over time, this grassroots strength has turned into a funding base as well. Progressive Coalition campaigns today are not just the most volunteer intensive, but often the best funded. This is true even though the Progressives still rely on small contributions rather than big-money fundraising, like the Democrats and Republicans.

By using a class-based message and grassroots organizing, progressive activists have also been able to raise voter turn-out in the city by a considerable margin. Reflecting the status quo in many communities across the country, the leadership of both major parties in Burlington were perfectly content to let local politics atrophy into lackluster contests in which candidates competed for the support of those few who voted. Between 1971 and 1979, voter turn-out for the mayoral elections fluctuated between a low of 22 percent and a high of 36 percent, with the average being in the upper twenties. Turn-out in the low-income and student areas were the lowest in the city. In 1981, however, roughly 1,000 new voters joined or rejoined the electoral process, largely as a result of the Sanders' campaign and the progressive get-out-the-vote effort. Without these new voters, Sanders would have lost. For the 1983 mayoral race, over 13,320 people cast votes, a level hailed by the local media as a record turn-out. While bad March weather has occasionally dampened turn-out, voter participation has generally remained high in all seriously contested races ever since the progressive movement broke onto the scene. From a turn-out of 32 percent in 1981 to a high of 49 percent in 1987, voter participation in the mayoral contests has averaged 40 percent during the 1980s. The only time since 1981 when the Progressives lost the mayor's office came in 1993, when turn-out dropped below 10,000—most of the decline coming in the progressive's strongholds.[2]

Progressive get-out-the-vote and registration efforts have concentrated on the low-income and working class areas of the city. Yet, they also fought and won a major battle over students' right to vote. In the mid-1980s, the Republicans and Democrats dominated the voter registration board and tried to undercut progressive strength by requiring all students to provide special evidence of residency not required of other applicants. With the help of the secretary of state and the city attorney, the Progressives successfully blocked this illegal discrimination. Progressive organizers have aggressively £ after absentee ballots as well. Many elderly and other "marginal" voters are not able to easily get to the polls, so activists have tried to contact many of these people directly—arranging to have an absentee ballot delivered to them and keeping track of people who fail to mail them back in.

In addition to the more quantifiable data on voter turn-out and registration, the progressive movement has generally reinvigorated Burlington politics. Since 1981, the city has seen far fewer uncontested local races. Local political debate is much more alive than the old politics as usual. To fend off the Progressives, Republican and Democratic organizers have had to reinvigorate their grassroots structures and engage in meaningful political discussion. Long-time progressive political activist and current co-chair of the Vermont Progressive Coalition, Ellen David-Friedman has characterized the city's new political climate as follows:

> Burlington has become a politicized town, with an uniquely informed and motivated electorate, with passionate contests waged for virtually every modest public post, and with debate proceeding on the true issues of political life: who has power and how are they using it.[3]

The Sanders' revolution did not just suddenly happen, but resulted from years of activism that established the crucial ground work for the 1981 triumph. The 1981 mayoral bid was neither Sanders' nor the progressive community's first foray into electoral politics. Bernie Sanders ran for office in 1972 as the Liberty Union Party's first candidate for governor, receiving 1 percent of the vote. In 1976, he ran again, this time reaching 6 percent statewide, with double that proportion in Burlington. Other progressive activists built up campaign experience in the 1970s. Through the Liberty Union Party, progressives ran for state and local office. In 1975, the Party's candidate for mayor of Burlington received 28 percent of the vote. Progressive activists also formed a local chapter of the Citizens Party around the presidential campaign of Barry Commoner in 1980. In 1981, Citizens Party candidate Terry Bouricius won an alderperson seat in Ward Two. This prior electoral activity meant that when conditions became favorable in the 1980s for progressives to seriously challenge the political status quo, they were able to do so with a core of activists who had built up considerable experience around political campaigning.[4]

The Progressive's victories were also grounded in a number of non-electoral organizing efforts in Burlington's low-income neighborhoods during the 1970s. For example, with up to two-thirds of the city's population renting their living arrangements, tenant organizing has been a key focus of progressive activism. By 1981, the tenant movement had formalized into an organization called People Acting for Change Together (PACT). That year, PACT found itself in a major battle with the board of alders. PACT had worked to develop a rent control agreement with local landlords, called the Fair Housing Proposal. The board of alders' refused to put this initiative on the 1981 ballot. PACT responded by collecting the necessary signatures to put a stronger version of the proposal before voters through a special April ballot. To head off this initiative, the board placed their own watered-down version of the Fair Housing Proposal on the ballot. Both measures went down in a four to one defeat, however, after a coalition calling itself Citizens Against Rent Control spent an estimated $10,000 campaigning against them. The local political establishment's hostility to PACT has meant that the Progressives have been the movement's only consistent political ally. Activists from the tenants movement thus became involved in Sanders' 1981 campaign.[5]

The People's Republic—Running City Hall During The Sanders' Years

With a self-professed socialist occupying the mayor's office, Burlington in the 1980s presents an interesting case for examining both the possibilities and limitations for progressive city government. Since Steven Soifer's detailed study, *The Socialist Mayor*, and other materials have well-documented these early years, our discussion will take advantage of this ample material to go into some depth.[6]

Constraints on Progressive City Government

Sanders' administration had to operate within several serious constraints. Seen from Sanders' socialist convictions, the overall capitalist economy placed a major limitation on what he could achieve. Obviously, city government does not have the power to seize major private economic assets and make them public institutions run by workers and the community. As a result, local government has to work within the logic of an economy that is privately owned and controlled. To promote a healthy and vibrant community within this context, city government has to ultimately encourage an active business environment, even while it seeks to direct business in a more socially beneficial direction.

In addition, progressive reforms also face the conservative structure of US government. Although our nation's system of checks and balances has traditionally been hailed as a democratic protection against possible tyranny, in reality, the system also ensures that government has a difficult time doing anything that upsets the standing order. The "founding fathers" were well aware that weak and constrained public authority ultimately favored those who had the economic power, while strong and efficient government could serve as a tool of the powerless. With state power divided among federal, state, and local levels, and with each level divided among legislative, executive, and judicial functions, popular movements have historically found themselves in control of the more accessible components of this system only to have their actions blocked at the other levels. To successfully enact sweeping changes, progressives ultimately have to take control of the entire system from top to bottom.

In Burlington, the obstacles of the political structure became clear at two levels. First, local governments often do not have complete authority over their own destiny. Despite the ideal image of New England town democracy, Vermont is one of the states that places the greatest restrictions on municipalities. Vermont is not a "home rule" state, meaning that local governments can not change their own charters. Even if both the locally elected officials and the general population agree to changes, any policy that is not allowed in the city charter must seek the approval of the state legislature. Historically, this restriction has most affected the issue of taxation. The state of Vermont has given its municipalities charters that permit property taxes as the only form of local revenues. Such taxes are regressive. Through years of hard work, senior citizens and low-income residents may acquire their own house only to find themselves paying the same level of taxes as people with similar properties yet much higher incomes. Even local governments that are not sympathetic to the tax fairness issue still run up against the state restrictions, since they are forced to face the ire of angry property owners every time they try to raise local revenues. Despite these difficulties with the property tax, local governments can use little else to raise money.

Second, within Burlington, the new socialist mayor faced an uncooperative local governmental structure. While the city's budget originates in the mayor's office and the chief executive does have a veto power over any legislation passed by the board of alders, the heart of Burlington's government lies elsewhere. Most of the city's departments are governed by commissions, which have a high degree of autonomy from the legislative and executive branches. The commissions, for example, hire and fire the departmental heads. With commissioners appointed for five-year terms (in 1983, the Progressives succeeded in getting this reduced to three years), this system places a serious break on rapid policy changes. Even worse, given the local balance of power, the board of alders, not the mayor's office, has the dominant voice in the appointment of most commissioners. This power has proven a major obstacle to the progressive agenda. Not until 1995 did the progressives achieve a majority on the board.

The progressives did come close to this majority several times, however. In 1982, they held five of the thirteen seats and a year later that climbed to six. Until 1995, the seventh seat proved just beyond reach. Beginning in 1984, the Progressive Coalition had repeated and varied chances to gain this seat only to see their candidates miss by narrow margins, often in run-off elections. Since the Republicans and Democrats have proven more than willing to work together in opposition to the Progressives, this split between a socialist mayor and a Republican and Democratic majority board has been one of the central limitations on progressive change. Only after the 1982 elections did the local establishment begin to give way, when the Progressives gained a bloc of five votes on the board.

Since then, city politics has involved compromises between the mayor and his supporters and the majority on the board. With five seats, the progressives established some leverage by being able to prevent the board from overriding a Sanders' veto. With six seats, the progressives established a clear stalemate on the city council. Made up of the thirteen alderpeople, plus the mayor, the council decides all commission appointments. With a seven-seven split, both progressives and the mainstream parties had to work out compromises if they were going to appoint anyone. Using this balance of power as leverage, Sanders eventually obtained approval for his appointments to such key city positions as the treasurer. Nevertheless, by the end of the Sanders' years, the Progressives held a majority only on a minority of commissions. Given this balance of power, Sanders' achievements are all the more remarkable.

Progressive Accomplishments

Between 1981 and 1989, Sanders and the Progressive Coalition achieved several significant accomplishments. Soon after being elected, for example, Sanders established a mayor's arts council to help bring art and culture into the broader community, where it was available to all. Over the years, the council has built up an impressive array of programs, including various concert series, neighborhood festivals, a senior arts program, a municipal art gallery, and alternative local cable programming. The council has also funded low-income and under-employed artists, and brought "touring artists" into the city and private workplaces. By the mid-1980s, the council was sponsoring over 200 events a year. More important, these programs have helped redefine the role of art, making it accessible to people of all incomes and, with events such as a Hiroshima remembrance, directly raising political awareness.

Another success story has been the mayor's youth office. Starting with no funding from the board of alders, the office set out to provide young people with a sense of belonging and involvement in their community. As with the arts council, the youth office's activities have mushroomed. While the former mayor had banned rock music in Memorial Auditorium, the youth office not only got the ban dropped, but sponsored an annual battle of the bands. It also established a Building Understanding between Seniors and Youth program, in which young people help older citizens in various ways, such as with snow shoveling and yard work. Over the objections of some adults, the youth office opened a teen center, designed by the young people who would be using it. The office established several after-school programs, a nationally acclaimed tree planting program, a youth-written and -produced newspaper, summer programs, an employment program, an annual kid's day, and several youth dance troupes. It also played an instrumental roll in establishing a nonprofit childcare center aimed at providing high quality service to low-income families. When opened, the center was one of the few facilities in Burlington to provide infant care and the only one to offer part-time care.

Sanders and the Progressive Coalition also challenged the capitalist model of rental housing by establishing several affordable housing projects that allow tenants to have a democratic voice in running their cooperative housing, including the eventual prospect of building up equity as collective owners. Under Sanders, Burlington became the first city in the nation to fund a community land trust. The Burlington land trust aims to remove a significant portion of the city's land from the speculative real estate market. The trust buys the land upon which housing has been built. People can then buy the living units, while the trust retains ownership and control of the land. This perpetually reduces the overall purchase price, helping more moderate-income people afford their own house. And the trust places the future use of neighborhood land in the hands of the community as a whole rather than individual home owners and developers. The land trust potentially gives the community the power to minimize gentrification.

Bernie Sanders has also been notable as one of the few US mayors to have a foreign policy. Throughout his terms as mayor, Sanders publicly denounced US policy in Central America. In the early 1980s, Burlington established a sister city relationship with Puerto Cabezas in northeast Nicaragua. As a result, the people of Burlington sent in 1985 over $100,000 in humanitarian aid to this community. Sanders personally visited Nicaragua that same year, being the only US official to attend the Sandinista's sixth annual celebration of the overthrow of the Samoza dictatorship. Although mainstream political observers questioned the wisdom of such actions, Sanders was successful in linking such foreign policy questions to local realities. After all, he noted, the nation's bloated military budget is part of the reason local programs are poorly funded. Furthermore, through such efforts, the citizens of Burlington had the unique opportunity to discuss and articulate their opinions on the nation's actions in the world. In 1982, voters approved a non-binding proposal by a three to one margin that called for the termination of all US aid to El Salvador. In 1986, voters rejected aid to the Contras.

The Sanders' administration succeeded in areas that are supposedly the terrain of conservative politicians. Contrary to constant right-wing mudslinging against bloated and costly left-wing "big government," one of the greatest accomplishments of Sanders' administration was to bring rational, efficient government to the city of Burlington. Previous administrations had left city finances in such a mess that the new Sanders-appointed treasurer's office soon discovered a $1.9 million surplus! The new city treasurer also found that 97 percent of all retired city workers were receiving incorrect amounts for their pensions. Through centralized purchasing, competitive bidding for city contracts, and intelligent investment of city funds, the Sanders' administration was able to save the city hundreds of thousands of dollars. The administration was then able to use the surplus funds for much needed projects, such as rebuilding roads and bridges, funding some of the policies discussed above, and initiating a small business revolving loan fund.

The Sanders' administration demonstrated a record strikingly similar to the Socialist municipal governments earlier this century. Because they are free from the cronyism and favoritism that can easily enmesh the mainstream parties, progressive administrations are often the ones that can truly deliver efficient and honest government to local residents.

The Sanders' administration was successful at promoting a vibrant local business climate as well. Despite the constant red-baiting that tried to portray the socialist mayor as anti-business, the Sanders' administration clearly saw the link between the welfare of working people and local business prosperity. Although he tried to steer business activity in more socially responsible directions, Sanders also aimed to keep Burlington economically healthy. His establishment of the Community and Economic Development Office (CEDO) embodied both goals. CEDO was created to provide the administration with an institutional framework for pursuing progressive economic priorities *and* to build bridges to the local business community. Over the opposition of three Democrats and two Republicans, the Progressives were able to establish CEDO as a body answerable to the mayor and the board, not a citizen commission. Since its founding, CEDO has been involved in hundreds of projects. It has not simply fostered progressive economic initiatives, but has encouraged economic activity generally. CEDO has initiated several projects to encourage small businesses. These include the revolving loan program, which secured $400,000 in federal funds for local use, and incubator business centers, which house a group of small businesses that share overhead costs through cooperative purchasing and rent. While business people used to automatically having their own way within city hall may not like having to work with CEDO and the Sanders' administration, most cannot deny that progressive city government has been good for business. Economic planning works. Sanders left the city with a healthy economy. Progressive success around quality of life issues such as these gained national recognition when the US Council of Mayors designated Burlington as the "Most Livable City in America" for populations under 100,000.

Partial Victories, Trade-offs, and Compromises

While progressives were able to directly pursue and implement their priorities in some areas, the constraints surrounding the Sanders' administration meant that many of his policy initiatives underwent a complex process of partial gains and trade-offs. Progressives have had to compromise on some of their goals in order to win on others. Since activists who come to political office in other cities will face similar dilemmas, the Sanders experience is worth examining.

Some Sanders' initiatives were blocked by combined opposition from the local political establishment and the state government. For example, to provide the public with better quality and cheaper services, as well as greater democratic control, Sanders appointed a committee in 1983 to explore the possibilities of municipal ownership of the local cable television company. Although the board initially passed a resolution in favor of the initiative, it later changed its position, joining the outspoken opposition of the local media, the Green Mountain Cable Company, and key city departments. The state's public service board made its opposition to the plan clear when it granted Green Mountain Cable's request for a rate increase to rebuild their system.

Sanders, however, was bolstered by the discovery that Green Mountain's cable franchise license had quietly expired in 1982. The Sanders' administration appealed to the Vermont Supreme Court to block the company from rebuilding its network and to rule on the city's claim to control the franchise. The stalemate was resolved when the cable company offered to pay the city $1 million plus an annual franchise fee of no more than 5 percent of its gross city revenues. In return, the city agreed to drop its legal appeal and let the company use the city's poles to put up cables. In the end, Burlington did get a far better deal from Green Mountain Cable than they had before. Local opposition combined with the insecurity of whether the state would even allow such an undertaking, however, pushed the idea of a municipal cable system off the political map. The establishment succeeded in blocking this overtly socialist measure.

The state proved an even greater obstacle to progressive hopes to bring greater tax fairness to local finances. The ideal solution, some combination of a local graduated income tax combined with other progressive taxes, was not a possibility due to the state legislature's ability to veto such measures. Instead, Sanders publicly opposed property taxes for hurting low- and moderate-income people. In office, he remained largely true to his pledge to hold the line on property tax increases, once again stealing one of the conservative's favorite issues. The state, however, undermined the mayor by forcing Burlington to implement a citywide property reappraisal, the first in twenty years. Progressives opposed this action since it was clear that a reappraisal would hit low- and fixed-income home owners the worst, while also shifting the tax burden from commercial to residential properties. This is exactly what happened, even worse than expected. Three out of four home owners saw the value of their homes increase, with the biggest rise hitting the poorest sections of the city.

Forced by the state to implement tax policies that made local taxes less rather than more equitable, the Sanders' administration set out to find ways to bring greater tax fairness in spite of Vermont's legislature. The administration first tried to alter the property tax classifications. Although their first effort was struck down by the state legislature, a more specific measure that taxed business property at 120 percent of its value, while leaving residential property at 100 percent, did survive state scrutiny.

In a long battle that spanned almost the entire length of Sanders' four terms as mayor, progressives eventually won a gross receipts tax on rooms and meals. Their first attempt died when voters rejected a 3 percent tax proposal following a well-funded campaign against the tax by the Burlington Chamber of Commerce. In round two, Sanders won approval for a 1.5 percent tax from the board of alders only to see the state reject the necessary charter changes. By 1985, Burlington began facing serious budget shortfalls, thanks to major cuts in federal revenue sharing.

Amid this atmosphere, Sanders won the support of the local business community which realized that some form of new revenues were going to have to take up the slack. This time, the new tax proposal was engineered in such a way as to conform to the existing charter. Although the legislature considered changing the charter to close the provision used by the Progressives to implement the tax, ultimately it decided not to make such a move against home rule. Throughout this battle, Burlington received the support of other Vermont municipalities who also wanted greater control over their tax base. In 1989, the Sanders' administration tried to expand the tax to cover beer, wine, and tobacco products in order to raise funds for a city childcare proposal. The measure went down at the polls, however, by a two to one margin.

In another attempt to get around the limitations of the property tax, Sanders attempted to compel the city's two largest tax-exempt institutions, the University of Vermont and the Medical Center Hospital of Vermont, to contribute to the city's finances. After all, he argued, both used taxpayer-funded services. Although voters approved charter changes that would allow the city to tax property like the university and the hospital at one quarter of their "assessed value," the measure was vetoed by the state. The effort was not wasted, however, as the university eventually agreed to make payments for the fire protection that it uses. In 1987, the city openly challenged the hospital's tax-exempt status by presenting it with a tax bill of $3 million. The Vermont courts struck down the city's actions, agreeing with the hospital's claim that it was a "charitable" organization that provided some "free medical care" to the community.

Overall, while the Progressives were never able to achieve the sweeping tax changes that they would have liked, they did win some important alternative sources for funding city government other than the property tax. Furthermore, through their constant proposals, the Progressives were able to define the tax issue in new terms, moving from the question of taxes—yes or no—to what kinds of taxes and who was paying them.

In other policy areas, the Sanders' administration had to contend with hard economic realities. These constraints became clear during the battle over the future of Burlington's waterfront on Lake Champlain. In 1981, Sanders ran against the plans of Burlington developer Tony Pomerleau to convert the land owned by the Central Vermont Railway into high-priced condominiums and expensive hotels and offices. Sanders' slogan that "Burlington is not for sale" effectively tapped into many people's desires not to see their waterfront turned into a playground for the rich. Although some environmentalists hoped to block all development on the waterfront, the Sanders' administration called for development that preserved it for public use by combining parks, public facilities, and mixed housing. Although Sanders initially spoke in terms of public ownership of the land, the legal reality seemed to require the city to purchase the property at very high prices. Without sufficient cash, Sanders decided to throw his support behind a plan proposed by the Alden Waterfront Corporation that seemed to fulfill the administration's vision. By the time the plan went to the voters for approval of a bond issue for its financing, however, it had changed considerably. To progressive critics, the plan looked like another attempt at handing over the waterfront to the wealthy. Sanders, however, claimed that it still fulfilled many of his initial goals. In the end, the bond issue was defeated, with Sanders' base in the low-income areas of the city rejecting it outright.

In retrospect, the working-class voters of Burlington saved their mayor from compromising far too much to the logic of the economic status quo than he needed. Following the rejection of the Alden plan, the administration again pursued the option of public ownership. A Progressive attorney rediscovered a Vermont statute dealing with public land that had been given over for use by private companies, such as the railroad. Using this provision, the Progressives scored a major upset in 1989 when the Vermont Supreme Court sided with the city of Burlington by ruling that the Central Vermont Railroad could only use the land for "railroad, wharf, and storage purposes." Once the land was no longer used for such purposes, the court said, it reverts back to the state. Burlington thus found itself in possession of thirty-five acres of waterfront property. Today, the waterfront is one of the Progressive Coalition's shining achievements. It boasts two miles of public beach, nine miles of public bike paths, a community boathouse, a children's science center, and ample community parks.

Despite his overall popularity, Sanders was not always able to gain public support for progressive measures. Even in cases when the majority of voters would benefit from a policy, the ability of opponents to mobilize public sentiment through the media has, at times, proven decisive. Despite the fact that the majority of Burlington residents rent their homes, for example, Sanders was unable to get rent control passed in 1981. In 1988, the Progressives went before voters again, this time seeking approval of an ordinance that would have protected tenants from arbitrary eviction. A landlord campaign against the measure convinced enough voters that it was a "thinly veiled attempt at rent control." It went down to defeat 53 percent against to 47 percent in favor, although it won in the Progressive Coalition strongholds.

Bernie Sanders also brought to the mayor's office some limitations. For generations, socialists have been criticized by other progressive groups for letting their class analysis get in the way of fully appreciating other forms of oppression. While independent political movements build their base strength by raising basic economic questions, they must do so by addressing all the dimensions of oppression in this society. In this regard, Sanders had clear limitations when he entered the mayor's office in 1981.

Although sympathetic to the issues raised by the women's movement, Sanders was not a feminist nor did he understand gender oppression as well as class exploitation. As a result, the Sanders' administration came under increasing criticism for not including more women in positions of authority. Indeed, Sanders' inner circle of advisors was all male. The Burlington women's council did eventually emerge from the Sanders' administration, and the Progressives have enacted significant programs and policy changes that have improved the lives of women. The council has sponsored conferences on women's issues, a media watch committee, a women's health day, affirmative action measures in the building trades, and a sexual assault prevention project. Progressives have also implemented the state's only municipally funded daycare center and shelter for battered women. Inside government, Progressives have fought to have city jobs reevaluated to establish comparable pay between male- and female-dominated work. While all these measures are notable, the women's council had to fight for its independence from the mayor's office, and was not one of the administration's top priorities.

Sanders also ran into conflicts with the environmental and peace communities. Some ecologists have criticized him for focusing too much on economic growth rather than questioning the desirability of growth as an end in and of itself. The well-known intellectual advocate of social ecology, Murray Bookchin, who lives in Burlington, became an outspoken Sanders opponent. A group of his supporters evolved into the Burlington Greens, which challenged the Progressive Coalition unsuccessfully for the mayor's office after Sanders stepped down.

During his first term in office, peace activists were angered at Sanders when he opposed their civil disobedience actions at the local General Electric plant. For these activists, the plant, which is the sole significant manufacturer of the high-speed, multi-barrel guns used against Nicaragua, was the natural local manifestation of the US military machine. Sanders, however, felt that demonstrations at the plant targeted workers who were simply trying to support their families, rather than the people in Congress and other decision-makers responsible for the policies. Although in negotiating around these issues Sanders agreed to set up a peace conversion task force, little was done. Similarly, anger flared again in 1985 when a newspaper reporter discovered that the local police had infiltrated the peace movement. In response, the Sanders' administration pushed the police commission to adopt guidelines for the use of undercover police officers. Yet critics from the peace movement did not see this measure as an adequate protection. The administration did not give this issue priority, perhaps due to the role that the police union played in Sanders' electoral success in 1981.

The Sanders years also present a mixed record on an overarching issue central to progressive activism: fostering real democracy. The Sanders' administration and the Progressive Coalition have clearly had a democratizing impact on Burlington politics. They have revitalized political debate and electoral competition. Turn-out and political participation among the less well off of the city's population have noticeably increased. Furthermore, city politics generally occurs in a much more open atmosphere than in previous years. Yet the Sanders' administration has failed in some of its most ambitious attempts to foster participatory democracy.

In 1982, the board of alders passed a resolution to establish neighborhood planning assemblies that would allow residents to make recommendations toward city policy and exercise control over some community development money. Set up in each ward, the assemblies were intended as an experiment in direct democracy. In actuality, with no money for fulltime organizers, many never got off the ground. Those that did had spotty attendance, generating openings for Sanders' opponents. Indeed, some became sounding boards for his mobilized enemies. Other assemblies accused the administration of dealing with them as if they were mere conveyor belts for its policies, rather than bottom-up institutions of citizen control. In order to foster genuine citizen participation on an effective scale, such democratic experiments require more activist energy and public financial backing than the assemblies received.

Sanders also took criticism for his own leadership style. Critics have argued that his administration involved a tight-knit inner circle and top-down decision-making. As such, Sanders had failed to break fully with the well-established politics of the status quo. Acknowledging that there may be some truth to these criticisms, Sanders himself has pointed to the difficulties involved. As he told researcher Steven Soifer:

> I think we have not done as good a job as we can do, I would say that frankly, but it really is not easy… The real issue is how you maintain the involvement of people in any kind of political process. The truth is, we have a very difficult time… How do you get them to come out to meetings? I think anyone who says our intent is not that is not telling the truth…have we gone about it always in the right way? I'd be willing to concede that we haven't.[7]

While none of the concerns raised here involve easy answers, the Sanders' administration would have had a better appreciation of the issues at the outset. To his credit, Sanders did develop, through experience, a better understanding of different segments of the progressive community and his administration did make real changes in response to criticism. In general, the lesson seems to be that promoting democracy and concrete policy changes involves a complex process that takes a great deal of time, effort, and creativity. Good intentions and a general commitment to democratic empowerment are not enough.

The Burlington Progressive Coalition

During Bernie Sanders' long tenure as mayor, the activists who supported him and helped him run city government coalesced into the Progressive Coalition. Despite the establishment's hope that Sanders' decision to move on to statewide politics would signal the peak of progressive power in Burlington, the Progressive Coalition did not fade after Sanders left the mayor's office. If anything, it has become stronger.

With Sanders' announcement that he would not run again as mayor following his 1987-1989 term, the Progressive Coalition reached a critical crossroads. Could the movement maintain its momentum without its charismatic leader or would the Republican and Democratic regulars get their opportunity to regain city hall? In December 1988, the Progressive Coalition held a meeting that nominated Peter Clavelle as Sanders' successor. Clavelle had gotten his first experience with local government in 1972, when, at the age of twenty-three, he was hired as the city manager of Winooski, just north of Burlington. During the Sanders' administration, Clavelle served competently as the director of CEDO—an office central to progressive policies. Not the same fiery orator as Sanders, Clavelle's candidacy gave the Progressive Coalition a chance to prove that the last eight years had not been about people's infatuation with a single charismatic figure, but rather about their support for progressive government generally.

To counter the Progressive Coalition in the 1989 race, the Republicans chose not to run a candidate, thereby giving Democrat Nancy Chioffi the best shot. The Progressive's mayoral race became more difficult, however, when Sandy Baird challenged the Progressive Coalition from the Left by running as a Green. On a frigid April election day, the Progressives proved that they were in Burlington to stay. Clavelle decidedly defeated Chioffi 54 to 42 percent. The Greens' candidacy did not cut significantly into Clavelle's support. Baird tallied only slightly more than 3 percent of the vote. Clavelle showed solid majorities in the Progressive Coalition's base of wards one, two, and three. He also won Ward Five by just four votes and lost only the more suburban Ward Four. At the same time, the Progressives held onto their six seats on the board of alders.

Today, the Progressive Coalition remains the single strongest political group in the city. When Clavelle ran for re-election in 1991, he faced no serious challengers. In 1993, Peter Brownell gained a surprise victory over Clavelle, winning 54 percent of the vote and becoming the city's first Republican mayor since 1965. In explaining Brownell's triumph, the local press pointed to the Clavelle administration's successful effort to provide domestic partner benefits for unmarried city employees. Indeed, opponents had made use of the issue, arousing homophobic sentiment and claiming, wrongly, that domestic partner benefits would cost the city a great deal of money.

Progressive activists point to deeper causes for their defeat. Twelve years of unbroken progressive rule had left many activists feeling complacent. In 1993, the Progressives did not mobilize as strongly as in the past, while the opposition did. The results can be seen in the election returns. Clavelle won four of the city's six wards. Despite this accomplishment, he lost the election because turn-out went down in these areas, while it climbed in the city's largest and least progressive ward.

Celebrations by the local media that the Progressives had finally been beaten back proved premature. In 1993, the Progressive Coalition maintained its strength on the board of alders. Then, in 1995, Clavelle swept back into city hall while seven progressives (five running as Progressives and two as independents) won seats on the now fourteen-member board. In addition, another independent candidate, and likely ally with the Progressive Coalition on many issues, also won election. This gave the Progressives seven solid votes, and the possibility for an eighth. In their campaigns for school board seats, the Progressives also won every race they entered. The 1995 election season demonstrated that the remobilized Progressive base was still solid and the dominant force in local politics.[8]

The 1995 election also served as a reminder that voters expect government to fulfill its more mundane functions, in addition to loftier ideological debates. When he won in 1993, Peter Brownell had campaigned on a classic Republican call to eliminate waste from city hall and cut the budget. Unfortunately for Brownell, when he got into the mayor's office he soon discovered that twelve years of a Progressive administration had left a very efficient and lean operation. Finding no fat to cut, Brownell fulfilled his campaign promises by reducing the city's snow removal budget. It took only one heavy winter to convince many voters who were not solidly Progressive that re-electing Brownell was not in their best interest.

The Structure of the Progressive Coalition

The organization of the Progressive Coalition has reflected the dramatic and sudden way in which progressives stepped into local power, as well as the small city nature of Burlington politics. Few, not even Sanders himself, expected an independent socialist to win the 1981 mayoral race. Although Sanders' victories demonstrated a solid and developed network of experienced activists within the city, the progressive community began running city hall before it had any formal citywide political organization. During most of the Sanders' years, the Progressive Coalition remained a loose-knit network of like-minded people. Indeed, during its first few years of existence, the Progressive Coalition did not have a written platform. What united people was support for Sanders and the direction of change coming from city hall. By the time the mayor's seat passed from Sanders to Clavelle, the coalition had developed a more formalized structure complete with official bylaws and elected leadership.

Even with this more structured organization, however, the Progressive Coalition today remains largely a coalition of individuals. Unlike LEAP, the Progressive Coalition has not been built on the formal membership and support of established progressive organizations. While coming from many progressive groups, activists participate in the Progressive Coalition as individuals, not as the leaders of organizations.

The Progressive Coalition is also not organized as a political party, as defined by state law. It does, however, have several party-like mechanisms. Its bylaws provide for semiannual membership meetings that adopt platform planks and elect the leadership. A steering committee is chosen with six ward and six at-large representatives. The bylaws require that half the steering committee be women. Steering committee meetings are open to all members. The Progressive Coalition makes candidate nominations either at the general membership meetings (in the case of citywide offices) or through the ward caucuses (in the case of city council candidates). The ward structures of the coalition vary across the city. The ward groups are strongest in the central areas of Burlington, where the coalition has its base, while they are largely nonexistent in conservative wards, such as the New North End.

Overall, the Progressive Coalition remains a relatively informal group. The coalition has no paid staff or dues-paying membership. Indeed, what constitutes the membership of the coalition is quite casual. Essentially anyone who volunteers for progressive campaigns, donates money, or attends gatherings will get on a mailing list and be kept informed of the coalition's meetings and activities. While this structure has served progressives well in many respects, it does have several limitations, of which activists are well aware.

The Progressive Coalition is heavily intertwined with local progressive government. While the coalition now has official platforms, its political agenda has largely developed out of the process of governing. Burlington's commission system, and offices such as CEDO, have given a significant number of progressives the opportunity to participate in the city's planning process, where many innovative ideas have been worked out. As welcome as these opportunities have been, they do pose a trade-off. Local activists have only so much time and energy. If they are attending city planning meetings and helping run the local government, then they have less time to be out in the community organizing.

Ideally, progressive officeholders should be backed up by grassroots activity. This "street heat" allows the community to speak for itself, pushes local progressive officials when they need pushing, and supports them when they face opposition. The power and reach of government institutions is limited. Fundamental political, economic, social, and cultural changes cannot simply come from the pens of legislators and executives, no matter how progressive. Ultimately, people create change through their own self-organization within their workplaces, neighborhoods, and communities. Political power merely supports this broader process.

Outside of its electoral work, however, the structure of the Progressive Coalition does not enhance this grassroots capacity. The electoral movement has generally drawn on the organizing groundwork laid by other progressive groups. Activists in these groups often face the difficult balance between helping run city hall and doing community work. A similar trade-off happens within the Progressive Coalition itself as questions of administering city hall and making policy intermingle with issues related to building the organization.

One of the problems with focusing so much on electoral contests at the expense of other forms of activism is that the campaign seasons run only part of the year. As a result, even the strongest progressive ward groups can lapse into dormancy during the periods between elections. While this does provide overworked activists and volunteers a break from the action, it also means that the group is constantly having to remobilize and reestablish its base once or twice a year. The Progressive Coalition's heavy electoral focus reflects, in part, the difference between a group that places some candidates in office yet remains in a minority position and a group that captures the reigns of government at an early stage.

The limitations of the Progressive Coalition's informal structure and its participation in running city hall have led some activists to desire a more developed party-like organization. Specifically, a higher level of organization, complete with a more formalized, dues-paying membership and paid staff, could deliver benefits in two important areas. First, it would help cultivate new leadership and activists. While electoral campaigning may do this somewhat, more ongoing community organizing (especially if designed to recruit new people) could accomplish even more. Second, an expanded community organizing focus could change the nature of the coalition's active base and leadership. The Progressive Coalition is still very much led and organized by college-educated, professionally trained activists who have made a life-long commitment to progressive change. Even when they enthusiastically support progressive ideas, many "mainstream" working people face concrete issues of time, money, and energy that make it more difficult for them to enter into positions of leadership or sustained activism. When the activists driving the coalition do not share the same material or cultural background as many working people, this distinction can create additional barriers to participation.

Progressives need to develop greater grassroots-organizing and leadership-generating strategies if they are going to further expand their base. The 1993 election loss was an indication of important demographic changes within the city. The fastest growing part of Burlington's population is in the New North End, the ward that swung the election against Clavelle that year. In recognition of its growing size, this ward is now represented by four alderpeople, while all the other wards still have only two. The most suburban part of Burlington, the New North End has proven the most resistant to progressive ideas. Clearly, to penetrate this area, activists have to develop an agenda and culture that will better resonate with working class suburbanites—something that can only be done by fostering leadership within this community.

To overcome these limitations, progressive activists need to build into their efforts deliberate strategies to go into "mainstream" communities and develop organic leadership. The Progressive Coalition has done events, such as picnics, to try to make itself more accessible to ordinary people. Encouraging new leadership, especially among "mainstream" working people, requires a more developed grassroots structure, more attention to non-electoral activities, and simply far more energy than the Progressive Coalition currently has.

A more developed grassroots structure would also help the group develop new candidates. Surprisingly, recruiting good candidates is often a far more difficult challenge than actually getting them elected. Because the election seasons in the United States are relatively long, candidates need to have a large amount of disposable time. This energy drain becomes even greater because elections are centered around the individual candidate rather than parties or political organizations. Therefore, every candidate literally has to develop, in its entirety, their own individual campaign. Our candidate-centered system also compels a progressive movement to find people who have a certain level of name recognition. Years of low-profile experience within the group and the ability to articulate the movement's goals and ideals effectively does not, in the ·eyes of our electoral system, necessarily make a person a well-qualified candidate.

All of the demands imposed make finding qualified candidates a difficult task. At times, the Progressive Coalition has had to endorse less than ideal candidates simply because they needed to find someone willing to run. It is a tribute to the Progressives' success that voters will support these candidates because they are affiliated with the coalition, even when they do not have the name recognition or other qualifications demanded by the political system. Nevertheless, a more formal party-like structure, more non-electoral work, and a more developed strategy for developing new leaders would all enhance the coalition's ability to find and cultivate effective candidates.

The Progressive Coalition needs to develop in the direction of an organized political party in the classical sense of the concept. Part of the problem is that no example of such a structure exists within mainstream US politics. Neither the Republicans nor the Democrats act as strong political organizations. Individual membership in either major party simply qualifies a person to vote in the primaries. Such membership brings little in the way of formal participation in the organization. Locally, both major parties have very loose structures. They rarely engage in non-electoral work. Nor do they have deliberate strategies to recruit new leadership or candidates out of the grassroots. For better models, we need to turn to the Populists and Socialists. Since progressives have neither the media access nor the financial resources of their Republican and Democratic opponents, they have to develop grassroots institutions instead.

Burlington's Progressives recognize the benefits of further grassroots organizing. Within the group, activists have discussed the possibilities of establishing greater non-electoral work and setting up more a formal, dues-paying membership that, among other things could support paid staff. The discussions today are taking place in a political context that is much different from the early 1980s. Progressive political activism has now spread throughout Vermont. Burlington activists have become one part of a larger movement.

Sanders Goes to Congress

Nine years after his stunning win in Burlington, Bernie Sanders once again made history by becoming the first independent elected to Congress in decades. In 1990, he knocked out the incumbent, Republican Peter Smith, by a landslide of sixteen percentage points. Today, he continues to hold Vermont's sole seat in the US House of Representatives, having been re-elected twice. The three successful campaigns of "Bernie for Congress" have helped energize independent political activity across the entire state of Vermont.

The Ingredients of Sanders' Statewide Success

Several factors combine to account for Sanders continued tenure in Congress. Eight years as mayor of Burlington was a clear political asset. One fifth of Vermont voters live in or around Burlington. As the state's largest city, Burlington and its chief executive constantly make the evening news in Vermont. Sanders' success, however, is not simply a Burlington phenomenon. His congressional campaigns have seen activism across the state. Furthermore, his votes come from a wide distribution of Vermont's citizens.

Crucial to Sanders' support base was Jesse Jackson's two presidential campaigns and the existence of the Vermont Rainbow Coalition. Vermont had a strong Rainbow Coalition movement. In 1988, Jesse Jackson won Vermont, the whitest state in the union. The Vermont Rainbow Coalition became one of the stronger of the state groups to come out of Jackson's two national bids. Shortly after Jackson's 1984 campaign, the group endorsed seven Rainbow Democrats for the state legislature with five winning election.

The Vermont Rainbow also had a complex and evolving history with the Democratic Party.[9] Initially, many Democrats greeted the Jackson activists as a healthy addition to the Party's base. As a result of Rainbow activism, Vermont Democrats have moved, over time, toward the liberal-left side of the political spectrum. Meanwhile, the Vermont Rainbow Coalition has remained true to its own agenda and acted with a mind of its own. In 1984, for example, the group refused to give into pressure from the Democrats to endorse Madeline Kunin for governor. Activists from the Rainbow Coalition made it clear that they would not support candidates who did not support their progressive agenda. The membership of the Vermont Rainbow Coalition also included substantial sentiments in favor of third party and independent politics. For many Rainbow activists, their work within the Democratic Party was a tactical question. Their long-term goal was to build an alternative to the two party system. Sentiment in favor of greater political independence was also furthered by the mainstream drift of some Rainbow Democrats. Upon getting into office, some of them developed stronger loyalties to the Democratic Party as a whole than to the Rainbow Coalition from which they came.

Bernie Sanders proved a decisive factor in bringing the tensions of the Rainbow's insider/outsider strategy to a head. In 1986, he declared his independent candidacy for governor and reached out to the Rainbow Coalition for key support. Rainbow activists were thus faced with a choice between supporting the incumbent Democrat, Madeline Kunin, who had managed to alienate and disappoint most of Vermont's progressive groups, or supporting Sanders, an independent who authentically stood for progressive ideals. In the end, the Rainbow risked the ire of the Democratic Party by supporting Sanders. Rainbow activists provided crucial support for Sanders' unsuccessful campaign.

In 1988, the Vermont Rainbow Coalition again chose Sanders over the Democratic candidate in his bid for the US Congress. Such political independence helped further drive the Rainbow down the road toward a break with the Democratic Party. In 1990, the Rainbow merged with independent progressives to found the Vermont Progressive Coalition. Sanders has clearly been aided by the Rainbow Coalition's ability to provide his campaigns with a solid core of experienced organizers and supporters who were part of a statewide network.

In addition to the Rainbow Coalition, Sanders has, over time, picked up the endorsement and support of many of Vermont's other progressive groups, including most trade unions, women's groups, and environmentalists. While many of these groups have had long-standing ties to the Democratic Party, Sanders' proven ability to displace the Democrats as the main alternative to the Republicans has gained the support of these groups. Although he lost his 1988 congressional race by a narrow margin, Sanders did relegate the Democratic candidate, who received only 3 percent of the vote, to "third party" status. Since then, his congressional races have been essentially Republican/Sanders contests. Thus, groups can support Sanders' independent candidacy as the logical alternative to the Republicans—the Democrats have become the spoilers, not Sanders. In 1990, for example, all of Vermont's major unions endorsed Sanders for Congress.

Sanders' statewide campaigns have also demonstrated the power of grassroots activism. By November 1990, the Sanders' campaign had at least 1,000 volunteers knocking door-to-door, getting on the phones, and handing out literature. In the opinion of the *Times Argus*, the local paper in Montpelier, the state's capital, Sanders established a serious community presence throughout the state, while his opponent "kept a low profile."[10] This grassroots activism even extended outside Vermont as the campaign conducted a major fundraising drive using national lists of progressive-minded people. The financial resources generated by this national fundraising combined with local grassroots efforts totaled over a half million dollars.

As in Burlington, Sanders' appeal is significantly class based. Statewide polling analysis done by his campaign organizers revealed that a person's income level predicts their support for Sanders much better than whether or not they describe themselves as liberal or conservative. Indeed, a significant segment of people voted in 1988 for both Bernie Sanders and George Bush. Sanders appeals to these voters because he speaks out about the economic and class issues that directly impact their lives. Furthermore, he is not part of the political establishment. His anti-establishment credentials help explain why some people vote for him as well as the Republicans. People are fed up with politics as usual. Both Sanders and the Republicans appeal to this sentiment, although Sanders is authentically not part of the establishment. Sanders has also distanced himself from politics as usual by his consistent refusal to engage in negative campaigning. Unlike many of his mainstream rivals, he does not attack his opponents personally, but instead trumpets his political principles, talks about people's reality, and promotes a positive vision of social change.

Finally, Sanders won in 1990 because he is persistent. His 1990 victory came after two statewide defeats. By running for governor in 1986, he suffered the status of being a potential spoiler as he was challenging an incumbent Democratic. In 1988, his much better organized and funded House campaign lost by a mere three percentage points. That campaign established a solid core of supporters, however. It also relegated the Democrats to spoiler status, setting the stage for his 1990 win. In running for office over the span of three decades, Sanders has also been persistent with his message. Ever since he entered politics in the 1970s, Sanders has stuck to his class-based, progressive ideals. He has done so consistently, even when his positions have not been popular. As a result, even his opponents have to admit that when people vote for him they know what they are going to get. In an age when people are quite cynical about politicians, Sanders' commitment to his principles helps to place him in a different category.

Accomplishments While in Office

When Bernie Sanders was sworn into his first term in office, political pundits questioned whether he would be able to achieve anything in the nation's capital. After all, what could one independent hope to accomplish in a sea of Democrats and Republicans? Most of the law-making in Congress is accomplished through the elaborate committee system. Yet committee appointments come from party-based bodies. So how does an independent get on a committee or subcommittee?

Sanders has proven the skeptics wrong. Despite the entrenched committee appointment structure, Sanders succeeded in gaining assignment to the Banking, Finance and Urban Affairs Committee and the Government Operations Committee. Furthermore, in an unprecedented move, the House Democratic Steering and Policy Committee granted Sanders "standing" in his committees. This allows him to accumulate seniority just like a Democrat and, thereby, move up the congressional power structure.[11]

Sanders has also proven to be more than just a lone voice for working people in the halls of power. In 1992, he co-founded the Progressive Caucus in the House of Representatives along with Ron Dellums (D-CA), Peter De Fazio (D-OR), Lane Evens (D-IL), and Maxine Waters (D-CA). The caucus now has fifty-two members. Unlike the mainstream Democrats, it has fashioned a broad intellectual and legislative response to the Contract with America. The caucus' "The Progressive Promise: Fairness" calls for a crackdown on corporate crime and tax loopholes, an increase in the minimum wage, single-payer health care, deep cuts in both the military and intelligence budgets, and a $127.7 billion investment over two years in infrastructure repair and environmental cleanup. The Progressive Caucus has worked with, and overlaps in membership with, the Black Congressional Caucus. The two groups have jointly sponsored alternative budgets that echo similar themes, such as cutting the military budget in half and transferring the money to much needed social spending.

The independent representative has displayed an ironic sense of humor as well. Following the passage of NAFTA, he introduced a bill to lower Congress' wages to their Mexican equivalent, so as to keep pace with the spirit of "free trade." Needless to say, the measure failed to win majority support. He has been more successful with other initiatives. Sanders has personally sponsored or co-sponsored a wide range of bills. In 1992, during his first term in office, he succeeded in getting a piece of legislation passed that was drafted by his office—a difficult task for a new member of Congress. On the last day of the 102nd Congress, members passed Sanders' Cancer Registries Act of 1992. The law established a nationwide network of uniform state cancer registries to lay the ground work for consistent and accurate reporting of incidents of the disease. The hope was that this would encourage a more coordinated approach to researching and fighting cancer. This specific bill linked well with Sanders' general call for a national health care system.

While the passage of one's legislation is the most dramatic form of success that a member of Congress can achieve, it is not the only form. Representatives can have a significant influence on national law-making through the amendment process. Even those amendments that do not win approval can force debate that requires other individual Congresspeople to go on the record with their public vote on an issue. In July 1995, the House passed an amendment sponsored solely by Sanders that stopped further funding for the Mexican peso bail out. In this effort, Sanders was joined by 156 Republicans and eighty-eight Democrats. Both the White House and House Banking Committee Chair James Leach, condemned the decision. In Sanders' view, it was wrong for the Clinton administration to provide $20 billion in loans and loan guarantees to a Mexican government that is only promoting the agenda of multinational corporations.[12]

During his political career in Congress, Sanders has not hesitated to speak truth to power. In early 1992, he spoke up during the floor debate over a version of the 1993 tax bill.

> *What our Republican friends are upset about is that for the last fifteen years their side has been winning this [class] war, and that we should concede. It is not that I want to identify with the Democrats, who threw in the towel years ago. As the only Independent in this body, what I concede and congratulate my Republican friends about is that "You won. Reaganomics and the trickle-down theory was a fraud, but you got enough of the Democrats to go along with you."*[13]

Also, that same year, he entered the floor debate about appropriations for the Defense Department:

> *With all due respect, perhaps let me inject a moment of reality into this debate for the American people... Five million children go hungry in America, one million children sleep out on the streets, and hundreds of thousands lack basic inoculations for diseases that should have been wiped out twenty years ago. We rank first in the industrialized world in terms of childhood poverty, with 20 percent of our kids falling in that category. Hundred of thousands of bright young people can not afford to go to college because the Federal Government is not adequately funding student financial aid programs. And today, despite the fact that the Cold War is over, that the Soviet Union no longer exists, that the Warsaw Pact no longer exists, this Congress and this President have the unmitigated chutzpah to vote $4 billion for B-2 bombers. In other words, not enough money available to wipe out childhood hunger, not enough money available for college education—but $4 billion is available to build B-2 bombers.*[14]

Given his background and principles, it should come as no surprise that Sanders has displayed an exemplary congressional voting history. In 1992, he had a 100 percent voting record with the AFL-CIO, the League of Conservation Voters, the American Federation of Government Employees, the National Education Association, Pro-Choice, the Consumer Federation of America, the American Civil Liberties Union, Bread for the World, the Human Rights Campaign Fund, and the National Catholic Social Justice Organization. This meant that for all of the legislation that these groups deemed most important, Sanders voted with them every single time.

A majority of voters in Vermont obviously feel that Sanders is accomplishing something in the nation's capital. They keep sending him back into office. In 1992, he won re-election easily. In 1994, he faced a more serious challenge. The Republican National Committee had decided the time was right to knock Sanders out of Congress and targeted the Vermont race as a top priority. They got behind a shrewd and well-funded candidate who ran television ads from August straight through to election day. To complicate matters, an element of complacency had settled into the Vermont progressive community. The Sanders' campaign was not as well organized or as energized as in past years.

Furthermore, in 1994, Sanders also faced the prospect of losing a small, but potentially key bloc of voters—the Vermont chapter of the National Rifle Association (NRA)—for his support of gun control. Living in a heavily rural state, hunting provides a popular form of recreation and sport for many Vermonters. In a close race, the NRA is a political force in the state, with the ability to swing a few percentage points of the vote one way or the other. While Sanders has generally not identified with the people in Congress who have been enthusiastic about gun control, during his third term in office, he did offer unenthusiastic support for the assault weapons ban found in the

Clinton crime bill. He reasoned that assault weapons are a far cry from hunting rifles or even handguns. Despite his vote being the exception rather than the rule for Sanders' position on gun control, even this mild action earned him the ire of the NRA, which set out to get rid of him in 1994.

Having this one narrow issue eclipse some people's broader economic interests frustrated many Sanders' supporters. As Phil Philmonte, Sanders' 1994 campaign manager, put it:

> It was heart-breaking to see mostly young, working-class guys driving around in trucks with "Bye, Bye Bernie" bumper stickers. Many of these same people had voted for him in 1990 and 1992. Because of one lukewarm vote over an assault weapon ban these people were willing to get rid of the only political figure that spoke to their class interests.

The staff person for the Vermont Progressive Coalition, John Galleger, put it this way:

> That's what the Right tries to do, strip people off with a divide and conquer strategy. They get people to focus on abortion, guns, gays, etc. as a way of bringing them into the fold.

In the end, Sanders' supporters were able to realize the warning signs and regain campaign momentum just before election day. Sanders won re-election by a close margin of 50 to 47 percent. In 1996, he won re-election again, using a platform that, among other things, called for raising the minimum wage, a federal jobs program, "fair trade" instead of "free trade," progressive tax reform, national health care, pro-worker changes to labor laws, and campaign finance and election reform.

The Vermont Progressive Coalition

While Sanders' election to the US House of Representatives is the most well-known example of statewide activism, progressive political organizing has spread throughout Vermont generally. In Rutland, the state's second largest city, progressives have gotten onto the city council. In 1994, progressive city councillor Kevin Jones ran for mayor against a five-time incumbent. Although Jones lost the election, the fact that he gained over two-fifths of the vote revealed a strong progressive potential. This can be seen in other races as well. Unlike Rutland and Burlington, most Vermont towns do not have mayors, but are run by select boards. Progressives have won election to these bodies in several towns across the state.

Most important, local Progressive Coalition groups have developed throughout Vermont. The pattern in this regard has been set more by the examples of the towns of Brattleboro and Montpelier than Burlington. Unlike the latter, the local Progressive Coalitions in these towns did not grow out of the sudden taking of political office. Instead, they have had to steadily build up strength by combining electoral and non-electoral forms of activism.

Two Model Cases in Brattleboro and Montpelier

In Brattleboro, for example, activists energized by Sanders' 1988 House campaign set out to develop a local political movement. A good part of their work has centered around educational efforts. They have sponsored a successful series of progressive forums to encourage local discussions of the big political issues. Brattleboro's population is not more than 14,000, yet progressive activists consistently witnessed turn-outs of over 100 at their forums. The local group also linked up with progressive Democrats, labor unions, and other groups around the state to campaign for a statewide single-payer health care system. While the measure was defeated, it did became a major political issue—something that would not have happened without grassroots organizing.

Brattleboro progressives have also plunged into local electoral politics. Although most of these campaigns have been unsuccessful so far, they have demonstrated that progressives can run credible campaigns and that the Democratic Party can be thoroughly displaced by a progressive alternative. They have come quite close on several occasions to sending someone to the Vermont legislature. One progressive candidate ran for state office three times in District Two—in 1990, 1992, and 1994. Yet victory remained elusive. In 1992, she failed to win when the liberal Democratic candidate proved a spoiler. Although the Democrat lost badly, he took enough votes away from the progressive to allow the Republican to win. In 1994, she faced off against a big-name Republican who had been born and raised in the area. Even given the Progressive's door-to-door campaigning, the Republican won by a narrow margin. That same year, progressive businessperson Mark Hutchins ran for a state seat in a neighboring district. Hutchins lost by a mere fifty-seven votes.

In town politics, Brattleboro activists have won outright victories. Their candidates have won several seats on the school board and they now have roughly two dozen people, one-sixth of the membership, on the town's representative body. The main problem, as experienced by all the groups that we talked to, has been finding qualified candidates willing to run for office.

Vermont's capital in Montpelier has also witnessed strong progressive political activism. With a core group of just over twenty devoted activists, the Montpelier Progressive Coalition has fostered an impressive array of activities and projects. One of their committees, for example, secured a $3,500 grant to provide low-income groups with free access to the internet. By the summer of 1995, they had trained around 100 people how to e-mail their state representatives and how to find basic information on corporate taxation, legislative affairs, and other issues. This group has also established a world wide web page and produced syndicated progressive opinion pages used by other activist groups in Vermont. Another committee held a series of forums around low-income advocacy and education policy. Activists also held a dinner and fundraising performance, featuring a theater group that does plays about poor peoples' issues. Another special dinner focused on hunger issues. During it, people were served different proportions of food based upon the average caloric intake of different social classes in our society.

The coalition's radio committee succeeded in getting Jim Hightower's progressive talk show program aired locally while at the same time organizing a boycott of sponsors of G. Gordon Liddy's program. The Montpelier group gained some national coverage for their successful store-front art displays showing the impact of the Contract with America on real people. Local activists also pulled together progressive artists to design a poster to be used at events funded by the National Endowment for the Arts, highlighting the funding and the Republican designs to eliminate it.

As in Brattleboro, Montpelier activists have run progressives for local office. One of their school board candidates missed election by only twenty-eight votes out of the 2,400 cast. Additonally, they have placed issues directly on the ballot. One of the most active campaigns focused on a referendum measure to block tax breaks to corporations. Although it did not win a majority, it created a debate and forced government officials to admit that they had been too liberal in handing out public money. All this activity has given the local Progressive Coalition a presence in the community and a sense of momentum. By the summer of 1995, the group decided it was ready to begin systematically evaluating the local political demographics with an eye toward running several people for the state legislature.

The Birth of a Statewide Movement

All of this activism in towns across the state has coalesced into a statewide organization called the Vermont Progressive Coalition. Formed in 1990, originally as the Progressive Alliance of Vermont, the coalition merged the Burlington group with the Vermont Rainbow Coalition. Also helpful in launching the coalition were two earlier state-wide progressive "Solidarity Conferences" that helped bring activists from across Vermont into contact with each other. For its first few years, the Vermont Progressive Coalition did not really take off. It was, and remains, a coalition, not a formal party. Many of the coalition members were activists whose time and energy was already devoted to local organizing. The looseness of the organization's structure is indicated by the fact that during election campaigns some candidates use the label progressive, while others simply run as independents.

Concern over these problems has led to change. In 1995, the group took a major step toward reorganizing the Vermont Progressive Coalition by hiring a staff person and establishing a state office. The goals were to aid the formation and development of new local groups as well as help coordinate the existing groups. "Our goal is to pull together local activists and progressively-minded people around projects within their own community," explains staff person John Gallager. "We want people to have a sense of making real changes in their community and then linking that up to the broader effort."

While much of this grassroots activism involves locally grown issues, the Vermont Progressive Coalition has developed several coordinated state-wide efforts. For example, under the rubric of the Vermont Coalition for a Fair Budget, the Vermont Progressive Coalition pulled together various progressive groups, as well as its local chapters, to campaign against the Contract with America. The coalition developed a four-page, newspaper-sized pamphlet that described the human impact of the Republican agenda through the real stories of eight fellow Vermonters. Organizers aimed to have grassroots activists place the handout at every household door in the state. Indeed, by the end of the campaign, over 85,000 copies had been distributed across Vermont.

The Vermont Progressive Coalition has also thrown itself into the battle to reform the state's tax codes. Progressives want to replace the regressive property tax with a more equitable system. As one of their brochures states: "In order to achieve justice for all people, a fair system of taxation must be developed that is based on the ability to pay. This must include fundamental tax reform that cuts taxes for the majority while compelling all to pay their fair share."

During the summer of 1995, Vermont Progressive Coalition activists were handed an opportunity to publicize their political priorities when the nation's governors picked Burlington for their national conference. In response, over seventy-five Vermont grassroots organizations co-sponsored a People's Conference for Economic Democracy in the city during the conference. An extensive list of speakers, which included Bernie Sanders and progressives elected to the state legislature, was complemented by entertainment, information booths, voter registration tables, and a parade through Burlington's low-income neighborhood. Although by big-city standards the event was fairly modest, the turn-out of over 2,500 made the protest the state's largest grassroots demonstration in recent memory.

Since 1990, the Vermont Progressive Coalition has also had either two or three of its members elected to the state legislature, all from Burlington so far. As with Bernie Sanders in the US House, these representatives have been a progressive island in a sea of mainstream politicians. Yet they have an impact greater than their numbers. As they have publicly argued, the legislative process is dominated by the Speaker of the House. Since, unlike their Democratic counterparts, they are not beholden to the majority party, Progressive representatives are free to directly express the desires and interests of their constituency.

While in the legislature, Progressive representatives Dean Corren, Terry Bouricius, and Tom Smith have proven a thorn in the side of the Democratic majority. These three have been among the most active members in the state House, sponsoring more bills and amendments than any of their colleagues. These bills and amendments have frequently put liberal Democrats on the spot, forcing them to vote with their party against progressive proposals that they know they ought to support.

Progressive legislators have been part of a grassroots movement that has forced the state leadership to debate a single-payer health care system for Vermont. The majority in the legislature has been able, for now, to get around the single-payer bills by coming up with alternatives that do little to solve the health care crisis, but which give the public the impression that they are actually doing something about it. Progressives have also led a campaign to amend the state's constitution with an equal education opportunity amendment, in which the state would pledge to promote equitable, well-funded public education for all of Vermont's children. This activity increases the visibility of the Progressives and the need for an alternative to the Democratic Party.

The Connection With Bernie Sanders

The current status of the Vermont Progressive Coalition is one of steadily growing local groups, on the one hand, and a statewide congressional seat filled by an independent, on the other. How is this local activism and Bernie Sanders' election and re-election to Congress related? The answer is a complex one. Sanders has not had immediate coattails. People who vote for him do not automatically vote for a Progressive running for a state or local office. In part, this separation reflects the US electoral system, where the public is encouraged to look at candidates as individuals rather than as members of a political party or slate.

Furthermore, as the Progressives have not yet founded an official party organization, Sanders is legally required to run on his own. While openly a member and supporter of the Vermont Progressive Coalition, Sanders has used the label independent on his ballot line rather than progressive. This decision comes from the observation that people are disillusioned with parties and politics generally. Therefore, being an independent can prove a more immediate political asset than being tied to a political formation, even if it is not the Republicans or Democrats. Yet if the Vermont Progressive Coalition establishes itself as a legitimate state party, Sanders will be among its best-known candidates. This can only help the Progressive's efforts.

Sanders' victories have shown that a voting base does exist for a progressive agenda. While organizers have to win over and mobilize this base for their own local campaigns, the Sanders' example identifies where sympathetic voters live and how they can be mobilized. Moreover, Sanders' campaigns have helped bring together the activists who often form the building blocks of local grassroots political activism.

Sanders has a long history of directly supporting the progressive movement. The value of Sanders' willingness to speak on behalf of progressive groups and at progressive events cannot be overestimated. While the media might be able to downplay local activists, Bernie Sanders cannot be ignored. As a member of the US House of Representatives, he commands a certain level of public attention.

Sanders has also devoted both his personal and staff time to helping lay the ground work for a state party. Sanders' outreach coordinator, Phil Philmonte, has spent considerable effort helping to bring different grassroots groups and constituencies together. Following Sanders' 1994 re-election, for example, Philmonte began setting up a series of statewide conferences that brought together distinct constituencies to discuss their common concerns. The first conference saw over 400 senior citizens from the state's major senior citizen groups attend over a dozen workshops. A labor conference, attended by over 250 people, brought together the leadership of Vermont's four major unions at the same podium for the first time. The event produced follow-up meetings between the unions to develop concrete coordinated campaigns. An economic and social justice conference similarly pulled together leaders and social workers from among the state's low-income communities.

The most surprising conference, however, was the one for veterans, which was co-sponsored by every major veterans' group in the state. With his consistent opposition to US foreign policy in general and his distinction of being one of the few members of Congress to oppose the Gulf War, Bernie Sanders would, at first glance, seem to have little in common with veterans. During the conference, however, the common class issues came to the forefront. Sanders and veterans found that they both opposed Republican cuts to veterans programs and both agreed that the nation's leadership had not made good on its promises to those who had risked life and limb for their country.

By early fall 1995, Phil Philmonte was laying the plans for other gatherings on small businesses, environmental protection, and health care. Other ideas included a gathering of low-income people to help them develop basic activist skills, and a meeting between Sanders and teachers in an effort to get students involved in speaking out at congressional hearings about the issues important to them.

Each of the conferences have accomplished a number of goals. They have gotten groups often isolated from each other to meet and discuss their common concerns and goals. This process has led to greater coordination between groups. Furthermore, during these conferences Bernie Sanders emerges as a clear champion of the participants' issues. By working with these groups, Sanders has encouraged them to see him as their strongest ally. The conferences have also been run in a way that encourages groups to broaden their conception of politics—to see how their specific concerns tie into a progressive political agenda. During the veterans' conference, Sanders spoke about how cuts in veterans' benefits were tied to continued and expanded corporate welfare. Finally, this kind of outreach helps to strengthen the grassroots groups that progressives need to build their politics. It establishes greater unity among these groups and fosters a sense of being part of a single progressive political agenda. In developing these meetings, Sanders is helping to bring together the audience and the network that Vermont Progressive Coalition organizers can then develop into a political movement.

The Future

The Vermont Progressive Coalition is now moving in the direction of founding a political party. Key to reaching this goal, it must further develop active local groups and build greater strength in the Vermont legislature. The media has proven capable of ignoring two or three progressive representatives in the House. It will more likely have to cover a bloc of half a dozen to a dozen officeholders. This number of representatives could also potentially represent the swing vote in many legislative debates.

Until those conditions develop, however, the Vermont movement will remain a more informal network. The group is hesitant to transform itself into a political party before it is ready. Operating as an independent coalition does offer some advantages at the current moment. Forming a party throws down a kind of political gauntlet, challenging individuals and organizations to openly break with the two party system. In contrast, progressive organizations can currently support Sanders, and other Progressives when they run, yet also maintain some connection to the Democratic Party for other political contests.

While Vermont's Progressives are proceeding carefully, they clearly intend to seriously contest for power throughout the state. This means eventually establishing a progressive political party. The question is not if, but when. As they have in the past, Vermont activists are likely to continue to make national news and political history. They may even point the way for activists in other states.

While Vermont can not be considered a typical state, its unique characteristics should not lead us to write off the Vermont experience as too exceptional. The advantages of their small scale and a ready supply of progressive activists did not create the Vermont movement. The progressive voting base and their overall agenda is no different than used by progressive movements across the country. The advantages simply help explain why, by the mid-1990s, Vermont progressives are already talking about founding a political party, and seriously contesting statewide political power. In comparison, progressives in many other states are just beginning to build active local groups. Vermont is not the only state heading toward a major progressive independent political challenge. As we will see in the next chapter, New Party activists are doing the same kind of grassroots movement-building in several states across the country.

Chapter Seven

National Third Party Time?
The New Party

On a mid-June Sunday afternoon, close to two dozen people sit around a backyard in a north Milwaukee neighborhood. With the charcoal going strong and plenty of beer and soda in the icebox, this scene looks like a typical American cookout—except, perhaps, for the social mixing of whites, blacks, and Latinos. These people have come together, however, to practice a much more profound American tradition: grassroots democracy. Steve Heinz, a union organizer in his twenties, starts the conversation. He asks people to introduce themselves and say the first thing they would do if they were president. "I'd slash the military budget," imagines the first person in the circle. "I would repeal GATT and NAFTA," exclaims another. Others would institute a Canadian-style, single-payer health system, or rewrite labor laws to favor workers, or invest far more money in schools. The ideas go on. The people sitting in this backyard have some fundamentally different priorities than the people running this country.

That is why they are here, to learn about an exciting and innovative political organization aimed at making their priorities a reality. It's called the New Party and, as Heinz explains, it's about building a grassroots movement of ordinary Americans from the ground up. As he goes through the party's basic strategy and then into the successes they have had both in Milwaukee and elsewhere in the country, the audience becomes more energized. Heads nod and people murmur in agreement. The question and discussion session is quite lively. Most of the people in that backyard join the New Party—several become sustainers by pledging a monthly contribution toward building the organization. Everyone goes away with the sense that they have become part of something meaningful. They have tasted real grassroots democracy.

This Milwaukee Sunday afternoon was not an isolated event. A few days later, several similar house parties occurred elsewhere in the city. Local organizers hoped to hold at least thirty such meetings. Overall, during the summer of 1995, New Party activists in eight cities throughout the country organized similar house parties to expose their friends and neighbors to this growing political movement. By the end of the summer, this person-to-person outreach had reached several thousand people. The house parties are characteristic of the New Party's commitment to building a grassroots political organization from the bottom up.

Founded in 1992, the New Party is still a fledgling organization, yet it has enormous potential. By early 1996, the Party had already developed an impressive winning record by electing ninety-four of the 139 candidates that it has run for office. The New Party's goals are much broader than simply electing people to office, however. Even more important, it has established active and growing local groups in many parts of the country. New Party activists seek nothing less than to rebuild American democracy by getting ordinary people involved in politics. This means building a new type of political party—one that embodies a mass movement, is based in a grassroots membership, and is controlled from below. Through its organizing, the New Party aims to foster leadership within local communities and among everyday citizens.

The goal of constructing a grassroots membership organization provides one reason why the group has taken a third party route. As a national pamphlet explains, even if progressives could succeed in "taking over" the Democratic Party, it would not be the organization that progressives need. The Democratic Party has no organic connection between the organization and its voting base. It has no mobilized grassroots structure to hold its officeholders accountable. Furthermore, the New Party is engaged in a political process that is fundamentally different than the vote-getting culture of the two major parties. "We don't wait until five months before the election to start to groom voters," stresses Milwaukee organizer Tammy Johnson. "We are building a movement 365 days a year."

The New Party's Basic Strategy

The major components of the New Party's strategy all revolve around this fundamental goal. For all tactical and strategic questions, activists ask if a given approach or action will help build the grassroots structure. So far, the Party has identified eight key components to successful movement-building.

1. Start Local, Think Global

Thinking about changing the course of Congress or even electing a progressive governor can seem like an overwhelming task. Starting local makes more sense. The New Party has learned a lesson from an unlikely source: the Christian Right. In the late 1980s, the Christian Coalition set out to alter the national debate. With major national battles now going on over school prayer, reproductive rights, school vouchers, and gay and lesbian rights, we are experiencing the fruits of their strategy. By the summer of 1994, the religious Right had taken control of the Republican state committees in a dozen states and were making serious inroads into several others.[1] How did they do it? They realized that the key to national power was to start in one's own backyard—running candidates for school boards, city councils, and county boards while using targeted local issue activism to build further momentum and membership.

The New Party rejects the Christian Coalition's party-within-a-party approach, their covert tactics of running candidates who conceal their affiliations, and their strategy of relying upon low voter turn-out to win through a disciplined voting bloc. The New Party has, however, adopted the coalition's wisdom that the key to national power is to start locally. While state and national races may seem to deliver a larger audience and greater publicity, in reality, such electoral bids do little to build a fledgling movement. Because they require a great deal of time and money, they can easily burn out activists, leaving little energy after the campaign to do the more important work of organization-building. Furthermore, unless a group has enough of a grassroots structure to give it a serious community presence, the corporate media will be able to largely ignore the alternative candidates anyway. Also, without a serious community presence already in place, state and national candidates are going to have little chance of success. People are not going to waste their votes on protest candidates. Activists are not going to spend their time and energy supporting candidates who are going to have insignificant returns.

At the same time, local efforts that simply remain local tend not to last. While local races are more accessible and local government can have a significant impact on people's lives, ultimately, the economic and political forces controlling people's futures have to be fought at a higher level. Local government does not have the power to change the direction of the country by itself. Therefore, activists need to have a sense that their small-scale, local efforts are adding up to something that is much larger and more powerful. People need to feel that they are a part of history in the making. Both the Christian Coalition and the New Party combine a national structure and strategy with local, grassroots-based activity. Such a strategy entails years of seemingly quiet local activity that is not going to make the evening news. Yet as the religious Right has shown, this strategy can create news-making results down the road. Representative Bernie Sanders agrees:

> *The New Party deserves a lot of credit because they are doing things at the local level—which is what we did in Burlington. That, to me, is critical. I get a little tired of people who make all the right analyses and decide they want to run for President of the world but they aren't willing to do the basic grassroots work.*[2]

2. Be Practical, Have Patience

Grassroots work requires practical people with patience. As a national New Party pamphlet explains: "We don't intend to run where we don't have a serious chance of winning... We want to build from positions of real strength, where we really can win, and gradually increase our capacity to do so at higher and higher levels of office." Even if only small scale, real victories that deliver real changes in people's lives makes the movement a serious effort that people want to join.

Holding some house parties may not seem nearly as important as running a candidate for mayor. Yet if the house parties are going to increase the membership base and help develop new leaders and activists, then such activities will expand the capacity of the movement. In contrast, if the movement is so young that a mayoral candidate has no chance of success, then such a campaign may simply use up the resources of the existing group while bringing in few new people. Similarly, running just a few candidates for local offices that can win is more important than trying to put together a more comprehensive local slate if most of that slate stands little chance of success.

The Christian Coalition's experience serves as a lesson. While aiming for national influence, they embarked on a long-range plan of a decade or more. Grassroots organizing takes time. "This is a project for life," Doug Kratch, co-chair of the Wisconsin chapter of the New Party, emphasizes. "We are not based on a charismatic leader that will deliver immediately flashy results. We are constructing a lasting political movement that is based solidly in our communities." As Steve Heinz stressed to the house party he hosted in Milwaukee, "We have a twenty-year plan."

3. Flexibility

While sticking firmly to its core values of democracy, economic justice, and equality, the New Party remains open in the tactics it uses to build the movement. The New Party's flexibility is especially clear in its relationship to the Democratic Party. It forcefully stands for building a new political organization and movement run by ordinary people. As a growing, yet still young movement, there are a great deal of offices that it does not yet have the ability to win, but that Democrats could. Furthermore, because the Democratic Party has traditionally offered left-leaning people the only realistic path to office, it contains within it some good progressive candidates who may not yet be willing to leap into third party politics. In such situations, the New Party believes the tactic of cross endorsement, or "fusion," offers a way to use these progressive-minded, major-party people to build the political movement.

Under fusion, more than one party nominates the same candidate for office. That person receives the combined votes cast on the major party's ballot line and the New Party's line. Fusion allows supporters to register their third party sympathies, while still being able to support good people within the major parties. The third party also does not become a spoiler in this scenario, taking away votes from a progressive Democrat and allowing a Republican to win. In fact, fusion can actually help progressive major-party candidates, since the New Party could use its own mobilization efforts to get non-voters to vote. Fusion is also important because it allows similarly minded third parties to pool their votes by running joint slates of candidates.

Fusion has been used historically by third parties, such as the Populists at the end of the nineteenth century. When the balance between the major parties is close enough, the third party's votes can be the margin of victory. Past third parties used such margins to increase their bargaining position with the major parties, even winning major party cross endorsements for their candidates. The tactic is still used today in such states as New York. During his years in office, Governor Mario Cuomo got re-elected as a candidate of both the Democratic and Liberal parties.

Clearly, fusion has to be used with great care and only in situations where it is appropriate. Used incorrectly, it could blur distinctions between the major and minor parties to the detriment of the latter. Many grassroots activists also have some pretty strong feelings about rejecting the Democratic Party. Nevertheless, the fact that it was made illegal in most states during the time when the Populists and other third parties used the tactic to great effect speaks to its value as a tool for fledgling political movements. Currently, fusion is legal in only ten states—and practiced in only two of those.

Thus, while trying to make fusion legal, many New Party chapters that enter partisan races have chosen to run their candidates in the Democratic primaries and then use the major-party label to win the election. In Missoula, Montana, for example, the Party has established a working majority on the city council by running candidates as Democrats. Roughly 10 to 15 percent of all New Party campaigns have used the Democratic Party ballot line. So far, only 5 percent of candidates in partisan races have been on the New Party ballot line. This, of course, is only the beginning. The most victories have all been for candidates running in non-partisan races. Combining such efforts with making fusion legal again allows for a flexible approach to build the grassroots strength now that will allow it to run explicitly third party candidates for those same offices in the future.

While both LEAP and the New Party enter candidates in Democratic Party primaries, their strategies are very different. LEAP intends to build a progressive bloc within the state Democratic Party and to pull the Party to the left. In contrast, the New Party is dedicated to building an independent party. It uses the Democratic Party line to produce the kind of winning campaigns that build up a grassroots structure necessary for the more difficult task of winning elections outside the two party system. This strategy is based on the assumption that real victories do more to build the movement than politically pure, but marginal candidates. The New Party is committed to avoiding the wasted-vote syndrome that has destroyed most fledgling third party efforts. When people support the New Party, they know that they are going to see concrete results. Furthermore, the New Party seeks a majority base. This means going after and trying to mobilize such large populations as Jesse Jackson's base as well as the labor movement's rank and file. A flexible strategy provides the best way of reaching out to these people and drawing them away from the Democratic Party. Obviously, such tactics are not problem-free. The New Party as it grows will have to continually negotiate its balance between third party strategy and Democratic Party ballot line tactics.

4. Electoral Campaigns Are Not Enough

The New Party also breaks with the major parties' practice of isolating electoral campaigns from other kinds of activism within the community. Indeed, the New Party was founded, in part, precisely to link issue campaigns, community organizing, and other sorts of advocacy work to electoral activity. While the progressive community is currently fragmented into single-issue campaigns and concerns, the electoral realm provides the one major arena in which progressives can get beyond their specific areas of struggle to formulate a more unified and forward-looking vision of the society they want to build. They can then apply this vision in electoral campaigns and win positions in the government. They can also take the vision back into their communities to enhance their non-electoral activism by linking it to this broader agenda.

Electoral politics, in this approach, provides a bridge for connecting people with other forms of grassroots organizing. Americans are taught to think of "politics" narrowly, as nothing more than electoral campaigns and voting. Grassroots organizing outside electoral politics can seem "radical" to many ordinary people. Yet, by putting an electoral face on movement politics, the New Party is providing a path to "radical" activism that many more people might feel comfortable joining once they get some exposure to the issues, activists, and successes of community organizing.

The New Party is also not content to simply compete in the existing electoral system. Dominated by the two major parties, our system has many aspects that are not democratic and do not favor third party movements. One important aspect of New Party organizing focuses on changing the rules of the game. This involves legally challenging prohibitions on fusion, increasing ballot access to third party candidates, and reforming campaign financing to take private money out of politics. In Minnesota, for example, the Twin Cities New Party succeeded in getting a bill called the New Democracy Act introduced into the state legislature by Representative Andy Dawkins and Senator Sandy Pappas. In the words of the New Party newsletter, "the Act is a package of a dozen new ideas designed to revitalize, open up, and generally make democracy something more than a spectator sport."[3] It includes provisions to legalize fusion, allow sixteen-year-olds to vote in school board elections, shorten campaign seasons, provide free airtime to candidates who agree to spending limits, and establish a citizen's campaign jury to monitor political advertising and convene public debates.

This substantial commitment to non-electoral grassroots organizing further demonstrates the New Party's dedication to building an independent political force. While some of its candidates win office under the Democratic Party label, grassroots New Party organizing draws people into the membership and leadership roles of a broad political movement that is clearly outside the status quo and the two party system.

5. Diversity

No progressive political movement can succeed in this country unless it unites the diverse groups that make up the majority of the nation's rich tapestry. This means crossing barriers of class, gender, age, and, perhaps most importantly, race. The grassroots organizers interviewed for this book, whether from Connecticut, Wisconsin, or New Mexico, all pointed to race as the single most difficult division facing the progressive movement. When attending local New Party meetings, examining the list of New Party candidates, or meeting New Party activists at a national leadership conference, one is struck by the mixture of black, white, and brown faces. As a result of hard work, the New Party is already a multiracial movement. Roughly a third of the membership is African American and 10 percent is Latino. Half the candidates that local groups have run for office have been people of color. Yet, even with these significant achievements, the task of promoting racial diversity is never ending. Without constant attention, specific chapters and levels of leadership will reflect the white character of their founding.

The New Party has also made a special effort to involve young people. In the spring of 1995, it sponsored teach-ins at a few dozen campuses across the country, calling the effort the Rock the Boat Tour: Take America Back Before They Drown Us. Later that summer, it pulled together a gathering of New Party student activists for a training weekend at a farm in Wisconsin. In October, students active in the New Party at the University of Wisconsin in Madison worked with other student groups to sponsor a major Midwest student conference. Over 100 students from Wisconsin, Michigan, Minnesota, Indiana, Illinois, and Iowa met to strengthen their organizing skills and develop their strategic perspectives. The next year, the New Party participated in Democracy Summer '96. Organized under the auspices of the New Majority Education Fund, the project recruited and trained young would-be activists in basic grassroots organizing skills. Supported with $100 a week stipends, these activists were then sent to projects in one of several states to join in campaigns around raising the minimum wage, equal education spending, and campaign finance reform.

In other areas, roughly two out of five New Party members are either in unions or have connections to the labor movement. One-quarter of the membership describes itself as having professional occupations, while the other three-quarters is working class. Half the membership is women, although efforts need to continue to promote women in positions of leadership.

6. Internal Democracy

A movement that hopes to democratize our society must itself be internally democratic. The New Party is organized in a decentralized manner. State and local chapters enjoy a high degree of autonomy, and the national office exists to serve their organizing efforts. While local and state chapters have a great deal of latitude over how they organize themselves, their bylaws and procedures have to be consistent with, although not identical to, those of the national organization. The fact that each local chapter has its own distinct name, such as Progressive Milwaukee and Progressive Dane in Wisconsin, symbolizes this grassroots autonomy.

Currently, the national party is directed by an interim executive board. Two representatives are elected by members in each state where there are active chapters. This structure is intended as a short-term measure until the New Party can hold a national convention. Until now, the New Party has resisted following the traditional path of political organizations, in which the group is founded through a large-scale national convention that draws up the formalities of a national organization. All too often, groups have a big founding national convention, their activists go home, and the organization is never heard from again. Consistent with its bottom-up strategy, the New Party has instead focused on building active local chapters. It will hold a national convention when this grassroots activism has developed enough, and has sufficient diversity, to make a founding convention a truly demo-cratic and meaningful undertaking. In the meantime, the New Party has sponsored leadership summits to bring activists together from across the country to discuss the movement.

A similar logic explains why the Party has not developed a national platform. It is easy for a bunch of activists to get together and draw up such a document. But for a platform to really represent the agenda of ordinary Americans, a party has to first develop the grassroots structure that allows people's desires and ideas to filter from the bottom up. This is the only way to produce a program that offers a vision understood and supported by party members. Meanwhile, national party literature does point to general progressive values, such as an environmentally sustainable, socially just economy; opposition to all forms of discrimination; democracy; and peaceful and equitable economic development worldwide. The New Party's slogan is: "A Fair Economy, A Real Democracy, A New Party."

7. Institutional Support

The New Party is an organization of individuals rather than a formal coalition of groups. Yet, like LEAP, part of the New Party's success comes from its ability to gain institutional support. The Association of Community Organizations for Reform Now (ACORN) has been a major contributor. As one of the nation's largest coalitions of community groups, ACORN's support has been one of the reasons that the New Party has had such success in mobilizing low-income neighborhoods and people of color. Many of the New Party's initiatives, such as living wage campaigns, have built broad coalitions and brought in institutional support in less formal ways. When we interviewed New Party organizers in Wisconsin, we found ourselves talking to major institutional figures, such as two secretary-treasurers of local labor federations, the director of a school reform organization, and the director of an innovative jobs training program. While the organizations had no formal membership in the New Party, the participation of their leadership has brought key connections, resources, and concrete skills.

The participation of organizational and individual institutional players has helped provide the New Party a level of professionalism that is very much evident in its activities. The New Party has drawn in people who have experience as major players in their community. The New Party has also proven successful, relative to other groups, in raising money, and was able to support a staff of roughly twenty people in 1996. Most of these paid organizers are out in the field, helping to build active and effective local party chapters.

8. Making Politics Enjoyable

Emma Goldman once said, "If I can't dance, I don't want to be part of your revolution." Yet, for most people, politics seems boring and tedious. It does not help if progressives come across as dour, heavy, and dogmatic.

The New Party was founded on serious needs and issues. It is involved in the life and death struggle over the future of people's lives and communities. The party promotes an internal culture that is welcoming and enjoyable, while not losing sight of the gravity of the situation. New Party publications often use humor as a part of their message.

Local New Party meetings which we attended also have a sense of energy and enthusiasm about them. People enjoy coming to New Party events. It is exciting to go into one's community and talk to people about a serious and practical political movement that is genuinely concerned with ordinary people. As Milwaukee resident Richard Berghofer exclaimed after spending two hours going door-to-door talking with people about the living wage campaign: "I could keep doing this for hours. People are so enthusiastic, this is really fun." We live in a society in which people often live quite isolated lives. A movement that pays attention to generating a positive and inclusive sense of community is going to go quite far. A hundred years ago, the populist and socialist movements were not just a political exercise for tens of thousands of local activists. They were a way of life.

Progressive Organizing in Wisconsin

To better understand how these eight principles operate in reality, its best to turn to New Party activity in Wisconsin, the group's strongest chapter. Wisconsin activists actually began organizing on their own a year before the national party even came into being. In their strategy and approach, the Wisconsin movement represents the basic model of New Party organizing across the country.

Progressive Milwaukee: One Chapter's Story

The spirit and energy of New Party organizing in Wisconsin is evident in the campaign for a living wage. One summer evening, Richard Berghofer, a local resident and union member, worked with several teams going door-to-door in one of Milwaukee's most diverse neighborhoods. The people living on his assigned street seemed quite familiar with the individual pain and community-destroying cruelty of poverty-level wages. He walked up to a modest-looking old wooden house and was greeted by Rosa Rodrigez, a young Latina woman in her mid-thirties, who cautiously peered through her screen door. "Hello," he said, "I'm a volunteer for an organization called Progressive Milwaukee that is dedicated to bringing family-supporting jobs back into our communities. If you have a moment, I would like to tell you about a campaign we have going to raise the minimum wage." With an encouraging response from her, Richard goes on to explain that we need to do something about the low wage jobs that are killing our community. She agrees, the minimum wage is just appalling. "People work hard, but you can't support a family on $4.25 an hour—that's just ridiculous," she stresses.

Berghofer continues to explain how it is about time that Milwaukee's political leaders take a firm stand for raising the standards in our communities and moves the conversation toward action. He asks her to support a city and county ordinance that would require all private companies that bid for public contracts to pay a living wage to their employees. Rodrigez gets a glint in her eyes as she imagines the possibilities: $7.70 an hour plus health and dental—that would be some job! This is only the first step, says Berghofer, "We want to raise the job standards in our community across the board." After signing a pledge card supporting the living wage initiative, Rodrigez enthusiastically takes a flyer announcing upcoming hearings on the city ordinance in her neighborhood. "I'll be there," she promises. "You know you are the first person that's come knocking at my door that I've enjoyed talking to."

When Berghofer crosses the street, he has even better luck. Three African-American men not only sign pledge cards, but also want to know how they can get involved in the campaign. Door after door, Berghofer and other volunteers are greeted with similar expressions of support as they talk about a problem that plagues these people's community. Whether they are black, brown, or white; male or female; low or middle income; young or old; everyone wants to sign a pledge card. Many want to know how they can get involved. After two hours of canvassing, the Progressive Milwaukee volunteers go back to their headquarters with almost 100 signed cards and a feeling that they have accomplished something.

Indeed, their activities that evening represent the flowering growth of a new progressive political movement in this city of nearly 700,000. Twenty-five years after the last Socialist mayor left city hall, Milwaukee is again seeing people organizing to gain control of their communities and to reclaim the ideals of democracy. The counter-attack against the right-wing political agenda of the 1980s and 1990s has begun.

Electoral Success

In the summer of 1991, activists from labor and community organizations began coming together to discuss a better approach to change. They formed Progressive Milwaukee. As Bruce Colburn, Secretary Treasurer of the Milwaukee County Labor Council and Progressive Milwaukee founder, explained:

> *Many of us had spent years fighting around our own battles—organizing our own groups to fight for decent jobs, for housing, for justice, for peace, and against discrimination. We realized, however, that power to control our own futures, our own jobs, our own communities was slipping further and further away. Some of us had rejected or given up on making change through elections. Others of us had worked tirelessly during elections finding over and over again that the political parties were, at their best, not accountable and clearly lacked any real plan for change.*

Progressive Milwaukee was originally founded to achieve a specific goal: to find, recruit, and support for political office people with a proven track record of fighting for progressive change. The group met with immediate success. In the spring of 1992, they ran or endorsed five candidates for the Milwaukee county board. Four of the five won, including Roger Quindel, who beat a twenty-four-year incumbent in a supposedly conservative working-class district. Beginning in the fall of 1992, Progressive Milwaukee took the plunge into state politics when it backed community activist Johnnie Morris-Tatum for a seat in the state legislature. She went on to win a stunning victory by defeating the incumbent in the Democratic primary. Considered a long shot when she first entered the race, Morris-Tatum now has such a solid base that she ran unopposed for re-election in 1994.

These initial victories were just the beginning. In 1993 and 1994, the group entered and won two special elections for county supervisors. On city council, incumbent Don Richards declared himself a member of Progressive Milwaukee and then won re-election in 1996. Also that spring, Roger Quindel was re-elected and a new member, James White, joined him on the county board.

In the spring of 1995, Progressive Milwaukee took on major segments of the mobilized local business community, the local media, and the governor in a fight over who was going to determine the future of Milwaukee's public schools.[4] Like school districts across the country, the Milwaukee Public School (MPS) system is in need of urgent reforms. The right-wing and the business community have exploited these needs to serve their own interests by promoting a "reform" agenda that includes privatization and school vouchers. For the 1995 local school board races, the Milwaukee business community placed itself behind five candidates who supported contracting out the school system to the Edison Project, a for-profit management company, and expanding currently limited voucher programs. In addition to helping two embattled incumbents, Progressive Milwaukee mobilized a major campaign to elect Rose Daitsman in the one citywide race.

This latter battle represented a classic struggle of people power versus corporate money. Daitsman's opponent, John Garder, who was both pro-privatization and pro-school-vouchers, received ample campaign funding from the business community. Almost none of his contributions came in amounts under $500. In addition to corporate wealth, all five business candidates enjoyed the support of the MPS superintendent, the mayor, and most of the local media. Progressive Milwaukee and other groups countered the establishment's power with grassroots campaigning and fundraising. Over 100 volunteers ran a large-scale phone and mailing campaign. Through house parties, friends writing letters to other friends, and contributions from union PACs, Daitsman's campaign raised over $30,000. Such resources allowed her to purchase airtime on local television. In the end, four of the five candidates who opposed privatization won, including two incumbents backed by Progressive Milwaukee. In the citywide race, where the business community had expected to win easily, Rose Daitsman came within 2,000 votes of defeating John Garder, out of 60,000 cast. The opposition to right-wing, business-oriented school "reform" had made its voice heard. Again, Progressive Milwaukee had proven itself a major and growing player in local politics.

Interestingly, in the group's experience of running candidates, the campaigns to get people elected have proven the easiest part of the process. "We have actually found it more difficult to recruit good candidates and also to then hold them accountable once in office," explains John Goldstein, president of the Transit Workers local. To help make candidacy a less daunting task, as well as to produce skilled campaigners, Progressive Milwaukee has developed a candidate training program. Through workshops, committed and potential candidates get a clear view of what the New Party is about and how it differs from mainstream politics in its process and expectations. The training also provides a good amount of practical preparation, such as how to talk with the media, how to formulate a coherent message, how to mobilize one's base supporters, and how to deal with attacks from opponents and the media.

A Grassroots Membership Organization

Although founded to recruit and run progressive candidates, Progressive Milwaukee has evolved into a broader political movement. The thrust of the group's organizing work is to build a grassroots organization within Milwaukee's neighborhoods that will not just elect people to office, but, also, hold those officeholders accountable once elected, and fight for the interests of ordinary people all year round. Such a grassroots structure would provide a space, which does not exist today, where ordinary people can get together to discuss politics as actual collective actors in the process.

To build the organization, Progressive Milwaukee is a dues-paying membership organization. For $36 a year ($12 for low-income people) individuals become formal members. Dues go to support, among other things, a fulltime staff person. Since its founding, the group has sustained a steady momentum of doubling its membership every year. Initially, Progressive Milwaukee consisted of only three dozen members. The next year, there were over seventy-five, and the year after, 150. By the summer of 1995, with the group on the eve of two major new grassroots organizing projects, Progressive Milwaukee had a membership of over 300. This membership cuts across the spectrum of the progressive community. In addition, Progressive Milwaukee aims to involve people who have never been active in progressive politics before.

Getting people's money and formal membership does not, by itself, create grassroots democracy. Real democracy means that people get together to decide their own collective futures. They participate in the organization so that it is propelled by them. Progressive Milwaukee clearly expects an active membership. "About once a month a member is going to get a call asking them to be active," explains staff person Tammy Johnson. "Whether it's helping with a mailing, going to a public hearing, attending a meeting, making phone calls, or staffing a table, we want our members to get involved in some tangible way." The organization also actively seeks the views of its membership. Since its founding, Progressive Milwaukee has conducted at least three membership surveys soliciting feedback on specific issues, elected officials, and electoral work generally. Furthermore, membership meetings have seen lively discussions over such topics as the goals and purpose of the group.

To get people active in a living, breathing organization requires grassroots leadership. A true grassroots organization needs to cultivate activists in the neighborhoods that it wants to represent. To build an active membership, Progressive Milwaukee has developed a Precinct Leader Action Network (PLAN). PLAN is an ongoing network of coordinated volunteers who commit to talking to their neighbors and handing out literature in their neighborhood. Several times each election cycle, PLAN volunteers will be asked to register voters, educate and identify supporters, mobilize them around an issue or campaign, and get them to vote on election day. Ultimately, organizers hope to develop PLAN activists whose efforts extend well beyond the election cycle. As genuine grassroots leaders, such activists would be spokespeople for their neighbor's concerns, get people to participate in efforts to do something about those concerns, and encourage them to join and be active in the organization. Progressive Milwaukee wants to provide ordinary citizens, especially those who are now politically apathetic, a channel to participate in political decisions in ways that make real changes in their lives.

Progressive Milwaukee organizes its electoral and non-electoral campaigns with this goal of generating grassroots leadership in mind. For example, when Richard Berghofer went out onto the streets for the living wage campaign, he did not just ask people to sign cards or attend a public hearing. He also sought to find out who was willing to get involved in the campaign. After handing in their signed cards, Progressive Milwaukee activists followed up with those rated as potential leaders, told them more about the campaign, and invited them to get involved.

The exact blocks covered were also not random. Campaign organizers concentrated the effort initially in Milwaukee's Ward Six. The idea was to send out volunteers week after week to contact every household in the ward. Not only would this generate visible support for the living wage campaign, but it would leave behind a list of contacts and activists. Through a focused effort, Progressive Milwaukee hoped the campaign would produce the human infrastructure to build a solid grassroots party. The sixth ward offered a good test case. With its multiethnic population, its range of middle to low income groups, and its progressive history, the ward could produce the kind of diverse grassroots structure that Progressive Milwaukee wants to mobilize.

Starting with a fairly modest volunteer pool, organizers set goals that could only be achieved if these initial volunteers succeeded in activating a much larger number of community residents.

The PLAN has been successful. On the Northside, the network had grown by the spring of 1996 to include eighty-six precinct leaders and several hundred people who had signed "activist contracts" committing themselves to working on electoral efforts as well as campaigns around living wage jobs, welfare reform, and the environment. During the following summer, New Party activists expanded their volunteer and leadership base through another series of house parties. They also looked toward continued expansion of their Northside PLAN and the possibility of setting up a new one on the Southside, which includes a significant Latino community.

Progressive Milwaukee's grassroots organizing has also begun to build concrete relationships with local unions. The local branch of the Service Employees International Union (SEIU) helped Progressive Milwaukee's living wage effort with funding and volunteer support. The union has been looking for new ways to mobilize their rank-and-file membership and to participate more directly in community activism. In the course of canvassing, Progressive Milwaukee volunteers are contacting SEIU members and drawing them into the community effort.

This commitment to grassroots organization-building is also clear in Progressive Milwaukee's election efforts. The group only develops or endorses candidates who are dedicated to the broader movement. While in office, they must be dues-paying members of the organization and actively work on Progressive Milwaukee events. This relationship is formalized through candidate contracts. Upon signing them, Progressive Milwaukee pledges to support a candidate's campaign with training, volunteers, and fundraising. In return, the candidates pledge to support the organization's growth by being open about their affiliation with it and helping in concrete ways to build the grassroots movement.

This kind of grassroots structure has promising potential. When participating in Progressive Milwaukee events, one is struck by the fact that the activists are not just the "usual suspects" from leftist groups, but ordinary people who know they're being screwed, and had never before found an avenue for fighting back. Rather than preaching to the converted, Progressive Milwaukee's basic goal is to build leadership and organization among ordinary people by reaching out to the large pool of frustrated citizens who want something better for themselves and their children, yet see no viable alternative. If the experience of Progressive Milwaukee, and the New Party generally, is any indication, there are hundreds of thousands of would-be grassroots leaders waiting to be contacted.

Practicality—Start Small, Think Big

In addition to its commitment to building a grassroots membership organization, several other characteristics stand out in the Milwaukee experience that illustrate the New Party's basic strategy. Progressive Milwaukee emphasizes bottom-up practicality. The group only enters elections that it has a reasonable chance of winning. Organizers see little utility in running protest candidates who will get few votes and do little to build the organization. Therefore, the still young organization has focused on local races when it can use volunteer power to bring victories.

For example, Milwaukee's school board races are routinely decided by margins of a few hundred votes because most people stay home on election day. In the 1995 spring school board races, only one out of five registered voters actually cast a ballot. An individual district race may see as few as 5,000 and no more than 10,000 votes. In 1995, only 60,000 votes were cast for the citywide school board seat. Similar margins hold true for city council and county board races, which also vary between 5,000 to 10,000 votes. With such a low volume of votes, these races can provide opportunities for a newly formed grassroots organization. By carefully picking their fights, activists can have a serious chance of winning.

And there is nothing like winning. In the eyes of Milwaukee activists, even successes that come on a small-scale build people's enthusiasm and give the organization an image of seriousness. Of the eleven races that the group has entered, it has won all but two. This is the track record of a serious political organization. When Progressive Milwaukee enters a race, they intend to win. People who join a Progressive Milwaukee campaign know that their time and energy is being well spent.

Not only are local races immediately winnable, but these offices can make a real difference in people's lives. When Progressive Milwaukee entered the school board races, it joined a fundamental struggle against business interests and the Christian Right over the fate of public education and the upbringing of future generations. Similarly, the Milwaukee county board has an annual budget of close to $1 billion and funds a whole range of social services. Local politics involves issues in which people can see a direct connection between electoral efforts and changes in their lives and communities.

The right-wing political agenda has, if anything, increased the importance of local offices. In its crusade against social spending and business regulation, the Right has tried to limit government power by shifting responsibilities for programs and policies from the federal level to the state and from the state to local government. In the area of social spending, this local "empowerment" is hypocritical since "decentralization" has brought lower levels of overall funding support. These changes do mean that state and local government will play an increased role in policies that were once seen as beyond the reach of grassroots political movements.

Another attraction of local races is that they are often non-partisan: people run as individuals with no party line appearing on the ballot. Although most people think of electoral politics as contests between two clear parties, in actuality, 70 percent of all elected offices in this country are non-partisan.[5] In an official political culture that considers anything outside the two party system highly unrealistic, third party politics means asking people to make quite a leap. In non-partisan races, however, the party ballot line is not a factor. There is no basis for rejecting candidates because they are supposedly not serious contenders simply due to their lack of official Democratic or Republican credentials.

In fact, a new political group can have an advantage if it endorses non-partisan candidates when the local major parties do not make such organizational efforts. The key task is to make sure that voters make the connection between the institutional political movement and the non-partisan candidates, in spite of the fact that the formal process does not recognize the link. Ironically, given the system's origins, Progressive Milwaukee has benefited from an electoral system that extends non-partisanship not only to the school boards, which is common, but also to city councils and county assemblies. Thus, the group has been able to launch a growing electoral effort to obtain local power without ever having to run full force into the "major"/"minor" party debate.

In moving to higher-level, partisan offices, Progressive Milwaukee has developed a flexible insider/outsider approach to the Democratic Party. In cases where the group has a realistic chance at success by running a candidate on the New Progressive Party line, they will do so. When this is not possible, Progressive Milwaukee is open to using the Democratic primaries to win that party's nomination for a specific office. With Johnnie Morris-Tatum, Progressive Milwaukee had the chance to send a grassroots activist with a proven record of challenging the system to the state legislature by displacing the Democratic incumbent through the primary system. The key is that even though Morris-Tatum is officially a Democrat, she has committed to building Progressive Milwaukee as an independent voice for ordinary people. Whether running on their own ballot line or the Democrat's, the group focuses its attention on replacing bad officeholders who are not representing the interests of working people with committed progressives.

Crossing the Racial Divide

Another striking characteristic of Progressive Milwaukee is the group's multiethnic composition. Go to a Progressive Milwaukee event and you will see all the colors of the human rainbow. While racism provides the Right with a major organizing tool, racial divisions continue to hamper progressive activism. Unfortunately, genuine coalition and multiracial participation among progressives is still all too rare. Yet Progressive Milwaukee is notable for the degree to which it has crossed the racial divide. This has not happened by itself, but has required constant effort. The initial organizers paid particular attention to having a diverse group of people at the outset. Many had the advantage of having worked in several multiracial coalitions during the 1970s and 1980s. The group has also tried to generate a public face that is multiethnic and welcoming. Their steering committee embodies diversity and they have run multiracial slates for office. Progressive Milwaukee's first staff person was an African-American woman.

Furthermore, the group has focused on issues that are of general interest to the broad community and of central concern to people of color, including education, jobs, and living wages. This is key to crossing the racial divide. Milwaukee has experienced one of the most dramatic deteriorations of a black community in the country. Because of a former concentration of unionized, industrial jobs, Milwaukee once had the highest paid African-American workforce in the United States. After twenty years of deindustrialization, however, the city's black workers now have the second lowest earnings of any major city. In addition, Milwaukee has a steadily growing Latino population with similar economic issues, such as the need for decent family-supporting jobs. If present trends continue, Latinos will be the largest minority group in the city by the year 2000.

Organizing this multiethnic base has not been easy. Milwaukee is a highly segregated city. Racial barriers continually threaten to separate activists and communities that ought to be part of a common political movement. Yet Progressive Milwaukee is committed to this task. It was founded in response to the political agenda of the Right, which exploits white racial fears as one of the primary justifications for its policies.

In 1993, Progressive Milwaukee witnessed firsthand the power of the city's racial system. That year, the superintendent of the Milwaukee public schools called for a referendum to raise $366 million to rebuild the crumbling inner city school system. Progressive Milwaukee took up the cause by organizing a broad coalition behind the measure and doing extensive grassroots work including phone banking, direct mail, and literature drops. The referendum's decisive defeat (30,984 in favor compared with 93,948 against) reflected the nation's racial chasm as whites voted overwhelmingly against giving more funds to what they saw as mostly minority schools. Voter turn-out and political alienation also played a big role, as voting in heavy African-American wards ran as low as 16 percent, while turn-out in predominantly white areas exceeded 50 percent.[6]

The centrality of race to US politics means that a progressive political movement can never afford to not deal with the issue. Even with its notable successes, "There is still a great deal more we can do," explains Bruce Colburn. "What we have achieved is very fragile. Unless we continually work at multiethnic participation, it can easily fall apart. Instead, we have to expand our diversity."

Coalition-Building and Community Organizing

With its emphasis on building a movement rather than simply electing a few candidates, it comes as no surprise that Progressive Milwaukee places as much emphasis on non-electoral activism as it does on electoral campaigns. The ultimate criterion in either case is whether or not the activity will build the grassroots organization and deliver real improvements in people's lives. By far, the group's greatest attempt to link electoral to non-electoral work has been Progressive Milwaukee leadership's role in initiating a bold economic organizing project called the Campaign for a Sustainable Milwaukee.

Sustainable Milwaukee is nothing less than a comprehensive community agenda for the city's future. It emerged out of the growing feeling among progressive activists that they needed to do something new and different. For years, a vibrant array of labor, environmental, religious, and community organizations had fought battles over individual issues, launched often innovative programs targeted at specific problems, and formed coalitions around specific concerns. Now, however, they were faced with a right-wing agenda and an economic transformation that threatened to overwhelm these efforts. Progressives were fighting too many defensive battles, increasingly defining activists in terms of what they opposed, not what they were for. Even worse, activists found themselves defending a status quo that they did not support.

Activists began to face this dilemma head on. Traditional progressive activism was not getting at the root economic and political forces that were producing the specific problems in the first place. What they needed was a common plan that would address both people's immediate needs and fundamentally change the rules of the game. An alternative model of community-driven economic development was needed to unite progressives and the broader community into a proactive, visionary effort—one aimed at turning Milwaukee into a sustainable, vibrant, and life-affirming city.

To start the process, leaders from Progressive Milwaukee, along with key labor and community groups, pulled together a broad coalition of people to discuss how to rebuild the city from the bottom up. From the beginning, the group focused on the need for family-sustaining jobs. Without the ability of ordinary people to support themselves and their families, a healthy, sustaining community would not be possible. While such a concern rings true for cities and communities across the country, Milwaukee is especially familiar with corporate America's economic restructuring. In the 1970s and 1980s, Milwaukee saw over 40,000 family-supporting jobs leave the city.[7] In their place, there was an explosion of low-wage, poor-benefit jobs. A recent study by the University of Wisconsin in Milwaukee ranked the city as the third greatest creator of low-wage jobs in the United States, following only Miami and Los Angles. Thirty percent of all job openings in the city paid $6 an hour or less. Sustainable Milwaukee organizers, however, did not want the project to simply become a narrow jobs initiative. Instead, they chose to define community economic development in broad terms that included areas such as education, transportation, and the environment as well as jobs.

For a year, the group engaged in a two-pronged process. It launched four task forces around the areas of jobs and training, credit, education, and transportation and the environment. Each task force went through a process of analyzing the problems and highlighting the general principles relevant to addressing them, formulating an outline of proposed solutions, and, finally, developing a list of specific recommendations that could be taken to the community for greater feedback and discussion. While the task forces worked on their specific areas, the larger group continued to meet. To encourage a process in which people stepped out of their traditional areas of concern, task forces reported back to the larger group at each step so that the broad coalition could discuss each specific area.

Organizers strove to create an open and inviting process that would involve a diverse array of people. As the group's final document explains: "A community plan for economic reconstruction, we believe, should be authored by the community, not outside 'experts.' As a community, we know better than anyone else what ails us, and as much as anyone else about what can work to solve our problems." The actual Sustainable Milwaukee plan contains many ideas and concrete projects that local groups had already pioneered, but that had not been connected to a more comprehensive strategy.

Sustainable Milwaukee organizers deserve a great deal of credit for establishing a process that came across as serious enough to attract the time and energy of busy people. As the planning developed, the group continued to grow. The four task forces involved almost ninety participants, including labor activists, teachers, elected officials, social service staff, religious activists, people from neighborhood organizations, environmentalists, and members of African-American, Latino, and Native American groups. Members and organizations involved in the process took the preliminary plan back to their boards, community groups, and to thousands of individual Milwaukee citizens. After a year of work, Sustainable Milwaukee unveiled its plan on October 22, 1994 at a six-hour "Community Congress" attended by almost 300 representatives.

The Plan

Entitled "Rebuilding Milwaukee from the Ground Up," the plan offers a bold vision for the city's future. It combines a broad analysis of the problems and necessary solutions with a concrete sense of the power that local government and the community have to make real changes. A brief summary of each task force area will provide an idea of what the plan is about.

In the area of jobs and training, the report highlights how deindustrialization, racism, suburban sprawl, and government giveaways to corporations have combined to gut the city's economy. Sustainable Milwaukee participants believe that the community must establish and fight for new standards. "A job at any cost"—which basically involves going along with whatever the business community wants to do—is simply not an adequate solution. The report distinguishes between "high" and "low" road business strategies. High road businesses develop lasting family-supporting, unionized jobs that enhance the community and protect the environment. Low road companies exploit the community by forcing people into low-paid, dead-end, and temporary work that drains local resources and damages the environment. Sustainable Milwaukee believes that local and state government have the ability to demand high road standards. The report recommends local and state legislation to raise the minimum wage and establish minimum health, family leave, and childcare standards. The authors estimate the city needs at least 50,000 new jobs to employ everyone who wants work. Local and state governments can stop giving away millions in tax dollars to low road companies that use the money to destroy the city. Instead, tax money should be channeled into businesses, large and small, that will provide good, community-sustaining jobs. Public money can also fund community-driven training programs and businesses as well as provide a framework for worker and community buyouts of local firms. Government can provide jobs directly by developing public service work. The report also highlights the role that the community can play through such concrete actions as union organizing and establishing a plant-closing early-warning system.

The credit task force pointed to the major redlining of the city by area financial institutions. Both city residents and businesses are starved for capital, while huge differences exist between the mortgage approval rates for whites versus people of color. The report offers a series of suggestions to strengthen, enforce, and expand the government regulations that foster socially responsible banking. It also recommends various alternative financing methods, such as capital provided by state government deposits, socially targeted pension funds, and the creation of "public purpose" banks dedicated to community development.

From the outset, Sustainable Milwaukee's environmental task force sought to move beyond mainstream political and economic wisdom that pits a defense of the environment against jobs for the community. The report also links traditional environmental concerns of pollution and nature preservation with inner city resident's battles over toxic dumping in their neighborhoods, workers' struggles for a safe workplace, and suburban residents' feelings of a loss of community among the sprawl. The group offers a comprehensive alternative conception for economic development, land use, and environmental standards—one in which citizens gain a much larger role in determining the destiny of their communities. Specifically, the plan encourages environmentally friendly jobs, while, at the same time, strengthening the ability of workers in existing jobs to identify and speak out against unsafe and toxic conditions. The report criticizes local and state transportation policies, which overwhelmingly favor cars at the expense of public transportation. The group calls for a priority shift by supporting the development of light rail and an expanded bus system. Viewing healthy urban centers as more environmentally friendly than suburban sprawl, the plan points to new land use policies that encourage concentration and spatially diversified, integrated communities. It calls for programs that would empower inner city residents to rebuild their urban communities by providing resources for housing reconstruction, bringing in family-supporting jobs, and encouraging neighborhood-based environmental advocacy and enforcement efforts. The plan also offers ways of expanding governmental regulation of corporate pollution.

Finally, Sustainable Milwaukee posits a fundamental connection between an economically healthy community and the education system. While defending public education from right-wing efforts at privatization and other attacks, the education task force was nevertheless frank about the need for genuine public school reform. The schools must be made more accountable to the community and must be tied to broader efforts at community revitalization. The plan highlights the need for equity both in school funding and in a curriculum that is multicultural and tied to students' reality. Toward these ends, the group advocates reduced class size, a more diverse teaching staff, the elimination of tracking, increased openness and accountability, and greater parental and community involvement. As part of the last point, the report suggests a reform of the state's Family Leave Act that would allow parents the equivalent of two days a year of paid leave from work to take part in school-related activities. Such a measure would make participation in their children's education open to all parents, regardless of their access to spare time. The plan also calls for major changes in the existing school-to-work programs. While these programs currently focus on technical skills, the group would add such topics as workers' right to organize, the history of the labor movement, health and safety protections, racial and sexual harassment, family leave laws, and the value of community service. Additionally, the task force encourages the rebirth of "lighted schoolhouses," an innovation pioneered during the city's early Socialist years. Such schools become community centers, open early in the morning to late in the evening, providing both jobs and services for neighborhood residents.

Overall, each component of the Sustainable Milwaukee plan shares several common themes. The plan seeks to unite the city with at least the inner ring of suburbs that are now suffering from many of the same economic and political forces. The plan combines the powers available to local and state government with community mobilization. Many proposals are formulated in such a way as to foster what the report calls "community capacity"—developing skills and organization within the community so that ordinary people can speak and act on their own behalf. Finally, Sustainable Milwaukee offers not just concrete analysis and alternatives, but it also upholds basic social and moral values, such as family-supporting jobs, healthy communities, racial and gender justice, responsible business practices, and democratic community participation. We live in an age when the Right appeals to people's sense of values, yet hypocritically engages in real policies that undermine those ideals. In contrast, Sustainable Milwaukee is about the community standing up and saying, "this is what we believe in," and then formulating a plan to actually practice those values in economic and political life.

Implementing the Plan

The Sustainable Milwaukee plan has not ended up on someone's shelf, but has provided a unifying agenda for community activism. Out of the Community Congress, the group established a forty-member steering committee dedicated to implementing the plan and then hired a growing staff. After discussions in general membership meetings, the group decided to initially focus on two specific areas: a campaign for a living wage and area mass transit.

The living wage campaign represents a first step in moving toward Sustainable Milwaukee's founding purpose to bring family-supporting jobs back into the community. In addition to Progressive Milwaukee's door-to-door canvassing, other groups involved in Sustainable Milwaukee have mobilized behind the initiative. For example, sympathetic politicians introduced the legislation and worked with their colleagues to try to get it passed; the Interfaith Conference has encouraged area churches to raise the campaign within their congregations; and unions such as the United Electrical Workers mobilized their members to turn-out at hearings in support of the ordinances.

By spring 1996, the campaign had already won several major victories. The school board voted to raise its minimum wage to $7.70 an hour, thereby liberating 3,800 service workers from poverty wages. The campaign also got the city council to mandate $6.05 an hour wages for businesses that hold city contracts. With these early victories, organizers have turned their attention to improving on the city ordinance, adding health care to the school board provision, and securing a county living wage measure.

In reaction to decisions going on in the state and local government, the group also chose to work on mass transit. Prompted by a 1995 grant of $289 million in federal funds to improve transportation in Southeast Wisconsin, elected officials began a planning process that will guide policy in the area for many years to come. At issue was a choice between automobiles or public transportation. Traditionally, state and local transportation policy has favored cars. If such policies continue, the bulk of the federal money, as well as state and local funds, will go to highway reconstruction and expansion. Many environmentalists, local businesses, community groups, senior citizens, and labor unions favor a light rail system as well as expanded bus service.

Advocates of the $600 million light rail proposal say that it would provide much needed transportation for carless, low-income families. In addition, the stations could provide centers of neighborhood revitalization. A light rail system produces much less pollution and congestion than cars, and costs less than freeway construction and maintenance. Furthermore, planning for light rail gives communities much greater control over potential development. It can also reduce suburban sprawl because it encourages concentrated development in contrast to the freewheeling chewing up of more and more farmland and woodlands for roads. With its community plan focused on alternative transportation methods, Sustainable Milwaukee decided to play a leading role in the fight for light rail. The group set out to make the formal process of community consultation more than a token gesture by mobilizing member organizations to turn-out local residents for the open transportation hearings.

In addition to these two central focuses, Sustainable Milwaukee began to carry out other parts of its plan. The environmental justice group, for example, has helped draft legislation to be introduced in the state legislature establishing a statewide environmental justice board. The board would conduct an inventory of affected communities as well as educate and provide assistance programs to people, groups, and local elected officials in those communities. The bill also places greater restrictions on licenses, permits, and environmental impact statements to make concern for environmental justice an integral part of the planning process.

The task force on credit is working to strengthen the city's socially responsible investment program and expand it to the county level. The group is also trying to steer pension funds into targeted inner city investments. Another group is continuing efforts to set up a plant-closing early-warning network, with plans to hire a staff person dedicated to the project. By the spring of 1996, the education task force had secured federal funding for three "lighted schoolhouses" demonstration projects.

Sustainable Milwaukee also put together a broad group of people to successfully secure a $5 million grant from the Annie E. Casey Foundation for the city. The foundation, which works in support of low-income children, realized that it had to find ways of bringing family-supporting jobs into poor communities if it was going to get at the root forces impacting the lives of youth. To do so, the foundation asked "conveners" in eleven cities, including Sustainable Milwaukee, to apply for one of five $5 million grants to help reform the local economy and connect people with decent jobs. Through the application process, Sustainable Milwaukee designated a targeted area encompassing the Near North Side and Near South Side neighborhoods. In drawing up a planning process for the actual projects, the group lined up two major community organizations to serve as conduits into the neighborhoods and developed a process for obtaining the required one-to-one matching funds. Keeping with Sustainable Milwaukee's commitment to grassroots empowerment, the application places a strong emphasis on community participation and decision-making.

The coalition secured the grant despite the mobilization of powerful opposition. A major conservative foundation dedicated staff resources to trying to undermine Sustainable Milwaukee, including planting an article in the *Wall Street Journal* that tried to discredit the organization. In the end, the Casey Foundation decided to stick with the coalition. The grant represents one of the largest private grants in Milwaukee's history and is one of Sustainable Milwaukee's biggest successes.

The very process of bringing a diverse group of people together delivered results as well. In developing Sustainable Milwaukee's transportation alternative, for example, suburban environmentalists had to deal with and learn from the skepticism of inner city residents who had seen similar multi-million dollar developments bring few economic benefits into their communities. As a result, coalition plans for light rail devoted careful attention to ensuring that the system's stations provided a real impetus for local development. In another example, Esperanza Unida, which offers an innovative job-training project that combines formal classroom work with hands-on, practical experience at non-profit businesses, directly benefited from its coalition work. For years, the group had tried without success to get the area technical school to certify its instructors. Yet, after mentioning such difficulties at Sustainable Milwaukee meetings, labor activists in the coalition, whose unions have several members on the school's board of directors, got their people to lobby from within the technical school to secure the certification and make other changes.

The Relationship Between the Party and the Coalition

Although people involved in Progressive Milwaukee have played a key role in founding Sustainable Milwaukee, it is a separate coalition and process. Progressive Milwaukee's initiative came from the group's realization that progressive politics requires a comprehensive agenda—both to help keep officeholders accountable and to move activism beyond defensive struggles into more visionary campaigns.

By forming a separate initiative, Progressive Milwaukee activists allowed this grassroots agenda-building process to develop a life of its own. Because it is formally separate from the New Party, Sustainable Milwaukee has been able to pull together an even broader coalition. It includes certain community organizations, unions, and individuals that are clearly uncomfortable with third party politics. Sustainable Milwaukee also has the participation of some local political and business leaders. For example, the Greater Milwaukee Committee, an organization of 175 top executives and business owners, participated in the application for the Casey Foundation grant. At Sustainable Milwaukee meetings, political figures who are not part of Progressive Milwaukee can be increasingly seen among the participants. Milwaukee's mayor, John Norquist, even attended the group's Community Congress. That such people have gotten involved testifies to the seriousness of Sustainable Milwaukee's momentum.

Although independent from each other, Progressive Milwaukee and Sustainable Milwaukee clearly build on each other. On the one hand, Progressive Milwaukee provides, along with other groups, the grassroots activism, such as the living wage campaign, that is crucial to Sustainable Milwaukee's success. Part of the difference between the city council passing a $6.05 an hour minimum wage and the school board's $7.70 an hour wage is the community organizing PLAN that Progressive Milwaukee developed. Through this grassroots network, Progressive Milwaukee was able to identify ordinary residents who earned poverty-level wages from the school system and get them to take an active role in the campaign, testifying before the school board. Furthermore, the third party offers an electoral component that is critical to changing government policy. Not only does Progressive Milwaukee help get pro-Sustainable Milwaukee candidates elected, but incumbents from the major parties recognize that if they oppose Sustainable Milwaukee, they could well face a progressive challenger willing to embrace the plan.

On the other hand, Sustainable Milwaukee provides Progressive Milwaukee with three major elements. First, it offers a much needed platform. When people ask organizers what Progressive Milwaukee stands for, they can point to "Rebuilding Milwaukee from the Ground Up." Sustainable Milwaukee's plan also provide a clear measure upon which Progressive Milwaukee can hold its candidates accountable. In addition, Sustainable Milwaukee's initiatives provide Progressive Milwaukee activists a framework for organizing the kinds of grassroots activities that build their political organization. The living wage campaign demonstrated this relationship most clearly. Progressive Milwaukee's door-to-door work provided key grassroots support for the city and county ordinances. Yet this campaign also helped build a neighborhood-based leadership structure and membership for the New Party chapter. Finally, Sustainable Milwaukee's plan will, in all likelihood, provide Progressive Milwaukee with more electoral momentum. Although currently the initiative has experienced little backlash from the area's political establishment, Sustainable Milwaukee's community-driven logic ultimately threatens the local power structure. By placing a community agenda clearly on the table, the initiative, as it moves forward, will force those in power to take a clear stance on the issues. When such battle lines develop, Progressive Milwaukee will probably be the only political party willing to fully embrace and support the community's vision of its future. Those who want the Sustainable Milwaukee plan to go forward will likely have to vote for Progressive Milwaukee's candidates.

Together, Progressive Milwaukee and Sustainable Milwaukee are clearly making an impact on local politics and economics. The director of Esperanza Unida, Richard Oulahan, has been involved in progressive activism in the city for over twenty years, and sees a clear change:

> *I have witnessed many coalitions come and go, but Sustainable Milwaukee is different. The group's meeting continues to be packed, whereas with other coalitions attendance tends to drop off after a while. People want to be there. I think part of the reason is a sense of urgency that comes with economic decay. However, I also credit the group's leadership. While many people talk, Sustainable Milwaukee has been committed to doing. I have been impressed by how well the group has moved from talk to action.*

The same can be said of Progressive Milwaukee. Although the group started on a small-scale, its activities bring real changes to real people. There is nothing like delivering concrete results for building a movement.

Progressive Dane—The New Party in Madison

While activists launched a political movement in Milwaukee, similar New Party efforts took on life in the state's capital of Madison. With a population of 191,000, Madison not only houses the state government, but also the main campus of the University of Wisconsin. With its college-town atmosphere, Madison has a long history of progressive politics. During the 1960s and 1970s, the university campus was a hotbed of radicalism with students taking advantage of the close proximity of the neighboring capitol building to frequently march on state government. This radicalism spread into city politics. During the 1970s, Madison elected a prominent member of the 1960s' protest movement as mayor. While the 1980s saw the intensity and scale of activism quiet down, the city government remained solidly liberal and Democratic. Increasing suburban growth, however, has produced greater conservatism. Today, conservative forces have a majority on the Dane County board of supervisors.

New Party politics began in Madison differently than in Milwaukee. Madison already had an active third party: the Farm-Labor Party (FLP). While maintaining statewide ballot status, the FLP was mostly a Madison phenomenon, electing several of its members to local office. By the early 1990s, the FLP clearly needed to find ways to broaden its base. At the same time, other currents of progressive activism began moving toward third party politics. As with progressives across the country, Madison activists had been involved in a range of coalition work that heightened people's desire to create something new and lasting. When the national New Party formed in 1992, several activists wanted to start a local chapter in Madison. These people linked up with FLP activists as well as the Greens, the Rainbow Coalition, and others to form Progressive Dane.

While Progressive Dane would eventually become the local branch of the New Party, it did not start out that way. Activists in the FLP already had a party structure and were reluctant to simply jump wholesale into the New Party. They, along with other activists, had questions concerning the New Party's relation to the Democrats—especially its tactic of running fusion and cross-endorsed candidates. People also wanted to ensure local autonomy. While working out such questions, the group decided to plunge into electoral politics as a coalition of the FLP, the New Party, the Wisconsin Greens, and the Rainbow Coalition.

Formed in 1992, the coalition had immediate success. With several FLP officeholders already on city council and a relatively healthy pool of possible candidates, Progressive Dane ran eight candidates for city council in the spring of 1993. Six of the eight won, with the two unsuccessful candidates losing by narrow margins.

In 1994, after ironing out its concerns, the FLP handed its ballot line over to the new organization and Progressive Dane became a formal chapter of the New Party. The group then went on to run and elect seven endorsed candidates to the Dane County board of supervisors and one to the school board. In a special election, they also elected a member to city council to replace one of their incumbents who was leaving town. In 1995, Progressive Dane increased the strength of its city caucus by one—winning seven out of eight races. The one unsuccessful candidate lost by only twenty-one votes! Over a three year period, Progressive Dane has accumulated an impressive track record, winning all but four of the twenty-five races it entered. In early 1996, Progressive Dane again elected seven of its members to the county board and one to the school board.

The people that Progressive Dane has placed in office are making a difference. For example, Progressive Dane member Merrill Miller was elected to a special one-year term in 1994 to replace a retiring council member. Having been on both the old council and the new one elected in 1995, Miller sees a difference. "Where before I found myself often voting in the minority, now I find myself in the majority," he explained. "I think that there has been a significant shift in the balance of power and that Progressive Dane is largely responsible for that shift." On the council, Miller is working to develop local transportation alternatives to decrease the city's dependence on the private automobile. Progressive Dane is backing him up by organizing a broad coalition to pressure the city to pass a measure that would increase support for bus, rail, pedestrian, and bike projects and raise money by requiring businesses to pay an annual parking stall fee. If the city council fails to pass the proposal, the coalition is prepared to put the matter before voters through a ballot initiative.

Miller's election is a testament to the New Party's commitment to opening the political process to new people. A graduate student and staff member of the graduate student union at the university, Miller had never been involved in electoral politics before volunteering for Progressive Dane races in 1993. The experience taught him that one did not need vast expertise to run for office if an organized group of people was there to help. When Progressive Dane needed someone to replace the retiring council member, Miller decided to run for office.

As in Milwaukee, Progressive Dane looks quite different from the mainstream parties. It is a membership organization designed to ensure member participation and control. Most of the group's decisions have been made by consensus at routine general meetings. In contrast to the candidate- and personality-driven politics of the major parties, Progressive Dane campaigns on its party program. As in Milwaukee, candidates sign contracts pledging their support for building the organization in return for campaign support. Within both city and county government, the group has organized a progressive caucus to discuss policies among its officeholders as well as with the broader organization. Such practices fly in the face of traditional local politics, where officeholders act as separate individuals accountable neither to each other nor to the people who elected them.

As in Milwaukee, Progressive Dane tries to spend as much time on non-electoral forms of activism as it does on electoral campaigns. For example, the group sponsors a neighborhood empowerment project focused on the city's poorer and minority areas. Through such activities as fundraising, joint forums, and volunteer projects, Progressive Dane aims to strengthen existing neighborhood associations and involve them more in electoral politics. One of the projects was a tutoring program, in the Darbo-Worthington neighborhood. Volunteers from Progressive Dane, the neighborhood, and elsewhere in Madison help elementary and junior high school kids learn basic skills. The project also provides a chance for children to develop positive, friendly relationships with adults who take an interest in their lives. This leads to empowerment. Through the tutoring program, students have launched their own newspaper, the *Lollipop Press*, performed plays, gone on field trips, and planned a variety of social activities.

Over time, projects such as this one are crucial for maintaining and expanding the diversity of the group. Although it has recruited and endorsed candidates of color, Progressive Dane remains a predominantly white organization. Progressive Dane would like to serve as the vehicle for the political empowerment of people of color. Not only would organizers like to see people of color become active members of Progressive Dane, but they would also like them to run for office with the organization's support. This project is not easy work. Organizers have found the process of building personal ties of mutual respect and trust quite time consuming. Yet, in the experience of all the activists interviewed for this book, white progressives who want to build a multiracial alliance need to get involved in supportive and egalitarian ways with the issues that directly confront communities of color.

Ron Richards, the key organizer of the neighborhood empowerment program, sees non-electoral work generally as crucial for the third party movement. "If we are going to not be like the other political parties," explains Richards, "if we are going to be a true democracy movement, then we can't confine ourselves to elections. It is the community activism, not the electoral work, that will keep our party rooted in the community rather than becoming a group of professional politicians."

Progressive Dane also has a semi-autonomous student chapter. Called Students for a New Progressive Party (SNPP), the group has been quite active, holding fundraisers, sponsoring forums, and writing articles for the student paper's op-ed section. During the spring 1995 semester, the chapter answered the national New Party's call for campus teach-in events. The SNPP's Campus Democracy Week included speeches, poetry readings, bands, and panel discussions. By coordinating their week with a nationally organized student demonstration against the Contract with America, the group co-sponsored a campaign that March that collected almost 1,000 signatures denouncing the right-wing agenda. When students across the Midwest contacted SNPP to find out how to set up New Party chapters on their campuses, the group decided to co-sponsor a large youth conference in the fall of 1995. Organizers hoped to bring together college students, high school students, and young people who were no longer in school to talk about building a progressive alternative and develop skills for organizing New Party chapters.

The student chapter is involved with the broader Progressive Dane effort as well. As co-chair of the statewide New Party, Doug Kratch, explained, "When we need volunteers we call up the students and explain to them what we need and they will see who will volunteer." The student chapter has tried to encourage students to vote in local races as well as to consider running for office themselves. "I think that the students help provide a sense of renewal," Kratch continues. "They keep us from getting bogged down. The Democratic Party around here is an aging organization. In contrast, I'd say the average age of people involved in Progressive Dane is in the twenties and thirties."

Like Progressive Milwaukee, activism in Madison continues to grow. The healthy attendance at Progressive Dane's monthly general meetings reflects both the vitality of the movement as well as the group's strategy of including an educational presentation and discussion on a topic of broad interest. Following a successful house party campaign in the summer of 1995, Dane activists had also secured sufficient funding to support a staff person—an action that typically helps move grassroots groups to new levels of activity. "I am just amazed at all the different kinds of people that we have got working together," comments Carol Weidel, Progressive Dane co-chair. "We run the spectrum from hard core leftists to liberal Democrats and even a few Republicans." Merrill Miller sees a similar vitality. "Progressive Dane has a lot of different projects involving lots of different people," he reflects. "All of this activity, however, contributes to the success and growth of our common organization."

Wisconsin's New Progressive Party

The Wisconsin New Party movement, begun in Milwaukee and Madison, is now spreading throughout the state. In the spring of 1994, Progressive Dane and Progressive Milwaukee formally joined the national New Party by holding a founding convention for the New Progressive Party of Wisconsin (NPP). The first order of business was ensuring their ballot access inherited from the Farm-Labor Party. To keep their ballot status, the NPP is required to win at least 1 percent of the vote in a statewide race every four years. To fulfill this requirement, the NPP launched its first statewide race that November by running Kathleen Chung for state treasurer. Chung, an AFSCME member and shop steward, had been active in the fight for women's liberation, racial equality, and social justice for workers. In the middle of a transition in employment, she also had the personal time needed to run. With 42,889 votes, Chung gained close to 3 percent of the vote, easily maintaining the NPP's ballot line. While 3 percent may not seem like much, it provided a base to build on. "In looking at the results, we found scattered all over the state pockets of progressive voters," explains NPP member Tammy Johnson.

The second order of business was building new local chapters. Less than a year after its founding, the NPP had grown from two to four chapters. Together, they represent a diverse movement. Of the two new chapters, Progressive Fox Valley is located in a conservative area of central Wisconsin centered around the small cities of Appleton, Oshkosh, and Fond du Lac. With the Democratic Party almost nonexistent in this area, the NPP promises to provide people the only alternative to the Republican's cynical conservatism. In contrast, Progressive Uplands holds the distinction of being the first rural chapter within the national New Party. Among other issues, the group is motivated by concerns for farmland preservation and other land use questions. Many of the key activists have been involved in fights against corporate and military pollution and environmental destruction. The NPP is hard at work developing contacts in most of Wisconsin's other major cities and towns. By the NPP's second convention, in the summer of 1996, activists welcomed three new chapters.

The third order of business was strengthening existing chapters. During the 1996 campaign season, activists in both Milwaukee and Madison are planned major efforts to expand the scope of their local activities. The spring will bring a new round of local elections for city councils, county boards, and mayors. The fall of 1996 will see the state elections followed by school board races in the spring of 1997. Party activists also hope to endorse at least three to five candidates for the state assembly. Although these people would run using the Democratic Party's ballot line, they would all be dedicated to building the New Party.

Within the movement, the mood of optimism and the sense of momentum runs deep. Every year, local activists have doubled the size of their organizations. Activists in both Madison and Milwaukee see their organizations emerging within the next few years as a major force within their city's politics. Similarly, in the near future, state leaders look to the NPP contesting up to a third of the seats in the state's legislature. "In the next couple of years, we should be able to supplant the Democrats in the areas of the state where they have become moribund," exclaims Doug Kratch. "Most of the left side of the Democratic Party is still out there, it is the Democratic Leadership Council that has abandoned them. It's our role to move into the vacuum created by the Democrat's retreat."

New Party Chapters Across the Country

Although Wisconsin has the most developed statewide movement, newly founded New Party chapters are rapidly developing the grassroots movement across the country. In the eyes of national New Party founder Joel Rogers, the same basic ingredients found in Wisconsin exist in communities throughout the nation:

> *The kinds of people who are driving the Sustainable Milwaukee project are to be found… in every major metro region in the country. If encouraged and supported, they could provide both the local face for national campaigns and a consolidating, forward-looking, this-is-what-we-want-to-do-right-here force for local economic restructuring.*[8]

The potential of this organizing can be seen in a sampling of New Party activity nationally.

Arkansas

On the same election day that put one former resident of Little Rock, Arkansas into the White House, five of eight New Party municipal candidates also won their election. Two of the Little Rock New Party candidates who lost came in third and fourth, out of a dozen people vying for the two at-large seats on the city's board of directors. The Jefferson County New Majority (as their local New Party group is known) ran three African Americans for the Pine Bluff board of alders and won two of the seats. The New Party also swept three municipal offices in rural Altheimer, electing two council members and the recorder-treasurer.

From this promising start, state activism continues to grow. For the 1994 fall race, Little Rock activists began building a Precinct Leader Action Network. With the help of this grassroots structure, the group placed two New Party members on the city council and one New Party-Democrat into the state legislature. At a July 1995 summit called Save Our Schools, New Party organizers developed a community-driven platform for school reform. They went on to build a broad coalition behind the campaign of New Party member Micheal Daugherty, who defeated a Christian Coalition leader in the primary and then won a seat on the school board in the general election. Daugherty joins two other New Party members on the board, including Linda Poindexter, the board president. Together with other progressive-minded members, they now have a voting majority.

Meanwhile, newly elected New Party city directors Gloria Wilson and Willie Hinton helped to lead a public campaign to block efforts to contract out Little Rock's garbage pickup to a notoriously anti-union firm. The New Party chapter also organized a campaign to direct surplus municipal funds to needed city services. "This is the first time in anyone's memory that there has been extensive public participation in the budgetary process," says New Party activist Neil Sealy.[9] Even more recently, the Little Rock New Party launched an effort to challenge real estate domination of the city's planning process. When Gloria Wilson attempted to launch the campaign with a rousing speech before her fellow city directors, the mayor tried to prevent her from speaking. More than seventy supporters came to her aid to overcome the mayor's efforts. Wilson came close to victory after her speech. In the end, the mayor cast the tie-breaking vote to reject the New Party's proposal to hold public interviews for planning commission candidates. While victorious this time, the local status quo was clearly shaken.

For its part, the New Party is not letting up. Together with ACORN, the Arkansas New Party is leading a broad coalition that has successfully placed a major campaign finance reform initiative on the ballot. The measure would limit campaign contributions to $100 for most state and local races, provide a tax credit up to $50 for such contributions, and tighten reporting and disclosure requirements. The coalition includes the Arkansas AFL-CIO, Common Cause, and United We Stand.

Washington, DC

In the nation's capital, the New Party chapter, dubbed DC New Democracy broke into local politics by running candidates for the city's advisory neighborhood commissions—a non-partisan elected body that has an impact on zoning, crime prevention, and neighborhood services. Fourteen of the twenty-two New Party candidates won.

The group has also fought budget cutbacks. In the summer of 1995, after running up a $700 million deficit, city council's fiscal authority was taken over by a financial control board appointed by President Clinton. Fearing that the board would simply cut services indiscriminately, DC New Democracy members hammered out a document entitled "Grassroots Solutions to DC's Budget Crisis." Later that summer, the group launched a drive around campaign finance reform. In 1992, DC voters had passed a finance reform initiative, which included a $100 limit on individual contributions, by a two to one margin. The mayor and city council ignored this mandate, however. Instead, council member John Ray introduced legislation to raise the ceiling for contributions to the pre-1992 level. Not only did the New Party mobilize to block the measure, but it drafted its own "DC Spending Limit and Clean Campaign Act" to further diminish the influence of big money and promote publicly financed elections.

Maryland

Just north of the nation's capital, New Party organizers are busy setting up rapidly growing local chapters in Maryland. In the spring 1995 races, the local New Party chapter Prince George's United ran half a dozen candidates for mayor and city council in several working-class towns in the Washington suburbs. David Harrington became the first New Party mayor in the country when he won his race in Bladensburg—and became the first African-American mayor in the history of the town. New Party member Otis Collins was also re-elected to the town city council. Two other New Party-endorsed candidates won seats to their local city councils.

The New Party's attention to building a diverse political organization is quite clear in Prince George's County. The local organization is half people of color and half female. "I'm an affirmative action organizer," stresses state New Party staff organizer and Brentwood councilperson Peter Shapiro. "I know that most of the lefty activists are going to show up to a meeting anyhow, so I spend most of my time going into the African-American and Latino communities."[10]

Other local efforts are underway. Baltimore New Party organizers have begun pulling together an active group to focus on city races and organize a local referendum to expand the city's minimum-wage laws to cover all workers. Maryland also has active New Party affiliates in Montgomery County and in Annapolis, the state capital. In the former, New Party organizers entered 1996 gearing up to tip the balance of power in the local school board. In the latter, according to organizing committee member Lucy Oppenheim, "progressives face a huge challenge from the Christian Coalition in this county, and with the exception of a few rare individuals, the Democrats aren't doing a thing about it." On University of Maryland's main campus, a Students for the New Party group ran a slate for the student assembly. They challenged the decidedly unprogressive existing party, called the Old Line Party. By winning eighteen of twenty-nine seats, the New Party students gained a majority.

At the state level, New Party Democrat Paul Pinsky, a leader in the fight for single-payer health care, was elected to a term in the Maryland state senate in 1994. Among other actions, Pinsky introduced a bill that would have substantially eased the state's ballot access requirements. The bill passed the senate, but was killed in the house. Also, in 1994, New Party member Salima Siler Marriott from Baltimore won re-election to the state house after a tough race against a well-funded opponent.

New Jersey

Also on the East Coast, New Jersey activists have mounted a series of campaigns. In 1993, Concerned Citizens of Union County brought together New Party people and environmentalists to fight back against the construction of a mass burn garbage incinerator. While their candidate for county board lost, their referendum to require the mayor to place two members of the citizens group on the utilities authority passed by a two to one margin. In the same election, the New Party ran three candidates for the county boards in Essex and Union counties and, while losing, laid the ground work for future campaigns.

New York

Across the Hudson River, Progressive New York, a local New Party chapter, entered 1996 by mobilizing for a major challenge to Republican Mayor Rudy Giuliani's attack against the New York city public schools. Through forums and door-to-door organizing, New Party activists organized people to oppose the mayor's education cuts and to develop community-backed candidates for upcoming school board elections. On Long Island, the New Party ran a strong campaign by Fred Brewington for the county legislature. While his 23 percent of the vote fell short of winning, his campaign helped to build an important cross-racial coalition. "This is the first time I can remember in Nassau County that the white progressive community worked with and built trust with the black community," commented New Party local co-chair Don Shaffer. "This was an important step toward building a strong coalition for the future."[11]

Illinois

In Chicago, the newly formed New Party chapter chose not run any candidates in the fall of 1994. Instead, it launched an aggressive voter registration drive, registering over 4,000 low-income voters. "This is part of our answer to the right-wing," explained Keith Kelleher of SEIU Local 880. "You can't create a new majority coalition by just fighting over the same batch of people who have voted in the past. If we want a new politics, then we have to create and expand an electorate who will demand it."12

Later that spring, progressives won a spectacular victory in Chicago's twenty-fourth ward when New Party city council candidate Michael Chandler beat out the fifteen-year incumbent, Jesse Miller in the Democratic primary. Chandler tapped into the growing frustration with politics as usual. In addition to the resident's common complaints, such as ignoring neighborhood demands that the city do something about a seven-story toxic waste dump, Miller added insult to injury by attempting to let the same company build yet another dump nearby. With a campaign chest of only $4,000, but armed with an organized cadre of volunteers, Chandler captured 55 percent of the vote in a crowded race. He was the only challenger in Illinois that year, out of 350 candidates, to beat a sitting incumbent.

More recently, the Chicago New Party has begun to launch a living wage campaign similar to Milwaukee's. The group has also developed a local program on school reform with an eye toward entering school council elections. The aim is to counter Mayor Daley's recent attempt to consolidate his power over the school system and substantially limit community control of schooling.

Other election results have been mixed. In early 1996, New Party activists suffered a heartbreaking loss when their candidate for state representative, Willie Delgado, lost in the hotly contested Democratic primary. New Party member Danny Davis won the Democratic primary and general election in the seventh congressional district, however becoming the first New Party member in the US Congress.

Minnesota

Farther north in Minnesota, the Twin Cities New Party (representing Minneapolis and Saint Paul) cross endorsed two successful Democratic state representatives in the fall of 1994. The group next plans to focus on library board, park board, and city council elections as well as vigorous initiative campaigns.

In St. Paul, Minnesota, New Party activists built a coalition that succeeded in collecting the 10,000 signatures necessary to place an initiative on the ballot to require companies contracting with the city to pay at least $7.21 an hour and to fill new job openings with residents from Saint Paul's poorer communities. Unfortunately, the initiative failed due to opposition from business leaders claiming that the initiative would force them to eliminate jobs and raise prices. Using similar arguments, the city's Democratic mayor, Norm Coleman, pulled strings to split the labor community by gaining some union opposition to the measure.

Although the initiative lost, the fact that it gained 41 percent of the vote has helped activists keep pushing the measure. The city councils of St. Paul and Minneapolis have set up an unprecedented joint task force to propose ordinances on living wage jobs. New Party supporters expect to have a strong presence on the task force. Meanwhile, New Party activists in both cities are organizing a Precinct Leader Action Network, similar to Progressive Milwaukee's, to mobilize neighborhood support for a living wage.

Montana

After more New Party victories in the fall 1995 elections, five New Party-Democrats joined with several other progressives to form a solid progressive majority on Missoula city council. These representatives have put together a 100-day plan for the council to advance a progressive agenda around such issues as housing, human rights, jobs, and the environment. In addition to the electoral victories, the local New Party chapter has also worked actively as part of a coalition to pass a citizens initiative protecting city open space. As local New Party steering committee member Pete Talbott describes:

> *In just two years, the New Party has changed the dynamics of the city council from an overwhelming conservative majority to a council that can start to pass some progressive legislation. We're real excited about what we've done and what we'll be able to do over the next few years.*[13]

Looking ahead, activists plan to expand their membership and hire a staff person. They plan to run school board races in spring 1997, gain another council seat, and organize a statewide living wage campaign. New Party activity has also begun to spread elsewhere in the state.

And the List Goes On

The New Party continues to grow. By early 1996, its newsletters and sustainer reports pointed to new organizing committees in Des Moines, Iowa; Brazos County, Texas; and western Colorado. In Massachusetts, a newly formed New Party group had built enough support among various progressive organizations and individuals that it was able to hire a fulltime organizer. The first New Party group in New England, the chapter plans a major house party member recruitment effort and looked toward local upcoming elections.

Overall, between 1993 and spring 1996, New Party chapters had run in 139 races, winning ninety-four elections. The organization's national membership also continues to climb at a steady rate. At the end of 1994, the New Party had 4,300 members. By the end of 1995, the number had increased to over 6,000 and, by May 1996, over 7,500 members had joined. The interim executive council has set a short-term goal of doubling the New Party's membership each year for the next two years. It looks forward to running at least 225 candidates in elections and strengthening the organization's financial base.

In 1995, the national New Party had a budget of roughly $300,000. The vast majority of all financial contributions to the New Party have come in small amounts under $250. The New Party pushes a sustainer membership in which people pledge $10, $20, or $50 a month to provide the organization with a steady cash flow. While this money is peanuts by American election standards, the New Party has been able to support a growing staff. It is convinced that paid organizers are critical to building sustained local groups. By being able to dedicate activists to New Party work fulltime, local chapters help ensure that the time-consuming task of pulling people together and keeping projects running gets carried out. Future membership growth will only aid the New Party's movement-building efforts.

In keeping with its emphasis on combining electoral and non-electoral activism, the New Party is actively promoting, along with its community and labor allies, living wage campaigns similar to the one in Milwaukee. According to the national New Party's 1996 winter newsletter, living wage ordinances were being introduced in Chicago, Los Angeles, and New York. Similar ballot initiative efforts were already underway in cities like Houston and, at a state level, in Idaho, Missouri, Montana, and Oregon.

The New Party's active involvement with living wage campaigns has earned it respect from organized labor. In an April 1996 meeting in Washington, DC, the new leadership of the AFL-CIO brought together over seventy labor and community leaders who are involved in living wage efforts across the country. As a key participant in many of these local campaigns, the New Party received an official invitation to the conference. A New Party newsletter heralded this invitation as probably "the first time in 75 years that a third party has been officially invited to a meeting by the top leadership of the American labor movement."

While no one can predict the future, the New Party's general model may be the wave of the future for progressive politics in the United States.

Chapter Eight

Fragments of the Rainbow

Other Progressive Party-Building Efforts

Part of the promise of independent progressive politics is its ability to pull together people from different social movements and unite them in a bid for popular self-governance. To greater or lesser extents, both Jackson campaigns, Connecticut LEAP, the Vermont Progressive Coalition, and the New Party embody this "majoritarian" strategy. In contrast, the Labor Party Advocates, the Campaign for a New Tomorrow, and the Greens have all sought to build third parties rooted in fairly distinct social milieus of protest. In this chapter, we will look at the strengths and weaknesses of these groups, and explore recent attempts to build greater operational unity among different progressive efforts.

Building a Labor Party

Of the three efforts discussed in this chapter, building a labor party tied to the union movement offers the single greatest base of popular resources. The ranks of organized labor have the largest resource pool of any social movement in the country. In 1990 alone, union political action committees spent over $84 million on political candidates—almost entirely for Democrats. In contrast, none of the other political efforts discussed in this book have a budget of even a half million dollars. This resource base is not just counted in dollars, however. The United Auto Workers' national magazine, *Solidarity*, reaches over 1.3 million readers—a circulation that most of the alternative press can only dream about. Furthermore, while racism has long been a problem for organized labor, today's union movement is racially diverse and many people of color play active leadership roles in local union politics.

In other countries, such resources have been used to build strong labor, socialist, or social democratic parties. This has not happened in the United States. Yet, with the collapse of the New Deal social contract, the cost of limiting union activity to collective bargaining and unwavering electoral support for Democrats has begun to become clear. When employers went on the offensive in the 1980s, organized labor suffered defeat after defeat. While the Republicans worked to undermine what legal rights workers had remaining, the Democrats awkwardly strove to distance themselves from the labor movement, their former ally. Having pursued a narrow agenda for decades, unions now found themselves without many allies or active support within the general population. As a steadily declining proportion of workers were in unions, some business leaders gleefully began talking of the death of the labor movement.

While typically not covered by the evening news, the labor movement has begun to show significant signs of renewal, especially at the local level. Some of this innovation can be seen in more independent political action. For example, local unions and labor leaders have been involved as key people in such efforts as the New Party and the Vermont Progressive Coalition.

Furthermore, even though most unionists are not yet willing to break with the Democratic Party, a growing number of labor leaders have begun to realize the need for creating new ways to politically activate their membership. Many unions' traditional political action focus has centered on raising campaign money, which has then automatically been given to the Democrats. Today, an increasing number of local unions and labor councils are experimenting with more creative and activist-oriented strategies. Such unions and councils have sought a more active role in electoral politics by recruiting progressive candidates, getting them elected by mobilizing rank-and-file members, and building coalitions with other progressive groups. Activists have also extended such grassroots techniques to include mass lobbying of local, state, and national legislatures, pushing public referendums, and revitalizing protest politics. Although working with candidates and officeholders who are officially Democrat in name, this grassroots activism does assert political independence by having much more of its own agenda and strategy. The LEAP coalition in Connecticut and related spin-off groups provide examples of this new union activism.

The fight against the North American Free Trade Agreement (NAFTA) is another example of this positive trend within the labor movement. In fighting NAFTA, unions mobilized their members and built coalitions with other progressive groups and the broader community. Although NAFTA was ultimately passed, the mere fact that there was a real debate and a close vote was due to a grassroots mobilization whose effectiveness in pushing the issue into public awareness surprised many pro-NAFTA policymakers. President Clinton's key role in getting the trade agreement passed also helped push more labor leaders, and rank-and-file union members, into questioning labor's blanket support for the Democratic Party.

Sentiment for more creative activism has also become visible within the national labor federation. In 1995, the uninspiring leadership of AFL-CIO President Lane Kirkland had become such an embarrassment that even the cautious leadership of the federation was compelled to replace him. In the first contested election in decades, the reform slate, led by SEIU President John Sweeney, won office on pledges to "put the movement back in the labor movement." To what extent the new leadership will fulfill its promises remains to be seen. Two of Sweeney's top initiatives were a call for a major campaign to organize new workers, especially in heavily non-union areas, and nationwide efforts to revitalize grassroots political activity by union members. In early 1996, for example, the federation set out to raise millions of dollars for an aggressive grassroots get-out-the-vote mobilization for the upcoming elections.

Enter the Labor Party Advocates

Quite aside from the national leaderships' specific actions, the changes within the AFL-CIO are reflective of broader trends within the labor movement that provide greater openings and legitimacy for the work of activist reformers within the ranks of labor.[1] The effort to lay the basis for a labor party in the United States is very much a part of this new progressive activism. In 1991, delegates of the Oil, Chemical, and Atomic Workers union (OCAW) passed a resolution to launch the Labor Party Advocates (LPA) to agitate within the ranks of labor for the founding of a labor party.

The organizers of the Labor Party Advocates had a broad vision. In working for a labor party, they sought not simply to establish a political party that would genuinely represent working people, but they also hoped to help transform the labor movement itself. LPA activists shared a vision of organized labor that went back to the social unionism of the early CIO, when the labor movement actively represented and fought for working people generally. A labor party could help redefine the labor movement by embodying this broader social vision. Specifically, through independent political activity, the labor movement could reach out to the general society and be seen as a vehicle for working people's interests. As LPA organizers argued, the fact that the Canadian labor movement represents over twice the proportion of workers as in the United States was connected to its support for the New Democratic Party. The Canadian party has provided greater public visibility to a progressive agenda, resulting in much better labor laws than in the United States and higher union awareness within the public. At the same time, the party has also provided a political context that has expanded the horizons of Canada's unions, so that they look much more like the social unionism of the old CIO than many of their American counterparts.

Elaine Bernard, a long-time leader and activist in the New Democratic Party, has drawn out the lessons for US labor activists of the Canadian experience:

> We commonly use the term "labor movement" to describe the world of organized labor. In most advanced industrial countries, that world includes organizations of working people in both the workplace and community. While unions are the main form of organizing in the workplace, labor-based political parties organize in the community. In these countries, when people talk about a "labor movement" they are talking both about trade unions and about this wider spectrum of organizations often including much of the progressive community. In the United States today there are trade unions...but there is really no wider social and political labor movement at all.[2]

She outlines several specific gains that a new political party could provide labor activists, including helping to place labor's progressive agenda into the public debate, expanding the labor movement's concerns and perspective, and fostering coalitions between labor and community groups.

Labor Party Advocates activists hoped that political organizing would similarly encourage broader and more creative thinking. Through independent political work, the labor movement could develop a comprehensive agenda that would allow unions, and working people generally, to move from the defensive battles of the 1980s to an offensive reply to the corporate agenda. Any labor party would also embody the ideals of labor reformers and thus bring to the forefront the best tendencies found within the movement. In short, by working to transform the nation's politics, organized labor could transform itself.

As the name suggests, Labor Party Advocates was not formed as a political party, but rather as a recruitment drive for the idea of a labor party. LPA organizers had no illusions as to the prospects of winning over most top labor leaders. Most national unions are firmly attached to the Democratic Party. Instead, LPA focused its energies on grassroots organizing among local labor leaders and the rank-and-file membership. Only after the group had recruited enough people to launch a truly representative and mass political party would it call for a founding convention.

LPA activists used a variety of tactics to promote the idea of a labor party. With modest resources at the national level, LPA sent former OCAW Secretary-Treasurer Tony Mazzocchi around the country as a national organizer to speak on behalf of a labor party. Officers of endorsing unions, such as OCAW President Bob Wages, also contributed their share of public speaking. Most LPA activity, however, came from the grassroots. Within local unions, activists conducted surveys of union members, asking them about their views on politics and the desirability of forming a new party of workers. Conducted by LPA members in union locals across the country, such surveys consistently revealed widespread dissatisfaction with both major parties and repeated majorities of workers who thought that a new political party of working people was a good idea. At the most formal level, LPA sympathizers placed before union meetings and labor council assemblies proposed resolutions endorsing the idea of a labor party. More informally, LPA members talked up the idea of a labor party among their co-workers and union members.

Labor Party Advocates also tried to gain attention by setting up and participating in public events. LPA activists could be seen handing out literature and talking with fellow workers in Labor Day parades, strike picket lines, and worker rallies across the country. Local LPA groups also sponsored activities of their own. For example, many locals organized public events to support ongoing labor struggles—such as the "war zone" in southern Illinois involving striking and locked out workers from Stanley, Caterpillar, and Firestone. LPA groups set up public hearings and conferences to discuss issues of concern to working people. In December 1994, activists in Ohio and Michigan pulled together a two-day Labor Education Conference in Toledo, Ohio. Several hundred union activists and sympathizers discussed a wide range of issues, including women's rights, labor law reform, national heath care, privatization, jobs, foreign policy, and independent political organizing. This common practice of combining discussions about various issues with education on the need for a labor party reflects one of LPA's central goals. LPA organizers worked to build a labor party not as a candidate-centered election machine, but as the mechanism for developing working people's agenda. In other words, LPA aimed not to build a worker equivalent of the Republicans and Democrats, but a political movement in which the vast majority of the nation's politically apathetic working population could come together and articulate what kind of economy, society, and government they wanted.

Between 1991 and 1995, the Labor Party Advocates had success in raising the debate about a labor party within the ranks of organized labor. In addition to the OCAW, the United Electrical Workers (UE), the International Longshoremen's and Warehousemen's Union (ILWU), and the Brotherhood of Maintenance of Way Employees (BMWE) officially endorsed LPA. None of these are among the most powerful of the nation's unions. Yet LPA never hoped to pull in such national leadership. The true testing ground of LPA's message lay at the grassroots. Success in this regard varied depending upon the area. In California, LPA won the official endorsement of such bodies as the San Francisco Labor Council and the 75,000-member California Council of Carpenters, as well as a dozen more local councils and unions. In Boston, the 12,000-member Service Employees International Union Local 285 voted to endorse LPA as did the 18,000-member New England Health Care Employees Union, District 1199, and the 20,000-strong Teamster Local in Chicago. All told, unions and labor councils representing roughly one million total members had formally given their support to the idea of a labor party by June 1996. More informally, and often much more quietly, other groups within major unions lent support to LPA. The Service Employees International Union, one of the country's largest unions, while not endorsing LPA specifically, did pass a broad resolution that expressed support for exploring the idea of creating a labor party. LPA achieved these successes with relatively few resources and a loose organization.

Despite such considerable activity, by 1995, the Labor Party Advocates had reached a turning point. In some areas of the country the group had not done as well. In Michigan, the home of the United Auto Workers with its firm ties to the Democratic Party, LPA made little official headway. More generally, LPA needed to evolve to a new stage. When originally founded in 1991, the group aimed to recruit as many as 100,000 people and 10,000 elected union officers to endorse the founding of a labor party. This ambitious goal would have produced the founding of a new party with a genuine, already established mass base. LPA never came close to this goal. Its membership leveled off at well below even 10,000 direct members. Part of the modesty of this number reflects a scarcity of resources—a problem faced by every group discussed in this book. LPA's turning point, however, also reflected the eventual limitations of the project. LPA activists had asked people to join an organization that supported the formation of a party that did not yet exist. LPA neither ran nor endorsed political candidates. Nor did it establish a formal platform or wage issue campaigns. These restrictions reflect the group's commitment to fostering a movement, not just an electoral machine. LPA activists also did not want to compete with or challenge existing union political action committees by entering electoral races.

As LPA's experience demonstrates, however, only the most politically involved individuals are going to actively join such an abstraction. Furthermore, when sympathizers did join, the project of recruiting for LPA often took secondary status to the primary grassroots activity in which they were already involved. To continue to grow, LPA had to offer something more tangible.

By 1995, LPA needed to establish an actual political party in order to move forward. Five years of organizing had revealed strong sentiment among union members, and the general public, for a new party of working people. This also seemed doable. When Tony Mazzocchi said that if LPA had in its possession a mere fraction of the millions organized labor gives to Democratic candidates every election, this country would have a labor party, he was not engaging in mere rhetorical flourish.

Between June 6 and 9, 1996, over 1,500 delegates elected from unions and local LPA chapters across the country met in Cleveland, Ohio to formally launch the Labor Party of the United States. The union base of the new party was obvious to anyone who walked into the convention hall. A large bloc of the attendees came from the four major endorsing unions: OCAW, UE, BMWE, and ILWU. Local unions and labor federations also provided a good proportion of the delegates, while representatives from LPA chapters and at-large members made up the remainder. Much of the convention was taken up by the rather unspectacular, but important work of approving the details of a constitution and a platform. Yet during these debates two major issues came to the forefront: the question of political strategy and the organizing base of the new Labor Party.

Political Strategy

The Labor Party Advocates was founded on an explicitly non-electoral strategy that aimed to build support for a new political party within the labor movement. Having founded that party, the leadership hoped to continue with a non-electoral focus. At the convention, the platform and constitution committees jointly submitted a strategic plan entitled "A New Organizing Approach to Politics" for approval by the delegates. The plan committed the Labor Party to build its base through the kind of issue campaigns and educational work that would promote a new political agenda among "hundreds of thousands of working people." Only after the Labor Party developed sufficient grassroots support and organizational development would it run candidates for office.

After a spirited debate, which spanned several hours, a majority of the delegates voted to adopt this strategy. Opinions on this question spanned the entire continuum—from those who hoped for national Labor Party election activity this year to those who hoped the Labor Party would always remain a non-electoral, educational, and agitational organization. Most views fell somewhere in between these two poles and broke into two major categories.

Those in favor of the non-electoral focus did not want the fledgling party to enter into electoral contests before it was ready. Proponents argued that for electoral campaigns to be done right they have to be well prepared. The party must run serious campaigns that it can win, not hopeless protest candidacies that the public will either never hear about or soon forget. One delegate pointed to union organizing as a parallel. Union organizers do not call for a certification election and then organize support. They build a solid base of support first, one capable of enduring the hostility and manipulations of management, and then call for an official vote. To act differently from the candidate-centered Republicans and Democrats, several delegates argued, the Labor Party must develop a level of grassroots organization that can hold its officeholders accountable to the people who elect them. Rather than using up the Party's scarce resources on election bids, advocates argued that, for the current time, the group's money and energy could be better spent promoting an alternative political agenda through other means.

A sizable minority of delegates, however, spoke out and voted in favor of running candidates now. Some held rather unrealistic expectations about the group's capacity to mount major national and statewide campaigns. Many pro-election delegates, however, looked toward targeted local races. The delegation from ILWU formally submitted an alternative proposal that would have kept the Labor Party out of national races, but provided the flexibility at the local level for individual chapters to run independent or Labor Party candidates when they felt they had sufficient strength and opportunity. Many delegates spoke out in favor of the proposal. Its logic was straightforward. Political parties run candidates. By not running any candidates, the Labor Party would be asking people to join and help build an organization whose actual activities were counterintuitive at best.

ILWU delegates agreed with the "New Organizing Approach" document that a Labor Party had to be different from the two major parties. That meant a significant focus on agenda-building and issue work. They also feared that if, after five years of non-electoral work, the Labor Party did not take some steps toward actually running people for office then the group would not only fail to grow, but could actually loose many of its existing grassroots activists. Instead, they argued, selective and carefully targeted electoral work could provide the Labor Party an added aura of legitimacy, as well as new channels for building coalitions with other groups and involving people who are not in unions. Many of those delegates who spoke in favor of an electoral strategy had themselves already been involved in local independent bids and hoped to continue to establish a framework for furthering these efforts.

Those who supported the Longshoremen's alternative did have strong precedents. Anticipation of major national bids were clearly unrealistic. Yet groups like the New Party have demonstrated that carefully selected local campaigns do offer a key tool for building active grassroots groups, ones which can pull in labor support, when they are combined with a broader strategy that includes substantial non-electoral activity.

The debate over the alternative strategy demonstrated the classic dilemma symbolized by the "which came first: the chicken or the egg" metaphor. To run realistic and effective candidacies, a new party needs a strong grassroots. But if the party does not run candidates as part of its strategy it may never build enough of a grassroots to run in elections. Groups like the New Party try to bridge this dilemma by moving the question to the local level, where activists can combine selective use of a broad arsenal of both electoral and non-electoral work. Entering local races that the party actually wins and putting real people in positions of power does add an element of seriousness to a group. Such victories also provide people a direct and immediate sense that they really can build a political movement. They also complement non-electoral efforts by establishing public figures who will introduce legislation and publicly support policies demanded by social movement activism.

The Longshoremen's proposal was ultimately rejected by a majority of the delegates—with the delegations from the other three endorsing national unions voting almost unanimously against it. Thus, the Labor Party emerged from its founding convention committed to popularizing a working people's agenda and building its organization through non-electoral campaigns. In two years, finances permitting, the Labor Party will hold a second convention at which time its political strategy will come up for renewed debate and consideration.

That the timing of electoral activity and concerns over entering into this realm prematurely proved such a central issue at the convention reflects the Labor Party's founding as a union-based party. At a concrete level, independent electoral campaigns do pose a special risk to union activists. The majority of unions are still very much tied to the Democratic Party. They have an entire institutional structure for organizing money and volunteers in this regard. If the Labor Party runs its own candidates, it could directly threaten that structure and even split labor between union-endorsed Democrats and its own candidates. In Wisconsin and Vermont, activists have been able to negotiate around this danger by gaining significant union backing for specific candidacies in ways that allow unions to continue their traditional Democratic-based activity. By contrast, as a fledgling national organization, the Labor Party could provoke the active hostility of the country's union leadership. Thus far, this has not happened. While not supportive of LPA, the AFL-CIO has not mounted a serious campaign to block its activities. The "New Organizing Approach" helps to avoid prompting such a polarization by promoting activity that hopefully will build the grassroots of the party and help reconstitute the ranks of organized labor.

The Labor Party's strategy also avoids potentially serious legal and financial issues. Under law, unions are restricted in their ability to use membership dues for political purposes. Funds raised to support candidates must come from voluntary member contributions to a separate political action committee. If the Labor Party were to run candidates prematurely, it could legally jeopardize much of the financial support it has received from endorsing unions.

Having chosen to remain a non-electoral organization, the Labor Party now faces the task of developing the kinds of issue campaigns and educational efforts that will provide activists with enough of a concrete purpose that the movement continues to grow and expand. The "New Organizing Approach" resolution briefly mentioned examples of non-electoral work, such as a campaign to restore the right to organize a union or a constitutional amendment providing all Americans with the right to a decent job at a living wage. The Labor Party could also build on the educational work developed prior to the convention. For example, LPA organizers had produced a series of attractive educational posters. Under the theme of "The Economic Facts of Life for Working People," the series provided a tool for discussion within unions and communities about current economic realities. A flyer distributed in the convention packet aimed to expand on this effort by announcing a Labor Party educational program called "Corporate Power and the American Dream." Designed for use with unions, community groups, and Labor Party chapters, it provides an easy-to-read workbook to promote debate and discussion on alternative economic agendas for working people. Questions include: why is there so much job insecurity, why are there not enough decent-paying jobs to go around, and what happened to the nation's wealth?

The Union Base

Like the other groups studied in this book, the Labor Party has a broad platform. Entitled "A Call for Economic Justice," the program approved by convention delegates included a host of progressive alternatives, such as the right to organize unions, a shorter work week, living wage jobs, tax fairness, an end to discrimination, universal health care, an end to corporate welfare, and protections for the environment. The Labor Party is based, however, in a particular social movement. Its concrete activity aims to recruit union members and leaders for independent politics.

The union focus is built into the very structure of the new party. While people can join as individuals, the constitution also opens membership to all labor organizations, including international unions, locals, districts, state federations, central labor bodies, and other worker-supportive bodies. Institutionally, this means that labor organizations will play a big role in the Labor Party. Individual members have two ways of participating in the party. They can join a local chapter or work as members of a labor organization that has endorsed the Labor Party. The size and influence of the former channel is something still very much in the process of evolving. Within LPA, formal local chapters had been a fairly recent creation. Indeed, the LPA leadership had been reluctant to establish formal chapters and did so only a year before the 1996 meeting in Cleveland.

At the convention, delegates debated the relative power that chapters should have in an interim organization between LPA and the Labor Party. The proposed Interim National Council has representatives from the major endorsing labor bodies—including the four endorsing national unions, the United Mine Workers, the American Federation of Government Employees, and other large endorsing organizations, such as the California State Council of Carpenters, the Farm Labor Organizing Committee, and the California State Nurses Association. Five members elected by an annual convention of Labor Party chapters are also on the interim council. The debate on the convention floor centered around a provision that assigned each chapter representative only one-fifth of a vote—thus giving all the chapter representatives combined only one vote on the council. Delegates from local chapters objected that they were being relegated to a marginal voice.

Those in favor of the one-fifth clause could point to the fact that the chapters were still modest organizations whose members were self-selected activists. By contrast, the labor bodies on the council had an elected leadership chosen from a membership of thousands and tens of thousands. The convention thus had to decide how to balance representatives chosen by chapters, which individually may have only a few dozen active members, with endorsing organizations like the California State Council of Carpenters, which represents 75,000 people. In the end, a clear majority voted in favor of the one-fifth clause.

The debate over chapter representation illustrated the union focus of the new party, which may prove limiting. Local chapters, while currently quite modest, provide the only avenue for people who are not in unions to join and participate in the Labor Party. The endorsing unions, by contrast, bring in resources and a substantial membership base—one potentially, but not necessarily, mobilized behind the Labor Party.

This strategy of building a party out of a particular social movement base is a double-edged sword. On the one hand, it allows the group to offer a powerful and specially designed appeal to mobilize a key element in the population for independent politics. We can not underestimate the benefit of mobilizing even a proportion of the relatively enormous resources of the labor movement behind a political revolt. The Labor Party hopes to maximize this possibility. The potential for Labor Party activity to strengthen and expand reform efforts within the broader labor movement is also quite valuable in its own right. In terms of a mass membership community-based organization, however, the Labor Party is building on an ultimately limited foundation. Only 15 percent of US workers are in unions, although far more would probably join if given a fair opportunity. While anyone can join the Labor Party, clearly union members, or people who come out of a union milieu, are going to feel most at home. This trade off in defining one's base underscores the need to develop coalitions and greater cooperation between progressive political efforts. The Labor Party is mobilizing one component, indeed a critical one, for a mass political challenge, but, by itself, it may not be sufficient. For example, the Labor Party does include people of color, but is this presence enough that such an organization can be seen as speaking effectively to and for the community-based struggles of people of color? At least some activists of color, particularly in the African-American community, think not. Several of these activists have organized their own third party efforts.

Black Politics and the Campaign for a New Tomorrow

Although a modest black middle class expanded due to the gains of the Civil Rights movement, and the 1965 Voting Rights Act led to a vast expansion in the number of black elected officials, the majority of African Americans find themselves at the forefront of our nation's falling standard of living.

Today, the conditions in America's inner cities are worse than they were during the ghetto uprisings of the 1960s. Hate crimes are up. And, everywhere, the victories of the 1960s are being rolled back by both Republicans and Democrats. Growing discontent and frustration has altered the terrain of black electoral politics, which has become less and less tied to the Democratic party. This trend is significant. As a growing electoral bloc, the black vote has been a key component in the Democratic Party's ongoing electoral coalition since the 1960s. In 1976, for example, the African-American vote accounted for the margin of Jimmy Carter's election to the presidency.[3]

Yet, at the national level, African Americans have been abandoned by the Democratic Party despite providing it with its most dependable bloc of voters. Bill Clinton illustrated this shift in June 1992 when he stood up in front of the leadership of the national Rainbow Coalition and criticized them for having invited rapper Sister Souljah to speak the previous day. According to her critics, she had made inflammatory and anti-white remarks in both her music and in an interview with the *Washington Post.* Sister Souljah replied that she, like many rappers, had been quoted out of context. The general attack on rap music aside, the fact that Bill Clinton chose to make Sister Souljah an issue was interpreted by many as a clear sign to the broader public that the Democrats were distancing themselves from blacks.

Instead of countering Republican race-baiting head on, the Democrats have chosen to cave in to white suburban fears. A 1991 survey by the National Opinion Research Center showed that 46 percent of all whites interviewed believed that "blacks tend to be lazy," 59 percent believed that "blacks prefer welfare," 53 percent agreed that "blacks are prone to violence," and 30 percent felt that blacks are "unintelligent."[4] The Democratic Party did not challenge this racism, but conformed to it. This abandonment in the face of deteriorating conditions has given birth to a fledgling effort to organize a people-of-color-led political party—the Campaign for a New Tomorrow.

This effort has deep roots. As James Jennings articulates in his groundbreaking book, *The Politics of Black Empowerment: The Transformation of Black Activism in Urban America,* a new kind of political activism has been growing in black America for some time.[5] In dozens of interviews conducted around the country, Jennings found a new generation of black activists had moved from demanding access to power to seeking power itself; from wanting a piece of the pie to redefining the pie; from wanting integration into the existing society to wanting to fundamentally change that society. By the 1980s, a much broader grouping of activists than the traditional black Left had begun to conclude that getting progressives, rather than just their traditional liberal allies, into positions of political power was necessary to address the problems faced by the African-American community. In the early 1990s, Jennings spoke to grassroots organizers who had spent the past decade and a half challenging the power structure of both white and black elected officials, and their corporate backers, through creative fusions of electoral campaigns and classic protest tactics.

This insurgent black activism took electoral form in a number of ways. During the 1980s, African Americans organized several major challenges to the established leadership of the Democratic Party. In 1983, for example, activists took on the Democratic Party machine in Chicago by running progressive legislator Harold Washington against the incumbent mayor. Demographic trends had made African Americans and Latinos a growing proportion of the city population. This change, coupled with a massive grassroots campaign that registered over 180,000 new voters, provided the basis for Washington's upset win in the Democratic Party primary. Large-scale increases in voter turn-out in black and Latino areas proved more powerful than the over $10 million that corporate donors gave to incumbent Mayor Jane Byrne. The battle did not end there, however, as long-time Democratic supporters got behind the campaign of Washington's Republican opponent. In the end, Washington won by less than 50,000 votes. Alliance-building proved key to his victory—both between African Americans and Latinos and to a minority (12 percent) of white voters.[6] Washington's victory opened the way for progressive activists and the broader community to participate city politics.

This "rainbow coalition" has repeatedly proven a key component in all the other insurgent campaigns. While newly mobilized voters placed Harold Washington in the mayor's office in Chicago, organizers in Boston further demonstrated the basic outlines of a new black insurgency by running long-time community activist Mel King for mayor. King's two campaigns grew out of years of vibrant community organizing around such issues as affordable housing, education reform, racism, and economic development. His 1979 mayoral campaign focused on four main elements: intense mobilization of black voters, an issue-oriented campaign, grassroots-dominated campaign leadership, and a black and white working-class coalition. While he received a modest 15 percent of the vote that election, his bid did pave the way for an even stronger effort four years later. In 1983, King came in second (trailing Ray Flynn by only 400 votes) in the city's preliminary election. This qualified him to be one of the two candidates in the final election. Although Flynn went on to become mayor, King's campaign demonstrated again a new and strong current of black activism. In particular, his bids showed the potential for building alliances with whites on the basis of class issues rather than middle-class liberal reformism. It also demon-strated the prospects for building broad coalitions with other people of color. By fostering such alliances and furthering community activism, the impact of the King campaigns continued on through movement politics well after 1983.[7]

This new black insurgency found national expression in the two campaigns of Jesse Jackson for the Democratic presidential nomination. Jackson's bids were similar to the experience in Chicago and Boston, where black activists led a broad coalition to challenge the mainstream of the Democratic Party. As such, they all represented independent political efforts within the Party. They also all demonstrated the central role of coalition-building.

Jackson's 1984 campaign highlighted two other trends. First, the race pointed to serious divisions between ordinary African Americans and the traditional black leadership. Although Jackson gained notable support in 1988, almost no Democratic black elected official supported his campaign in 1984. Birmingham Mayor Richard Arrington actively told blacks not to "waste" their votes on Jackson, while others, such as Atlanta Mayor Andrew Young and Coretta Scott King, openly championed Walter Mondale. Black activists thus had to challenge the official leadership in their community in order to campaign for Jackson. In the end, black voters defied their elected leaders by choosing Jackson by an over two-thirds margin in 1984.

Second, the Jackson campaign revealed the emerging potential power of the black electorate. In 1984, the national media tried to ignore Jackson's bid as a marginal candidacy. Yet the level of activism within the black community forced media coverage. With voter turn-out in black communities soaring, African-American voters were having a much greater impact relative to their proportion of the population. In many areas, black turn-out not only caught up to white voting rates, but even exceeded them by considerable margins. In the southern primaries, for example, 45 percent of all African Americans voted, while only 30 percent of whites went to the polls. Nationally, an estimated one-fifth of Jackson voters had never gone to the polls before.[8] After 1984, Jackson claimed that his campaign registered over two million new voters.

Enter the Campaign for a New Tomorrow

Ron Daniels, former executive director of the national Rainbow Coalition, was one of the many activists who felt that Jackson should have used the aftermath of his campaigns to build an autonomous grassroots political organization. Instead, Jackson and the national leadership centralized the Rainbow Coalition and allowed its grassroots to wither. In response to the decline of the Rainbow Coalition, Daniels set out, in 1992, to cultivate this neglected potential by running his own independent campaign for the presidency.

Ron Daniels' first experience in running for office had come in 1977 when he ran for mayor of Youngstown, Ohio. In a three-way race, he won 18 percent of the vote—a local record for an independent. From 1974 to 1980, Daniels served as president of the National Black Political Assembly

(NBPA). When founded in 1972, the NBPA brought together a diverse array of African-American leaders—from elected Democrats to black nationalists. The founding convention revealed strong sentiment among many participants for a black political party and a radical political message. Internal tensions, especially between nationalists and elected black officials, soon divided the organization. An attempt to create a National Black Independent Political Party, with Daniels elected as chair, never really got off the ground, despite a founding convention in 1980 attended by 1,500 to 2,000 activists.[9]

In 1992, Daniels decided to use an independent presidential bid as a way of pulling together some of the activists who had been fired up by Jackson's two bids, only to be left hanging. His long-term goal was to begin to lay the ground work for a multiracial, people-of-color-led, independent political organization. Specifically, he hoped to pull together groups of local activists and begin developing a broad progressive political platform. His campaign called for the elimination of all forms of discrimination, equality for women, creation of a socially responsible and sustainable economy, a domestic Marshall Plan, a 50 percent cut in the military budget, respect for the sovereignty and treaty rights of Native Americans, and reparations for African Americans.

Initially, the Daniels' campaign targeted fourteen states and the District of Columbia for building active local and state committees. His campaign generated enthusiasm among a number of progressive and left-leaning groups and individuals. The campaign, however, never achieved a level of material resources, political support, or organizational infrastructure equal to its goals. In the end, it secured ballot status in nine states and official write-in campaigns in five others. With a budget of only $25,000, the campaign gained 25,000 votes in states where it was on the ballot and 10,000 votes through write-ins. Few progressive activists were willing to participate in a campaign that did not meet the standards of grassroots mobilization and visibility set by Jackson's insurgency. The 1992 Daniels' campaign underscores the necessity of obtaining a significant level of grassroots support before mounting a national campaign.

Daniels was aware of these limitations. His race aimed to identify and bring together a modest coalition of grassroots activists. In this goal, his campaign had some impact. Activists tried to build on his 1992 campaign in two ways. First, they launched the National People's Progressive Network as a coalition of third party and independent groups. Second, Daniels' campaign network continued as an organized group under the name used during the race, the Campaign for a New Tomorrow.

As specified in its statement of purpose, the Campaign for a New Tomorrow "is a nationwide, independent, progressive political organization led by Blacks and people of color—Latinos, Native Americans, Asian Pacifics, Arab Americans, other minorities of color—whose goal is to build a grassroots, independent political party, separate from the Democrats and

Republicans, rooted in our community struggles, and having the interest of oppressed groups, working people, and the poor as its core political agenda." The Campaign for a New Tomorrow continues the goals of Daniels' campaign to develop a popular platform and build support for independent politics. The group's statement of purpose rejects the current socioeconomic system and calls for a fundamental social transformation as the only way for oppressed groups to achieve full freedom, equity, and self-determination. Under the slogan "we are the leaders we have been looking for," the group seeks to develop activists and leadership among African Americans and people of color.

The 1992 campaign left a network of contacts in thirty-one cities in twenty-five states. In three of these cities—Pittsburgh, Washington, DC, and New York—activists managed to develop active and ongoing chapters. In New York, local members organized teach-ins on Martin Luther King Day and planned forums on critical community issues. In 1994, they ran educator and community activist Mary France for New York's thirty-fourth assembly district. The Campaign for a New Tomorrow chapter in our nation's capital has worked with a broad-based grassroots coalition—the District of Columbia Community Action Network. DC CAN has played a leading role in fighting attempts by the Republican Congress to slash city services. Through a series of speak outs, demonstrations, radio programs, and marches through the areas of the city hardest hit by the cuts, DC CAN has challenged political leaders who are not responsive to the community. By pulling together labor, peace, students, homeless, and social justice groups, the coalition aims to develop a community-driven alternative agenda to help save the city.

The strongest chapter of the Campaign for a New Tomorrow group developed in Pittsburgh. Eight thousand residents signed petitions for Ron Daniels in 1992. Since then, the chapter has remained quite active in the community, developing a steadily growing paid membership and support base. In the past couple of years, the group has organized a number of community forums, run a youth education workshop, appeared on local radio talk shows, and played a leading role in a community response to a case of police brutality.

Campaign activists got behind Rick Adams' 1994 independent campaign for city council. With a strong showing of nearly one-third of the vote, the Adams' campaign demonstrated the potential for broad-based progressive electoral coalitions. This campaign built on local maverick Duane Darkins' earlier campaign as an independent running for mayor. By winning 15,000 votes, Darkins placed second to Tom Murphy, the first Democrat in sixty years to lose Pittsburgh's African-American vote.

Currently, the Pittsburgh Campaign for a New Tomorrow is attempting to reactivate the city's community advisory boards as a way of developing a base from which to challenge the city's one-party Democratic regime. The community advisory boards originated in the 1970s as an elite response to a movement to replace the at-large city council elections with a ward-based system. Under the at-large system, black candidates found that they could not win election, despite African Americans comprising a quarter of the city's population. To try to derail this movement for a ward-based alternative, the city council came up with the community advisory boards. The twenty-four boards were given the power to call a mandatory meeting with the mayor and council once a year and department heads at any time. When the effort for ward representation momentarily faded (in the mid-1980s a revitalized movement did win ward elections), the city's leaders undermined the active community boards and let the system as a whole fall into dormancy. The community advisory boards remained that way until recently, when members of the Campaign for a New Tomorrow got hold of the city charter and discovered their existence. Seeing an opportunity to build community-controlled political institutions, organizers set out to mobilize targeted communities to activate their boards and run people for these elected offices.

Through its electoral and non-electoral work, the local Campaign for a New Tomorrow has reached out directly to the black community. Volunteers have literally gone door-to-door to contact ordinary people and talk with them one to one. This is slow, time-consuming work. Yet this direct contact, coupled with the group's constant involvement in public actions, has produced a momentum that has pulled in working-class people. As Campaign for a New Tomorrow organizer Claire Cohen commented:

> It is really exciting to see the significant number of people involved in our group who have never been politically active before. These are regular, working-class black people who have gotten really excited and involved in what we are doing.

Outside of Pittsburgh, Washington, and New York, the Campaign for a New Tomorrow has not been able to translate individual interest into active, ongoing groups. A significant handicap in this regard has been the organization's lack of resources. While most third party groups are resource-poor, the Campaign for a New Tomorrow is the poorest. Unlike the Labor Party Advocates, it has not been able to draw upon related movement organizations or activist networks for financial support. Furthermore, the Campaign for a New Tomorrow is organizing among communities that are themselves poor—both financially and, as a result, in terms of spare time.

This lack of resources has meant that the Campaign for a New Tomorrow has been unable to fund staff to support local groups. Local activism has been entirely dependent upon volunteers to hold the group together. As anyone who has done all-volunteer grassroots organizing can attest, such groups can live or die based upon the willingness of a few individuals to dedicate a significant amount of their time and energy to call people together, maintain regular meetings, and jump into the breach when something needs to be done. The Pittsburgh chapter has grown because dynamic and effective individuals have been willing to take on that role. In other cities, Ron Daniels and the Campaign for a New Tomorrow have gotten people interested in starting local chapters. But without key organizing volunteers willing to make the enormous time commitment, the groups have faded. Organizing in a community where many people are struggling just to survive makes the lack of staff all the more difficult.

The resource problem was also evident in the fall of 1995, when organizers had to postpone a founding convention in Philadelphia for an Independent Progressive Party. The planners wanted to extend the experience of the Campaign for a New Tomorrow in establishing people-of-color-led grassroots initiatives to other cities. By launching a new organization that was officially a political party, the initiators hoped to encourage people and groups who had shown an interest in independent politics to go the next step by setting up active local chapters. The Independent Progressive Party never got off the ground, however. Faced with scarce resources and little momentum, the planners found themselves stretched beyond the capacity to organize an effective launching.

The concept of the Campaign for a New Tomorrow as a people-of-color-led organization raises a basic dilemma that progressives need to face around the issue of race. As Ron Daniels argued in an October 1991 column, "Vantage Point":

> *As I move around the country promoting the idea of an independent presidential campaign in '92, I frequently encounter potential supporters in the Black community who are very skeptical about entering into a multi-racial coalition with progressive Whites. There is intense concern that white folks will dominate the coalition and that Black issues will be lost in the drive to present a "peoples' agenda."*

The inclusion of communities of color into positions of substantial leadership and initiative has been a fundamental difficulty for all of the other progressive political efforts that we have discussed in this book. By and large, all of these organizing projects have been initiated by white activists. The problem with many existing groups is that, despite their ideological opposition to racism and their awareness of the need for broad coalitions, they remain largely white organizations. The Labor Party Advocates, for example, has not been able to avoid reflecting the white, male-dominant character of leadership within the labor movement. Historically, organizations that do not start out with a multiracial leadership and membership have found it difficult to change their composition once they have been established. Of the national organizations, the New Party has the best overall record for fostering internal diversity. Yet even New Party activists understand that more needs to be done. Building a truly multiracial party is a never ending task.

The question facing the progressive movement generally is how to develop forms of organization and activism that will establish and maintain the central participation of communities of color—both in terms of the movement's activists, members, and leadership as well as ensuring the centrality of African Americans' and people of colors' agendas. As Ron Daniels has stressed, "Black people and people of color must function within an environment which insulates/protects their interests from the potential effects of racist and paternalistic attitudes and practices which might surface in any coalition effort." Whatever its limitations, the Campaign for a New Tomorrow does just that. Can other progressive third party efforts do the same?

No easy answers to this dilemma have emerged. Some groups have tried to bring together whites, blacks, and other people of color within their organization. Others have sought to build external alliances between groups. Some predominantly white organizations have actively attempted to provide appropriate aid to efforts within communities of color. While the best approach may vary depending upon the circumstances, clearly progressives who hope to foster a strong progressive political movement in this country must, from the very beginning, think seriously about how to cross the racial divide that is so strong in our society. The strengths and weaknesses of "going it alone" are perhaps best represented by the Greens, the oldest of the new national progressive third party efforts.

Green Politics

The Greens are not simply a US phenomenon, but part of an international Green movement that has developed throughout Europe and elsewhere. In recent European parliament elections, for example, Green parties won as much as 10 percent of the vote and a solid Green delegation exists within the parliament. Green mayors govern in cities such as Dublin and Rome. The flagship of the international movement is the German Green Party, which made world headlines when it broke into that country's party system in 1983. In that year, a new kind of politics entered the electoral arena when twenty-seven members of the newly elected Green delegation to the West German parliament arrived in Bonn, the nation's capital. While taking their seats, the Greens, clad in bright shirts and dungarees, entered a parliamentary room filled with legislators in drab business suits. During their festive entrance, the Greens carried large potted plants to add some life to German officialdom. German politics has never been the same since.

While the word Green is associated with ecological ideals, the Green movement is not just another term for the environmental movement. Not all environmentalists identify with the Greens and, more importantly, Green activists come from movement currents of which environmentalism is only one part. Both in Europe and the United States, the Greens are perhaps best described as the electoral expression of the New Left. Three major social movement strands came together in the Greens: the environmental movement, the women's movement, and the peace movement. Individual Green activists, for example, fought against nuclear power and the deployment of US Pershing II and Cruise short-range nuclear missiles. They worked for laws protecting the environment, for pay equity for women, and for paid parental childcare leave. They set up alternative papers, food and housing cooperatives, women's shelters, and coffeehouses.

These "post-material" movements can all trace their origins to the 1960s revolt by middle-class students and disgruntled professionals against the post-war boom society. In their own ways, each of these New Left movements saw the existing society as repressive, destructive, and spiritually dead. Within the Greens, ecological principles provided the glue for joining these currents together. With its emphasis on holistic thinking and interconnectedness, ecology provided a common ideological reference point upon which activists from the environmental, peace, women's, and other New Left and countercultural movements could come together in a common political effort.

A central characteristic of the Green movement has been the considerable diversity, and at times even sharp division, within its own ranks. While appreciating the complexity of Green thought, we can identify several general principles that help define the movement. One of the German Greens' early federal programs begins with a representative statement of these principles:

> The Establishment parties in Bonn behave as if an infinite increase in industrial production were possible on the finite planet Earth. According to their own statements, they are leading us to a hopeless choice between the nuclear state or nuclear war, between Harrisburg or Hiroshima. The worldwide ecological crisis worsens from day to day: natural resources become more scarce; chemical waste dumps are subjects of scandal after scandal; whole species of animals are exterminated; entire varieties of plants become extinct; rivers and oceans change slowly into sewers; and humans verge on spiritual and intellectual decay in the midst of a mature, industrial, consumer society. It is a dismal inheritance we are imposing on future generations... We represent a total concept, as opposed to the one-dimensional, still more production brand of politics. Our policies are guided by long-term visions for the future and are founded on four basic principles: ecology, social responsibility, grassroots democracy, and nonviolence.[10]

While traditionally more comfortable with nonviolent direct action campaigns and building alternative institutions, Green activists have sought to become an electoral force for change since the 1980s. This has compelled the Green movement to translate its visionary principles into concrete policies. The results have been striking.

The German Greens call for large-scale efforts to increase environmental protection—from a ban on nuclear power, a conversion to renewable energy, a sharp restriction in the use of industrial chemicals to tough regulations ensuring massive waste reduction and recycling. Yet, in contrast to some environmental groups, the Greens also push policies leading to far-reaching structural changes in the economy. Green governmental policies aim, for example, to dramatically transform the workplace. With a distrust of large bureaucracies, the Greens naturally gravitate toward reforms that encourage greater worker participation and control within the workplace as well as community- and worker-owned businesses. They also call for a major reduction in the workweek (to as low as thirty hours) and vastly expanded paid family leave (up to three years). Through these provisions, combined with tougher anti-discrimination and pay equity laws, the Greens also hope to strike a fundamental blow against patriarchal gender roles by allowing women and men to share equally in childcare, housekeeping, community work, and paid work outside the home.

Given their commitments to social responsibility, the Greens seek to uphold and extend a democratized welfare state. For example, they call for a universal, guaranteed income that provides minimum basic needs to all people not currently working in the market, regardless of their individual circumstances or reasons. Thus, if willing to live quite modestly, people will be free to pursue socially beneficial activities, such as childcare, personal development, and community work, that the market fails to assign a monetary value. For the German Greens, such policies can help provide a sphere of personal and community life that is shielded from the ravages of the capitalist market. The Greens also aim to uphold the national single-payer health care system by decentralizing it to enhance community control. Additionally, they propose policies to transform the health care system from one based on the one-dimensional logic of Western medicine, with its emphasis on drugs, surgery, and disease treatment, to a more holistic and preventative conception of health.

With nonviolence and holistic thinking at the center of their politics, the Greens offer a fundamental challenge to traditional foreign policy. They have long campaigned against military alliances like NATO, and have seriously proposed nuclear disarmament and "transarmament" to a nonviolent civilian-based defense system. They have also called on all the industrially developed countries to place 1 percent of their gross domestic product in an international climate fund, which would provide third world countries resources to aid them in their struggle with the environmental destruction caused by Western corporate interests.

Such policies, while quite radical, resonate among a significant sector of voters. In 1983, the German Greens crossed the 5 percent vote threshold required to send a delegation to the national legislature. With seats in the parliament, the Greens gained nationwide visibility from which to advocate their ideas. Parliamentary representation has also brought with it state-provided financial resources. While the total votes for Greens in Europe have gone up and down over the years, the Greens have become an established part of the political scene. In 1994, for example, the Greens became the third largest party in Germany when they received 7.3 percent of the vote in the national elections. That same year, they won over 10 percent in elections for Germany's seats in the European parliament—an increase of 1.6 points over the 1989 election. Several other countries also sent Greens to the European parliament. While observers usually look to national and European races for signs of success, the Greens strongest showings have come at the local level, where they have won enough votes to become partners in coalition governments, such as in Hesse, Lower Saxony, and the city-states of Bremen and Berlin.

The Green's electoral and parliamentary work has gained publicity for their ideas and helped place movements associated with the Green's into public debate and discussion. Indeed, other parties in Europe have responded by taking up many specific Green policies and causes, although clearly restructured for their own purposes.

Enter the US Greens

Green activists in the United States, inspired by the successes of the European parties, have sought to make a similar impact on US politics. The organizational roots of the US Green movement date back to a 1984 meeting of sixty-two activists in St. Paul, Minnesota. This gathering produced two major outcomes. First, activists wrote a basic statement of Green thought called the "Ten Key Values" (which embraced ecological wisdom, grassroots democracy, nonviolence, social justice, decentralization, community-based economics, feminism, respect for diversity, personal and global responsibility, and future focus). Expanding upon the German Green's four basic principles, these ten key values have served to guide US Green activism and given the movement a sense of identity. Second, after often passionate disagreements over structure, the group founded a fledgling organization called the Committees of Correspondence (CoC)—named after an organization of the same name that helped promote the American Revolution two centuries ago—later renamed the Green Committees of Correspondence.

The Committees of Correspondence was not a political party, but a loose network intended to tie together existing local and regional groups and encourage new ones to develop at the grassroots. In different parts of the country, local Green groups did develop, some achieving notable early success. For example, in New Haven, Connecticut, the Greens won as much as 23 percent of the vote when they ran candidates for mayor, town or city clerk, and alder seats. Many of these returns placed the Greens ahead of the Republicans as New Haven's main opposition party. The Maine Green Party played a major role in a successful referendum campaign to require a statewide vote to approve any radioactive waste disposal plan. In Vermont, the Burlington Greens helped to mobilize opposition to Bernie Sanders' early compromise plan on the waterfront development. In Chapel Hill, North Carolina, the Greens ran a campaign for mayor that gained significant publicity. In California, the Central Coast Greens and East Bay Green Alliance succeeded in blocking the release into the environment of Frostban, a genetically engineered microorganism manufactured by a firm in Oakland.[11]

In 1991, in Elkins, West Virginia, at their first fully delegated congress, Greens attempted to establish a national party structure. Delegates approved the first national green program and formally launched the Greens/Green Party USA. As the name suggests, the new organization sought to unite the movement (the Greens) with a political party (the Green Party USA) into a structure that would be more formalized and national in scope, yet controlled by the movement at the grassroots. This founding, however, produced a new level of controversy and division among the Greens. With various individuals offering quite different views on the nature of the disagreements, fully detailing the specific divisions is a difficult task. Opponents of the Green Party USA, and dissidents within the national party, have raised issues concerning such matters as the relative weight and independence assigned to electoral and non-electoral work, whether the Green Party USA should have a dues-paying membership (and, if so, what this would mean in terms of decision-making), how binding national decisions should be on local groups, and other organizational questions.

One group who chose not to join the new national organization formed a smaller and less formalized Green Politics Network. Among other projects, the Green Politics Network set up a Confederation of Autonomous Green Parties as a more loosely structured network of state Green parties. At the same time, several state Green parties, including California and Hawaii, chose not to affiliate with either the Green Party USA or the Green Politics Network. In part, their decision reflected a desire not to get involved in the GPUSA-GPN split. Their hesitation also involved some basic organizational dilemmas. The California Green Party, for example, has developed a far more formalized state structure than other state and local Green organizations. The California Greens have almost 100,000 residents who have formally registered as Greens. The Green Party USA, however, worked out its structure based upon a direct dues-paying membership. How to reconcile the two different forms of organization has been one of the structural questions that the national party and the California Greens had to work out between them.

Building Effective Grassroots Democracy

At the heart of such debates is the question of how to best build a democratic, bottom-up organization in the midst of a hierarchical society. Grassroots democracy, decentralization, and respect for diversity serve as three of the Greens' Ten Key Values. Greens have tried to build these values into the very structure of their organizations. As a 1992 statement from the national committee of the Green Party USA states:

> *The Greens believe we must build from below, city by city and state by state. A party of the people cannot be called forth from one national center, but must be the construction of grassroots people in communities all across the country.*

We can see these principles in the structure of the Green Party USA. The group can best be described as a loose federation of largely autonomous local groups. A brief introduction flyer provided by the national Greens/Green Party USA clearinghouse provides the following overview to explain Green organization:

> *The Greens are structured as a democratic association of locally-based activists groups. Our local Green chapters coordinate with each other at the state and regional level; through a regionally-elected Green Council which meets biannually; and nationally through mandated (instructed) and recallable representatives to conventions and coordinating bodies.*

The strength of Green politics lies in its literally hundreds of largely independent local chapters. Within these local experiences, Greens tend to place considerable emphasis upon broad participation, consensus decision-making, and respect for diversity. The challenge that the Greens have faced is how to combine these core values to produce effective and coherent strategies.

At the local level, such practices are fairly straightforward. Meeting in relatively small groups, Greens can easily emphasize inclusion and participation. With the ability to gather people together both routinely and when needed, activists can maximize participation and consensus-building while ultimately arriving at clear decisions and strategies. Such grassroots-level activism can also rely entirely upon volunteer time and energy and still function effectively.

The difficulties have come as the Greens have attempted to move such experiences to higher levels of organization. We live in a society in which the official institutions of power do not value participatory democracy and, thus, offer few ready-made models to draw upon. The challenges involved in integrating participatory, decentralized structures into a coherent organizational process is most clearly demonstrated within the Greens at the national level. In its actual operation, the Green Party USA's national structure is relatively weak. For example, where the New Party has a national office with staff who provide a focal point for developing an overall strategy and targeting resources, the Green Party USA has a clearinghouse that coordinates the passing of information to different groups and the broader public.

For national coordination and direction-setting, the Green Party USA relies upon an annual membership congress as well as an elected interim council, which meets twice a year to develop overall strategy. This decision-making structure has both its strengths and weaknesses. On the positive side, every Green can have a sense of participating directly in the national movement. All Greens can attend national gatherings, and delegates to the Green congresses and councils come directly from among their own ranks. Yet the Green Party USA has faced major problems in national level planning.

In the time between the congress and council meetings, the local and state chapters operate largely on their own. This autonomy has produced a rich diversity within the Greens in terms of local activities and strategies. Green publications and meetings show lively and energized debates. As with the German Greens, however, this level of decentralization also encourages internal fragmentation. Some Green congresses, for example, have witnessed sharp and heated debates between different Greens. Indeed, the Green movement has developed a reputation for internal disagreements and a culture among some activists for a strong distrust of authority. This experience suggests that decentralization does not automatically mean internal democracy, but can produce disorganization instead. At its best, autonomy can provide the movement with sophisticated strategies that combine varied local activity into an effective umbrella movement. Local diversity can also paralyze higher level decision-making by pitting differing local perspectives against each other. Instead of producing creative synthesis, national meetings, for example, can become battlegrounds between firmly entrenched localized perspectives.

By trying to make national decisions through a mass consensus-building process driven by initiative from the grassroots, the Greens have also risked making no decisions at all. The number of people involved, coupled with the tight timeframe of a weekend gathering, can place severe constraints on the ability of a meeting to produce clear decisions and overarching plans.

While these internal structural difficulties played themselves out, the Green Party USA also found itself in financial trouble. With the 1992 national conference running up a considerable deficit, coupled with other spending, the national party contracted a serious debt. As a result, the party had to strip down its operations and pull back on its publications. It has been unable to support a staff of field organizers to help inspire and sustain volunteer activity. Reflecting these internal difficulties, the number of national dues-paying members dropped from about 2,500 to 1,000 in two years. During roughly the same period, the organization went through four different coordinators of its national clearinghouse.

The Green movement, however, has always been driven by grassroots activism. Thus, although efforts to establish a unified and effective national structure fell into crisis, the Green movement continued to expand.[12] Several of the fledgling state and local efforts came into their own in the first half of the 1990s. While no organized Green parties formally existed in 1989, by 1994, eighteen states had electorally active Green parties: Alaska, Arkansas, California, Colorado, Florida, Hawaii, Maine, Missouri, New Mexico, New York, North Carolina, Ohio, Oregon, Pennsylvania, Rhode Island, Virginia, West Virginia, and Wisconsin. While membership in the Green Party USA dropped, membership in local and state Green parties continued to increase. Indeed, their total membership far exceeds the combined totals of all the national organizations. By 1995, the Green state parties had achieved official ballot status in five states: New Mexico, California, Maine, Alaska, and Rhode Island.

In 1994, the New Mexico Greens ran Roberto Mondragon, a former Democratic lieutenant governor turned Green, for governor. Not only did he win 11 percent of the vote, but other statewide Green candidate's totals ran as high as 33 percent in a two-way race. These returns qualified the New Mexico Greens as the first third party in the state's history to achieve "major party" status. In Santa Fe County, the two-and-a-half-year-old Greens had developed a particularly strong electoral movement. In 1994, their two candidates for state assembly won 32 and 43 percent of the vote respectively. Earlier that year, Chris Moore, was elected to the Santa Fe city council as a Green. In looking ahead to the next couple of years, the New Mexico Greens hope to spread active local groups throughout the state, win more local races, and break into the state legislature with one or two elected Greens.

In California, the Greens faced a choice of legally establishing a party by either winning 2 percent of the vote in a statewide election or convincing at least 80,000 people to register as Greens (out of a population roughly around 25 million). In 1992, the Greens chose the latter route and qualified as an official party after a major grassroots mobilization. Roughly 83,000 voters registered as Greens. The California Greens have also teamed up with the Peace and Freedom Party and other progressive groups to fight referendum battles for immigrant rights and a statewide single-payer health care system. In 1994, Greens won re-election or election in eight non-partisan races to offices on city councils, resources conservation boards, and school boards. In three California cities, the Greens have emerged as the second party with their candidates solidly beating the Republicans. In the partisan race for secretary of state, Green activist Margaret Garcia garnered about 4 percent with over 310,000 votes.

The Maine Green Party won ballot status in 1994 when Jonathan Carter, its candidate for governor, won 6.5 percent of the vote in a four-way race.

Rhode Island Greens gained 6.1 percent of the vote that same year when they ran Jeff Johnson for lieutenant governor. The Alaska Greens were the first state Green party to achieve ballot status when, in 1990, Jim Sykes, their candidate for governor, received 4 percent of the vote. The Greens then went on to elect Kelly Weaverling as mayor of Cordova (although he failed to win re-election two years later). In 1992, Mary Jordan, their candidate for the US Senate, won 8 percent of the vote. Candidates for the state legislature have achieved as much as 25 percent of the vote.

The Green parties with state ballot status embody only one part of electoral activism. In 1992, Hawaiian Greens made history by electing the first third party candidate since the islands became a state. Keiko Bonk-Abramson not only won election to the island of Hawaii's governing council, but won re-election in 1994 despite a strong effort to unseat her. Currently, she is the highest Green elected official in the United States and the only one to win in a partisan race. Ironically, the internal dynamic of the Hawaii council resulted in her being selected as chairperson for that body. As a result, Keiko Bonk-Abrahamson has become a powerful figure in state politics. When the Greens ran several ultimately unsuccessful candidates for the state assembly in 1994, they garnered 41 percent and 38 percent of the vote in a couple of two-way races and 17 percent and 10 percent in two multichallenger contests.

Elsewhere, active Green groups combine electoral and movement activism at the local level. In Chapel Hill, North Carolina, two Greens have been elected to local office and over a dozen more Green-supported candidates have won elections. The local Green group has combined this electoral activism with a host of issues work, such as establishing a citizen energy task force and a community land trust; promoting affordable housing, gay and lesbian rights, and racial justice; and protecting open space. Much of this work has been done through broad coalitions.

Other local groups have downplayed electoral work and focused primarily on non-electoral strategies. For example, in New Orleans, Greens have promoted community gardens, developed a community showcase of a Green image of urban renewal, and protested the granting of an honorary doctorate to the state's leading polluting industrialist. In upstate New York, Buffalo Greens fought against a nuclear waste facility and established a solidarity buying club to support family and organic farming. In nearby Syracuse, activists helped develop a Green cities youth project with Native American, white, and black children. They also adopted some empty lots for use as gardens. In Ithaca, the Greens have developed a pioneering example of an alternative money system, the Ithaca Hours, in which people use a local currency to barter and trade their labor time. Elsewhere in the state, Green groups worked to stop a hydroelectric project, block a toxic chemical-releasing cardboard recycling plant, and prevent timber harvesting in Allegheny State Park. In Wisconsin, the Greens organized against a sulfide mine, worked to reduce the use of bovine growth hormone, and developed a campaign against "Project Elf," a gigantic transmitter system designed to send secret one-way orders to submerged nuclear submarines.

Within this diversity, two polar ends have emerged in Green thinking. At one pole, activists express a deep suspicion of electoral politics. They fear the co-optation of the Green movement by a government apparatus tied to the existing society and oriented toward limited reforms. For example, once local Green parties qualify for statewide ballot access they have to conform to state election laws, which, in many cases, promote party structures at odds with Green desires for decentralization and grassroots control. Activists also argue that electoral politics can, by its own success, threaten non-electoral activism by bringing in many new recruits interested in elections, but not necessarily oriented to the Green social movement. Diana Balto Frank of the Lehigh Valley Greens in Pennsylvania expressed her concern this way:

> For North American activists, participating in electoral games serves one purpose: to divert us from working to make real, fundamental change. No matter how you play—whether it's running your own candidate or supporting someone else's—electoral politics devotes time and money to working within a system that cannot work for us, rather than to building grassroots movement which can become the basis for a new social system.[13]

Other groupings within the Greens see this as dead wrong. Many Greens look to winning state power and making concrete policy changes as a necessary component in the battle for fundamental change. These Greens want to enter electoral races not just to educate, but to win power and govern. David Spero of the Green Party of California is a strong advocate of this perspective:

> Those who claim an opposition between electoral work and "movement" work choose to ignore the tremendous power and resources of the state. Ignoring it will not make it go away. You have to engage the state and do the tremendously difficult work of transforming it and dragging it closer to the people. That is why the main business of the Greens should be electoral. Not because we want to "administer an oppressive system," as Left Greens put it. And not to get the message out. The message is already out. We run to win, and we win to use government resources to help organize and empower communities.[14]

These two positions represent the logical poles between which most Greens practice considerable diversity in their actual synthesis. Even the most election-oriented groups, for example, also sponsor movement-related projects. And even for Greens who do not reject electoral campaigns out of hand, their main focus may still lie primarily in terms of non-electoral activism.

The Green Party USA represents one version of this synthesis. It was founded upon the principle that the party should grow out of, and be responsible to, the broader movement. As an August 1992 statement by the national committee describes:

> We need a party of the movement, one that integrates electoral and extra-electoral action. It must be a party that grows out of, is rooted in, and is accountable to a grassroots movement based on popular action, counter-institutions, and an oppositional counter-culture.

The very name Greens/Green Party USA reflects the idea of the Greens as a broad movement and the party as its electoral expression. In contrast, the Green Politics Network has long sought to make electoral activity a key focus of activism in its own right, with greater organizational autonomy for the electoral wing from the larger Green movement.

Ideally, electoral and non-electoral work must complement each other. The co-optive dangers of electoral politics and governing do pose real problems. Non-electoral work alone, however, risks leaving the Greens, and progressives generally, stuck at our current level of scattered single-issue activism. To counter the Right and move off the defensive, progressives must begin to mobilize the broader population around a comprehensive movement for an alternative direction. Electoral politics provides the natural terrain to synthesize single-issue efforts into a broader movement.

Activists should not be forced into a trade off between the two poles. A nationally based political effort can tie single-issue activism into a broader movement. Electoral organizing should not simply revolve around the question of winning votes, but of building the broader movement. Similarly, decisions made concerning non-electoral work needs to consider questions beyond the specific issue at hand. For example, how does a particular single-issue project link up to and help build the broader political movement? Does a specific project help build coalitions with new groups or does it simply call out all the familiar faces? Does an action allow activists to raise awareness of the broader issues and expand the political base for other actions and electoral support or does it preach to the converted or simply educate on the specific issue at hand? In short, non-electoral work can deliver concrete changes while also providing building blocks of a political movement capable of taking state power and using that power, in return, to support non-electoral work.

In spite of the sometimes heated debates on strategy, electoral work by Greens has continued. By 1995, the Greens had thirty-five people in elected office and forty more in appointed positions of power. Such performances prove that the Greens are a potentially serious electoral force. Indeed, if this country used proportional representation, the US Green movement would follow their German counterparts by becoming a political bloc in at least several state legislatures, if not nationally.

The electoral victories of the German Greens compared to the Greens' many losses in the United States demonstrates the advantages that a proportional representation system provides for progressive movements. In Germany, half of the national legislature is elected in a winner-take-all process similar to our own, in which voters elect one representative from their area. The other half of the seats are distributed to each party according to their proportion of the votes. Thus, with similar vote totals, the German Greens are represented in their national legislature and the US Greens are not. As a result, unlike in the United States, most Germans know that the Greens exist and are a legitimate party. The nature of US electoral law is a serious obstacle to national Green success. Greens in the United States have not fully developed a strategic approach to overcome this problem.

Yet, by 1995, more promising signs became visible at the national level of the Green movement. The Green Party USA had begun to work out its internal difficulties. The Greens' national clearinghouse has moved to Blodgett Mills, New York, where a Green with extensive office managing experience has taken the job of coordinator. The level of internal tensions between different Green groups has also lessened. In the summer of 1995, the New Mexico Greens sponsored a national conference in Albuquerque that brought all the different Greens together. Coming out of the two-day gathering, activists from all the major Green groups, including the Green Party USA, the Green Politics Network, and several unaffiliated state Green parties, all agreed to be part of a unity-building process called Green Coordination/Green Roundtable. The initiative will bring Greens from all the different groups together to engage in continuing and non-binding dialogue about Green organizing in the United States.

Given the nature of the US electoral system, the Greens face two key strategic questions. The first is when to run or not run candidates for office. The second is whether to continue to primarily appeal to their natural base or to work more with others to build a winning majority coalition. These issues are not unique to the Greens, of course. As we have seen in this chapter, these questions are at the forefront of debates within the Labor Party Advocates and the Campaign for a New Tomorrow as well.

When to Run and When Not to Run for Office

In comparison to other groups, Greens have sought the widest range of public offices. While the New Party and the Progressive Coalition enter only those races that they feel they have a good chance of either winning or of making a very strong showing, many Greens have been willing to run for state and national offices that are currently quite out of reach. With the exception of Vermont, no progressive group running as independents or a third party has yet won seats in either state legislatures or in Congress, let alone statewide offices such as governor. Thus, in entering such races, activists are placing their time and energy into contests that, because of our winner-take-all system, currently will not produce any formal representation in the government. This can lead to demoralization, marginalization, and wasted effort.

Faced with such a prospect, the Greens have had to make serious choices. Some currently hopeless races are done for purely tactical reasons. For example, to qualify for an official line on most state election ballots, an independent party must run someone for a statewide office and receive a certain percentage of the vote. Thus, although Jonathan Carter received only 6.5 percent of the vote in a four-way race for Maine's governor in 1994, by crossing the 5 percent mark his campaign won statewide ballot status for the Maine Green Party. Jeff Johnson's 6 percent for lieutenant governor similarly qualified the Green Party of Rhode Island for their official line on the state's election ballot.

Other Green groups have run candidates for higher office because they perceive an opportunity to gain more publicity and enough votes to appear credible. For example, in running a former lieutenant governor, Roberto Mondragon, for governor, New Mexico Greens knew that they had a high profile candidate who would receive public attention. New Mexico activists with whom we spoke felt that his strong showing, plus similarly solid returns in other state races, gave a clear boost to the New Mexico Green Party, which has witnessed a large influx of new activists and supporters.

In many races, such as for state assembly seats or even for Congress, the major-party incumbents run unopposed. Under the right conditions, such races can provide progressives an opportunity to raise their profile. Since the third party candidate would be the only alternative, they can hardly be accused of being a spoiler who takes away votes from a second major-party candidate. And, since the vote is only split two ways, the progressive's returns may be higher than usual. In addition, the media may have to provide progressives with more coverage simply because they are the only alternative. But, because it is a two-way race against an incumbent that the other major party felt incapable of challenging, a progressive's chance of winning is also unlikely.

In all of the above examples, Greens have made strategic decisions concerning the potential for ballot access, media coverage, coalition-building, and fostering grassroots activism. Some Green campaigns, however, have also revealed a more candidate-centered logic. Because of the nature of our electoral process, finding qualified candidates is a constant dilemma for progressive organizers. Thus, a specific campaign can be governed as much by the availability of someone to run as by broader strategic considerations. This arguably was the thinking behind some Greens' efforts to have Ralph Nader's name in the California Greens state presidential primary. Seeing Nader as a high profile candidate, many Greens decided to seize what they saw as a unique opportunity to mount a major nationwide presidential campaign. Indeed, some activists had already been considering and even seeking such a bid. In this instance, and in other more local cases like it, activists ultimately responded to an individual's willingness to run rather than to a strategic plan out of which specific candidates would come.

Such candidate-driven campaigns can have their downsides. Given all of the obstacles they face in the media, the political culture, and with finances, third party campaigns need to rely upon strong grassroots activity to provide their advantage. When this grassroots structure is not in place, running a candidate may result in such a poor showing that the campaign discredits the party and demoralizes activists. The more a group has an overall plan at the local, state, and national levels, and the more it has active mechanisms for recruiting and grooming candidates from within its own ranks, the less likely the availability or scarcity of candidates will dictate a group's activities. Such planning and candidate cultivation, however, does require a significant investment of activist energy and resources—something always in short supply.

Unfortunately, running for offices that are well beyond a group's current reach can become a substitute for the steady and painstaking task of locally-based grassroots organizing. In entering high profile races, such as for governor or US Congress, activists may be lured by the prospect of media coverage and publicity. Indeed, under the right conditions and when used as part of a broader strategy, such a tactic may help promote the movement if it can win some media visibility. Progressives, however, cannot build a grassroots-driven movement using the tactics of the major parties. Such campaigns do not provide a viable means for activists to build their party. A grassroots base can only be developed through the relatively low profile, time-consuming, person-to-person work of locally-based, winnable election and issues work. At an electoral level, activists who spend more time running for higher offices than they do fighting the battles for city council, school boards, and mayors are not only going to lose elections, but are, at best, going to develop loose and temporary networks of volunteers incapable of sustaining an active long-term presence in their community.

Appealing to Your Natural Base versus Seeking a Majority

Like the two other national party-building efforts discussed in this chapter, the Greens come directly out of specific social movement currents. This is both a strength and a weakness. On the one hand, these groups arise in the first place precisely because they give political expression to a distinct milieu of social protest. On the other, their very origins place limitations on their ability to appeal beyond that milieu.

In a country with a more representative election system, appealing to distinct segments of the population would not be such a problem. In many cases, it would be an asset. Parties would be able to freely develop in ways that speak directly to their base without having to worry about whether or not this will deliver an electoral majority. In proportional representation systems, different progressive political parties can comfortably grow out of, and be culturally oriented toward, specific sections of the population, win seats in the legislature, and then negotiate with each other to form coalition governments or oppositions. This has been key to the success of the German Greens. Because of proportional representation, the German Greens can mobilize their base, win 5 to 10 percent of the vote, and then directly represent their supporters using the seats gained in the legislatures.

In the United States, however, parties have to win majorities or, if more than two candidates run, pluralities to take office. To gain a political presence, US parties cannot forever maintain a base of 10 percent of the voters. The dilemma here is real. To broaden its appeal, a party may end up abandoning the very perspective and politics that attracted its base in the first place. By avoiding such efforts, a party maintains its marginality. Neither is a promising outcome.

The natural solution for the Greens, and other parties, lies in alliance-building. Internally, Greens keep what is distinct about themselves intact, while at the same time working with other groups around specific actions and campaigns. Today, most forms of coalition-building come from alliances with non-electoral groups. At this stage, the strength of specific third party groups varies enormously by geography. Strong groups often do not overlap. For example, Chris Moore attributed both his own and the Greens' general success in Santa Fe to their efforts to build coalitions. Outside of elections, the Greens worked with other community groups around such projects as a living wage campaign, preserving a neighborhood grocery store, reforming property taxes, opposing NAFTA, raising awareness around the 500th anniversary of the European conquest of America, and starting a tenant-land-lord association.

For each of these issues, the Greens were able to use their own distinct perspective to support concrete projects that other groups may have come to in very different ways. All of this non-electoral work established the contacts, and mutual trust, and understanding that allowed candidacies that represented and spoke to a wide range of groups at election time. In particular, the largely white Greens were able forge a successful coalition with the city's growing Latino activist community.

This can likely be reproduced in many other localities. Given the difficulties in obtaining ballot access in this country, Green parties that do gain a ballot line can offer a coalition of groups the necessary mechanism to directly enter independent electoral politics. The task is to build the kind of ongoing interactions with other groups so that a diverse array of popular causes and progressive activists can look to the Greens and see their ballot line as a collective asset. This could increasingly happen. The Greens' holistic perspective, respect for diversity, and appreciation of the need for multiracial efforts make them potentially promising coalition partners.

Alliance-building can also be party-to-party. In cases where the Greens operate in an area in which other progressive third parties are active, such alliances can take the electoral form of running joint slates of candidates. For example, such cooperation has developed between the Greens and the Peace and Freedom Party in California. This may be the wave of the future. For progressives to reach enough of a critical mass to gain national public attention, they must eventually pool their efforts. Obviously, a formal merger of the different party-building efforts into a single progressive organization would represent the most direct solution. Certainly, such a combination of existing efforts—each with their particular strategic focuses, issues, membership base, and internal organization—is a complicated and involved task. There are, however, several important steps to be taken toward a single merged party.

Coalition-Building Efforts

In the United States, several groups are currently attempting to network among the different progressive political organizations to foster greater cooperation and operational unity. The oldest, the National Committee for Independent Political Action (NCIPA), dates back to 1984. NCIPA is a national network of organizers involved in progressive political efforts, not a mass membership organization. It aims to bring existing groups together and build strategic alliances around party-forming initiatives. It also promotes the idea of independent politics within the social movement community. People involved with NCIPA participate in a diverse array of groups, including the Greens, the Campaign for a New Tomorrow, the New Party, the Labor Party Advocates, the Peace and Freedom Party, the United Electrical Workers, Black Workers for Justice, the new socialist-oriented Committees of Correspondence, and the Southern Rainbow Education Project. NCIPA publishes the Independent Political Action Bulletin, an excellent source of information about progressive political efforts going on around the country.

In 1992, NCIPA not only helped Ron Daniels' presidential campaign, but also assisted the founding of the National People's Progressive Network (NPPN). Launched in August 1992 by 350 activists who met in Ypsilanti, Michigan, the network was intended to be what its name suggests: a network of progressive organizations, coalitions, and political parties to support independent politics, grassroots activism, and coalition-building. Yet the National People's Progressive Network has been handicapped by a lack of resources. In 1993, no follow-up national meeting was held.

NCIPA and NPPN organized the first annual National Independent Political Summit during the summer of 1995. This gathering brought together over 220 activists from twenty-five states, representing over 100 different grassroots party and movement organizations. At least one quarter of the participants were people of color, and the gathering was roughly balanced between male and female activists. For three days, activists met in workshops and plenary sessions to discuss potential joint projects, communication between groups, work with progressive Democrats, and building multiracial coalitions. The summit sponsored several caucus workshops, including ones for people of color, whites against racism, women, men against sexism, youth, and lesbians, gays, and queers.

The greatest achievements of the summit were probably the most intangible. That weekend, a wide diversity of people met together, got to know each other, and exchanged information. The summit helped to build direct grassroots-to-grassroots contacts within the movement for independent progressive politics. Yet, visibly missing, were many of the larger institutional players. While key people from the Greens/Green Party USA and the Campaign for a New Tomorrow were clearly evident, many other national and regional organizations, including the New Party, the Vermont Progressive Coalition, and the Labor Party Advocates, did not play a formal role. While activists who were members of these groups did attend as individuals, the organizations as a whole did not participate in either the planning or the decisions made during the three-day meeting. Thus, the summit was still more of a gathering of individuals rather than a meeting of organized groups.

Nonetheless, attendees discussed four major proposals for coalition work among progressive groups:

> *1. A National People's Pledge Campaign—in which grassroots activists would contact people in their communities to sign a formal pledge calling for the founding of a progressive third party. The campaign aims to collect up to one million signatures—enough to provide a mass base for creating a strong national party.*

> *2. Building a National Slate of Local Independent Candidacies—which would tie existing independent electoral campaigns together by having candidates, who keep their particular group affiliation and official ballot line, at the same time sign onto a common umbrella name and platform. Forming this slate would be tied to coordinating progressive activism around such related activities as voter registration, media work, and campaign training.*

> *3. A National Caravan/March for Social Justice in 1996—with Wall Street as its eventual destination to highlight economic, social, and environmental racism.*

> *4. A Movement-Generated 1996 Independent Presidential Campaign.*

The momentum of the 1995 gathering has continued. A second summit in April 1996 of about 100 people in Atlanta established the meeting as an annual event. The gathering set up a new institutional framework for continuing the groups' activities. The summit established the Independent

Progressive Politics Network by drafting a set of unity principles and approving an organizational structure. Through the Independent Progressive Politics Network and its annual summits, activists aim to further the initiatives discussed in 1995. In Atlanta, participants adopted a short platform, "A People's Vision: A Peace and Justice Program," to be used to develop a concrete national slate of local independent candidates. The 1996 summit also formally launched the people's pledge campaign, further discussed a 1996 presidential campaign, and reaffirmed the group's support for the caravan/march for social justice.

Third Parties '96—Building a New Mainstream

In the summer of 1995, activists from a diverse array of groups also met in Washington, DC to draw up a common statement of principles. With Republican victories the previous November, and the bankruptcy and ineffectiveness of the Democratic Party all the more clear, the need for deliberate cooperation among progressives had become more urgent. The Third Parties '96 conference met with the explicit goal of producing a common statement of principles that a broad coalition of independent political groups and participating movement organizations could agree to support. After four days of meetings, during which the group at times struggled with pushing along a challenging consensus-building process, the gathering did produce a Common Ground Declaration in which attendees agreed, by consensus, to seventeen principles.

1. We support proportional representation.

2. We support campaign finance reform to provide a level playing field in elections.

3. We support initiative, referendum and recall. We oppose their use in restricting civil and human rights.

4. We support more open and fair access to the ballot in all elections.

5. We believe that all economic activity should improve and protect the health of the earth, while promoting the happiness and prosperity of its inhabitants.

6. We must end corporate welfare.

7. We support public policies which respect all forms of life, preserve and promote biodiversity, protect endangered species, conserve natural resources, and eliminate pollution.

8. We support developing and promoting environmentally friendly, energy efficient technologies and renewable energy sources, especially all forms of solar power.

9. We would encourage, through economic measures and education, the practices of source reduction, reuse, and recycling, and we advocate the elimination of toxic, nuclear, and environmentally harmful substances.

10. We oppose race and class discrimination in exposure to environmental hazards, in communities and workplaces, including the siting of toxic waste facilities, employment in hazardous industries, and the location of energy and mining facilities.

11. We support people's right to control their own sexual and reproductive lives.

12. We propose an end to the war on drugs and its replacement with policies that treat addiction as a health matter, not a crime.

13. We would cut military expenditures dramatically, and provide for displaced workers.

14. We support the elimination of US military bases in foreign territories.

15. We believe that economic decisions should be made democratically, with participation by all affected workers, communities, and consumers.

16. We support the maximum empowerment of people in their communities, consistent with fairness, social responsibility, and human rights, to meet local needs, and to defend those communities against exploitive forces.

17. We support community courts and justice centers with emphasis on intervention, prevention, and mediation; alternative sentencing for juvenile and nonviolent offenders. We support community controlled law enforcement to handle lesser offenses and disputes and to maintain community order.

In addition to these seventeen principles of consensus, a strong majority agreed on twelve other statements, including further electoral reforms; fair taxation; equal funding for public education; several stronger statements against discrimination based on race, class, disability, sexual preference, and gender; housing as a basic right; and community-owned and -managed communication systems.

Even more than the National Independent Politics Summit, the Third Parties '96 meeting was a grassroots rather than institutional effort. The Common Ground Declaration was endorsed by people as individuals, not as official group representatives. Nevertheless, the roughly 100 individuals who attended came from over four dozen parties and organizations. The parties included various local, state, and national Green parties, Virginia and Maryland Libertarian parties, Pacific Party of Oregon, West Virginia Mountaineer Party, Socialist Party USA, Democratic Socialists of America, DC Statehood Party, New Party, Natural Law Party, Communist Party USA, Committees of Correspondence, Democratic Party of Maryland, Democratic Party of Virginia, Patriot Party of Virginia, and Independence Party of Kansas.

This list includes groups, like some Perot spin-offs and the Libertarians, that would not fit the conventional label of Left or progressive. Their participation did raise the issue of whether progressives wanted to seek alliance with such currents. Some activists wanted to stick to the progressive community. Organizers founded Third Parties '96 to foster a broad dialogue that included all groups who respected the coalition process and the principles agreed to in the Common Ground Declaration. Indeed, as Perot supporters and Libertarians talked to Socialists and Greens, all sides realized how much of an agenda they had in common. Attendants with whom we spoke were struck by the learning process in which people with quite different political backgrounds began talking to each other. Their agreement in the Common Ground Declaration provides a further indication that basic progressive principles have potentially widespread support within the general population.

Ralph Nader for President

By the winter of 1995, further activity aimed at building on the Common Ground Declaration was, at least momentarily, eclipsed as key activists in the initiative joined the draft Nader campaign. At gatherings such as the National Independent Politics Summit and the Third Parties '96 meeting, some activists showed clear interest in the prospects of a independent progressive presidential campaign in 1996. That sentiment remained fairly abstract until November 27, 1995, when long-time consumer advocate Ralph Nader made the surprise announcement that he would let the California Green Party enter his name into their presidential primary. The Greens had sent a letter to Nader asking to use his name as a way of generating greater publicity for their statewide efforts. Nader's decision in California sparked a nationwide draft Nader campaign, as Greens and other third party activists across the country sought to nominate this nationally known and trusted figure.

Nader, however, had only agreed to let the California Greens use his name in their primary. This decision did not mean that he was running for president. As Nader wrote in his reply to the Greens in California:

> I am permitting the Green Party of California to put my name on their March 1996 primary ballot to broaden the narrow agenda that the "major" party candidates parade before the electorate. I intend to stand with others around the country as a catalyst for the creation of a new model of electoral politics, not to run any campaign. The campaign will be run by the people themselves and will be just as serious as citizens choose to make it. It will be a campaign for democracy waged by the private citizens who choose to become public citizens. I will not seek nor accept any campaign contributions—but I welcome civic energy to build democracy so as to strengthen and make more usable our democratic process for a just, productive and sustainable society.[15]

Several groups sought to take Nader up on his call for a citizen-driven campaign. Early in 1996, Nader agreed that, if certain stipulations were met, he would allow his name to be placed on the Green Party's ballot in Maine. Groups in at least eighteen other states, including the Alaska and New Mexico Green parties and the Consumer Party in Pennsylvania, expressed interest in using a Nader candidacy.

Not everyone involved in independent politics, however, believed that a presidential race in 1996 was a good idea. While hoping for such a national campaign further down the road, many activists felt that a bid in 1996 was premature. Dan Cantor, a national New Party organizer, summarized the arguments against a Nader campaign when he commented:

> *There won't be a serious third-party challenge from the left this year; nor should there be. The base can't sustain it. We have to build our base at the local level before we try a Presidential run. Over time we can move up. But there's no substitute for building our power. It has taken the American left a long time to get as weak as it is. To think we can rebuild our strength by running for President is just unpersuasive. There is just no substitute for the unglamorous work of building a base city by city, state by state.[16]*

Without the resources and grassroots infrastructure to make a Nader bid a visible event, a progressive presidential campaign could easily be ignored by the media and simply use up activists' energy in a process that delivers only a few votes. Furthermore, the outright meanness of the Republican Contract with America and the budget confrontation between the president and Congress had made Bill Clinton a true "lesser evil" in the eyes of many progressives. As a result, many voters who might support Nader would vote for Clinton simply to prevent the Republicans from having unrestricted control of the federal government. By focusing on more local and winnable races, progressives avoid being labeled spoilers who pave the way for conservative electoral victories.

Nevertheless, Nader advocates pointed to the possible local benefits of his candidacy. With 5 to 10 percent of the vote in a state, a Nader candidacy could help local activists fulfill their state's guidelines for winning an official party line on their state's ballot. Such a showing could also qualify for some public campaign money. Furthermore, in areas where organizers are not running their own candidates, campaigning for Nader could provide a concrete activity to begin to pull together local groups.

During 1996, Nader remained aloof from the campaign. His caution seems warranted. In the past, high profile, candidate-centered efforts have not left behind the same level of grassroots structures that the more painstaking focus on local elections and issues work brings. Presidential bids should come as an expression of the strength and success of grassroots organizing. A national presidential race would thus provide a way for a network of established grassroots groups to break into the national spotlight in order to move their progressive political organizing to a new level. With local organizing today still at a rudimentary level, a presidential campaign runs the danger of becoming a substitute, rather than a complement, for the less glamorous task of mounting campaigns for school boards, city councils, and local ballot initiatives.

Whatever the limitations of these early efforts at coalition-building, projects like these have promise. Such activist-to-activist contacts are valuable in their own right. Yet, their long-term promise is that they can, in the not too distant future, lead to party-to-party alliances involving all the key institutional players.

New Zealand's Alliance: A Possible Model for the United States?

Recent coalition-building efforts in New Zealand might well serve as a valuable model for US party-to-party common projects. While a very different country, by the end of the 1980s, New Zealand progressives faced a situation that US activists would find quite familiar.[17] Corporate restructuring and right-wing attacks on the country's welfare state had caused a widening gap between rich and poor and a growing sense of economic insecurity among much of the population. Painfully, these changes had been led not by the conservative National Party, but by Labor, the supposed party of the Left. Only one Labor minister of parliament, Jim Anderton, a one-time party president, openly defied his party's leadership. This resulted in his expulsion from the parliamentary caucus and his resignation from the party. Anderton took with him several thousand disillusioned party members to form the New Labor Party. At the same time, other groups founded new political parties, including the Maori party, Mana Motuhake, the Greens, the Democratic Party, and the Liberal Party (formed by National Party members disenchanted with their party's rightward drift). As with the current situation in the United States, none of these groups was particularly large. Certainly, none by themselves was capable of making a significant impact on national politics.

In 1991, these small parties got together to form a coalition called the Alliance. The Alliance maintained the organizational autonomy of each party while running joint slates of candidates under a single name. Organizers did not have to wait long to see the fruits of their efforts. In 1992, the Alliance won control of the municipal authority that manages the regional assets of Auckland, the country's largest city. Challenging efforts to privatize the city's port facilities, the Alliance won 42 percent of the vote. A year later, the coalition won 18 percent of the national vote. Unfortunately, New Zealand's winner-take-all election system held the Alliance to only two out of ninety-nine parliamentary seats. That same year, however, the Alliance scored a major victory when the electorate passed a national referendum replacing the winner-take-all national elections with a mixed, half-proportional representation system similar to Germany's.

Today, New Zealand's corporate and political establishment is clearly worried. The new mixed election system promises to give the Alliance a greater number of parliamentary seats, better reflecting its percentage of the vote. Furthermore, for each seat that the Alliance wins, it gains a staff budget of $700,000. This can be used to hire more organizers in a country whose population is only around three million people. Of the twenty-five unions once affiliated with the Labor Party only four remain. The Alliance has begun evolving toward becoming a party itself, rather than just a coalition. Recently, the five member parties dropped their individual veto rights on Alliance decisions. They also changed the coalition's ruling body so that half of the representatives are chosen directly by regional Alliance caucuses, not by the individual parties.

While the obstacles to independent party politics in the United States are still formidable, they are not insurmountable. Indeed, the independent politics movement faces significant opportunities as well as obstacles, and the obstacles can be overcome.

Part Three

The Path Ahead

Can We Win?

Obstacles and Opportunities Facing the Progressive Movement

The prospect of building an alternative to our two party system can seem a daunting task. The obstacles are serious: an electoral system rigged against new parties, a hostile corporate media, and a society in which financial resources are concentrated in the hands of the few. In our nation's history, only the Republican Party provides an example of an outright victory in which a new party succeeded in breaking into the two party system. As this book has argued, however, the prospects for a progressive movement are not at all grim. Indeed, the political and economic changes of the past decade, and the inspiring responses of people at the grassroots, give amble reasons for optimism.

The Obstacles

It would be folly, of course, to ignore the problems facing activists. The obstacles built into US politics do make third party organizing quite difficult. The key question is how to understand these barriers. Are they challenges that can be overcome or are they reasons why a progressive movement will not work? In this chapter, we will examine four of the most significant stumbling blocks and discuss what activists are doing to overcome them. We then turn from these difficulties to the unique opportunities and advantages that progressives face today. These, too, should not be ignored.

Obstacle 1—The Legal Structure of Elections

In a country where laws are set by two major parties, it should come as no surprise that the legal arrangements that govern elections are hardly favorable to third party activism and political diversity. The difficulties go back to the writing of the Constitution. As a group of mostly wealthy white men, over half of whom owned enslaved human beings, the "founding fathers" were quite concerned to develop a system of government that would protect their privileges from the leveling spirit of the majority. As James Madison wrote in his defense of the Constitution:

> Those who hold and those who are without property have ever formed distinct interests in society.[1]

Later he proceeded to elaborate on what an "unjust and interested majority" of those without property might do if they got control of the government. This included "a rage for paper money [going off the gold standard], for an abolition of debts, for an equal division of property, or for any other improper or wicked project."[2]

Despite their hostility to the ideals of real democracy, the founders of our government had a problem. Many wanted to keep ordinary people from having any say in the national government at all. Yet, as armed revolts such as Shays' Rebellion testified, a new government that was too blatantly authoritarian in its design might spark a new revolution. The founders solved this dilemma by allowing some popular representation, which they then filtered and restricted so that it would not become the dominant voice in state affairs. Their filtered democracy had a number of levels. The founders established the House of Representatives elected by a popular vote of white men, although initially many states had property-ownership requirements to vote. They limited the power of this potentially popular branch by splitting the legislature in half. The founders created the Senate to block any "radical leveling" notions with which the House became infected. They also gave the presidency the power to veto legislation as well as set up a Supreme Court, which soon asserted its authority to declare any action of any branch of government unconstitutional. As originally formulated, none of these other branches were popularly elected. For over a century, the Senate was chosen by the state legislatures. The president is elected by the electoral college, which was also originally chosen by the state governments. Still today, Supreme Court justices are appointed for life by the president with the approval of the Senate.

Contrast this system with the constitution drafted by the small farmers and artisans of Pennsylvania. During the American Revolution, the Philadelphia militia sponsored a constitutional convention to provide their state with a new form of government. This Pennsylvania constitution provides some sense of what kind of national government we might have had if ordinary people had been given any say in the matter. It had a one-house legislature elected on a yearly basis, and required governmental authorities to clearly explain, publish, and distribute all proposed pieces of legislation to the public. Furthermore, the constitution prevented new legislation, except in the case of emergencies, from being voted upon until the next session of that body, after a new round of elections. Thus, candidates would have to campaign on the concrete issue of how they were going to vote on legislation about which the population had been well informed. The small farmers and artisans placed a great deal of faith and power in their democratic legislature. They established a weak executive branch made up of a council of twelve with no veto power. Their supreme court was elected by popular vote every seven years and subject to recall in the state assembly. Their constitution also set up a fourth branch of government, an elected council of censors, charged with overseeing the government's performance and with the power to recommend a new constitutional convention if changes in its structure were needed.

Replacing The Winner-Take-All System

While our basic constitutional structure hampers real democracy, the greatest legal obstacle facing progressive activists today is not found in the Constitution, but in state and federal laws that govern how we choose our representatives. The Constitution does not specify the way in which members of the House of Representatives are elected, but leaves this to state legislation and the Congress. Unfortunately, throughout our nation's history, lawmakers at the local, state, and national level have chosen the so-called winner-take-all system (also called a single-member plurality system) as the dominant method for electing representatives. Inherited from Great Britain, our winner-take-all system divides voters into distinct geographical areas in which each selects one person to represent it.

This method contrasts sharply with the classical, party-list style of proportional representation. Under a proportional representation system, each party receives a certain number of seats in the legislature equal to its percentage of the vote. The winner-take-all method ensures that only those who win a majority of the votes will get into office—or in the case of races involving more than two candidates, those who receive the largest minority. This system can render the wishes of large numbers of voters unrepresented. For example, in a two-way race, if one candidate wins 51 percent of the vote and another 49 percent, the latter's votes are wasted as only one person can fill the available slot. In a proportional representation system, by contrast, no one's vote is wasted since every party that gets a minimal threshold of votes (typically 5 percent) will get some seats. Thus, a party that wins only 10 percent of the vote will get 10 percent representation.

Since most new parties start out by winning over only a minority of voters, the winner-take-all system works to their disadvantage. In a proportional system, even 5 percent of the vote would give a new party representatives in the government and, hence, more public visibility. Indeed, even a small number of seats could provide the balance of power in a closely split legislature. In our system, however, a new party will often simply keep losing elections until it builds up a majority in each separate geographical area—something more difficult to do when it has no visibility in the legislature.

The founders were well aware that the winner-take-all system blatantly favored those who were already in power. As James Madison argued in *The Federalist Papers*, the system of representation must be designed in such a way as to break up the majority interest of the population (that is, those without property) by dividing them into separate geographical units in which parochialism, ethnicity, race, and other divisions could be used to cloud people's common interests. As Madison wrote:

> *Whilst all authority in [the government] will be derived from and dependent on the society, the society itself will be broken up into so many parts, interests and classes of citizens, that the rights of individuals, or of the minority [i.e., the wealthy], will be in little danger from interested combinations of the majority.*[3]

History has proven the founders shrewd defenders of their interests. The winner-take-all system has functioned quite well to prevent the majority from forming a party that would genuinely represent their needs.

The winner-take-all system is not written in stone, however. In 1967, Congress passed an act mandating that all seats in the House of Representatives had to be chosen by single-member districts. Congress could change the law to mandate a different system or simply relax the law to return to the historical experience in which each state determined its own method. Even with the 1967 law, individual states as well as local governments could adopt alternative systems for electing their own legislative bodies.

A strong case can be made for some form of proportional representation. The winner-take-all method hampers third parties and squelches political diversity. It also means that large numbers of people are not represented by a candidate of their choice. The Center for Voting and Democracy in Washington, DC has compiled what they call a "Representation Index" for the 1994 congressional elections. Researchers compare voter turn-out with the number of voters who cast ballots for the winning candidates to come up with the percentage of eligible voters who actually chose the elected members of Congress. The ratings went from a high of 35 percent in South Dakota to a low of 12 percent in Florida. These findings demonstrate that even in the best case only around one-third of the public actually chooses their representative.

The system of single-member districts also creates a host of problems related to how the authorities draw the actual boundaries of each voting district. Every ten years, current congressional districts are checked and redrawn according to population changes and other political criterion. Ever since the beginning of our nation, those in power have tried to draw the political boundaries in a way that benefits them. Known as "gerrymandering," this designing of boundaries for political ends can create all manner of oddly shaped districts as mapmakers concentrate one side's supporters or split up another side's voters. Although Congress has mandated that congressional districts be drawn in as compact and continuous a way as makes sense, this has not solved gerrymandering. In examining the 1991-1992 round, Sherly Seckel found that in states where one party was able to oversee redistricting, the redrawing of boundaries produced fewer competitive races in subsequent elections than in states where the process was more bipartisan.[4]

Our winner-take-all system, combined with the specific manner in which many districts are drawn, are two of the major reasons why elections for Congress are not competitive. For decades, incumbents who run for re-election win over 90 percent of the time. In 1986 and 1988, over 98 percent of all incumbents won re-election. In the 1994 House races, only 157 out of 435 seats were won by a vote margin of 20 percent or less. The rest were all landslides.[5]

The winner-take-all system of single-member districts also makes it difficult to bring racial fairness to US elections. With many whites commonly voting racially, African Americans and other candidates of color have a hard time winning elections in areas where people of color are not in the majority. Historically, district boundaries have been drawn in ways intended to deny black majority districts. The single-member district system is part of the reason why the racial composition of Congress does not look like the American population. For example, while African Americans make up nearly 12 percent of the US population, there were no African American senators in the 102nd congress. In the House, only 6 percent of the representatives were African American. A similar pattern exists for Latinos and Asian Americans.

This issue of how to draw political boundaries recently went to the US Supreme Court when North Carolina's newest district was challenged as a product of "racial gerrymandering." Under the direction of the US attorney general, who sought to apply the requirements of the 1965 Voting Rights Act, North Carolina drew the boundaries of this new district to ensure a black majority, thereby hoping to increase black representation in the state. Five residents challenged the redistricting by arguing that the plan was done solely to segregate races for the purposes of voting and, therefore, was unconstitutional. In hearing the *Shaw v. Reno* case in 1993, the Supreme Court agreed with the plaintiffs and by a five to four decision ruled that the five residents did have a valid claim for relief under the Equal Protection Clause of the Voting Rights Act. The justices ordered the case sent to the US District Court for trial. In 1995, in *Miller v. Johnson*, a majority of justices similarly declared a black-majority congressional district in Georgia racial gerrymandering and unconstitutional.

This question of supposed racial gerrymandering simply would not be an issue in a full proportional representation system. Anyone who wanted to be represented by a member of their race would win a proportion of representation equal to their percentage in voting. This is arguably a much fairer way of addressing problems of racial gerrymandering.

The winner-take-all system has also not worked well for women who attempt to break into the political system. Although women are over half the population, in 1994, they made up only 11 percent of the members of the House of Representatives. In Germany, which has a split system (in which half of the national legislature is chosen through a proportional representation system of party lists and the other half by single-member districts), women won 13 percent of the contested seats in single-member districts, but received 39 percent of the seats filled by proportional representation.[6]

To move elections from winner-take-all to proportional representation requires two logical steps. First, we have to replace current single-member districts with multi-member schemes. For example, a state with twelve representatives could set up three four-member districts, or two six-member districts, or one twelve-member district. Yet multi-member districts are not, by themselves, the answer. While some states, such as Vermont, and many local governments currently use multi-member districts for their own legislative bodies, most of these cases still maintain a winner-take-all system by using plurality voting. Under this method, voters get to choose up to as many candidates as seats in the district. So, in a four-member district in which 51 percent of the public supports party A and 49 percent support party B, party A still takes all the seats.

There are several ways of organizing elections in multi-member districts that will prevent a winner-take-all result. The most direct system is called limited voting. Under this method, people vote for fewer candidates than the actual number of seats. The most extreme example of this is to allow each voter only one vote. Thus, in a four-member district, the candidates supported by the top four voting blocs would be elected, rather than simply the largest group that votes for all of its candidates.

A second method is cumulative voting. Here, voters cast as many votes as the number of seats, however, they can vote for one candidate more than once. In our four-member district, voters could, for example, cast all four votes for a candidate that they really wanted to ensure was elected. Thus, a minority could still elect at least one candidate by concentrating their votes.

Preference voting offers a third alternative. Under this system, voters rank their choices in order from first to last. The formula for determining preference voting results sounds complicated, but a computer can determine the results quickly and accurately. Basically, in a race for just one office, the ballots are scanned to see if any candidate has won an outright majority of people's first choice. If not, the candidate who received the least first choices is eliminated and those voter's second choices are then added to the evaluation. If, at this point, one of the surviving candidates has still not won a majority, then the next lowest candidate is also eliminated and that person's voters are redistributed. This process continues until someone is elected. With a modified formula, preference voting can be used in the same way to elect a number of candidates in a multi-member district.

All of these systems have been used in the past and today for state and local representative schemes. During the first half of this century, nearly two dozen cities adopted proportional representation, including Boulder, Kalamazoo, Sacramento, Cleveland, Cincinnati, Toledo, New York, and Wheeling. At the state level until 1980, Illinois used cumulative voting for its state legislature. Cambridge, Massachusetts has used preference voting for all of its local elections. Not surprisingly, Cambridge has experienced higher voter turn-outs and a lower decline in voter registration than similar neighboring communities, such as Somerville, Medford, and Worcester, which do not use this system.[7]

These alternative methods have also been used by other countries to select their national legislatures. Prior to 1994, Japan used limited voting. Today, both the Irish legislature and Australia's upper chamber use preference voting. While each system has its own merits and limitations, all of these alternatives have proven to promote greater diversity than the winner-take-all method. Under these systems, a candidate does not have to have the support of the majority or even the largest plurality to win office. Thus, a much greater number of voters will actually get some representation in the government.

The system used by most of the world, including most of Europe, Latin America, and the nations that emerged from the breakup of the Soviet bloc, is the party-list version of proportional representation. Under this system, each party develops a ranked list of candidates that run under its name. People vote for the party, not individual candidates. Each party is then granted a number of seats equal to its proportion of the vote. Typically, the specific candidates sent to the legislature are selected in order of the party's list. Thus, if a party won ten seats, its top ten candidates would be the ones to take office. Of the methods discussed so far, the party-list system is the most removed from the candidate-centered norm of US elections. At a national level, however, it is arguably the best of all the possibilities because it encourages strong parties. Progressive activists can only benefit from changes that strengthen a party-based, rather than candidate-centered, brand of politics.

Such systems may sound desirable, but can activists succeed in getting them adopted? New Zealand is the most dramatic example of a popular victory in this regard. In 1992, voters went to the polls and rejected their country's 140-year-old winner-take-all system by an overwhelming majority

of 85 percent. A follow-up referendum put a German-style system in place
in 1993.

Pressure for proportional representation is growing in this country as
well from a number of different sources. Obviously, many progressive
groups would like to see such a change. Some right-leaning groups would
also like to see an alternative system. This would allow conservative groups
to break off from the Republican Party. In the short run, even the
Republicans might benefit in some sense from a proportional system as the
Democratic Party tends to get slightly more representation in the House than
its straight percentage of the vote. According to the Center for Voting and
Democracy, for example, Democrats received 50.8 percent of the overall
vote in 1992, but won 59.3 percent of the seats. In 1994, however, this
contrast dropped to 46.6 percent of the vote and 46.9 percent of the seats.[8]
Such conservative possibilities, while making for strange temporary allies,
should not dissuade progressives from seeking real change. Although
proportional representation may open up some opportunities for the Right,
progressives would clearly, in the long run, be the major beneficiaries.
Because we live in a country whose official political spectrum is tilted
decidedly to the Right, the greatest political growth area is to the left of the
two major parties.

Progressives might also get some help from the court system. In striking
down what it called racial gerrymandering in North Carolina and Georgia,
the Supreme Court has left proportional representation as the only remaining
way of fulfilling the Voting Rights Act's mandate for racial equality in
elections. In 1992, the NAACP filed suit against the small town of Atlanta,
Texas. They pointed out that no black had ever won election to the
five-member school board chosen by a winner-take-all system. Black
candidates tended to gain the number of votes roughly equal to the number
of black voters—a result not sufficient to win. (Blacks comprised 20 percent
of Atlanta's population in 1990, and 31 percent in 1995.) In the settlement,
the town authorities agreed to adopt cumulative voting. Casting all their
votes for their one candidate, black voters succeeded in getting Veloria
Nanze elected to the school board in May 1995. By that time, over two dozen
municipalities in Texas had similarly adopted cumulative voting. Despite
continued racially polarized voting, many of these places experienced
significant gains in black and Latino representation that same year.

Several cities, such as Peoria, Illinois; Alamogordo, New Mexico;
Sisseton, South Dakota; and Chilton County, Centre, Guin, and Myrlewood,
Alabama have recently adopted cumulative voting as a way of increasing
fair representation for blacks, Latinos, and Native Americans. In 1994, in
Cane v. Worcester County, a federal judge became the first to order
cumulative voting as a remedy for a case against a local government.
Activists in Eugene, Oregon spent the fall of 1995 collecting signatures to
place a referendum on the ballot establishing preference voting for city

council elections. They hope to have a vote in 1996. In San Francisco, an elections task force has recommended placing a two-part referendum before voters. The first question asks if voters want to change the current at-large, plurality system for selecting the city council. The second part asks them to choose from among four alternative plans: single-member district, preference voting at-large, cumulative voting, and preference voting in five three-member districts.

We should note, however, that even though proportional representation would make the task of building a progressive political movement easier, building a third party within our current system is not impossible. In spite of the winner-take-all system, both the Populists and Socialists developed serious third party movements that were not foreordained to eventually decline. The bottom-up strategy used by the New Party and other groups provides a realistic strategy for building organization and momentum even within the current system.

The United States is also not the only country that uses a winner-take-all, single-member district system to elect its national legislature. Indeed, the system is dominant in the Anglo world, including Great Britain, Canada, and Australia. France also uses a winner-take-all method. We have only to look north to find an example of a successful challenge to a two party system like ours. From 1962 to 1993, the New Democratic Party of Canada plugged away within a winner-take-all environment. Thanks to the grassroots and financial support of organized labor and other progressive groups, the NDP climbed from 13 percent of the vote in 1962 to a peak of over 20 percent in 1988. In 1962, it held nineteen seats in the federal legislature; in 1988, it held forty-three. These kinds of strong showings have made the New Democratic Party a recognized force in Canadian national politics. Even more significantly, the Party took power in several provincial governments, including Saskatchewan, British Columbia, and, for a while, Ontario, the nation's largest province. Whatever the strengths and weaknesses, the New Democratic Party experience proves that, under the right conditions, a winner-take-all system does not have to be a deciding obstacle to third party politics.

Ballot Access

While overcoming and, ultimately, replacing our winner-take-all system is probably the greatest rule-changing task facing progressives, four other legal concerns affect independent political organizing.

The first is ballot access. For people to vote for progressives, candidates and/or parties must be on the ballot. While it makes sense to have some requirements for ballot access—so that people cannot simply walk in off the street and clutter up the ballot up with their names—the United States has more restrictive ballot access laws than most other liberal democracies. As Richard Winger, editor of *Ballot Access News*, points out, other countries such as Great Britain and Canada have winner-take-all systems in which two parties predominate. Yet these electoral systems still support long-standing third parties that are a permanent institutional part of their country's politics with a credible impact on political debate. The United States is one of the few systems in which third parties are virtually absent from national politics. Winger argues that the main reason for this contrast lies in the more restrictive ballot access laws operating in our country.[9]

In the United States, ballot access laws are set by state legislatures. Would-be parties and independent candidates have to wade through a wide spectrum of requirements ranging from extremely restrictive to relatively fair. Typically, states require candidates and parties to collect a certain number of petition signatures to qualify for the ballot. In the 1971 *Jenness v. Fortson* ruling, the Supreme Court upheld a Georgia law that set petition requirements for each candidate at 5 percent of registered voters. Under this law, a third party has to collect roughly 100,000 signature for *each* person it wishes to nominate for state office. Georgia law does allow an organization to qualify for party status, which frees it from this requirement. Yet party status is only granted after a group has received 20 percent of the vote in a statewide election. In the 1940s, when these requirements were originally established, this margin would have disqualified the Republican Party had it not already had ballot status.

By upholding the Georgia laws, the Supreme Court gave a green light to other states to raise their requirements. In the decade after the ruling, thirteen state legislatures increased their requirements. None voluntarily lowered them. In Arkansas, for example, a new party needs to get a number equal to 7 percent of the last vote cast. In some states, any registered voter can sign a petition. In others, only those voters who did not vote in a primary can sign a petition for a new party or independent candidate. Some states either require or give the option to parties of registering voters under the party's name. In California, for example, a new party qualifies either by submitting a petition signed by 1 percent of the last vote cast or by persuading that same number of voters to register as members of the party. States can also set the requirements at different levels for different offices. Often candidates can find it easier to run for president than for a more local office. In 1992, for example, Florida required a third party or independent presidential candidate to collect 60,312 signatures, but a third party or independent running for a statewide office needed 180,936.

While such numbers may not seem great, to a fledgling organization they can prove a serious barrier. Richard Winger estimates that if, in 1994, a new party had tried to run a full slate of candidates for all federal and state offices, it would have had to collect 3,501,629 valid signatures. In Russia, by comparison, a party needs 100,000 signatures to get on the ballot for all offices, and in South Africa only 10,000. The laws in Great Britain and Canada require no petition signatures. Instead, candidates to all parties simply pay a filing fee. In Great Britain, paying such a fee gives a candidate two free mailings to all the voters, and an equal amount of free TV and radio time.

Ballot access laws in the United States show a clear double standard. The law sets much lower standards for the already established Democratic and Republican parties, which have nearly automatic ballot access due to their major party status. Only individual candidates seeking the Republican and Democratic nomination in a primary need to collect signatures. While, in 1994, a new party would need to collect 1,593,763 signatures nationally to run a complete slate for the House, the Democratic candidates only needed 138,996 to place themselves on the primary ballots in all 435 contests.

Even for parties and candidates who get a sufficient number of signatures, the battle may not be over. Authorities can challenge petition signatures. In 1993, for instance, supporters of a successful local referendum initiative in Tampa found their efforts struck down by the Florida supreme court. Despite the fact that the initiative had been approved by voters, the court declared the original petition invalid because some of the people who signed were on the inactive portion of the voter registration rolls. State law defined "inactive" voters as those who had not voted in the preceding two years, but had voted in the preceding five.

Depending on the state law, would-be candidates and parties also need to get started early, often well before their two party rivals. In some states, new parties have to qualify more than a year before an election. In 1994, a party that did not organize to fulfill state legal requirements before July would have found itself off the ballot in thirty states. Had the current laws been in effect in 1854, history would have been quite different. On July 6, of that year, organizers founded the Republican Party, which then went on to win more congressional seats and state governorships than any other party in that year's fall elections. In most countries, the deadlines for qualifying for the ballot are often only a month before the election. In South Africa, Chief Buthelezi's Inkatha Freedom Party qualified for the ballot less than a week before the election!

In tracing the origins of ballot access laws in the United States, Richard Winger sees a history clearly aimed against third party and independent challenges. Until 1888, no ballot access laws existed because the state did not print ballots. Instead, voters brought their own or used those provided by the parties. As late as the 1920s, most ballot access laws were fairly mild. In 1924, for example, only 50,000 signatures were needed to place a new party on the ballot in 48 states. In 1920, such low requirements allowed the Socialist Party to run candidates for over half of the seats in the House of Representatives.

Beginning in the 1930s, however, states began raising their requirements, typically in response to insurgent challenges. For example, frightened by the growth of the Communist Party, the Illinois legislature increased statewide petition requirements in 1931 from 1,000 to 25,000 signatures. They also required the petition to include 200 signatures each from at least fifty counties. That same year, Florida changed its laws to define a political party as a group that polled at least 30 percent of the vote for any statewide office in either of the last two presidential elections. The Communist Party sued, but lost its case before an unsympathetic court. When the Republicans failed to meet the 30 percent criterion in 1932 and 1936, the limit was retroactively lowered in 1937 to 15 percent. After Henry Wallace's 1948 Progressive Party campaign for president, Ohio amended its laws to prevent presidential candidates from using the independent candidates' procedure to get on the ballot. At the same time, Ohio increased the requirements for independent candidates for other offices from 1 to 7 percent of the last gubernatorial vote. In 1967, the Texas legislature responded to the growth of the Constitution Party by changing from a system that had no petition requirements to one with a 1 percent threshold of signatures from people who had not voted in the primary. The law also gave activists only fifty-five days to conduct the petitioning. Similarly, in 1969, New Mexico went from a no petition system to a petition one, requiring over 15,000 signatures after the People's Constitutional Party tried to build representation for Latino voters.

Not every state has restrictive laws. Mississippi and Vermont both allow any party on the ballot that can show it is organized. New Jersey requires only 800 signatures for a statewide third party candidate. Tennessee restricts third parties, but allows independent candidates to get on the ballot with only twenty-five signatures. Unfortunately, few other states have followed these examples. Between 1930 and 1950, eight states increased their ballot access requirements. In the 1960s and 1970s, twenty-two states did the same. This pattern has only changed somewhat recently. In the 1980s, while five states significantly increased their ballot access requirements, eight other states decreased theirs. Most did so because of court rulings. Thus far, in the 1990s, only Alabama has seriously increased its requirements, while five states have eased access—Massachusetts did so by an initiative, the four others by acts of their legislatures.

Overall, the court system has proven unreliable on the ballot access issue. In 1968, the Supreme Court struck down Ohio's new restrictive changes. Yet it upheld equally restrictive laws in Georgia in 1971, in California and Texas in 1974, and in Washington state in 1986—all with the argument that such laws are necessary to avoid "voter confusion" and to preserve "stability." In 1994, the Court also upheld Kansas' early petition requirements on the grounds that the state has an interest in "voter education."

Efforts do exist across the country to ease ballot access. In 1994, Connecticut lowered the number of signatures for a statewide third party or independent candidate from 1 percent of the last vote cast (about 15,000 signatures) to a flat 7,500. That same year, Nebraska dropped its provision banning petitioners from collecting signatures outside of their own county. Virginia loosened a similar law restricting people to their congressional district. Rhode Island moved from requiring a new party to win 5 percent of the vote in the race for governor before it could get recognized party status to allowing activists to qualify the party by collecting signatures. A federal judge in Colorado ruled that the state cannot require 1,000 signatures to get a third party or independent on the ballot for state legislative elections as long as it requires only 500 signatures for the US House of Representatives.

Not all of the news was good. In New York, the US Court of Appeals overturned a lower courts' ruling that had thrown out a state law requiring all signatures on petitions to include the signer's precinct number and legislative district number. Because of the law, activists often had to spend hours looking up this information since few people know their precinct number.

The ballot access hurdles, however, are not insurmountable. Indeed, in the experience of the activists interviewed for this book, even an "infant" progressive political movement should have the grassroots strength to collect the individual signatures or registrations to get on a specific ballot. Petition signatures collection requires door-to-door outreach, work that progressives should be doing in any case. The task does become more difficult as a group expands its scale of operation to run more candidates and/or gain recognized party status. The effort needed to get several candidates on the ballot uses valuable time and energy that could be better spent elsewhere. In a less restrictive environment, new parties and candidates could get on with the task of educating and mobilizing people.

Voter Registration

Access is not the end of the story. Once a party or candidate gets on the ballot, a person must still be registered in order to vote for them. The United States is one of the few countries in the world that requires each individual citizen to register themselves. Most governments take on this responsibility. For example, many countries automatically register voters permanently upon achieving voting age. In Canada, before a national election, the government sends thousands of state workers out into the streets to complete a national census that updates the registration rolls for all Canadians.

The lack of such a government mandate in the United States reflects the origin of our registration laws. They came at a time when the two major parties were trying to purge people from the electorate in order to stave off political challenges by citizens groups, such as the Populists and Socialists. We can thank the Civil Rights movement, which won the Voting Rights Act of 1965, for battering down many of these obstacles. Still, the fact that each individual has to track down the procedures and registration offices in their state means that many Americans remain unregistered. In 1984, for example, only 127 million people, or 73 percent, were officially listed as registered out of a population of 174 million eligible voters. On examining the year's data further, Frances Fox Piven and Richard Cloward put the estimate more in the mid sixties percentile.[10] Reforming these laws would clearly help raise registration levels. Some states do practice same-day registration, whereby people can register when they go to vote. These states experience voter turn-out levels about ten percentage points higher than the national average, with about two-thirds of that difference attributable to these simplified registration procedures.[11]

In May 1993, President Clinton signed the National Voter Registration Act into law. This could potentially increase voter registration significantly. More popularly known as Motor Voter, the new law requires state agencies to offer to register citizens to vote when they get a driver's license, Food Stamps, Medicaid, AFDC, and WIC as well as at agencies that provide services to people with disabilities. The law mandates that states accept mail-in registration and bans states from removing people from the rolls simply because they have not voted. By 1995, millions had registered to vote using these new procedures. In May 1995, Human SERVE, a national organization dedicated to ensuring that Motor Voter is fully implemented, estimated that twenty million new voters would be on the rolls for the 1996 elections.

Unfortunately, many state governments have not embraced the new law with open arms. In particular, Republican governors and state legislatures fear that since those who are not registered are more likely to be poor, a minority, and/or young, any increase in registration will produce more Democratic voters. California, Illinois, and Pennsylvania were the first to openly declare their intention to block the law. Illinois and Pennsylvania dropped their challenges only after losing several lawsuits. California lost its initial appeals. In response, citizen lawsuits have been filed in Louisiana, Michigan, Mississippi, New Hampshire, and South Carolina in an attempt to force these states to implement the law.

Politicians who want to sabotage Motor Voter often cry that it is an "unfunded federal mandate." They say they do not have the money to provide people with this basic democratic right. Governor Carroll of Georgia, for example, vetoed a $570,000 appropriation for implementing the law, claiming that this amount, equal to a mere 0.005 percent of the state budget, was an unreasonable financial burden![12] Some states, such as New York, Oregon, and Kentucky, have decided to stick to the letter rather than the spirit of the law. Since officially Motor Voter applies only to federal elections, these states have established two separate voter registration forms: one for federal races and another for state and local races.

Our country could also benefit from other reforms to encourage people to vote. For instance, there is no reason for having our elections on a Tuesday, other than to discourage working people from voting. Other countries either hold their elections on a weekend or declare election day a national holiday. For its historic first democratic elections in 1994, South Africa's polling places were open for three days. Our government could also take responsibility for providing its citizens with complete and up-to-date information on the procedures and locations for voting.

Fusion

Another set of legal obstacles face progressive activists who try to pursue a flexible fusion-candidate strategy, as used by the New Party. Fusion allows third parties to run common candidates with each other and/or with a major party—thereby increasing their chances for victory. Most states have passed laws that ban two parties from endorsing the same candidate. These laws date back to the Populist era when the People's Party used fusion to noticeable advantage. Currently, fusion is legal in only ten states.

This legal restriction may not survive long. The New Party has legally challenged laws that ban fusion. Although the New Party lost its first case in Wisconsin in 1992, in the early 1996 Twin Cities *New Party v. McKenner* decision, the US Court of Appeals for the Eighth Circuit ruled that Minnesota's ban on multi-party fusion is unconstitutional. In April 1994, the Twin Cities Area New Party had nominated Andy Dawkins, an incumbent state representative, as their candidate for that office. When the secretary of state's office rejected the nomination because Dawkins had already filed on another party line, the New Party took its case to court and won. The new ruling also renders the anti-fusion laws in Iowa, Missouri, Nebraska, and North Dakota invalid. More significantly, the Eighth Circuit Court's ruling has been appealed and the Supreme Court has agreed to hear the case. If the Court upholds the ruling, bans on fusion will be wiped out nationwide. Such a legal victory would open up a whole new level of third party activity as organizers would no longer have to face an either/or trade off between running candidates on their own ballot line or running them as Democrats. Equally important, coalitions of third parties could easily run common slates.

Such efforts will likely face other obstacles, however. In Minnesota, the New Party recently voted to cross endorse progressive Democrat Paul Wellstone for US Senate and three other progressive Democrats for the state legislature. Volunteers collected the 25,000 signatures needed in fourteen days. Yet the chair of the state Democratic Party attempted to block cross endorsements by adjusting internal party policy. The attempt at fusion did win significant support from institutional players in the African-American community and the labor movement. This bodes well for the New Party's future efforts.

Term Limits

Finally, a movement is afoot in the United States to limit the amount of time that candidates can hold office. In recent years, term limit proposals have increasingly been put on state ballots and passed by voters. A popular version of congressional term limits restricts senators and representatives to twelve consecutive years in office. Voters in several states have passed term limits for state offices as well. The base of this movement has come from conservatives aiming to break the Democrats' forty-year lock on Congress. Having achieved this in 1994, their enthusiasm for term limits has waned. Yet polls have shown that anywhere from two-thirds to four-fifths of the American people still favor term limits. From a progressive perspective, such limits would not bring about a vast political change by themselves. Replacing an incumbent politician dedicated to politics as usual with another mainstream candidate also committed to the status quo accomplishes little. In trying to break into the two party system, however, progressives do have to face the dilemma that incumbents get re-elected at an alarmingly high rate. Progressive candidates would benefit from more open, and hence more competitive, races. Unfortunately, the Supreme Court has declared its opposition to such limits by striking down congressional term limits as unconstitutional. In the Courts' opinion, if people want term limits for national offices they will have to amend the Constitution.

Obstacle 2—Money and Corporate Media

Bob Dylan once said, "Money doesn't talk, it swears." Few would argue with the statement that money drives American politics today. In 1992, the winner of a seat in the US House spent, on average, $543,000, and the loser $201,000. In the Senate, those numbers go up to $3.9 million for a winner and $2 million for a loser. What is worse, these figures represent steadily climbing campaign costs. Just nineteen years ago, the average cost of winning a campaign for the House was a mere $55,000![13]

Our money-driven electoral system does not benefit the general public. According to the Capitol Hill newspaper *Roll Call*, fewer than 900,000 citizens gave a direct individual campaign contribution of $200 or more in 1992. Yet, that same year, 81 percent of congressional campaign money came from these high amounts. While some political action committees (PACs) do exist that represent ordinary people, most represent corporate America. In 1992, business PACs gave almost $127 million to congressional races, outspending labor PACs by a three to one margin. When combined with the contributions of wealthy individuals, business outspent labor by $295 million to $43 million. The wealthiest environmental PAC, the Sierra Club, gave $612,000 in 1992, while polluting industries contributed over $20 million.[14]

Adequate campaign funds are not impossible to raise. Progressive candidates and parties can convert grassroots activism into significant financial support. While most progressive candidates will be outspent by their mainstream opponents, a few progressive campaigns, such as some of Bernie Sanders' in Vermont, have actually raised more money than their Republican and Democratic opponents. Yet, as progressives are more successful, they will be running more candidates and, hence, dividing the available funding pools in more directions. Unfortunately, as long as activists can not break out of our country's candidate-centered politics, they will find themselves having to support a separate campaign for each individual they are running.

Access to financial resources is a major difficulty for a progressive political movement, but not for the reasons most mainstream observers highlight. Mainstream campaigns use a great deal of money because they focus on what we termed the high-tech campaign methods. Most of a mainstream candidate's dollars go toward buying television and other media space as well as hiring professional campaign consultants and pollsters. Progressives do not have to, nor should they, imitate mainstream methods. For example, since progressives develop their agenda out of the life experience and participation of the broader community, they should not need expensive pollsters to carefully craft their campaign message. Bernie Sanders did not have to listen to the polls. The specific way in which he presents his message comes from his direct experience interacting with groups of ordinary people.

Similarly, progressives should not become overly enthralled with thirty-second television spots. Political scientists continually debate the affect such ads actually have. While a television spot can potentially reach millions of viewers, given people's general cynicism about politics, the most common response from the audience may be to simply hit the mute button. The widespread public disgust with the predominantly negative character of most campaign ads has led some scholars to wonder whether or not all the mud-slinging is simply driving people away from the polls. Progressives are arguably better suited to rise above the mudslinging. Sanders, for example, has never run a negative campaign, but always stuck to the real issues.

The overall utility of campaign commercials for progressives is still unclear. Obviously, such ads would provide public visibility to a movement that faces a major problem in getting media coverage. Yet television ads aim mainly to promote a candidate's image and name recognition, not to discuss a comprehensive agenda or the complexity of issues. Such image appeal works well for mainstream candidates who want to campaign on personality. A lasting progressive political movement must transform people's basic political understanding, however, not just create a momentary positive image for a few individuals or even a party. To accomplish this educational goal means either redefining the way television is used (for example, by running half-hour or hour-long programs), or utilizing the kinds of grassroots educational work and community organizing highlighted throughout this book.

The corporate media is not just expensive, either. It is biased against any social movement that seriously challenges corporate power and its control of our government. This does not mean we should ignore the mass media. All of the groups discussed in this book have won some favorable media attention, mostly from local sources. The proceedings of Third Parties '96, a national gathering of third party activists in the summer of 1995, was even covered by C-SPAN. By and large, of course, the media as currently organized will never give independent political movements fair coverage. As Gil Scott Heron sings, "The revolution will not be televised."

The only long-term solution to the media problem is grassroots organizing that translates volunteer energy and resources into a community presence. Just as the Populists and Socialists proved, this local energy can also support and fund an alternative media. For example, while there are many progressive publications today, nothing exists nationally aimed at ordinary working people. In their writing style and presentation, most progressive organs appeal to college-educated activists with a lifetime commitment to progressive politics. These publications do not look at all like the magazines and papers that most working people read on a routine basis. In some ways, this is not all negative, as progressives should establish better, more informative standards for publishing and media work. Still, new progressive publications and media could take the same basic ideas found in existing progressive sources and reformulate and repackage them. Imagine a progressive magazine that used more human interest angles to bring the stories and voices of ordinary working people to the center of its articles. Such a publication could also offer a more visually attractive, less text-heavy presentation. Some of the better labor presses, such as the United Auto Workers' popular monthly *Solidarity*, offer inspiring examples of how to publish a progressive message for a large audience.

Yet even grassroots organizing that builds an alternative media requires money. A serious and growing movement needs to have office space. It needs published materials. Most importantly, movements can get only so far on volunteer energy. The powers-that-be in government and business get paid for what they do. Progressive activists, however, often have to support themselves with other jobs and conduct their political organizing as volunteers. A serious political movement needs to have people dedicated to it fulltime. The absence of staff to follow up with fledgling local groups and interested individuals has been a major obstacle to the growth of several organizations.

While most of the groups examined in this book do support a modest staff, they all need more. The national staff person for some groups, for example, is not even fulltime. Progressive politics needs to have far more paid organizers going into communities to do the time-consuming work of pulling people together and helping them get in motion. Today, in comparison to the mainstream parties, the resources that are helping to build the progressive movement are tiny. None of the groups that we have studied has a budget of even a million dollars a year, and most are far below that. Compare this scale to the $43 million that organized labor spent on the Democrats in 1994. Just imagine what a New Party could do with even a fraction of that money.

To help their specific campaigns as well as fund more long-term work, progressives should push for comprehensive campaign finance reform. Political leaders have talked about campaign finance reform for decades. Time and time again, Congress has passed laws supposedly intended to reform the election system. Today, for example, all candidates must make full public disclosure of their expenditures and major donations. Current laws limit individuals to giving $1,000 to any one congressional or presidential candidate. PACs are similarly limited to $5,000. For the presidential general election, the two major party candidates are given a federal grant of $46.1 million under the provision that they not accept individual or PAC contributions.

Current finance reform laws, however, are riddled with loopholes. An individual can give a candidate $1,000 for the primary, another $1,000 for a primary runoff, another $1,000 for a convention, and then $1,000 more for the general election. The laws also do not restrict the number of candidates to which an individual or PAC can contribute. This makes it possible for people to swap contributions along the lines of "I'll contribute $1,000 to your favorite candidate, if you contribute $1,000 to mine." Wealthy individuals gather up separate checks, each to the maximum individual amount, from their spouse, children, other relatives, and employees and then hand over the bundle to a campaign in such a way that the candidate knows where the money really came from. Infants only a few months old have even been known to write out checks for campaign contributions!

Additionally, laws allow people to give a great deal of "soft money" to state parties to spend on general campaign activities, such as get-out-the-vote drives, ads directed toward state campaigns, and buttons and bumper stickers. The laws governing such contributions vary by state. Some states have no limitations, thereby allowing wealthy donors to give as much as they want to a party by channeling it through the appropriate state organizations. Some state laws even allow corporations and unions to spend money on parties and candidates directly out of their own funds, something that cannot be done at the federal level. In 1988, the Republicans raised $22 million in soft money, while the Democrats raised $23 million. Campaign laws also do not stop wealthy contributors from setting up their own "independent" committees, which happen to engage in activities that help their favorite candidate. The Supreme Court has upheld such activity on the theory that people should have the right to express their free speech by paying for ads backing the candidates they favor. The Court ignored the obvious reality that some of us are more free to pursue such expensive speech than others.

The use of these and other creative tactics might leave one wondering if real campaign finance reform is possible. A persuasive case can be made that the current laws are designed to have loopholes. Most European countries have substantially greater public financing of elections and/or restrictions on private contributions. The lawmakers enacting US reforms are the very same people who benefit most from the current state of affairs. Calls for campaign finance reform are usually blatantly partisan and self-serving. Republicans focus on restricting PAC contributions, while Democrats seek limiting individual contributions. The arguments on both sides serve their own interests: Democrats rely more heavily on PAC money, Republicans on individual contributions. Typically, Republicans and Democrats agree on reforms that directly favor the two party system. For example, while the major parties get $46 million for their presidential campaigns, third party candidates and independents receive a much lower amount, and then only after the election and only if they receive more than 5 percent of the vote.

The alternative to current loophole-ridden and politically biased reforms is obvious: full public financing. Under such a system, all private contributions would be rendered illegal. Instead, all parties and/or candidates would receive an equal amount of money provided by the government. The state could even go one step further by buying up or otherwise acquiring media time directly, and then parceling it out to political contenders on an equal basis. Such media access, if distributed in half-hour or hour-long blocks, could even be used to encourage more thoughtful media programming than thirty-second sound-bites. Full public financing would not only take private money out of elections, but would also support new parties and independents with the same level of resources as the two major parties.

The Working Group on Electoral Democracy, based in our nation's capital, has developed a model reform proposal called "Democratically Financed Elections." Many of the groups that we have examined are either directly involved in this effort or in reforms quite similar to it. While the authors frame their proposal in terms of congressional races, it can easily be adapted to presidential as well as more local contests. The proposal, as currently written, tries to get around the Supreme Court's protection of a wealthy individual's right to "free speech." Thus, it does not ban private contributions outright, but instead offers alternative funding.

To qualify, a candidate must raise a relatively high number of $5 contributions within the district that they are running (for example, 1,000 for a candidate for the US house). A party that receives at least 20 percent of the primary vote (based on the total vote received by all candidates) will then have its chosen candidate's general election campaign fully funded by public money. Parties who win between 5 and 20 percent would receive a proportional amount of public financing. Candidates who take the money must agree not to accept any private contributions, and must accept specific format restrictions on their radio and television advertisements that encourage accountability and substance. They are further required to participate in public debates set up by state authorities.

Under this proposal, the government also takes responsibility for providing additional funds to publicly financed candidates who face privately funded opponents, so that everyone spends at the same level. Similarly, the proposal provides such matching for state-funded candidates who face the "independent expenditures" of non-candidate-affiliated groups and individuals. It also limits the amount of money that a person can contribute to a party to $100 per year. The Working Group estimates that its system would cost $500 million annually, an average of about $5 for each individual taxpayer. Polls show that a majority of the public would contribute such modest amounts to help ensure genuinely democratic elections. Arguably, the taxpayer would save billions of dollars every year that currently go to special tax breaks, subsidies, regulatory exemptions, and other legislative favors shamelessly bought by private campaign money.

The Working Group's proposal is not without its limitations. For example, the 20 percent full-funding threshold would still work against new parties and independent candidates as these groups rarely achieve such support when first starting out. The model also maintains the candidate-centered focus of US elections rather than encouraging more party-based campaigning. The most critical funding need for progressives is in building grassroots-based party structures, not in running individual candidates' election campaigns. The proposal, however, represents an enormous step forward in taking private money out of politics.

Bills based on the Democratically Financed Elections model have been drafted in Missouri, Hawaii, North Carolina, Vermont, Massachusetts, and Connecticut. The New Party in Arkansas has joined a broad coalition to place a campaign finance reform initiative before voters. Dirigo Alliance activists in Maine have succeeded in placing an initiative on the ballot for the 1996 election. Their proposal generally follows the Democratically Financed Elections model, although rather than relying on new tax revenues, it targets specific cuts in the state budget to cover the cost of the system. As a sign of how broad based these democratizing issues are, the Maine campaign has brought together progressives with Perot supporters and even the Christian Civic League. Progressives need to take advantage of the opportunity to build broad coalitions around democratizing reforms. While some conservative grassroots groups may see real opportunities for themselves, obviously progressives would benefit enormously from a more democratic electoral system as well.

Elsewhere, activists have tried using ballot initiatives to limit personal campaign contributions. In 1994, a successful initiative drive passed a $100 limit and other election reforms in Missouri, Oregon, and Montana. In 1996, similar efforts were underway in Alaska, Arkansas, Colorado, and Washington, DC. In California, efforts at campaign finance reform split, getting two initiatives on the ballot for 1996. One backed by the California Public Interest Research Group, labor, and community groups would place a $100 contribution limit on local and legislative contests and a $200 limit on statewide races. Another backed by Common Cause sets the limits at $250 and $500 respectively.[15]

People aiming to get money out of politics have also tried using the court system. Council member Sal Albanese and a group of New York City voters recently filed suit challenging the constitutionality of current campaign finance laws, specifically the Federal Election Campaign Act of 1971, which allows for the use of private money in federal elections. In 1992, Albanese ran for Congress. He was outspent $524,000 to $267,000 by his victorious opponent. Albanese and thirteen voters claim that they were not allowed equal participation in the electoral system because of the financial disparity. In April 1995, a federal judge ruled that Albanese did not have standing to challenge the current system. The National Voting Rights Institute is appealing the decision. Two months later, the governor of Tennessee signed a bill that makes it illegal for anyone running for any state office to spend more than $250,000. This law directly contradicts past Supreme Court rulings. Therefore, even if Albanese never gets his day in court, finance-reform advocates hope that the issue of campaign financing will eventually be heard again by the Supreme Court.[16]

Obstacle 3—
The Candidate-Centered Culture of US Politics

Seen in a global perspective, US politics is distinctive for the emphasis placed on candidate-centered elections. In this country, the two major political parties, as well as most mainstream third party challengers, are very weak institutionally. Scholars have demonstrated how, during this century, the Republican and Democratic party labels have undergone a marked decline in importance for how people vote. Candidates typically appeal to voters based on their own attributes and image rather than their party name. Indeed, candidates often leave their party name off their campaign ads entirely. Electoral campaigns in this country are built around the individual candidates, who each have their own separate campaign organization. Parties do not run for offices, candidates do. Politicians build their own image and their own base among voters. The comparison to other countries is often stark. During the fall of 1995, for example, the New Democratic Party of Canada selected a party leader. The convention and the choice made front-page headlines. Yet, in this country, most Americans would not know the names of our Democratic or Republican party chairs because such figures hold much less significance.

Such a candidate-centered system works well for defenders of the status quo, but not for progressives. In his classic comparative study of political parties, French scholar Maurice Duverge noted that political efforts that come out of mass social movements tend to be the ones that favor strong parties. In looking at European political development, he observed that parties that came from the privileged sectors of society tended to be weak and relatively fragmented internally. In contrast, those founded by ordinary people, such as the labor, socialist, and social democratic parties, tended to produce strong organizations focused on platforms and other ways of adhering to collective decision-making. These mass-based parties also emphasized an active membership—making party life part of the leisure and culture of their community.[17]

The practices of the groups studied in this book point toward a similar conclusion. Progressives typically prioritize issues and a comprehensive platform over individual personality or general image appeal. For progressives, the task is not just to get officeholders elected, but to transform our country's political culture so that ordinary people can empower themselves. Candidate-centered politics works against this democratic project. Single-candidate campaigns do not build an organization as well as party-based efforts. Progressive ideas can get lost in debates over the personal merits of an individual. Scarce resources get divided by separate candidate campaigns. Candidate-centered politics can place such a burden on the individual seeking office that progressives often have difficulty recruiting people to run. Following a mainstream model of politics also steers activists toward narrow efforts at vote getting and election campaigns at the expense of non-electoral work and movement-building.

In the long run, progressives have to redefine electoral politics. Legal reforms could transform the election system in this direction. Yet, besides such reforms, progressives need to conduct their own politics here and now in a different manner than the major parties. Progressive electoral efforts must maintain a sense of themselves as a mass movement, rather than a mere candidate-electing machine. Making this distinction is not always easy. Progressives operate in a political environment organized to promote just the opposite. When progressive candidates run for office, the media will tend to focus on them as individuals. Jesse Jackson and the alternative press made many references to the Rainbow Coalition. Yet the mainstream media ignored the organization almost entirely. The media will not be an ally in party-building. It will focus the glare of its camera lights on the candidates, even when the candidates themselves try to emphasize their connection to a broader movement and organization.

Obstacle 4—Suburban Blues

Today's progressives must organize in a society quite different from that of their Populist and Socialist predecessors. One key difference is where and how people live. At the turn of century, our country was on the move from a still predominantly rural population to a vast urban society. Today, the nation's cities have given way to the sprawling suburban ring. This change from city to suburbs has political significance. Indeed, during the 1990s, the suburban vote has begun to surpass city returns in overall weight of votes.

Progressive politics can ill afford a split in their ranks between urban and suburban realities. The movements that we have studied in this book are mainly urban based. Be it in old cities like Milwaukee, Hartford, or Pittsburgh, college towns such as Madison, or the rural towns and cities of Vermont, current progressive political organizing operates in locations originally designed to be communities. Within the city, people can live isolated lives, of course. Yet the physical organization of space, combined with many urban institutions, does provide people the possibility of some collective options and human interaction. In contrast, suburbia physically embodies the isolated individualism promoted by modern capitalism. Surrounded by their subdivision yards, suburbanites often live isolated and rootless lives. Fewer and fewer people know their neighbors. Driving in cars to the strip malls to shop, relaxing in private enclosed backyards, and traveling the freeways over the top of the city, suburbanites can live day after day without having to meaningfully interact with the people surrounding them. Many of the religious and secular institutions that helped build community in the past have lost their strength or never emerged in the suburbs, leaving those living there fewer collective options.

The isolated living that suburbia embodies works against progressive politics in many ways. Social movements grow by bringing people together and encouraging human interaction. Suburbia does the opposite. Progressives often assert the interconnectedness of social life. Life in the suburbs can reinforce a narrow, media-generated reality. Activists are already grappling with the dilemmas posed by the suburbs. The progressive voting bloc in Burlington noticeably ends at the boundaries of the New North End, the most suburban section of the city. In Milwaukee, the returns from a referendum to increase funding for the public schools went from strong support to weak as one moved out from the center of the city toward the more suburban, whiter parts of the school district. The forces of right-wing reaction have built themselves in the suburbs. People who live isolated lives provide ample recruits for right-wing politicians to spread their message of fear. Indeed, the Right's political agenda is based upon white peoples' paranoia about blacks and their corresponding suburban fear of the "dark" city.

The progressive alternative is not just for urbanites, however. The fundamental fall in the US standard of living impacts most people. Even those suburbanites who express staunch support for the Republican agenda arguably also hold deep distrust of established institutions and politics as usual. People in both the city and the surrounding suburban ring want change. Progressives have to develop concrete political activities and overall political cultures that can span both city block and suburban subdivision. Movement activists need to think carefully about and confront the problem of this potential divide.

In seeking ways of organizing in the suburbs, progressives should keep in mind that the isolation that can prove an obstacle to activist hopes, can also provide an opportunity. Many people today, especially in the suburbs, have a strong yearning for community. People's lives are often far too lonely and meaningless. This is part of the reason why the religious Right has had success. It offers isolated individuals the possibility of connecting with other people. The literature that religious Right activists hand out when they go door-to-door, for example, speaks directly to people's sense of loneliness. Their message is straightforward: "Do you feel alone and afraid? Come join us, we will provide you a sense of community and family." Right-wing fundamentalism is not the only movement capable of fostering community, of course. Charles Derber, in his book entitled *What's Left?*, argues that progressive activists need to rediscover the politics of community. Raising the banner of economic change, respect for diversity, and political and social democracy are a central part of a Left agenda, but not enough. Using several historical examples, Derber demonstrates how activists in the past have used community-building as a bedrock of progressive politics.[18]

We can see this same community-building focus in the historical cases that we have examined. Being a Populist or a Socialist was a way of life. These past movements even used community-building as a tool for spreading the movement among populations whose isolation might, at first glance, seem to have worked against progressive politics. For example, when the Socialists went into the Southwest they were organizing among people who often lived miles from each other. Socialist Party functions, with their built-in picnics, parades, and celebrations, could literally provide the social life for many family farmers.

The suburbs may not involve such physically vast expanses, but the personal loneliness of people has meaningful parallels. How a political movement can also serve as a movement for community is a question for which contemporary progressives need to find answers. There are hopeful signs of beginnings in this regard as activists, who have built up strength in urban areas, begin to grapple with the surrounding sprawl. Some independent organizing has even started out in suburbia. For example, the New Party has developed active local groups in two working-class suburban counties just north of Washington, DC. Through such efforts, New Party activists elected the first African-American mayor in Bladensburg's 200-year history. Peter Shapiro lost his bid for mayor of Hyattsville by a mere seventeen votes! In Montgomery County, New Party activists are also directly battling the Right. In 1990, conservatives succeeded in hamstringing the county's budget process through a successful ballot initiative requiring a super majority to approve any spending over arbitrarily restrictive limits. In the six years since this change was made, three right-wing county board members have been able to block adequate funding for public schools and other needed services. As a result, local residents have seen three-fourths of the county's all-day kindergartens close, increasing class sizes, and the dismantling of interscholastic sports at the middle schools. In an attempt to deal with the funding crisis, the school board even proposed charging families $50 a year for their kids to ride public school buses! As New Party activists entered the 1996 fall election season, they were gearing up to place before voters a ballot initiative that would restore a simple majority rule to the budget. Progressive organizing in the suburbs is difficult, but possible. It is also badly needed.

The Opportunities

While appreciating the real challenges discussed here, we need to avoid thinking that the "grass is always greener" somewhere else. Some of the successful historical movements in this country and elsewhere may look like they enjoyed many relative advantages. Yet today's progressives not only face unique challenges, they also enjoy particular opportunities. Indeed, as both the living and historical examples in this book make clear, progressive politics is possible in this country despite all the problems of resources, culture, media, and difficult legal structures.

Some of the opportunities activists face today are the flip side of the obstacles. This is true in suburban organizing. The same is true in other dimensions of our political life as well. The high-tech, hyper-media, candidate-centered electoral politics of today seems to offer little to progressives who have neither money nor significant access to the mainstream media. Yet, it was in developing today's dominant electoral practices that the two major parties lost much of their grassroots strength. Progressive activists who organize in their communities do not have to face anywhere near the level of local organization that the two major parties had in the past. Populists and Socialists confronted entrenched Republican and Democratic party machines in which party loyalty could be passed down for generations. In places where patronage networks were strong, people who voted Republican or Democrat could expect concrete material favors, such as jobs, help with the government bureaucracy, or contributions to community events. Today, in contrast, loyalty to one of the major parties means less and less. The large number of people who register as independents testifies to this transformation. Furthermore, the two major parties have mainly surrendered grassroots organizing to political outsiders. In the cases examined in this book, the local Republican and Democratic party chapters that have been threatened by progressive organizing have shown little ability to produce a strong, vigorous grassroots reply. As the only grassroots effort in town, progressives enjoy unique advantages. The progressive ability to get-out-the-vote can make a critical difference.

More generally, the high-tech, media-driven politics pursued by the major parties has alienated many Americans. The statement that most people are cynical and distrustful of politics would get few disagreements. Both out of necessity and because of their political beliefs, progressives have to engage in politics in alternative ways. Among people who have learned to hate politics as usual, "politics by another means" can have an enormous appeal. We have to ask ourselves which would be more appealing to most people: watching a political candidate sling mud in a thirty-second television ad or attending a small discussion with their neighbors where they learn about a new political alternative, are welcome to speak their minds, and have their opinions valued? Today, the two party system rests not on people's active support, but on the apathy and marginalization of the vast majority of the public. Both parties rely more upon people's sense that there is no realistic alternative than on their enthusiastic allegiance. Much of the public is aware that it has been marginalized and is, therefore, potentially open to a new kind of politics that places them at the center. Even the obstacles presented by our political system provide progressives with further popular rallying cries. For example, many people who have not been won over to third party politics still support basic democratizing reforms, such as campaign finance reform and easing ballot access.

Building democracy from the ground up is an ambitious strategy that requires a huge amount of time and energy. Yet we must not forget that grassroots political organizing does work. None of the activists interviewed for this book had encountered a situation where they placed their message directly before a group of ordinary people only to have it significantly rejected. Progressive political organizing is exactly what most Americans want. People want change. Polls also routinely show that the majority of people want an alternative to the Republicans and Democrats. Progressives do not have to convince people that something different is desirable. Rather, the difficulty lies in getting the message out and in convincing people that it really can be done.

Progressives also benefit from the fact that, at least in the foreseeable future, the two major parties will be unable to offer real alternatives to their current agenda. In contrast, both Populists and Socialists had to contend with the ability of the major parties to steal significant parts of their platform. Both Republicans and Democrats realized that the best way to prevent more radical alternatives was to adopt those reforms that seemed the least dangerous. Better to inconvenience business owners with minimum wage laws and basic safety protections than have workers calling for the collective ownership of the factories. At the turn of the century, the major parties were able to reconcile such reforms with the nation's capitalist economy. Indeed, many of these measures helped rationalize and modernize a growing American capitalism.

The major parties now have much less room to maneuver. The century-long rise of US capitalism to world predominance has clearly reached its limits. More generally, we now live in a globalized world economy dominated by forces that seek to knock down government regulation and pit working people against each other in a race to the bottom. Challenging this basic logic of the world economy is difficult enough for progressives who benefit from being able to seek democratic alternatives. For those in power, who are unwilling to even question the logic of the capitalist system much less all the other power relationship intertwined with it, the task of finding alternatives is even more daunting, if not outright undesirable.

The dilemma faced by the Democratic Party for over a decade points to the lack of reform possibilities among the present powers-that-be. Other countries, such as Japan and many European nations, do offer policy models that uphold capitalism and the interests of those in power, yet which differ from the free market ideology embodied by the Republicans. In the past, social democratic countries have been able to give capitalism a human face while maintaining high profit margins for corporations using such mechanisms as industrial policy and relying on a highly trained, well-paid workforce. Yet, despite these examples, few voices have been heard within the Democratic Party pushing for such alternatives. Indeed, in other countries, even social democratic parties find themselves under great pressure from the world economy to conform to the free market agenda.

Formulating a progressive alternative in the United States in the 1990s will require moving far more to the left than the nation's economic and political leadership dares to go. Such basic strong-government measures as a coordinated industrial policy are beyond the bounds of acceptable official debate. This is true even though these policies have been key to the rise of such capitalist success stories as Japan, and they can be applied without any connection to a progressive agenda. Indeed, both major parties refuse to defend a strong activist government as being anything desirable. The political and economic structures of this country are so deeply entrenched in free market ideology and economic culture that such innovation appears beyond the reach of US corporate and governmental policymakers. Painful as this is, it presents real opportunities for independent politics.

Because of the narrow reform options among the powers-that-be, the task of challenging the right-wing agenda has fallen almost entirely into the laps of the progressive community. As the progressive movement grows, there seems little reason to expect that either major party will be able to steal a significant part of its new agenda. A future New Deal that co-opts popular sentiment does not seem to be in the cards. Progressives are, and will continue to be, the only political force offering real solutions.

The right-wing agenda does not address the reason for the fall in people's standard of living. Attacking "big government" and the supposed "handout" to minorities and immigrants might win votes among the minority of Americans who still bother to vote, but it does not solve problems. To the contrary, the current agenda is only going to make matters worse. As people's economic opportunities continue to decline they will find that even the minimal safety net protections are no longer there. For example, less than a year after the Republicans swept into Congress in 1994, polls showed that the majority of Americans did not support the kind of assaults on government social spending and regulation that the Republicans and many Democrats were pushing. In the years ahead, the Right can only offer to play more on people's fears: attacking gays and lesbians, feminists, people of color, "leftist-liberals," and so on. The Right's public agenda is a very cynical message that does not even pretend to give people real hope for a better future. Instead, it seeks to scare people into holding onto whatever they have now by supporting narrow, reactionary politics.

Only progressives offer people hope and a positive vision. Furthermore, those basic values that progressives espouse are also values shared by most Americans. Most ordinary people believe in fair play, democracy, equality, opportunity, peace, mutual respect, community, and freedom. This is why, when progressive activists and volunteers go out into their communities, they have an inspiring experience. People respond well to a believable alternative. Progressives are working with, not against, the basic desires of most Americans. The primary struggle is getting the message out and organizing a movement so that enough people can believe that real change is possible.

Chapter Ten

What Price Victory?

Overcoming Co-optation and Drift

Many of the concerns progressive activists express toward electoral politics and third party organizing revolve around a skepticism that such undertakings are realistic or possible. In this book, we have attempted to show that real groups, both in the past and today, have demonstrated that independent politics, while a difficult road, is not an impossible one. Indeed, in many ways the conditions in the United States today have never been better. Yet even conceding that progressive electoral politics might be possible, some activists point to a second area of concern. They worry that, if they build a political movement, they will only see their elected officials and parties absorbed into the political mainstream. These activists fear that electoral politics will inevitably seduce winning progressive candidates and organizations away from their movement roots to become yet another instrument for maintaining the status quo.

Some skeptics argue that this is due to the co-optive pressures built into the very logic of the electoral system. To win power, a candidate or majority-seeking party has to unite a sizeable bloc of the electorate. Building such coalitions by left-leaning movements has often meant reaching out to more moderate voters, with the consequence of watering down one's agenda. Similarly, in a legislative body where progressives hold some seats, but not the majority, they will have to compromise with others in order to pass legislation. The same is true of a progressive executive who is not backed up by a majority on the respective legislative body. Furthermore, the ability of elected officials to enact meaningful social change is often quite proscribed by the bureaucratic apparatus of the state as well as by private economic power. Elected officials constantly feel pressures to compromise with these power structures in order to succeed in implementing some of their agenda. In addition, governmental and electoral structures have not been designed with democratic accountability in mind. Instead, individual officeholders have a great deal of personal discretion and are not bound by party platforms.

Others point to the hazards of large organizations. Roberto Michels, now famous for his "iron law of oligarchy," developed his idea by observing the gradual bureaucratization and undemocratic maneuvering that developed within Europe's socialist and social democratic parties. He concluded that these outcomes are inevitable for any large organization.[1] Once developed, a party oligarchy, with its careerist and party professionals, will always compromise the movement in order to gain favor with the establishment. Furthermore, he argued, large organizations loose the capacity for flexibility and creativity, characteristics needed by any social movement seeking fundamental change.

Both of these concerns point to real dangers and pressures that progressives need to understand and develop effective ways of countering. Yet, unless qualified by a more complex picture, they can easily lead progressives to just as dangerous conclusions. Activists might decide that electoral politics is simply a waste of time because it will inevitably compromise the movement. They might also develop a kind of blind, automatic distrust for any form of national organization, fearing an inevitable tyranny by bureaucrats.

These explanations can also encourage a narrow sectarianism as activists declare their refusal to work with any individual or group who does not have true "revolutionary" credentials and is instead labeled a sellout or "reformist." Such a narrow view can be seen in the blanket rejection that some activists have to any form of cooperation or interaction with progressives who run as Democrats. While the Democratic Party as a whole is part of the establishment, this does not apply to everyone who runs under the Party label. Until recently, the Party has provided the only realistic electoral game in town. Therefore, progressives who wanted to get sympathetic people into office often made a tactical decision to run candidates as Democrats. While such a strategy does have its contradictions, the choice does not make activists any less progressive or more pro-establishment. For example, in their overall desires for social change and rejection of the status quo, the activists involved in LEAP are no different than those involved in the New Party or the Vermont Progressive Coalition. Similarly, the Democratic Party itself contains activists and legislators who sincerely believe in progressive versions of the New Deal only to see their party's mainstream move to the right. A progressive independent political movement needs to seriously consider the best way to interact with such people, rather than rejecting them out of hand.

A Cautionary Tale—
The New Democratic Party of Canada

The dilemma of co-optation is a real one, though, with a long and disappointing history. One only has to look to Canada for the most recent instance. Over the last few decades, the New Democratic Party of Canada (NDP) has been a shining example of what independent political organizing can accomplish. Working within a similar winner-take-all electoral system as the United States, Canadian labor and other social movements have built up the New Democratic Party as a solid progressive, social-democratic alternative to the two major parties. The NDP has been instrumental in the formation of Canada's more progressive labor laws, national health care system, and more generous safety net. By gaining 20 percent of the national vote by the late 1980s and taking power in 1990 in Ontario, Canada's largest province (as well as having a long history of governing in several western provinces), the NDP looked inspiring indeed.

Yet, in 1993, the NDP suffered a stunning defeat at the polls when it dropped to a mere 7.4 percent of the national vote. In the national legislature, it went from forty-three to nine seats. Soon after this calamity, voters threw out Bob Rae's NDP government in Ontario in a sweeping conservative victory. In its place, the "Common Sense Revolution" of the new Michael Harris government seemed to try to outdo our Republican Congress in slashing social spending and gutting regulations. Today, the NDP faces a struggle for its very existence. Most alarming, however, these electoral disasters were foreshadowed by growing complaints among progressive groups, especially in Ontario, that the NDP had lost sight of the cause and sold progressives out. The decision of the Canadian Auto Workers, the largest union in Canada, to pull its funding out of the Ontario NDP and use those resources to support grassroots community organizing symbolizes the depth of the crisis between the Party and its social movement base.

Disaster in Ontario

The title of George Ehring's and Wayne Roberts' book on the Ontario NDP, *Giving Away A Miracle*, conveys the sense of disillusionment that many party supporters must have felt toward the NDP government. In 1990, Bob Rae did not expect to become premier of Canada's largest province. Indeed, the Party was surprised when it found itself elected to power. Three years before, the incumbent Liberal government had been swept back into power with the largest majority in provincial history. As Rae later admitted, he had planned to retire after the 1990 election into a more private life. Although unexpected, with governing power in the nation's most powerful province, the New Democratic Party seemed poised to demonstrate to Canadians just how different a social democratic government of the people could be.

The Party was not prepared to govern, however. Following a series of scandals and broken promises, the Rae government earned the official condemnation in 1993 of one its key supporters, the Ontario Federation of Labor, when it announced its infamous Social Contract. After three years in office, the NDP government had become obsessed with lowering the province's budget deficit. To this end, the Social Contract canceled all public-sector contracts and forced $2 billion in concessions on unionized public-sector workers. Nine hundred thousand provincial employees were forced into a three-year wage freeze plus an additional twelve days of "unpaid leave" each year—the latter sarcastically became known as "Rae Days." How could a social democratic party with its founding base in the labor movement produce a government that out did its Liberal predecessor in implementing right-wing austerity measures? Indeed, the Social Contract offered only the most notorious example of NDP policies that increasingly appeared divorced from the values and ideas for which the Party supposedly stood.

The story of the Ontario NDP is a complex one. The NDP has both triumphs and follies to its credit around issues such as gender and race, for example. Here we will focus on two other ingredients to the Ontario NDP's experience that seem key to its crisis: the economic question and internal democracy.

The Economic Question

A surprising element of the NDP experience is that a social democratic party, complete with close ties to the labor movement, would have no distinct ideas for economic policy. Yet the Ontario NDP took power with no economic plan. The common assumption within Party ranks was that they would remain in opposition. Having spent decades in this role, the NDP had gotten used to simply attacking the policies of the governing party. Opposition politics permits the luxury of not having to have a realistic alternative of one's own. Specific efforts to develop an economic plan a few years prior to the 1990 win were fairly abstract and vague, in part because the exercise seemed a largely academic project.

The problem runs deeper, however. The NDP's failure to produce workable and innovative economic policies also reflects a general intellectual crisis found in many social democratic parties. The new global economy has rendered many of the old social-democratic formulas of redistributive social spending and Keynesian economics obsolete. Speaking in the context of Canadian social democracy, Leo Girard, International Secretary-Treasurer for the United Steelworkers of America (which also represents Canadian workers), wrote:

In this changed economy, our traditional methods of regulating economic activity are less effective. Unless social democrats identify new, more effective ways of regulating economic activity, our problems will get worse.[2]

Girard argues that activists can no longer seek to simply redistribute the pie from an economic prosperity that no longer exists. Rather, social democrats must find ways to redistribute power so that workers and communities have greater control over the decisions that impact their lives. In other words, activists must move from the battle for simple economic equality to the deeper question of economic democracy. This new agenda requires innovative and creative solutions—such as shortening and restructuring the workweek, establishing concrete community and worker controls over multinational corporations, redefining the norms of international trade, and harnessing popular energy and organizing as a counter-weight to corporate power.

In contrast to the clear need for new thinking, the Ontario NDP had nothing to offer. For years it had blasted the priorities of those in power, called for greater and more equitable social spending, downplayed the question of deficits, and pointed to greater taxes on the rich. Upon taking office, the NDP government found that these rallying cries did not add up to an economic plan. When Rae and his cabinet tried groping their way toward some kind of coherent economic policies, they ran full force into the militant hostility of the business community and its media. At the same time, Ontario entered a major recession. This helped drive up the government's budget deficit by increasing outlays for social spending while decreasing the tax base.

With no creative plan of its own, let alone a vision of economic democracy, the Rae government succumbed to the forces that have propelled many liberal and conservative governments down the road to right-wing austerity. With no progressive, movement-oriented solution to the job question, Rae gave incredibly generous deals to multinational corporations in exchange for vague promises of new jobs. The NDP government also became preoccupied with the debt question. In *Rae Days,* his book on the Ontario NDP, economist and journalist Thomas Walkom concluded that the business community successfully convinced Rae and his cabinet that they had only one fiscal option. Ontario, they argued, was heading for a kind of apocalyptic crisis in which the growing provisional budget deficits would lead to an outright denial of further credit from corporate financial institutions. This context of panic, induced by believing this scenario, prompted the government to unveil its Social Contract.

Internal Democracy

That the NDP had no new thinking on the economic question points, in part, to the difficulties of finding workable solutions. There are no easy and obvious answers. Yet the NDP's crisis also reflected serious problems within the internal life of the Party. By the time the Ontario NDP came to power in 1990, it did not look or function like an alternative, movement-driven party.

Part of the problem was leadership style. Inside the NDP government, premier Rae often seemed to make decisions without regard to a collective process. By 1993, the voices of many NDP supporters could be heard criticizing the Rae government for its top-down decisions. The Rae government implemented its infamous Social Contract, for example, over the vocal objections of its supporters. Furthermore, on popular issues such as state-run auto insurance, the government simply dropped this key long-time platform plank when it decided that the policy was not realistic. Yet the decay in the internal life of the Party involved deeper issues than merely the personal style in which NDP representatives made decisions while in office. In particular, three alarming trends had been evident for years.

First, mass debate within the Party had increasingly given way to rallying behind the official leadership. In the 1970s, the NDP, especially in Ontario, was torn by a basic ideological debate that has affected, in one way or another, all parties on the Left. A group known as the "Waffle" argued that the Party should return to its more socialistic roots. The Waffle attempted to infuse the NDP with the energy, issues, and, some critics would say, arrogance of the New Left. In contrast, the Party's mainstream sought to moderate its program in order to build larger voting blocs and win a greater share of elected governmental positions. These factions also disagreed on whether or not Canada should integrate itself into a continental economy with the United States and Mexico. Both sides accused the other of producing this split's final outcome. In the end, however, the Waffle faction was expelled from the Party. Not only did this action drive many left-leaning activists out of the NDP, but it also helped foster an internal culture that distrusted dissent. As a result, with no left opposition to challenge the reigning leadership and its policy ideas, the NDP traveled through the 1980s with an increasingly stale and obsolete platform.

Secondly, instead of engaging in a mass debate over basic economic and social questions, the increasingly election-oriented NDP leadership looked toward the more short-term goal of winning votes. Thus, it offered policy ideas, such as public auto insurance, that proved popular among voters and highlighted the limitations of the governing parties. Over time, this one-dimensional focus on elections produced a party that was intellectually more image than substance. The NDP told voters that it was the more caring party—the party more identified with working people and oppressed groups. As the Ontario NDP government proved, however, such slogans have to be backed up with real policies. Ideally, the Party's program should reflect ideas that the rank and file have debated and developed through a mass participatory process. Not only will the specific policies be more fully worked out, but the Party will take power with a grassroots membership committed and mobilized to fight for its agenda. The NDP chose to avoid such a mass process. Instead, NDP campaigns became more and more like those of the mainstream parties, who are driven by the wisdom of the pollsters.

This caused an increasing rift between the Party's leadership and its base. Progressive political parties are not just election apparatuses, but political expressions of broader mass movements. The NDP once believed this. It drew its original ideas and supporters from the ranks of organized labor and other social movements. Yet by the time the NDP took power in Ontario, a visible gap had developed between its elected officials and the grassroots movement. Many within the NDP's leadership, especially among its officeholders, had developed a distrust of the influence that popular movements might have on the Party. They worried that the movements would push the Party "too far" and "too fast"—giving the NDP an image of being captured by "radical" groups and causes. They also feared that energy would be drained into single-issue causes and protest campaigns that would not translate into voter support. On the other side, many grassroots activists distrusted political dependence on a party organization. Activists within the popular movements, while supporting the NDP, nevertheless sought to maintain their autonomy through their own base and organizations. The gap between the two sides reflects a fundamental difference in the role they assigned to the Party. Was the Party's goal to win elections and use state power for progressive ends or was it to help build broader social movements by educating, organizing, and mobilizing people around progressive politics?

Obviously, the two positions are not mutually exclusive or inherently incompatible. Yet, when the NDP government took power in Ontario, it treated them as such. As a result, it was not able to mobilize mass action in support of its policies. This proved disastrous for, by itself, the state's powers can prove quite limited. Pursuing a progressive agenda entails recognizing that governmental authority alone cannot offer a solution. Instead, a progressive government may have to admit its limitations and call on popular mobilization to challenge the power of the status quo.

Similarly, popular movements must be prepared to fight on behalf of a progressive government. According to Thomas Walkom, for example, the Rae government felt that it had been left hanging in its battle to enact major progressive reforms to the province's labor laws. While the government had to endure a powerful business backlash, complete with scathing criticism in the press, labor leaders had not been able to mobilize a strong campaign, complete with visible grassroots support, to defend the government. The Ontario NDP experience reveals the importance and difficulties of maintaining a mutually supportive relationship between the party and the popular movements that it serves.

The Federal New Democratic Party

At the national level, the NDP suffered from many of the same overall problems afflicting its Ontario organization. On the economic question, the NDP had been noticeably silent during the debate on the North American Free Trade Agreement. Its national economic plans offered few new ideas. For example, leaving aside a plan for a national childcare system and some vague calls for worker and community participation, the NDP's 1993 "Strategy for a Full Employment Economy" read like something that a liberal business think tank would have written. The plan's main emphasis on job creation aimed at providing investment pools, research support, and worker training to promote business growth and international competitiveness. Its environmental agenda of developing environmentally friendly technology and efficient energy use sounded a great deal like the brand of environmentalism being promoted by corporations. While the plan belatedly criticized the North American Free Trade Agreement, it championed the General Agreement on Tariffs and Trade as a way of opening markets to Canadian goods, thus ignoring the threat that GATT posed to Canada's labor and environmental laws. While maintaining its rhetorical commitment to trade unionism, equality between men and women, ending racial discrimination, peace, economic justice, and ecology, the NDP often sounded remarkably out of touch with the popular movement that lives these ideals. The Canadian labor movement, for example, remains split on whether or not to remain as active supporters within the Party. Generally, the Party has experienced major difficulties in how to translate its ideas into the real world.

More seriously, the NDP has lost a sense of itself as a mass movement. In examining the current crisis of the NDP, Buzz Hargrove, President of the Canadian Auto Workers, compared the NDP's present practices with the activities of its precursor, the Cooperative Commonwealth Federation, founded in 1933. In a paper endorsed by his union, Hargrove argued:

> Only a movement, with its commitment to a new world, could generate the excitement and energy to build a new party. Only a movement, with a long-term vision and active in every facet of people's lives, could keep people going through the inevitable disappointments and ups and downs... As a movement, the focus was on educating, organizing, mobilizing...
> Educational activity was paramount as reading lists were distributed, study groups formed, and leaders traveled the country not to get a sound-bite on the news but to teach and debate the issues. New people were constantly brought into "politics" by creating new institutions for fighting back—like the councils of unemployed... What is so striking about the present is the virtual absence of such activities in the culture or life of the NDP.

Hargrove continued this same theme later on:

> An electoral strategy without a politics of building movements alongside it will... inevitably frustrate activists and alienate potential supporters. While

*social democratic parties might, in certain circumstances, get into office
without a movement, the movement is the only guarantee that its mandate
will be fulfilled... The NDP has paid lip service to such a movement,
remaining suspicious about its independence. There is no way to escape that
tension. Movements... can't be reduced to being a tool of a political party or
they will wither and die. The NDP can only earn the support of these
movements by having its own activists participate directly in the movements,
and by demonstrating its ability in further building those movements.*

*This suggests dramatic changes in the party. It challenges the NDP to move
beyond being just an electoral machine and to become an integral part of a
movement-building agenda which extends into every workplace and every
community. It demands that we transform structures, like riding associations
[ridings are similar to US congressional districts], from being primarily
fundraising bodies to forums that develop ideas and work to build movements
and solidarity groups engaged in those daily struggles—big and small—that
introduce people to politics and nurture the confidence that change is
possible.*[3]

In the 1993 election season, the NDP did not look like the party
envisioned by Hargrove and other left-leaning activists. Like the mainstream
parties, the NDP launched a high-tech media campaign in which the party's
message was fine-tuned by pollsters and campaign consultants. The resulting
7 percent of the vote that the party received serves as a reminder to all
progressive activists of the need to build a party that creatively embodies
the quest for state power and the realization that fundamental change
ultimately comes from building popular movement power.

The Ghost of Social Democracy

Activist's fears of being sold out by electoral politics are strengthened
when they realize that the experience of the NDP is not an anomaly or
aberration. There is a long history behind this fear. The classic case is the
co-optation of the European socialist movement in the first half of this
century.

The basic issue that divided European socialism was the strategic
question of reform versus revolution. All socialists agreed that capitalism had
serious problems and was responsible for a good part of the misery
experienced by large sections of the working population. Most also shared
a vision of a future society in which capitalist competition was replaced by
democratic control of economic resources and where wealth was shared by
all. The catch, which split the movement, was how to bring this new society
into being. One camp, the reformers, or "revisionists" as their opponents
labeled them, saw the seeds of a better society growing within capitalism.
Their strategy was to use parliamentary power to eventually reform capitalism out of existence. In contrast, the other side of the split saw capitalist

society as heading not toward a better world, but continued immiseration and a growing economic crisis. These revolutionaries called for increasing confrontation with the established authorities in order to polarize society so that capitalism could be overthrown in a dramatic mass revolt.

The differences between reformist and revolutionary tendencies showed up around many specific questions of strategy, such as whether or not the party should try to appeal to voters who were not working class; whether or not elected parliamentary delegations should enter into coalition governments; and whether or not campaign material should emphasize immediate issues or the bigger picture of social transformation. For years, both tendencies co-existed within Europe's socialist parties—each contributing to the growth of the movement. The final showdown came when historical events, such as World War I and the Russian Revolution, forced the movement to make clear decisions and, as a result, the two sides could no longer exist within the same organization.

In looking at the history of the early socialist movement, many on the political left tend to sympathize with the concerns of the revolutionaries. Coming from various social movement backgrounds and traditions, they, too, share a hope for fundamental social change. This sympathy is understandable. Historically, the reformers won the upper hand within most socialist parties (today, more commonly called social democratic parties). They then embarked upon a course that seems to have sold out the socialist movement's original goals. One of the great betrayals in this regard came at the start of World War I. In country after country, the "revisionist" majority voted to support their respective nation's war efforts—thereby sending their working class off to kill workers from other countries. After the war, the historic flagship of the socialist movement, German Social Democracy, earned the hatred of many revolutionaries when it was handed parliamentary power by a German elite fearful of a mass revolt. The party then ordered the military to put down a series of popular uprisings where the working class seized power in several German cities. During this brutal repression, Rosa Luxemburg and Karl Liebknecht, two key leaders of the battle within the original party against "revisionism," were murdered by the authorities.[4]

In countries such as Germany today, social democracy has become a solid part of the establishment, having long abandoned any sense of wanting to mount a fundamental challenge to capitalism. Indeed, during the 1980s and 1990s, many European social democratic parties seem to have followed the same choice as our Democrats. Faced with a new economic order and growing right-wing politics, the dominant leadership has chosen to move social democracy not to the left but to the right.

The most spectacular example of this trend comes from France. Campaigning on a sweeping program for radical change, which included the nationalization of large sections of French industry and major democratization of economic decision-making, the Socialist Party swept into national power in 1981—electing Francois Mitterrand president. Yet, by 1984, Mitterrand's government had made a complete U-turn. Given the seriousness of the economic difficulties facing them, the Socialist leadership quickly abandoned the agenda that had gotten them elected.

The Historical Dilemma

To fully understand the debate between socialist reformers and revolutionaries, we have to realize that neither side had the full answer. The debate between reformers and revolutionaries did not break out simply because one side wanted to sell out the movement or the other was naively utopian in its revolutionary sentiments. Rather, the conflict reflected a concrete turning point caused by two major developments. First, the movement had achieved notable success, with socialist parties gaining considerable support among the working population. Because of these gains, the movement faced the question of how to continue to grow into an outright majority by gaining new supporters. Second, the capitalism that socialists faced in the early parts of this century looked quite different from the capitalism analyzed by Karl Marx. The gradual victory of liberal democracy and limited social reforms, on the one hand, and imperialism and colonialism, on the other, confronted socialists with difficult questions as to how to react to these new realities.

The revisionists were right in their argument that, at that time in Europe, revolution was not on the agenda. Instead, capitalism was about to enter a major transformation in its operation. Although often reluctantly, the corporate class accommodated such major reforms as the legalization of unions and the collective bargaining process, the development of the welfare state, and enhanced government intervention in the market. Through such changes, capitalism was able to enter, at least in the short run, a period in which it delivered unparalleled material prosperity to much of the working population in the West for several decades. While the Great Depression brought mass immiseration, the majority of the population did not look to revolution, but to more reforms. In the 1930s and 1940s, such changes offered real improvements in people's lives and were far more within reach than a complete overthrow of the established system.

If the socialist movement had not tried to implement a reform agenda structured by its own vision, then it would have surrendered reform efforts to the corporate parties, who would then enact more limited reforms. Progressives in the United States should well appreciate the difference between the mild and incomplete welfare state that came from an elite party such as the Democrats here and the full-blown social citizenship pushed by genuine working-class parties in Europe. We must also recognize that the reformism of social democracy did not come simply from those at the top of the party, but also reflected the desires of large parts of the parties' membership base of ordinary working people. Calls to reform, not revolution, have most often inspired the political loyalties of the majority of working people.

The revolutionaries proved accurate in several of their judgments, however. The reforms initiated by social democracy did not lead to further steps toward transforming capitalism in the direction of economic democracy. Indeed, the welfare state and Keynesian state economic intervention helped, at least in the short run, to rationalize and legitimize the capitalist order. The revolutionaries were also correct that the reformism promoted by the leadership lost sight of its founding ideals by seriously compromising the traditional socialist program. In many countries, social democratic parties have largely become part of the very establishment that they first set out to overthrow. Ultimately, as the experience of the French Socialists attests, the clearest sign of social democracy's failure came not in the 1930s, when it first accepted reformism, but in the 1980s. In the 1930s, the social democratic parties could accurately lay claim that they were supporting and giving voice to the desires of their base. The same was not true in the 1980s. In the face of the right-wing transformation of capitalism, many social democratic parties failed to provide new ideas. Instead of serving as vehicles for a mass discussion of the new realities, and for a popular mobilization against them, many of the parties seemed more like entrenched bureaucracies out of touch with their social movement origins. Such bureaucracies, when confronted with the growing obsolescence of their old programs and with little sense of mass mobilization, have often caved into right-wing calls for austerity as their only available path.

The tension between immediate reforms, with the compromises they often entail, and the long-term goals of fundamental change are questions that movement activists must still confront. During the 1980s, for example, the contending factions within the German Greens split into two major camps around roughly similar dynamics. On the one side, the "fundamentalists" focused upon the life-threatening magnitude of the current ecological crisis and its source in the very organizing principles of western civilization. They tended toward strategies that emphasized educating the populace as to the need for fundamental social change. On the other side, the "realists," which shared many of the same ecological concerns as the fundamentalists, more often sought to win immediate reforms to establish concrete policy gains. Reflecting their basic disagreement, the fundamentalists tended to subordinate electoral work as a means to aid the development of the non-electoral movement. In contrast, the realists tended to see parliamentary power as an end in its own right.

When considering the possibilities for coalition governments, the fundamentalists refused to compromise on their agenda or principles. By doing so, the fundamentalists hoped to push the Social Democrats to transform their agenda along Green lines. Alternatively, if the coalition stance failed in this regard, the Greens would then be in a strong position to highlight the differences between them and the now-revealed, hopelessly pro-establishment nature of the Social Democrats. By contrast, the realists emphasized an approach that sought compromise in order to ally with the left-wing of the Social Democrats. In doing so, they hoped to try to strengthen that group's influence within the Social Democrats and allow Greens to participate in governing. The tensions between the realists and the fundamentalists were ultimately resolved when the former gained the upper hand within the Party and the latter subsequently split, with many of the more strident members of the fundamentalist camp leaving the Greens.

We have to ask ourselves: "Can't we do better than this?" A key lesson for progressives today is to avoid turning these historical splits into universal conclusions that apply to situations of completely differing times and conditions. The trade-offs between reformism and more fundamental change represent a tension that has to be negotiated by activists in terms of their particular historical situation, not separate positions from which one has to choose one perspective or the other. A political movement has to recognize that, because of the complexity of the strategic issues involved, it will incorporate people with various positions along this spectrum. By focusing on differing aspects of a complex reality, conflicting tendencies can highlight and correct the excesses and limitations of each other's agenda. A party needs a structure and internal culture that can best channel these differences into productive and creative strategies, rather than infighting and paralysis. Understanding how such tensions either enhanced or split movements in the past is certainly one necessary step for activists today.

Charting A Different Course

The New Democratic Party's disastrous experience, and the experience of European social democracy, requires critical analysis. Looked at carelessly, this experience seems to confirm the notion that electoral politics is inherently co-optive and futile. In actuality, it illustrates the tough strategic choices and difficult historical conditions that must be squarely faced by progressives today. Co-optation and elitist bureaucracy are not inevitable. Strategic decisions and organizational choices matter. Different choices can lead to different outcomes. New historical conditions can also present progressives with a very different selection of choices.

Internal Building Blocks for Avoiding Co-optation

Progressives can help themselves avoid such experiences the more they move in the following three directions in their own organizations:

1. Build a Movement, Not an Electoral Machine

One lesson is clear. Activists must not follow the lead of the status quo parties, but develop their own brand of electoral politics instead. The more progressives can build a political movement, rather than a candidate-centered, vote-getting machine, the less the likelihood that officeholders will be absorbed into the mainstream.

Movement politics offsets co-optive pressures in several ways. First, activists and the public focus more on building a party with a platform that means something, rather than relying upon charismatic individuals. Secondly, the basis of movement activism lies in developing grassroots organizations and motion both within the party and among allied social movements. Elected progressive officials need such an active base. Grassroots "street heat" can back up elected officials when the limited powers of their office, combined with the inevitable opposition from the establishment, undermine their efforts. Pressure from below can also hold elected officials accountable to their supporters.

Additionally, a movement-building focus encourages activists to develop their policy agenda more fully before seeking to place candidates in office. A group that clearly works out how to translate its general goals into a realistic policy program will be better able to hold its elected officials accountable than a group that places someone in office only to leave it up to that person to work out ad hoc policies while governing. Historically, the greatest examples of splits between officeholders and the progressive party that supported them have come from situations, like the Ontario NDP, in which the movement came to power through a surprise win and was not prepared with a fully developed plan for governing. The more activists can anticipate the obstacles facing their agenda, the more they can work out ways in which they and their candidates can deal with them once in office. Furthermore, lively grassroots discussions of potential policy obstacles allows the movement, as a group, to confront policy trade-offs and other potentially divisive issues. In this way, disagreements can be channeled into innovative and sophisticated policy, rather than ugly fights among progressive officeholders and/or their grassroots supporters.

2. Develop Internal Democracy and Group Cohesion

All of the party groups discussed in this book are committed, in one way or another, to fostering democratic debate and control within their own groups. The same is true with past progressive efforts. For example, the US Socialists had their candidates sign official letters of resignation as a prerequisite for their support. If the Party membership did not feel that an officeholder had remained true to their mandate, they could turn in the letter, forcing the person to either step down from office or resign from the Party. New Party activists in Wisconsin have pursued a similar concept through the contracts candidates must sign in return for the group's endorsement. Implementing such mechanisms in an effective manner is not entirely without potential difficulties. Faced with the minutia of governing, some officeholders can feel hamstrung if held too tightly to the letter, rather than spirit, of a party's program. In local politics, for example, officeholders often deal with rather mundane issues that do not fit into clear ideological or political categories.

Brazilian politics provides a recent and well-documented example of how a commitment to internal democracy can translate into the structure of a large-scale national party. The Brazilian Workers Party grew out of a resurgent labor movement during the early 1980s. By developing this base, and building alliances with other social movements, it has grown to become not only the largest party in Brazil, but arguably the largest left-leaning party in the world. In 1989, its presidential candidate, Luis Inacio Lula da Silva, nearly won the election by receiving thirty-one million votes. Today, the Party runs the governments of several major Brazilian cities.

The Workers Party looks quite different from its mainstream competitors. For example, the Party has developed an internal structure through which decisions develop from the bottom up. Before its yearly national convention, the Party holds preliminary meetings at all levels—municipal, regional, and national. At the grassroots level, it has also developed the so-called "party nucleus." These groups are set up in neighborhoods, workplaces, and within social movements. Through this structure, ordinary members debate and propose policies that filter up, through elected representatives, to the higher levels of the Party. By uniting trade unions, peasant organizations, women's groups, environmentalists, Christian base communities, and slum dwellers into a rainbow coalition of participatory democracy, the Party has significantly transformed Brazilian politics at the grassroots level.

For a considerable time, the Workers Party also attempted to handle its internal diversity by providing mechanisms for officially recognized "tendencies" within the Party. These factions could operate as semi-autonomous groups, complete with their own internal organs to publicize their views. The experience of this innovation has been mixed. The internal life of the Party has been quite lively. This has benefited the Party by opening the way for creative and dynamic thinking. On a number of occasions, however, factional battles have threatened to tear the Party apart. Also, sectarian groups have tried to use this open system to push their own separate agenda. In response, the Party passed rules that more precisely defined what constituted a tendency and denied recognition to factions that operated as independent parties. According to Sue Branford and Bernardo Kucinski in their recent book on the Workers Party, no one single group is in control of the Party today. Instead, the Workers Party is run "somewhat hesitantly by a coalition of all the factions."[5] To avoid sectarian take-overs, the Party has further democratized its decision-making with requirements for debating every proposal and holding debates according to strict rules.

The experience of the West German Green Party during the 1980s also well illustrates the strengths and hazards of developing internal democracy. With its high degree of local group autonomy, mechanisms for equal representation of women, consensus decision-making, and mandatory representation for minority factions in Party offices, the German Greens tried to build their political ideals into the very structure of the Party. On the positive side, these democratic measures helped establish a high level of diversity, active debate, and potentially creative decision-making within the Greens.

By the mid-1980s, however, the degree of group autonomy fostered by the Party's internal organization had led to some intense infighting and a certain level of organizational chaos. Different tendencies within the Party developed strong lines of demarcation between each other. Yet, to be effective, they also had to work together in an internal structure that required high levels of goodwill, self-discipline, and cooperation to function. While different groups sometimes agreed to disagree successfully, the Greens witnessed intense disagreements that, at times, paralyzed strategic thinking and often grew into intense personal animosities. By the end of the decade, some Green activists talked of a sense of weariness and exhaustion as a result of the continual factional struggles. In the end, a significant number of the members of one of the two major factions, the fundamentalists, left the Party in the early 1990s.

The experience of the German Greens suggests that progressives have to find ways of walking a complex and tricky path between fostering democratic debate and accountability while steering this diversity into productive channels rather than internal balkanization. The pressures for fragmentation become all the more severe when a movement, like the German Greens, faces a situation where they are forced to decide between major strategic options.

The question of internal organization is further complicated by US electoral laws. As mentioned before, progressive parties have to conform to state election laws to qualify for ballot status. This network of state-based laws does not lend itself well to the development of extensive national structures that allow for strong planning, identity, and accountability. Indeed, one could argue that national parties do not really exist in the United States. Both the Republican and Democratic parties are legally organized at the state level. It is through state laws that parties qualify for the ballot, run their primaries, and structure their organizations. The Republican and Democratic national committees are just that—small bodies that coordinate the fifty state-based parties. Progressives have to legally conform to this kind of national federation of state organizations.

While formal rules and structures that promote democratic debate and control are necessary, by themselves, they are not enough. When the Populists and Socialists experienced their decisive splits, the more conservative factions of the party were able to use rather undemocratic bureaucratic maneuvers to ensure internal victory to their cause. As any grassroots activist can testify, even without the intention of dominating the group, a great deal of organizing energy is typically done by a relatively small group of dedicated activists. This can foster factional internal politics. The most open structures possible do not ensure that people will participate responsibly in them. The task of internal democracy is a never ending goal. In addition to formal institutional rules and structures, activists need to establish mechanisms for encouraging participation and for continuously developing new leadership. Such mechanisms must include a welcoming internal culture that invites participation as well as the time-consuming efforts to cultivate and encourage new people.

3. Keep a Focus on the Big Picture

From day one, a political movement must recognize the limitations of electoral politics and the power of elected office to change society. While state power is a key component in the struggle for fundamental change, it is only one part. Progressive elected officials and party organizing can only go as far as the rest of the broader struggle in all its different social movement manifestations. The question for activists is how to link electoral politics to this broader activism.

One ramification of this challenge is that the party and its candidates must cultivate an internal perspective that is prepared to lose elected power when such an action is in the best interests of progressive activism generally. Worse events can happen than losing political office. For example, individuals and parties who stay in office longer than they and their surrounding social movements are able to implement their agenda run the risk of seriously compromising their ideals. In Europe, Social Democrats have stayed in office only to preside over major cost-cutting austerity policies because their traditional agenda is no longer adequate and they have yet to develop a real alternative. While such actions may keep parties in power, in the long run, they risk alienating their base supporters. By losing state power and returning to the role of opposition, a party can place itself in a position to help lead a major strategic rethinking and process of innovation within the progressive community. It could also encourage greater non-electoral forms of grassroots organizing at a time when such a focus may prove more productive than just governing for the present.

As progressive political activism grows at the local and state level, groups may well find themselves with political power, but under highly constrained conditions. Developing an internal culture that places winning office within a broader context of popular movement-building, rather than simply doing the best with what state power candidates hold, will help steer a political movement through the dilemmas of power. Similarly, knowing when to seek majority power—and perhaps compromise to build that majority—and when to remain out of power —and keep one's principles intact—is an important strategic question that groups need to negotiate in a flexible and sophisticated manner.

Revolutionary Reforms:
Building Blocks for an Effective Program

Today, we live in a new era of a global capitalist economy. Correspondingly, the meaning and options of progressive reform politics has changed. All reform efforts are not the same. From the socialist movement's earliest days, in various different forms, the notion of "revolutionary reforms" has animated the strategic thinking of those who have sought fundamental change.[6] The basic idea is simple: develop reforms that can deliver concrete gains in the short run, yet also lead the way into more fundamental transformations in the long run.

The way in which the welfare state is structured can have a critical political impact on future politics, for example. In his thorough study of Scandinavian social democracy, *Politics Against Markets*, Gosta Esping-Anderson points to the ability of the social democrats to enact social programs that have universal reach as a key factor in both their staying in power and staving off a right-wing, anti-state backlash in the 1980s and 1990s.

We can see this lesson by contrasting the United States with Sweden. In the United States, a good part of our inadequate welfare state consists of means-tested programs. Only those who are destitute enough can qualify for such meager aid—be it income support, food, or health care. This not only helps stigmatize those who receive public assistance, but the selective nature of government aid also allows right-wing politicians to pit those who do not receive such state aid against those who do. The fact that many Americans do not think of themselves as ever being able to benefit from welfare spending, coupled with the racism that is deeply entrenched in our society, permits right-wing anti-tax and anti-government sentiments to grow roots within the population.

In contrast, the Swedish Social Democratic Party (SAP) pushed for a much different welfare state. Because it held the reins of parliamentary power, the SAP established the concept of social citizenship, in which the entire population directly benefits from the welfare state. Be it state-run health care, collectively controlled pension funds, childcare allowances, sick pay, unemployment insurance, accident compensation, or housing policies, the Social Democrats aimed to provide programs with universal and equal access to the entire population. They institutionalized the concept that society, not the marketplace, should be responsible for providing and guaranteeing basic levels of welfare for all of its citizens. With all Swedes enjoying widespread concrete and direct benefits from government spending, the Right has found it more difficult to develop anything resembling our Republican's Contract with America. Indeed, when the Right momentarily did come to power in Sweden in the early 1990s, interrupting decades of social democratic rule, it did so without calls for cut backs in social entitlements. The SAP regained power in the next election.

Esping-Anderson also detected a "revolutionary reform" potential in the wage-earner fund initiative developed in Sweden in the 1980s. Faced with the fiscal and economic pressure of the global capitalist crisis, the Swedish labor movement sought to reconcile the need for wage concessions from workers to maintain Swedish competitiveness with the long-term interests of workers. Their proposed solution was for workers to trade wage restraint for greater worker-ownership of their firms. The original plan sought to convert a certain portion of a firm's profits each year—say, twenty percent—into new shares in the company that would be collectively controlled by elected worker representatives. The higher the rate of profit, the more shares the workers would own. The plan's architects predicted that within twenty-five to fifty years workers would have effective control of most major companies. Obviously, had the original plan been enacted and succeeded in meeting its goals, the fundamental nature of economic ownership in Sweden would have been completely redefined. Indeed, opponents of the plan denounced it as "creeping socialism." Unfortunately, the Social Democratic Party only took up a watered-down version of the plan. With the failure of this "revolutionary reform" initiative, SAP reached the late 1980s with no alternative but to implement major austerity measures.[7]

The notion of revolutionary reforms can certainly be applied to the United States. At the local level, examples already exist of community-driven redevelopment.[8] With the proper resources, such resident initiatives could easily include alternative, cooperative, and ecologically sound forms of economic enterprises, such as worker- and community-owned businesses. Similarly, people could revitalize their housing and public space in a manner that establishes laws and norms of greater collective public control over land use. The good of the community would supersede the currently dominant rights of private developers. By using such alternatives as a way of rebuilding our cities, progressives would not only address the crisis of urban blight, but also create inner cities that provide living examples of a better, more democratic, and community-oriented society.

Furthermore, revolutionary reforms could take the form of measures designed to increase the ability of social movements to grow and develop. Today, for example, US labor laws are structured in favor of employers. Major progressive reforms are needed to provide critical help toward rebuilding the labor movement. Such reforms might include an easier process for workers to gain legal recognition of their union, harsher penalties for employers who violate the law, and repeal of laws that ban certain kinds of worker solidarity. We can also envision even bolder changes. Labor laws could be dramatically changed to establish a legal framework for state-mandated sectorial bargaining. Through such a system, the government would recognize unionization not just of individual firms, but of entire industries. Laws which ban companies from using scab workers during strikes would also increase the power of organized labor.

Similarly, tackling racism is a key to the overall success of any progressive agenda. Racism has too often crippled progressive social movements and provided a tool for reactionary politics. While fully eliminating racism requires major structural changes in our society, even partial efforts could make highly significant inroads. For example, real multicultural education in the public schools and a cadre of political leaders who talk honestly about racial problems would help to combat many of the myths that drive white supremacy and racial fears. Additionally, social programs with universal access would begin to both better equalize the standard of living between whites and communities of color, and undermine the ability of right-wing politicians to pit white suburbanites against inner city communities of color.

Progressives should also join the debate over who will control the emerging high-tech forms of communication. They could pass laws that not only prioritize public over private control of the new technologies (such as the internet and new cable systems), but that also lead to a reconsideration of past laws that granted access of the public airwaves to private television and radio networks. Establishing a truly public media in this country would clearly represent a major step toward altering the balance of power, both in politics and in American culture. Similarly, the political reforms already being advanced by progressive groups around campaign finance reform and proportional representation would structurally democratize our political system in ways that could open the door for further popular power.

Such a strategy places a basic faith in ordinary people that, as they become more organized and involved in politics and their communities, they will seek more fundamental changes. Indeed, over time, the basic contradictions within our society and the resistance of the powers-that-be will play itself out by pointing the way toward further, more fundamental changes. Thus, through what we have called revolutionary reforms, a progressive political movement can strive to alter the balance of power in our society in favor of the movements of ordinary people. The more activists tie their reform policies to this broader strategy of societal change, the more their movement will be able to resist the co-optive pressures of the political system.

Visionary Thinking for a "New World Order"

The idea of revolutionary reform, suggests that new, visionary thinking is needed if electoral success is going to be meaningful. Canada's New Democratic Party is not alone in finding its traditional policies no longer adequate. Throughout Europe and elsewhere, traditional social democratic movements find themselves in a desperate search for new ideas. The emerging global economy has placed the welfare state in severe fiscal crisis, while rendering traditional social democratic mechanisms of national economic planning ineffective. At the same time, the corporate centers of power have broken with the old social compromises of the boom years to go on a right-wing, free trade, deregulation, cost-cutting offensive. Today, the task of a progressive political movement is not how to better redistribute a booming prosperity, but how to subordinate destructive private economic decision-making to society's needs. While this task has many dimensions, two of the most pressing are rethinking economic democracy and social citizenship.

Economic Democracy

The old social democratic/New Deal-type reforms came in response to the realities of the Great Depression. Within this context, as well as the emerging post-war boom, the welfare state and Keynesian full employment policies did represent an answer to the "economic question." Today, such mechanisms simply do not provide an adequate response to the new global economy. For one thing, these mechanism assume a large common interest between popular well-being and corporate success. Proponents argue that by helping business do well, guided by the proper state policies, real gains could be delivered to a large part of the population. Business growth and increasing living standards seemed inherently linked. Such an assumed compatibility of interests has much less validity today.

One of the great ironies of the US economy in the mid-1990s is that, for the first time, the recovery of business from a recession has not corresponded to improvements in working people's daily lives. Indeed, many multinational corporations have built their record profits precisely by further degrading the US standard of living by eliminating jobs, moving production out of the country, suppressing wages, and offering more and more part-time and temporary work. Policies that simply encourage business will only enhance these practices. Instead, our basic standard of living will recover only when sharp inroads into corporate decision-making authority place society's well-being at the center of economic rationality. The rallying cry of today's progressives cannot be limited to government intervention to offset the downturns of the business cycle. The call must be for economic democracy.

Economic democracy involves far more than traditional bread and butter questions. With worker-manager "teams" in their automobile industry leading the way, the Japanese have forced managers in US industry to rethink their basic notion of decision-making within the workplace. Left to their own logic, they are copying their Asian rivals by replacing traditional top-down methods with even more insidious control techniques that use the trappings of "cooperation" and "employee input" to drain ever more energy from their workers. Yet, in countries where workers have the political space and legal supports to formulate their own independent models, such as in Sweden and Germany, they have produced visions and experiments of real workplace democracy that offer pro-worker alternatives. In an age when companies talk of greater "employee involvement" and "flexibility" as keys to increasing productivity, progressives have an ideal ground from which to push for genuine forms of popular control within the workplace. We are no longer just talking about wages and benefits.

Similarly, the environmental movement has clearly revealed the ecological crisis that our society faces. Limited reforms within our current economic social structure, such as recycling or relatively energy-efficient cars, while certainly welcome, simply do not provide an adequate response to the accelerating destruction of our environment. On ecological grounds, the old social democratic/New Deal liberal faith in continued economic growth is no longer viable. As environmentalists have shown, we have to rethink the basic assumption of boundless growth upon which our economy is founded. Since growth for growth's sake is a central component of our capitalist system—so much so that slowed growth will signal a major economic crisis—a genuine solution requires imposing a popular, environmentally sustainable logic on economic decision-making.

Our society has also reached a point where changes in family life and the role of women has surpassed our present economic structure—one founded on a nuclear family ideal where women stayed home, while men went off to work. Today, only a minority of the US population lives in a "traditional" nuclear family. The crisis of the family, which conservatives are so fond of trumpeting, has a material aspect. As parents scramble to make ends meet, more of their energy goes to their employers and less to their homes and families. As a society, we need to rethink the basic balance between work inside and outside the home as well as the gender roles associate with it.

The need for such rethinking has become even more urgent as our capitalist economy continues to produce more work with fewer workers. In the past few decades, our industrial society has witnessed a vast expansion in the productive power of the average worker. Yet, rather than producing less work time for all of us, corporations have used this greater productivity to shed workers. Policies that try to create new employment through further economic growth are not an adequate solution. Instead, we now face major decisions over basic distribution of jobs and the very definition of fulltime work.

To thoroughly address both the redefinition of gender roles and the restructuring of work, we need to seriously decrease the workweek. In Europe and the United States, proposals have been advanced by various progressive groups to lower the workweek to between thirty-five and thirty-two hours.[9] Such a change would provide both women and men with more home time while addressing the growing problem of unemployment. Vastly expanded paid family leave (the German Greens proposed three years) for both parents coupled with a national childcare policy are also necessary to provide more family time as well as to help equal out gender roles. Pay equity legislation and childcare allowances are similarly needed to address the economic strains of single-parent households, and to further enhance women's opportunities.

We also need to rethink the link between work and retirement. As people live longer, the established economic norms that simply warehouse people after they have reached a certain age is neither fiscally sound nor in the best interests of those forced to retire only to find themselves marginalized by society. Here again, the balance between paid work and other aspects of life must be reformatted. To address these issues, society must establish greater social and political controls over an economy whose basic rationality does not foster such rethinking and reorganization. The necessary reforms, such as the reduced workweek and paid parental leave, involve changes that remove a greater proportion of people's lives out from under the direct logic of the capitalist economy.

Such changes will be difficult. While the obsolescence of the national economy can, at times, be overstated, certainly today we live in a global economic order. Any progressive program for economic democracy has to address the pressures of international competition, operation, and investment. As the elite energy expended over negotiating and approving NAFTA and GATT demonstrate, trade policies matter. Ordinary people in different countries can avoid being pitted against each other by establishing alternative international agreements that force companies to compete on the basis of the highest standards rather than reduce everyone to the lowest. Similarly, national tariff and trade policies can provide one mechanism for forcing corporations to pay the full social and environmental costs of business operations that they chose to pursue.

In short, any effort to seriously address the basic social problems caused by our economy necessitates major popular inroads into capitalist prerogatives and controls. A progressive political movement needs to translate this general notion into concrete policies that enhance the ability of workers, communities, and governments to control corporate decision-making. Reviving old models of economic control are not enough in today's global economy. A progressive economic agenda has to find innovative ways to establish greater popular controls on corporate actors who are global in their reach and power.

In the long run, developing a realistic model for promoting economic democracy is one of the central theoretical and programmatic challenges facing progressives. While different grassroots efforts and progressive think tanks have taken some steps in this direction, efforts to produce comprehensive and active alternatives are only now beginning to emerge through such experiments as Sustainable Milwaukee and the jobs coalitions in Connecticut and Massachusetts. A growing progressive political movement provides a natural framework and sense of purpose for such rethinking. Engaging in actual political organizing that aims at state power transforms economic discussions from mere theorizing to a concrete platform to be put before voters and fought for. If progressives can develop a viable program, the potential response appears quite promising. Economic democracy is not only a necessity, but, arguably, something that most Americans would support. In an era when most people have become cynical about the morality and intentions of those in any position of power, a call to hold corporations responsible to popular mandates could prove quite appealing.

Social Citizenship—Creating Community

Given the present social crisis and the underdeveloped nature of the US welfare state, the classic social democratic demand for public programs that guarantee people's basic needs must become a core part of a progressive agenda and can be seen as a revolutionary reform. Already progressives have pointed to a variety of demands, such as national health care, government work programs, public childcare, a guaranteed income, and housing supports. Especially when developed in a manner that promotes community and enhances democratic controls and participation, such a welfare state would not only meet people's basic needs, but also transform our political culture. Under the current cultural climate, most people are forced to meet their basic needs by competing individually in the marketplace. In contrast, social citizenship pools part of the nation's wealth to provide collective public services for everyone. Such a system encourages people to see their personal interest in terms of the collective health of society.

When looked at in a comparative perspective, the prospects for universal public programs seem contradictory. While the need for such programs increases as standards of living fall, the pressures of the global economy place a greater strain on already declining fiscal resources. Indeed, progressives need to study the crises in which many social democratic systems find themselves today. At the national level, the situation in this country does have several unique characteristics that could provide relatively greater fiscal maneuvering room. For example, as the "world's policeman," the United States allocates far more of its revenues to military spending than any other country. Both Japan and Germany spend roughly a tenth of what our country spends on the military. Estimates of the cost of these huge US outlays vary depending on the source, but they run from the official government figure for 1994 of 22 percent to over half the budget, as claimed by the War Resisters League (who add in the portion of the national debt they say went to the Reagan military buildup the 1980s). In any case, a redirection of this taxpayer money could pay for many new programs. Similarly, with its generous corporate welfare, the United States also has one of the lowest corporate tax rates in the industrialized world. Again, the estimates vary, but clearly hundreds of billions of dollars are involved. A real peace dividend combined with fair taxes (both measures that most Americans arguably support) would deliver the fiscal basis to finance major efforts to establish social citizenship.

While vastly expanding state social provisions is worthwhile in its own right, progressives can take the concept of social citizenship far beyond simply meeting basic material needs. What policies such as the welfare state or public transportation can do is to establish areas of people's lives that are insulated from the logic of the marketplace. Social citizenship should mean that people do not have to subordinate all aspects of their lives to the needs of buying and selling. An ever expanding and democratic public sphere can provide spaces where people can live under a humane, rather than a capitalistic, logic. Thus, for example, reductions in the workweek and greater family-leave free more of people's time and energy for use in their homes and communities. Publicly owned media, national health care, public parks, community events and celebrations—all are examples of concrete reforms that create and expand a community sphere that transfers more of people's lives out of the marketplace. In applying a broad conception of social citizenship, progressives can develop an agenda for rebuilding the infrastructure of community life that offers people more areas for life-sustaining human connections.

Social citizenship is obviously a key concept in an era when reactionary politics is built by pitting people against each other. Yet we need to move beyond merely economistic notions of social solidarity. In addition, a progressive political movement must directly embrace, embody, and celebrate diversity. Gone are the days when one dimension of oppression (such as class) and one constituency (such as the working class) could define progressive politics. A progressive political movement must encompass social activism from across the spectrum of groups. It must espouse a universal commitment to fight injustice at all levels of society and to establish a truly "rainbow" community.

Bringing different people with different backgrounds together is a process that requires a great deal of hard work and creativity. We believe that struggles around questions of political and economic democracy, environmental sustainability, adequate support for families, and social citizenship and solidarity are potential umbrella projects to drive a politics where many people can find their home. Electoral and non-electoral victories by parties creatively representing these movements and their sympathizers offer real hope for the future. Indeed, it may be the best way to rebuild the progressive movement in this country. While the pressures toward co-optation and drift exist, they can be identified and resisted. Organizing an independent political movement is not pre-ordained to end in defeat or hollow success.

Conclusion

What an Independent Political Movement Can Do for You

Contesting for power at the local and state levels provides an avenue for building the kind of grassroots strength that will allow progressives to break into national politics. While getting progressives elected to office is a significant goal, it is not the only one for third party politics. Real change comes when ordinary people, organized into diverse social movements, push for it. Progressives seek to establish the true ideal of democracy where people themselves participate in organizing and leading society. While winning elected positions of state power is one part of this process, a progressive politics can substantially further the cause of broader movement activism. Indeed, organizing an independent political movement is a likely key to rebuilding the Left in this country. By organizing around independent politics, activists will help to solve three of the central difficulties facing the progressive community today.

Moving From Fragmentation to Working Unity

In today's political climate, the fragmentation of social activism into disconnected single-issue work can often place activists in a weak position. For example, at a recent forum to discuss the ongoing attack on the nation's welfare programs, the speakers and audience spoke quite passionately about the pain and suffering that budget cuts were going to inflict on people at the bottom of our society. While organizers hoped to rally the audience to fight back, the mood of the gathering was quite depressed. Within the existing political framework, there appeared little that activists could do to stem the right-wing tide. The Democrats were either unwilling or unable to challenge the Republican agenda. The general public also did not appear, on the surface at least, to support welfare programs. Furthermore, many of the activists in the room felt uneasy about defending programs that are inadequate and disempowering. As a result, many of those who attended the gathering went home with a sense of powerlessness and despair.

Could the meeting have had a much more hopeful character if its context had been different? Discussions at the gathering would have likely moved beyond the narrow confines of the current political debate had there been a sense of the possibilities for a progressive political movement. People could then have discussed alternatives to current programs, such as raising the minimum wage, reducing the workweek, and social citizenship reforms, including universal health care, childcare, education, and child tax allowances. A mood of optimism might have crept into the room as people began to envision the appeal that such ideas would have among the general population.

Currently, much of progressive activism remains limited to a fragmented single-issue focus. While such specific activism must continue, achieving significant progressive change in the future requires confronting authorities and presenting the public with comprehensive alternatives. In today's climate of rampant cynicism, isolated changes are not going to transform people's perspective to one of hope. Hope, a key ingredient in inspiring people's activism, can best come when people see that society in general can be far different from what it is at present. Political parties and movements provide the best context for thinking about comprehensive change. They offer a mechanism by which movements for social change have traditionally come together and articulated their common alternative.

Talking to Ordinary Americans

Progressive activists often have a sense of being marginalized in our society. While activists feel that their progressive values have universal appeal, they see few avenues for getting their ideas out to "mainstream" America. In the worst cases, the progressive community has gotten quite used to simply talking to itself.

Political parties are about setting the public agenda. Quite aside from actually electing people, parties provide a forum for developing an agenda and then placing it in the public debate. We can see this ability quite clearly in US politics, where the Right has been able to use electoral activism, coupled with non-electoral movements, to place its agenda of "family" values, deficit reduction, and attack on "big" government into popular view. In doing so, the Right has not only publicized its ideas, but has transformed the very nature of political debate in this country so that its concerns and worldview provide the frame of reference for political discussion. Thus, the public increasingly debates individual morality and the limitations of government rather than corporate restructuring, racism, welfare for the wealthy, or violence against women.

What works for the Right can work for progressives as well. Canada, for example, despite having a strong right-wing movement, nevertheless has a much broader political debate relative to the United States. Canadian news more routinely runs programs covering unions and issues raised by working people. Most US progressives would be astonished to turn on their television and see a twenty-minute special examining the contradiction between record corporate profits and continued downsizing and layoffs. Part of the reason for this difference is the fact that the Canadian Broadcasting Corporation is a publicly owned and financed television network.

The existence of the New Democratic Party has also helped widen the political debate. As a legitimate party, the NDP forces the media to recognize a progressive viewpoint. Canadian media cannot simply interview liberals and conservatives and say they have "both sides of the issue," as their US counterparts do routinely. They have to include a "third side" because a party that embodies a comprehensive "third" perspective is publicly visible and recognized. We should remember that Canada's single-payer health care system, so admired by progressives in the United States, would not have happened without the New Democratic Party. The Party, for all of its faults, used its public visibility, and governmental power in the western provinces, to place national health care into the country's official political debate—despite holding only a minority of seats in the national legislature.

The same pattern holds true in US history. The Populists and Socialist never had much of a physical presence in Congress, in terms of elected officials. Nevertheless, their agenda was very much evident in the nation's capital and many state legislatures. The Populists and Socialists altered the official political debate by raising questions with a loud enough voice that key issues could not be ignored.

Most concretely, by generating a political movement, progressives will be building ways to interact with "mainstream" America. Not only does electoral activism provide a platform from which to place progressive ideas before a broad audience, but it compels activists to organize among "mainstream" communities where they might currently have little involvement. Political organizing also provides an avenue for getting ordinary people involved in progressive politics. A movement that goes beyond the present boundaries of progressive activism will be built not just by the people who are already politically active, but by the tens of thousands of ordinary people who are currently uninvolved and apathetic. These people include many of the future leaders and organizers of political change.

The political process provides a ready-made channel for reaching and mobilizing such people. Electoral politics and party organizing represents a form of activism that is officially recognized and celebrated in our political culture. While many Americans are cynical about politics, party work often has more perceived legitimacy than joining a demonstration. Furthermore, the connection of party-building to elected state offices with real power, coupled with the ability to discuss comprehensive alternatives, gives a political movement a certain aura of seriousness and believability. Almost all of the political efforts researched for this book involved significant numbers of enthusiastic people who had never been involved in progressive politics before. Because many of these political groups have only just gotten started, their current access to elected power is typically limited to carefully targeted local offices. Nevertheless, even these modest efforts appear serious enough that people join them because they see a believable alternative that is concrete and accessible.

Going on the Offensive

Finally, with the Right setting the national political agenda, progressives often find themselves fighting defensive battles to hold onto what they have. In the long run, such a stance is a losing one. At best, activists fend off the worst changes. When they lose, the dynamic of the country moves further right. Ultimately, progressives cannot defeat the right-wing agenda piece-meal. Activists cannot try to rally public sentiment in terms of what they are against; rather, they must be for something positive.

A political movement permits progressives to go on the offensive. It allows people to develop a comprehensive alternative to the current agenda and then to take that agenda before the public. By using the political process to point the way toward a better society, progressives can seize the initiative from the Right and force the powers-that-be to respond to them, rather than progressives responding to those in power. Most immediately, being part of a movement to take political power will help expand the horizons of activism so that progressives can begin contemplating bold and creative alternatives to the present.

Unfortunately, today's efforts to articulate such a creative comprehensive vision exist mainly as abstract exercises unconnected to real movements. Individuals and small groups of activists and intellectuals have articulated many bold programs. These ideas, however, remain largely unconnected to concrete practice. Reflecting this limitation, they often acquire a very general and theoretical character. It is common, for example, to call for an end to racism or assert support for workplace democracy. But what do these slogans actually mean? What are the tangible, step-by-step changes that will make these ideals a reality? As long as such calls for comprehensive social change remain unconnected to movements with the power to implement them, they will largely be intellectual exercises and hollow rallying cries. In contrast, the task of having to explain a party's program to the public and the prospect of actually taking state power to implement it, compels activists to work out alternative ideas, and to do so in very concrete ways. It comes as no accident that such bold, forward-looking economic initiatives as Sustainable Milwau-kee or the Massachusetts and Connecticut jobs coalitions have come out of explicitly political organizing.

Because of its ability to address the three central dilemmas confronting the progressive community, we believe that a progressive political move-ment must become a task that defines progressive activism as we enter the next century. Progressive activism in this country has always taken a diversity of forms. At various times in history, certain currents of activism have exploded with such force and momentum that they have defined their era. The labor movement of the 1930s and the Civil Rights movement of the 1950s and 1960s are examples. They seized the national imagination. They not only involved considerable popular energy in their own right, but also provided a catalyst that inspired other social movements. In looking ahead, we believe that activists should view political organizing as a movement with a similar potential. The early parts of the twenty-first century could be an era defined by the progressive community's breaking up of the two party monopoly.

Thinking the "Unthinkable"

We believe that activists have ample reason to think in such big terms. While a political movement has to build from the ground up, we should not rule out the possibility of outright victory by breaking into national politics. The crisis of our two party system has never been as severe. A fall 1995 CNN/*USA Today*/Gallop poll is simply one example of a long-term trend in public opinion. The pollsters found that only 32 percent of the public was satisfied with a Clinton/Dole match up. Almost two-thirds wanted to see a third party alternative. The current political status quo is not based upon people's active endorsement. Rather, those in power have to convince people that no alternative exists.

A political order based upon the denial of alternatives is a fragile one indeed. Progressives do not have to persuade a majority of Americans to support their agenda, they only have to demonstrate that such an option can actually happen. We can look to history to see just how quickly our society has changed when the conditions were right and people saw a viable alternative.

Who would have thought in 1930 that the country was on the verge of an explosion of union organizing? In Michigan, for example, the introduction of the assembly line and an aggressive employer offensive during the 1920s had wiped out skilled, craft-based unions. Home to the auto industry, Detroit was a non-union, open-shop town. Yet, a decade later, Detroit would become the nation's premier union city and autoworkers would be helping to lead a massive social movement that propelled many industrial workers into the middle class. Similarly, who would have thought in 1940 that Jim Crow apartheid in the US South was on its last leg? And who would have believed that the politically demobilized, Cold War-driven suburbia of the 1950s would produce a generation of students a decade later who would lead the charge in transforming our country?

In short, massive social awakenings are not something that can be worked out in advance. The task facing activists is to realize the emerging potential and to begin laying the ground work upon which the larger movement can grow. Each of the above historical examples had precursors in smaller, less far reaching efforts. At the time, many of these projects may have seemed hopeless in their ability to effect major societal change. Yet, in hindsight, we can see that they paved the way for further greatness.

Ultimately, mass movements grow because people dare to think the "unthinkable." They do not wait for "the movement" to make its appearance, rather they launch it. Today, progressives must do the same. Currently, only a relatively small proportion of progressive-minded people are actively involved in independent politics. To alter the current direction of our society, this situation must change. To paraphrase a popular slogan, "We are the movement we have been looking for."

Addendum: The Ball Keeps Rolling

The continued Republican-Democratic split in our nation's capital should not leave Progressives glum about fall 1996 elections. The ongoing lackluster performance of both major parties underlines the political opening available to progressives which we have outlined throughout the book. And while not reported on the evening news, progressives scored a number of outright victories in November 1996.

Bernie Sanders won reelection for his fourth term as Vermont's sole member in the House of Representatives and the Progressive Coalition sent three members to the state house. The struggle to gain more state seats should intensify in the years ahead.

Newly elected New Party member Danny Davis of Chicago will join Sanders in the 105th Congress. His overwhelming 85 percent victory, running as a New Party Democrat, was clearly not welcomed by the city's Democratic Party who notably tried to ignore his existence. Also in Chicago, Democratic Socialist of America activist Steven De La Rosa Democratic mounted a strong, although ultimately unsuccessful, challenge against a high ranking Republican congressman. The grassroots support shown for his campaign promises an even stronger performance next time round.

In President Clinton's Arkansas, voters approved a New Party-sponsored referendum on campaign finance reform and sent a third New Party member to the Little Rock city council and two to the county board. The New Party also handily defeated the Arkansas state chair of William Bennet's right-wing "Empower America" for a seat on the country board. While in Maryland the ballot initiative to free up school funding lost by a narrow margin, the campaign did leave behind a broad coalition of progressive groups that promises well for the future.

In December the U.S. Supreme Court heard the New Party's fusion case. Activists are optimistic that the justices will uphold the lower court ruling—

thus opening up fusion candidacies across the country. In the mean time, in November all five Democratic state legislative candidates in Minnesota who agreed to run fusion candidacies with the New Party won by healthy margins. Running on the Green Party ticket for state assembly, New Party member Cam Ryder also had a strong showing with 25 percent of the vote in a three-way contest .

As a result of November wins Greens now hold a majority in Arcata, California and picked up local offices in Berkeley and Santa Monica. In New Mexico the Greens maintained "major party status" by winning 11 percent in a statewide race. At the end of 1996, at least 36 Greens held elected office in the United States, the majority of the them in California.

The ability of progressives to use election reform campaigns to change the rules of the game, while simultaneously building grassroots support, was confirmed in 1996 with New Party campaign finance referendum wins in Arkansas and in two districts in Massachusetts. Even more spectacular, Maine voters passed the sweeping reform referendum supported by the Dirigo Alliance. The measure establishes a system of full public financing for all Gubernatorial and state legislative candidates who forgo private money. Throughout New England, LEAP-style coalitions boasted major wins in November including electing New Hampshire's first women Governor, five incumbent Republican members of Congress ousted by Democrats, and four state legislative chambers moving to Democratic control. Most important, issue work around money and politics, decent jobs, health-care, state budgets, and multi-racial coalition-building continues to move New England progressives down the road of a pro-active, forward-looking, and comprehensive agenda.

Ralph Nader's campaign for U.S. President confirmed the skepticism expressed in the book concerning running for higher offices before progressives are ready. Nader received 580,000 votes nation-wide—110,000 more than the Libertarian candidate. His best showing was in California where he won 3.5 percent. While the campaign may have inspired some new people to become active in progressive politics, Nader's poor showing could have also potentially re-enforced the pervasive cynicism most people hold about political change. However, the Nader campaign was not very reflective of the current possibilities. According to Brian Tokar in the November 1996 *Z Magazine*, the "Draft Nader Campaign" was an ad hoc effort. The Greens split over whether or not to actively promote the campaign.

The Nader bid also did not enjoy the explicit support of most state Green parties or of any of the national groups studies in the book. To be really serious, progressive should attempt Presidential politics only through a solid coalition of progressive groups.

Most important, 1996 confirmed that bottom-up, grassroots organizing does pay off. The power of patient local organizing is shown by the New Party 's continued success. Not only has it won 110 of the 163 race it has entered, but organizers continue to establish new local chapters. Through grassroots organizing, flexible tactics, and concrete wins, the New Party continues to demonstrate an ability to build broad and effective coalitions which include a strong presence of people of color and growing union involvement and recognition. In short, progressive politics works. Proven paths are out there. We need only take up the challenge.

Notes

Introduction

1. For a scholarly overview of third party politics from a mainstream perspective, see Steven Rosenstone, Roy Behr, and Edward Lazarus, *Third Parties in America,* 2nd ed. (Princeton, NJ: Princeton University Press, 1996). The authors offer some interesting analysis of voting behavior and opinion data. However, they completely miss the mass movement character of progressive organizing that is the centerpiece of our examination.

Chapter One: Rediscovering Our Legacy

1. Quoted in Lawrence Goodwyn, *Democratic Promise* (New York: Oxford University Press, 1976), p. 33.
2. Reprint from *Farmer's Alliance* found in a collection of Populist writings edited by Norman Pollack, *The Populist Mind* (New York: The Bobbs-Merrill Company, 1967), p. 21.
3. Goodwyn, p. 26.
4. Pollack, pp. 3-4.
5. Kirk H. Porter and Donald Bruce Johnson, *National Party Platforms 1840-1956* (Urbana: University of Illinois Press, 1956), p. 183.
6. Ibid., p. 168.
7. Socialist Party, *Socialist Congressional Campaign Book* (Chicago, IL: The Socialist Party, 1914), p. 1. Located in the rare books room of the Industrial Labor Relations School at Cornell University.
8. Ibid., p. 89.
9. Goodwyn, p. 264.
10. Quoted in Goodwyn, p. 273.
11. Pollack, p. 62.
12. Goodwyn, pp. 196-97.
13. Socialist Party, p. 1.
14. Quoted in Ira Kipnis, *The American Socialist Movements 1897-1912* (New York: Monthly Review Press, 1952), p. 136.
15. Socialist Party, p. 8.
16. Ibid., p. 109.
17. Ibid., p. 5.
18. Richard Judd, Socialist Cities (New York: SUNY Press, 1989), p. 65.
19. *Appeal to Reason,* February 3, 1917, reprinted in John Graham, *"Yours for the Revolution": The Appeal to Reason, 1885-1918* (Lincoln: University of Nebraska Press, 1990), p. 213.
20. It should be noted that the electorate had expanded due to women winning the national right to vote that year.
21. "Jimmie Higgins and the Reading Socialist Community," in Bruce Stave, ed., *Socialism and the Cities* (Port Washington, NY: Kennikat Press, 1975).
22. The information for the Ohio cases comes from Judd, chap. 4.
23. Quoted in Kenneth Hendrickson, Jr., "Tribune of the People: George Lunn and the Rise and Fall of Christian Socialism in Schenectady," in Stave, p. 77. Our account of the Schenectady experience is based on this article.

24. Judd, p. 19.

25. Ira Katznelson, *City Trenches* (New York: Pantheon, 1981).

26. James R. Green, "The 'Salesmen-Soldiers' of the 'Appeal Army': A Profile of Rank-and-File Socialist Agitators," in Stave, p. 34.

27. Goodwyn, p. 354. In his classic work on Southern history, C. Vann Woodward also points to the importance of the Populist press for the development of the broader movement. See *Origins of the New South 1877-1913* (Baton Rouge: Louisiana State University Press, 1971), pp. 194, 247-49.

28. Woodward, p. 194; Goodwyn, p. 175.

29. Kipnis, p. 247. James Weinstein has provided a list of Socialist periodicals from 1912-1918 in *The Decline of Socialism in America: 1912-1925* (New Brunswick, NJ: Rutgers University Press, reprinted 1984), pp. 93-103.

30. Kipnis, p. 248; Graham, p. 1. For an extensive discussion of Wayland's business techniques and the criticisms they received from other Socialists, see Elliot Shore, *Talkin' Socialism: J. A. Wayland and the Radical Press* (Lawrence: University of Kansas Press, 1988), chaps. 5, 6 and 7.

31. The most famous radical exposé of the age came from Upton Sinclair's description of the horrible conditions in the meat-packing industry. *The Jungle* was originally published serially in the *Appeal to Reason*. Subsequent editions of the work have deleted much of Sinclair's open support for socialism. Gene DeGroven has compiled the original version as published by the *Appeal* in *The Lost First Edition of Upton Sinclair's The Jungle* (Memphis, TN: Peachtree Publishers, 1988).

32. An extreme case is Populist Tom Watson's *The People's Party Paper,* which had press runs of up to 20,000, but whose paid subscribers never exceeded 474. See Goodwyn, p. 355.

33. The more contemporary experience of the *Guardian* (New York), a major left weekly newspaper, illustrates the distinction between a press that gains a readership from the general atmosphere and a press that is actively promoted by the movement. Contemporary currents of left activism and left academia provided the *Guardian* with a national readership. In 1992, however, when the paper entered a major financial crisis, it largely had to seek its own aid— primarily by appealing to its readership—as its supporters were not part of a nationally organized political movement that could have self-consciously supported the paper. By the fall of 1992, the *Guardian* suspended publication.

34. *The Party Builder,* no. 47, September 27, 1913 (Westport CT: Greenwood Press, 1970). *The Party Builder,* an internal publication designed to promote Socialist organizing, is an excellent source for primary information on Party activity.

35. Ibid., p. 5.

36. Kipnis, p. 246.

37. Theodore Mitchell, *Political Education in the Southern Farmer's Alliance 1877-1900* (Madison: University of Wisconsin Press, 1987), p. 56. Goodwyn has a similar view of Alliance lecturing; see pp. 73, 111, 128, 174, 224, 235, 243, 331, and 374. This dynamic interaction may not have been universal. Scott G. McNall's research into the records of one regional lecturer in Kansas, S. M. Scott, found that he avoided sparking controversy and offered little opportunity for debate and discussions of complex ideology. See *The Road to Rebellion: Class Formation and Kansas Populism 1865-1900* (Chicago: University of Chicago Press, 1988), p. 208.

38. Woodward, pp. 195 and 273.

39. Goodwyn, p. 314.

40. Kipnis, p. 255; Judd, pp. 51 and 57. As the national office established *The Party Builder* initially as a tool for promoting the Lyceum Bureau, the publication provides a rich source of information on national lecturing efforts.

41. Oscar Ameringer, *If You Don't Weaken: The Autobiography of Oscar Ameringer* (Tulsa: University of Oklahoma Press, 1983), p. 274.

42. In 1909, the school had an average enrollment of 200. See Kipnis, p. 258.

43. Judd, p. 55.

44. McNall, pp. 193-94.

45. Ameringer, pp. 263-67.

46. Reprinted in James R. Green, *Grassroots Socialism: Radical Movements in the Southwest 1895-1943* (Baton Rouge: Louisiana State University Press, 1978), p. 154.

47. *The Party Builder,* September 27, 1913, p. 7.

48. Judd, p. 55.

49. While modern society may appear to be characterized by an erosion of community, it also contains a longing for such community. Evangelicalism, for example, has demonstrated an ability to grow at the grassroots, in part, by offering people an opportunity for community.

50. McNall, p. 186.

51. Mitchell provides a detailed discussion of these educational strategies in chap. 4. He points to a parallel between Macune's Educational Exercises and the modern techniques of Brazilian educator Paulo Freire. See note 53 on page 121.

52. *The Party Builder,* December 4, 1912, p. 3. The continual sporadic presence of such articles in this publication, reminding local activists that Socialist activity continued year-round, suggests that such a conception was not automatically universal or unproblematic.

53. Reprinted in Stave, p. 195. Long-time Socialist presidential candidate Eugene V. Debs held similar views on the limited role of elections. See Green, p. 126, and Nick Salvatore, *Eugene V. Debs Citizen and Socialist* (Chicago: University of Illinois Press, 1982), chaps. 7-9.

54. Quoted in Mitchell, p. 172.

55. Ibid.

56. Elsewhere I have developed more detailed discussions concerning the dialectic between the role of the Party and the role of experience as understood among leading left-wing figures of the early international Socialist movement. In "Rediscovering Western Marxism's Heritage: Rosa Luxemburg and the Role of the Party," I use Luxemburg to examine this left-wing approach in depth. See *Research and Society,* no. 3, 1990, pp. 1-34. One of the common vulgarizations of the Left's understanding of this dialectic has been the so-called theory of the vanguard party. In "A Revolutionary Vanguard? Lenin's Concept of the Party," I argue that Lenin's understanding of the revolutionary process was far more sophisticated than the vanguard practices that many interpreters erroneously ascribe to him. See *Nature, Society and Thought,* vol. 5, no. 2, pp. 133-60. For a reading of Marx that parallels my own approach, see Hal Draper, *Karl Marx's Theory of Revolution* (New York: Monthly Review Press, vol. 1, 1977, vol. 2, 1978, vol. 3, 1986).

57. Goodwyn, pp. 196-97.

Chapter Two: Insignificant Movements

1. This is a verse from "God is Marching On" by J. W. Nichol. Originally published by the *Appeal to Reason,* July 2, 1898.

2. E. E. Schattschneider, *The Semi-Sovereign People* (New York: Holt, Rhinehart, and Winston, 1960), pp. 76-77.

3. Judd, p. 143.

4. Quoted in Goodwyn, p. 188.

5. Ibid., p. 271.

6. Ibid., p. 362.

7. Ibid.

8. Quoted in Green, pp. 272-73.

9. From the *Coming Nation,* December 30, 1893, quoted in Shore, p. 52.

10. Ibid., p. 367.

11. Quoted in Green, pp. 272-73.

12. Jack M. Bloom, *Class, Race and The Civil Rights Movement* (Bloomington: Indiana University Press, 1987). The statistics come from pp. 43 and 49. For a general discussion of the Populist challenge and the Democratic counter-attack, see pp. 37-58. Goodwyn also argues that disenfranchisement aimed at the Populist base. See Goodwyn, p. 536.

13. From "Appearance and Disappearance of the Voter," in Walter Dean Burnham, *The Current Crisis in American Politics* (New York: Oxford University Press, 1982), p. 139.

14. J. Morgan Kousser, *The Shaping of Southern Politics: Suffrage Restrictions and the Establishment of the One-Party South, 1880-1910* (New Haven, CT: Yale University Press, 1974), p. 238.

15. Burnham, p. 142.

16. For a review of this controversy, see Piven and Cloward, *Why Americans Don't Vote* (New York: Pantheon Press, 1988), pp. 78-95.

17. Robert Dinkin, *Campaigning in America: A History of Election Politics* (New York: Greenwood Press, 1991), p. 96.

18. Burnham, p. 142. More generally, see pp. 137-52. See also Piven and Cloward.

19. Quotes from Kousser, pp. 252-53.

20. Our account comes from Ronald Edsforth's excellent study of the creation and recreation of the working class in Flint: *Class Conflict and Cultural Consensus: The Making of a Mass Consumer Society in Flint, Michigan* (New Brunswick, NJ: Rutgers University Press, 1987). The Socialist rise and fall is detailed on pages 54-69. The system of corporate paternalism and the reestablishment of elite-dominated politics are the subjects of chaps. 4 and 5. Edsforth also shows how the Great Depression destroyed this "politics as usual" and gave rise to the mass movement of the United Auto Workers.

21. See Eric Foner, "Why is There No Socialism in the United States?" in William Tabb, ed., *The Future of Socialism: Perspectives from the Left* (New York: Monthly Review Press, 1990), for a good summary.

22. Edsforth, p. 36. Edsforth's second chapter provides an elegant overview of the growth of the mass consumer society in the United States generally.

23. Eric Leif Davin and Staughton Lynd, "Picket Line and Ballot Box: The Forgotten Legacy of the Local Labor Party Movement 1932-1936," in *Radical History Review,* 22, winter 1979-80, pp. 43-63.

24. The term "mainstream" can imply a number of different things. On the one hand, it can describe the large bloc of people who would not consider themselves Left or radical. On the other hand, as used by many political observers, the term often implies that the Left is somehow "extreme" and, hence, inherently marginalized—that given full exposure to both ways of thinking, people would self-consciously choose a more "moderate" establishment agenda. Since many

progressive activists would consider their views to be much more in line with the interests and desires of the vast majority of Americans than the political establishment, I use the term in quotations in order to avoid the second connotation.

25. Kim Moody, *An Injury to All: The Decline of American Unionism* (New York: Verso Books, 1988), p. 96.

26. Samuel Bowles, David M. Gordon, and Thomas E. Weisskopf, *After the Waste Land* (New York: M. E. Sharpe, 1990), p. 149.

27. Institute for Labor Education and Research, *What's Wrong With the U.S. Economy* (Boston: South End Press, 1982), p. 318; Bowles, Gordon, and Weisskopf, p. 19.

28. Richard Flacks, *Making History: The American Left and The American Mind* (New York: Columbia University Press, 1988), chaps. 1-3.

29. In 1992, radical economist Herbert Gintis reflected a similar attitude when he wrote: "There was a time, not too many decades ago, when it was still reasonable to hold that working class revolutions are the likely medium of progressive social change in the advanced capitalist world... That time lies squarely in the past... The issues facing the oppressed in the present and future include nuclear holocaust, environmental destruction, racism and sexism, the exploitation of the Third World, the violation of human rights, and the suppression of national self-determination, among others." His approach assumes that issues related to the material well-being of white working-class Americans have forever been eclipsed by the evolution of capitalism. In short, he argues that the issues of the new social movements have replaced, rather than simply enlarged, restructured, and diversified, the issues of the old. See "The Analytical Foundations of Contemporary Political Economy," in Bruce Roberts and Susan Feiner, eds., *Radical Economics* (Boston: Kluwer Academic Publishers, 1992). For a critique of these arguments, see Rick Fantasia, *Cultures of Solidarity: Consciousness, Action and Contemporary American Workers* (Berkeley: University of California Press, 1988), which explores the dynamics of US working-class consciousness, rejecting notions that they lack such an understanding.

30. Another term for interest-group liberalism is pluralism. This is the name given to the dominant way in which social scientists examine political and social reality. It is identical to the individualistic, interest-group model that we describe above.

31. Obviously not all unions fit this mold. For example, organizing in the public sector often experienced instances of strong militancy. See Leon Fink and Brian Greenberg, *Upheaval in the Quiet Zone: A History of Hospital Workers' Union Local 1199* (Chicago: University of Illinois Press, 1989). In addition, in the major industrial unions the rank and file did not always passively accept the status quo, or corporate attempts to "increase profitability." For an overview of rank-and-file rebellions, see Moody, pp. 83-94. For a discussion of consolidation of "pure and simple" unionism after World War II, see Moody, chaps. 1-3, and Art Pries, *Labor's Giant Step: Twenty Years in the CIO* (New York: Pathfinder Press, 1972).

32. The "middle class" nature of these movements does not always hold true today. For example, the environmental movement includes mobilizations of minorities around issues of environmental racism. On the contemporary environmental movement, see a special issue of *CrossRoads,* no. 20, 1992.

33. For an overview of the so-called New Social Movements, see Carl Boggs, *Social Movements and Political Power* (Philadelphia: Temple University Press, 1986) and Barbara Epstein, "Rethinking Social Movement Theory," *Socialist Review,* vol. 90, no.1, pp.35-66.

34. The women's movement, for example, had elements that could be considered "post-material," while, at the same time, the movement also encompassed those who demanded an equal share of the post-war economic pie.
35. While the origins of the Great Depression remain a subject of debate among economists, the inability of the population to purchase the goods produced by US corporations arguably represented a contributing factor. Bowles, Gordon, and Weisskopf list underconsumption as one of three major causes (see p. 23). See also James Devine, "Underconsumption, Over-Investment, and the Origins of the Great Depression" in *Review of Radical Political Economics Summer 1983,* pp. 1-26.
36. Bloom, pp. 59-87 and 155-86.

Chapter Three: Our Time Has Come

1. I use the term "right-wing" to distinguish the current agenda from its New Deal liberal predecessor. The new agenda is a bipartisan program—being not simply the property of the Republican Party, but shared by the dominant forces within the Democratic Party as well.
2. The term "crisis" is admittedly an overused reference. I employ it here to refer to a situation in which the economy had reached a turning point. It was in crisis because it could no longer continue in the old ways. Indeed, as I argue, the New Deal regime was replaced by a new right-wing program.
3. For both aspects of the declining position of US capital internationally, see James F. Petras and Morris H. Morely, "The Imperial State in the Rise and Fall of U.S. Imperialism," in Arthur MacEwan and William K. Tabb, *Instability and Change in the World Economy* (New York: Monthly Review Press, 1989); Paul M. Sweezy, "U.S. Imperialism in the 1990s," in *Monthly Review,* vol. 51, no. 5, October 1989, pp. 1-17; Giovanni Arrighi, "A Crisis of Hegemony," in Samir Amin, et al., *Dynamics of Global Crisis* (New York: Monthly Review Press, 1982), pp. 55-108; Robert Gilpin, The *Political Economy of International Relations* (Princeton: University of Princeton Press, 1987); and Robert O. Keohane, *After Hegemony* (Princeton, NJ: Princeton University Press, 1984), chap. 8.
4. Bowles, Gordon, and Weisskopf, pp. 75-77.
5. Frances Fox Piven and Richard A. Cloward, *Poor People's Movements* (New York: Vintage Books, 1977); Manuel Castells, *The City and The Grassroots* (Berkeley: University of California Press, 1983), pt. 1, chap. 6; Bloom, chap. 7. For a detailed argument that state welfare programs are intended to control the poor and popular protest, see Frances Fox Piven and Richard A. Cloward, *Regulating the Poor: The Functions of Public Welfare* (New York: Vintage Books, 1971).
6. Bowles, Gordon, and Weisskopf, pp. 72-75.
7. Moody, especially chap. 4, and Mike Davis, *Prisoners of the American Dream* (London: Verso Books, 1986), pp. 121-27.
8. Kevin Phillips, *The Politics of Rich and Poor* (New York: Harper Perennial, 1990), pp. 76, 78-79, and 82-83.
9. For general discussions of the corporate offensive, see Michael Goldfield, *The Decline of Organized Labor in the United States* (Chicago: University of Chicago Press, 1987); Moody.
10. Some of these programs, on the surface, may seem to offer workers greater participation in workplace decisions. Critics, however, have argued that such schemes are intended to foster greater management control and to undermine unions. See Mike Parker, *Inside the Circle: A Union Guide to QWL* (Boston: South End Press, 1985); Mike Parker and Jane Slaughter, *Choosing Sides: Unions and the*

Team Concept (Boston: South End Press, 1988); and Michael Burawoy, *Manufacturing Consent: Changes in the Labor Process Under Monopoly Capitalism* (Chicago: University of Chicago Press, 1979).

11. For a yearly list of the actual number of decertification attempts, see Goldfield, p. 52.

12. Joblessness officially climbed from 5.8 percent in 1979 to 9.5 percent in 1982, the result of what Bowles, Gordon, and Weisskopf have described as a deliberately engineered recession. See p. 124.

13. For a brief overview of the role of unemployment, see Juliet B. Schor, "Class Struggle and the Macroeconomy: The Cost of Job Loss," in Robert Cherry, et al., eds., *The Imperiled Economy, Book One* (New York, Monthly Review Press, 1987), pp. 171-81. For a discussion of the governmental role in the restructuring of the labor force, see Sam Rosenberg, "Restructuring the Labor Force: The Role of Government Policies," in Robert Cherry, et al., eds., *The Imperiled Economy, Book Two* (New York, Monthly Review Press, 1988), pp. 27-38.

14. As capitalism interpenetrated with other forms of domination, its rightward drift was accompanied by specifically non-economic forms of reaction. The pro-life movement is an example. The right-wing program supported efforts to ban abortion, even though, from a strictly economic standpoint capitalists may have an interest in controlling the ability of female employees to have children. On this later contradiction, see Judith Van Allen, "Capitalism Without Patriarchy," in Karen V. Hansen and Ilene J. Philipson, *Women, Class, and the Feminist Imagination* (Philadelphia: Temple University Press, 1990), pp. 292-300.

15. Fred Block, Richard A. Cloward, Barbara Ehrenreich, and Frances Fox Piven, *The Mean Season: The Attack on the Welfare State* (New York: Pantheon Books, 1987).

16. Phillips, p. 88.

17. Clarence Lusane, *Pipe Dream Blues: Racism and The War on Drugs* (Boston: South End Press, 1991).

18. Ward Churchill, "The Third World At Home: Political Prisoners in the U.S.," in *Z Magazine*, June 1990, p. 93-94.

19. Brian Glick, *War At Home* (Boston: South End Press, 1989). The Reagan era also ushered in renewed attempts by the state and private groups to restrict the free flow of information critical of governmental and corporate policies. See Eve Pell, *The Big Chill: How the Reagan Administration, Corporate America, and Religious Conservatives are Subverting Free Speech and the Public's Right to Know* (Boston: Beacon Press, 1984).

20. For a progressive response to such right-wing notions, see Sarah Griffen, "Poor Relations: the Backlash Against Welfare Recipients," in *Dollars and Sense,* May 1992, pp. 6-9; and Steven Wineman, *The Politics of Human Services: A Radical Alternative to the Welfare State* (Boston: South End Press, 1984).

21. See Susan Faludi, *Backlash: The Undeclared War Against American Women* (New York: Anchor Books, 1991).

22. For a discussion of the ideological offensive, especially as it relates to racism, see Sheila Collins, *The Rainbow Challenge* (New York: Monthly Review Press, 1986), chaps. 1-2.

23. While the focus here is on changes in the domestic economy, the economic restructuring of capital has occurred worldwide. See Joyce Kolko, *Restructuring the World Economy* (New York: Pantheon, 1988).

24. For a description of some of their deregulation triumphs, in their own words, see the Republican Party platform in *Congressional Quarterly,* August 20, 1988, pp. 2369-73.

25. For an extensive treatment of the deindustrializing of the United States, see Barry Bluestone and Bennett Harrison, *The Deindustrializing of America* (New York: Basic Books, 1982).

26. At the same time, the Bureau of Labor statistic predicted that services would account for 75 percent of all new jobs created between 1982 and 1995. See Gilda Haas, *Plant Closures: Myths, Realities, and Responses* (Boston: South End Press, 1985), p. 29. According to William W. Goldsmith and Edward J. Blakely, services accounted for 90 percent of all new jobs in the 1980s. See *Separate Societies: Poverty and Inequality in U.S. Cities* (Philadelphia: Temple University Press, 1992), pp. 61-69 and 99. State policies have facilitated this shift. For example, among America's immediate neighbors, right-wing foreign policy has attempted to reduce the barriers to overseas trade and investment through such efforts as the North American Free Trade Agreement. While placed in the rhetoric of free and fair "trade," such agreements are more about investment than trade. They seek to allow US capital the freedom to chase favorable investment climates abroad (cheap labor, low taxes, lax regulations, etc.) and to strengthen the threat of capital flight here at home. See "The Gospel of Free Trade," *Dollars and Sense*, November 1991.

27. For an explanation of how the Immigration Reform and Control Act of 1986 aided employers, see Mary McGinn, "Unions Switch Position on Immigration," *Labor Notes*, June 1992, p. 1. For an overview of women and the US economy, see Teresa Amott, *Caught in the Crisis: Women and the U.S. Economy Today* (New York: Cornerstone Books, 1992).

28. In the words of Harry Magdoff and Paul Sweezy, the relative importance in the US economy of "making money" as distinct from "making goods" has risen dramatically. According to their estimates, in 1950 the financial sector's contribution to the overall Gross National Product equaled 21 percent of the contribution from goods production. By 1985, that had risen to 40 percent. See *Stagnation and Financial Explosion* (New York: Monthly Review Press, 1987), pp. 21-22.

29. Phillips, p. 88.

30. Petras and Morely, p. 44.

31. For a brief overview of the new generation of counterinsurgency and destabilization strategies, see *NACLA: Report on the Americas*, April/May 1986.

32. For a brief analysis of the role of military intervention in the competition between the United States and its Western allies, especially in relation to the recent war with Iraq, see Eqbal Ahmad and Noam Chomsky, "The Strategic Blue Print," in *CrossRoads*, March 1991, no. 8. For a longer version, see Noam Chomsky, *Deterring Democracy* (New York: Verso Books, 1991).

33. Giovanni Arrighi argues that during the post-war boom working-class social power and mass misery separated between the industrialized nations, on the one hand, and the third world, on the other. Today, according to Arrighi, the two conditions are converging as mass misery spreads back to the core countries while working-class power develops in the periphery. See Samir Amin, et al., *Transforming the Revolution: Social Movements and the World-System* (New York: Monthly Review Press, 1990).

34. Lawrence Mishel and David M. Frankel, *The State of Working America: 1992-93 Edition* (New York: M. E. Sharpe, 1993), p. 133.

35. Lawrence Mishel and David M. Frankel, *The State of Working America: 1990-91 Edition* (New York: M. E. Sharpe, 1991), pp. 1-2; Goldsmith and Blakely, chap. 3.

36. John Miller, "Silent Depression: Economic Growth and Prosperity Part Company," *Dollars and Sense*, no.175, p. 6.

37. Mishel and Frankel (1991), p. 130.

38. Chris Tilly, "The Politics of the New Inequality," *Socialist Review*, vol. 20, no. 1, January-March 1990, p. 108.

39. Mishel and Frankel(1991), p. xii; Goldsmith and Blackely, pp. 67-68.

40. Miller, p. 6.

41. Mishel and Frankel(1993), p. 286.

42. Ward Churchill, "The Third World At Home: Political Prisoners in the U.S.," *Z Magazine*, June 1990, pp. 94-95; also Goldsmith and Blakely, chap. 2.

43. Mishel and Frankel(1991), pp. 81 and 161.

44. Tim Wise, "Being Poor Isn't Enough," *Dollars and Sense*, September 1990, p. 11; see also Goldsmith and Blakely, pp. 35-38.

45. Juliet Schor, *The Overworked American* (New York: Basic Books, 1992).

46. Randy Albelda has argued that the so-called crisis of family values raised by the Right is, in fact, a crisis of family and community caused by the economic restructuring. See Albelda, "Whose Values, Which Families," *Dollars and Sense*, no. 182, December 1992, pp. 6-9.

47. Mishel and Frankel(1991), pp. 46 and 143.

48. Frank Clemente with Frank Watkins, *Keep Hope Alive* (Boston: South End Press, 1989), p. 143.

49. As she explained, Jackson supports the working class—"he is for restoring jobs and supporting America." *Post Standard,* Thursday, April 14, 1988, p. C-5.

50. Polls cited in Kevin Phillips, *The Politics of Rich and Poor* (New York: Harper Perennial, 1990), pp. 28-29.

51. Steven Rosenstone, Roy Bahr, and Edward Lazarus, *Third Parties in America* (Princeton, NJ: Princeton University Press, 1996), p. 248.

52. Labor Party Advocates newsletter, April 1993, vol. 2, no. 6, p. 7.

53. The US Bureau of Labor Statistics projects that by the year 2005, 87.5 percent of the new entrants into the labor force will be either minorities and/or women—by then, they will make up nearly half of all workers. For a sample of the new ideas emerging within the ranks of labor in response to this reality, see *Labor Research Review* 20, "Building on Diversity: The New Unionism," spring/summer 1993, vol. 2, no. 1. In responding to the conditions of struggle fostered by contemporary US capitalism, organized labor has increasingly sought coalitions with community groups and other social movements (Jeremy Brecher and Tim Costello, eds., *Building Bridges: The Emerging Coalitions of Labor and Community* [New York: Monthly Review Press, 1990]).

54. For example, labor suffers not simply from a management offensive, but from overt efforts by many individual state governments and the national government to dismantle worker rights and protections. The poor do not suffer simply a hostile economic environment, but also active efforts by government to dismantle the safety net.

55. See Thomas Ferguson and Joel Rogers, *Right Turn: The Decline of the Democrats and the Future of American Politics* (New York: Hill and Wang, 1986). The rightward shift of the Democratic Party has also been noted by scholars who identify with its more liberal side. James MacGregor Burns, et al., *The Democrats Must Lead: The Case for a Progressive Democratic Party* (Boulder, CO: Westview Press, 1992) offers a collection of scholarly essays devoted to the argument that the Party can win by moving to the left. In this collection, an article by William Crotty specifically charts the Party's rightward drift.

56. See Ferguson and Rogers, chap. 1. Our own research into the CBS/*New York Times* polls concerning voter's issue priorities that ran throughout the 1988 primary season support Ferguson and Rogers' findings.

57. Quoted in a campaign position paper in the edited collection by Frank Clemente with Frank Watkins, *Keep Hope Alive* (Boston: South End Press, 1989), p. 63.

58. David Reynolds, *Movement Politics: Grassroots Progressive Political Action As Seen Through Jesse Jackson's 1988 Campaign* (Ph.D. Dissertation, Cornell University, 1993).

59. The individuals who composed the core groups, the majority of whom the author interviewed, came from a wide variety of backgrounds. In terms of race, gender, and sexual orientation, the groups contained a noteworthy mixture. The activist history of the core members collectively encompassed the entire range of post-war social movements with some member's activism stretching back to the Civil Rights movement and earlier. Literally every core person interviewed, in all three regions, pointed to the wide diversity of people who volunteered for the campaign as one of their outstanding memories.

60. Clemente, p. 32.

61. Sheila Collins describes a number of precursors to Jackson's rainbow strategy, including the "Stop Rizzo" movement in Philadelphia, and the mayoral campaigns of Harold Washington in Chicago and Mel King in Boston. See *The Rainbow Challenge* (New York: Monthly Review Press, 1986), chap. 3.

Chapter Four: Beating Big Money and Media

1. Clyde Wilcox, "Financing the 1988 Prenomination Campaigns" in Emmet H. Buell, Jr. and Lee Sigelman, eds., *Nominating the President* (Knoxville: University of Tennessee Press, 1991), pp. 96-98.

2. Schattschneider, p. 101-100.

3. A detailed presentation of the data for Ithaca and Binghamton, as well as an analysis of voter registration patterns, is provided in my dissertation, Reynolds, chap. 7.

4. James Philip Thompson, *The Impact of the Jesse Jackson Campaigns on Local Black Political Mobilization in New York City, Atlanta, and Oakland* (Ann Arbor: University of Michigan, 1990).

5. Curtis Gans, "1994 Congressional Elections," in *Voting and Democracy Report* (Washington, DC: Center for Voting and Democracy, 1995), p. 43.

6. Quoted in Frederick Clarkson, "Christian Coalition: On the Road to Victory?" in *Church and State,* January 1992. For a short overview, see Kate Cornell, "The Covert Tactics and Overt Agenda of the New Christian Right," in *Covert Action Information Bulletin,* winter 92/93.

7. Wilcox, p. 97. Dukakis began the primary season with a much more substantial superiority. By the end of the season, however, his official finances had reached federal limits. This enabled Jackson to close the gap somewhat by the end of the campaign. These figures do not include PAC and other so-called independent expenditures on behalf of the candidates.

8. One campaign organizer kept a complete record of the information on each petition, including who carried the petition, where and from whom they collected signatures, and the dates involved.

9. Michael Robinson and S. Robert Lichter went as far as to argue that the media engaged in a kind of "affirmative-action journalism." They argue that because Jackson was black, "it was obvious all along that the Democrats would not nominate him." The media thus "never went negative with him," since they knew he could not win. See "'The More Things Change...' Network News Coverage of the 1988 Presidential Nomination Races," in Buell, Jr. and Sigelman, pp. 196-212.

10. Ferguson and Rogers have documented the public's adherence to New Deal values in chap. 1 of *Right Turn*. Similar themes can be found throughout the numerous polls taken by Gallop or CBS/*New York Times* during the primary season.

11. *Press & Sun-Bulletin*, April 8, 1988, p. 8A.

12. *Post Standard*, April 18, 1988, p. A9.

13. *Ithaca Journal*, April 6, 1988.

14. *Press & Sun-Bulletin*, April 3, 1988, p. C1.

15. C. Anthony Broh, *A Horse of a Different Color* (Washington, DC: Joint Center for Political Studies, 1987), p. 78.

16. Ibid., p. 80.

17. Charles P. Henry, *Jesse Jackson: The Search for Common Ground* (Oakland, CA: The Black Scholar Press, 1992), p. 108.

18. The poll was taken during March 10-12. See *Post Standard*, March 23, 1988, p. A-8.

19. The poll was taken during March 30-31. See *Post Standard*, April 6, 1988, p. A-8.

20. Referenced in the *Ithaca Journal*, April 20, 1988, p. 2A.

Chapter Five: Building a Party Within a Party

1. Louise Simmons, *Organizing in Hard Times: Labor and Neighborhoods in Hartford* (Philadelphia: Temple University Press, 1994), pp. 44-66.

2. Simmons, p. 1.

3. *Hartford Current*, April 12, 1992, p. A1.

4. Quoted in a debate between Springer and Bruce Colburn of the New Party in Milwaukee entitled "Inside or Outside the Democratic Party," published in *Labor Research Review*, no. 22, p. 94.

5. Ibid., p. 90-91.

Chapter Six: Independent Politics in Vermont

1. In addition to interviews we conducted, progressive state legislator Terry Bouricius generously provided a copy of his monograph, "Building Progressive Politics: The Vermont Story"—a particularly insightful analysis of both the Progressive Coalition's success in Burlington as well as Sanders' election to Congress.

2. The numerical information is taken from Steven Soifer, *The Socialist Mayor* (New York: Bergin and Garvey, 1991), pp. 91-94.

3. Ellen David-Friedman, "Bernie Sanders and the Rainbow in Vermont," in Mike Davis, et al., eds., *Fire in the Hearth: The Radical Politics of Place in America* (New York: Verso, 1990), p. 143.

4. This history is taken from Bouricius.

5. Soifer, pp. 94-100, provides an overview of tenant organizing. We also spoke with an activist who had been involved in these activities.

6. The material for this section comes largely from Soifer's study, supplemented with our own interview material.

7. Soifer, p. 146.

8. Voting information for the 1989, 1991, 1993, and 1995 elections are taken from the campaign coverage provided by the *Burlington Free Press*.

9. As the former co-chair of the organization, Ellen David-Friedman's detailed article, cited above, was invaluable in preparing this section on the Vermont Rainbow Coalition.

10. *Times Argus,* October 23, 1990.

11. In addition to interviews and information from Sanders' Burlington office, in preparing this section we have relied on materials from an article by William Grover, "In the Belly of the Beast: Bernie Sanders, Congress and Political Change," in *New Political Science,* winter-spring 1994, no. 28/29.

12. Press release, Bernard Sanders, July 24, 1995.

13. Congressman Bernard Sanders, floor speech, *Congressional Record,* February 26, 1992, H 622. Quoted in Grover.

14. Ibid., July 2, 1992, H 5832.

Chapter Seven: National Third Party Time?

1. Cornell, pp. 46-47.

2. Quoted in *The Progressive,* April 1996.

3. *New Party News,* vol. 4, no. 2, summer 1995.

4. In addition to interview data, information on the school board race comes from the coverage provided by *Rethinking Schools,* a progressive school reform journal based in Milwaukee.

5. In part, this reflects the legacy of anti-party Progressive Era reforms. To help defeat the growing third party challenges, these turn-of-the-century reformers passed laws that converted elections into candidate- and personality-centered contests that avoided the ideological and comprehensive policy questions raised by the popular political movements. For example, in Wisconsin, non-partisan races were introduced after the 1910 Socialist sweep in Milwaukee.

6. *Rethinking Schools,* winter 1993/94.

7. Nationwide manufacturing employment is down 10 percent from its 1978 high. Seventy percent of the 1.9 million manufacturing jobs lost from 1978 to 1988 came from only sixteen cities: Chicago, Flint, Gary, Hammond, Detroit, Newark, Buffalo, New York, Cleveland, Toledo, Youngstown/Warren, Allentown/Bethlehem, Philadelphia, Pittsburgh, Providence/Warwick, Houston, and Milwaukee (data taken from Sustainable Milwaukee report, p. 9).

8. "How Divided Progressives Might Unite," paper presented to the May 20-22, 1994 meeting at the Highlander Center, p. 39. Copy provided by the New Party.

9. Quoted in *New Party News,* vol. IV, no. 2, summer 1995.

10. Interview by author, May 1995.

11. Quoted in *New Party News,* vol. V, no. 1, winter 1996, p. 6.

12. Quoted in *New Party News,* vol. IV, no. 1, winter 1995, p. 5.

13. Quoted in *New Party News,* vol. V, no. 1, winter 1996, p. 6.

Chapter Eight: Fragments of the Rainbow

1. The monthly magazine *Labor Notes* is dedicated to profiling the thoughts and actions of progressive labor activists. For more information, contact *Labor Notes,* 7435 Michigan Ave., Detroit, MI 48210, 313-842-6262.

2. "The Difference a New Party Would Make," *Boston Review,* vol. XVIII, no. 1, January/February 1993, p. 7.

3. Manning Marable in his introduction to Rod Bush, ed., *The New Black Vote: Politics and Power in Four American Cities* (San Francisco: Synthesis Publications, 1984), p. 3.

4. James Jennings in his introduction to *Race and Politics in the United States: New Challenges and Reponses for Black Activism* (New York: Verso, forthcoming).

5. James Jennings, *The Politics of Black Empowerment: The Transformation of Black Activism in Urban America* (Detroit: Wayne State University Press, 1992).

6. Data on Washington's campaign is taken from Abdul Alkalimat and Doug Gills, *Harold Washington and the Crisis of Black Power in Chicago* (Chicago: Twenty-first Century Books, 1984).

7. James Jennings, "Blacks and Progressive Politics," in Bush.

8. Marable, pp. 8-10.

9. Lusane, pp. 45-47.

10. Quoted in Charlene Spretnak and Fritjof Capra, *Green Politics* (Santa Fe, NM: Bear & Company, 1986), p. 30.

11. Spretnak and Capra, pp. 234-39.

12. The details of various Green efforts are taken from the national publication of the Greens/Green Party USA, *Green Politics*, and the publication of the Green Politics Network, *Green Horizon,* as well as several articles written by Greens published in other places, including: Howie Hawkins, "Green Party Challenges," *Z Magazine*, October 1994; Bill Bradley, "Building the Santa Fe Greens," *Z Magazine,* June 1995; Marcia Wolff, "New Mexico Greens Making History," *Independent Political Action Bulletin,* fall 1994; "Inila-Wakan Electorate Meets Green Horizon," *Independent Political Action Bulletin,* winter 1995; and a paper presented by Anthony Affigne to the 1995 annual meeting of the American Political Science Association in Chicago, August 31-September 3, "Transforming the American Political Landscape."

13. "Electoralism a Diversion from Community," in *Regeneration,* no. 4, fall 1992, p. 28.

14. "Green 'Movement' Unexists: Green is an Electoral Concept," ibid., p. 12.

15. From a November 27, 1995 media release by the Green Party of California.

16. Quoted in an article by John Nichols, "California Dreamin'," in *The Progressive*, March 1996, p. 32.

17. The information for this section comes from an article written by Penelope Whitney and Peter Camejo, "Alliance for Progress," *In These Times,* August 7, 1995.

Chapter Nine: Can We Win?

1. James Madison, Alexander Hamilton, and John Jay, *The Federalist Papers* (New York: Penguin Books, 1987), p. 124.

2. Ibid., p. 125.

3. Ibid., p. 125.

4. "The Mapmakers and Competitiveness," in *Voting & Democracy Report 1995,* published by the Center for Voting and Democracy, p. 51.

5. "Dubious Democracy and the 1994 Elections," in *Voting & Democracy Report 1995,* p. 47.

6. Ibid., pp. 47-48.

7. Amy Dougals, *Real Choices/New Voices: The Case for Proportional Representation Elections in the United States* (New York: Cambridge University Press, 1993), p. 79.

8. Ibid., p. 56.

9. Our discussion of ballot access comes largely from the extensive and thorough material collected by Richard Winger. Specifically, we made use of several

conference papers that he has presented as well as his *Ballot Access News* and direct interviews.

10. Frances Fox Piven and Richard Cloward, *Why Americans Don't Vote* (New York: Pantheon, 1988), pp. 256-59.

11. Bernard Grofman, "Questions and Answers About Motor Voter," in *Voting & Democracy Report 1995,* p. 125.

12. Rebekah Everson, "Motor Voter in the States," ibid., pp. 121-23.

13. Numbers are from: John Bonifaz, "Losing Our Vote in the Wealth Primary," ibid., pp. 130-31; Marty Jezer and Randy Kehler, "Big Money Wins Again," in *Independent Political Action Bulletin,* winter 1995, pp. 11-13; and from the Working Group on Electoral Democracy.

14. Ibid.

15. John Nichols, "Taking the Initiative," *The Nation,* April 22, 1996.

16. Bonifaz.

17. Maurice Duverge, *Political Parties* (New York: John Wiley & Sons, 1963).

18. Charles Derber, *What's Left: Radical Politics in the Postcommunist Era* (Amherst: University of Massachusetts Press, 1995), part two.

Chapter Ten: What Price Victory?

1. Roberto Michaels, *Political Parties* (New York: Collier, 1962).

2. "Redistributing Power in a Changing Economy: Defining a More Modern Militancy," in Steven Langdon and Victoria Cross, eds., *As We Come Marching* (Windsor, CT: Windsor Works Publications, 1995), p. 61.

3. Buzz Hargrove, "Labour and Politics: Rethinking, Redefining, Rebuilding—The View from the Canadian Auto Workers," in Langdon and Cross, pp. 34-39.

4. This sense of betrayal felt among revolutionaries is well conveyed in German journalist Sebastian Haffner's book on the failed German revolution entitled, *Failure of a Revolution* (Chicago: Banner Press, 1986).

5. *Brazil Carnival of the Oppressed: Lula and the Brazilian Workers' Party* (London: Latin American Bureau, 1995), p. 50. See our annotated bibliography at the end of the book for further references on the Workers' Party.

6. Gosta Esping-Anderson discusses this notion throughout his book, *Politics Against Markets* (Princeton, NJ: Princeton University Press, 1985). Similarly, in the midst of the rethinking of the Gorbachev era, Soviet leftist Boris Kargarlitsky developed a path between reform and revolution by reexamining the classic debates with the early socialist movement as well as political practice in both Western and Eastern Europe. See *The Dialectic of Change* (New York: Verso, 1990).

7. See Esping-Anderson, chap. 9, and Jonas Pontusson, "Sweden After the Golden Age," in Perry Anderson and Patrick Camiller, eds., *Mapping the European Left* (New York: Verso Books, 1994), pp. 23-54.

8. For example, Peter Medoff and Holly Sklar offer a detailed and engaging account of Boston's successful resident-run Dudley Street Neighborhood Initiative in *Streets of Hope* (Boston: South End Press, 1994).

9. The French writer Andre Gorz has been a major intellectual figure in Europe who has pushed the concept of a reduced workweek. The essays in his collection *Capitalism, Socialism, Ecology* (New York: Verso Book, 1994) are devoted to examining this issue both in terms of a fundamental crisis of capitalism as well as concrete solutions.

Annotated Bibliography

History of Progressive Politics

Early Years

Colonial and Revolutionary America

Herbert Aptheker's series of short volumes on early US history provides a wealth of easy-access material on political conflict in colonial America and the early days of the republic. See *The Colonial Era* (New York: International Publishers, 1959) and *Early Years of the Republic* (New York: International Publishers, 1976). The American Social History Project's *Who Built America?* (New York: Pantheon Books, 1989, 1992) is an excellent two-volume history of the United States from the viewpoint of ordinary people.

Philadelphia Militia

Steven Rosswurm, *Arms, Country, and Class: The Philadelphia Militia and the "Lower Sort." During the American Revolution* (New Brunswick, NJ: Rutgers University Press, 1987).

Electoral Activity of the Knights of Labor

Leon Fink, *Workingmen's Democracy: The Knights of Labor and American Politics* (Urbana: University of Illinois Press, 1983). In particular, Fink focuses on the story of five communities: Rutland, Vermont; Rochester, New Hampshire; Kansas City, Kansas; Milwaukee, Wisconsin; and Richmond, Virginia.

Women's Suffrage Movement

A voluminous literature exists on the early women's movement and the fight for the vote. A good place to start is Barbara Ryan, *Feminism and the Women's Movement* (New York: Routledge, 1992). The first two chapters provide a good brief overview of the movement and a wealth of references. Eleanor Flexner's *Century of Struggle* (Cambridge, MA: Belknap Press of Harvard University Press, 1979) is a classic account (originally published in 1959 and revised by the author in 1979) of the women's movement up to the winning of the vote.

Populism

The history of populism has been shrouded in controversy. Many early sympathetic portrayals gave way to a scholarly campaign to smear the movement. Books such as Richard Hofstadter's influential *The Age of Reform* portrayed the Populists as a backward-looking, racist, and nativist bunch of ignorant rednecks who stood in the way of the nation's march toward progress. In 1976, Lawrence Goodwyn launched a major reconsideration of the Farmers Alliance and the People's Party. Much of our discussion of the movement comes from his work. In *Democratic Promise* (New York: Oxford University Press, 1976) and the abridged version, *The Populist Moment* (New York: Oxford University Press, 1978), Goodwyn attacked much of the prior scholarship on populism for focusing on what he called a Shadow Movement. In contrast, Goodwyn convincingly argued that the core of populism lay not in the pro-silver effort or the presidential campaign of William Jennings Bryan, but in the cooperative crusade and the grassroots activism of millions of ordinary working people. Goodwyn's book remains the seminal work on the movement. As a staff person for one of the national third parties we researched commented, "That book should be the bible for current activists."

Robert McMath's *American Populism: A Social History 1877-1898* (New York: Hill and Wang, 1993) provides a short and more recent overview with a good annotated bibliography.

Studies of Individual States

A large body of literature provides state and regional studies on the movement that is rich in local details. Three examples are: Scott McNall, *The Road to Rebellion: Class Formation and Kansas Populism 1865-1900* (Chicago: University of Chicago Press, 1988); Barton Shaw, *The Wool Hat Boys* (Baton Rouge: University of Louisiana Press, 1983) on the Farmers Alliance in Georgia; and William Warren Rogers, *The One Calloused Rebellion: Agrarianism in Alabama, 1865-1896* (Baton Rouge: Lousiana State University Press, 1970).

Educational Stategies

Theodore Mitchell's *Political Education in the Southern Farmer's Alliance 1877-1900* (Madison: University of Wisconsin Press, 1987) is a detailed, fascinating, and crucial read.

In Their Own Words

Norman Pollack, ed., *The Populist Mind* (New York: Bobs-Merrill Company, 1967) contains a wealth of material from Populist writings and speeches.

Socialism

General Histories

James Weinstein's *The Decline of Socialism in America: 1912-1925* (New Brunswick, NJ: Rutgers University Press, 1984) is sympathetic to the Right tendency of the Socialist Party. In contrast, Ira Kipnis in *The American Socialist Movement 1987-1912* (New York: Monthly Review Press, 1952) sees the heyday of the Party coming during the prominance of the Left.

Municipal Socialism

Richard Judd's *Socialist Cities* (New York: State University of New York Press, 1989) is an excellent study of municipal socialism, mostly in Ohio. Several collections have also examined the subject, including Bruce M. Stave, ed., *Socialism and the Cities* (Port Washington, NY: Kennikat Press, 1975) and Donald Critchlow, ed., *Socialism in the Heartland* (Notre Dame. IN: University of Notre Dame Press, 1986). For his dissertation in 1943, Henry Gruber Stetler did an excellent study entitled the *Socialist Movement in Reading, Pennsylvania* (Storrs, Connecticut) that is well worth the read.

Socialism in the Southwest

James R. Green, *Grassroots Socialism: Radical Movements in the Southwest 1895-1943* (Baton Rouge: Louisiana State University Press, 1978) is an excellent study that places the Socialist experience within the broader social context of life in the Southwest.

Major Figures

Sally M. Miller, *Victor Berger and the Promise of Constructive Socialism, 1910-1920* (Westport, CT: Greenwood Press, 1973) details the life of a key leader of the Socialist Right. Nick Salvatore, *Eugene V. Debs: Citizen and Socialist* (Chicago:

University of Illinois Press, 1982) profiles this Left Socialist. For the Center, see Norma Fain Pratt, *Morris Hillquit: A Political History of an American Jewish Socialist* (Westport, CT: Greenwood Press, 1979).

Women and Socialism

Mari Jo Buhle, *Women and American Socialism 1870-1920* (Urbana: University of Illinois Press, 1981) examines this long neglected aspect of American socialism.

The Socialist Press

No progressive editor or writer should go without reading about the life and methods of Julius A. Wayland, creator of the *Appeal to Reason.* Elliot Shore's *Talkin' Socialism: J.A. Wayland and the Radical Press* (Lawrence: University of Kansas Press, 1988) provides an excellent presentation. John Graham offers a fine selection of material from the *Appeal* in *"Yours For The Revolution": The Appeal to Reason, 1895-1922* (Lincoln: University of Nebraska Press, 1990).

In Their Own Words

Several works have collected the words of Left Socialists. See Phillip S. Foner and Sally M. Miller, eds., *Kate Richard O'Hare: Selected Writings and Speeches* (Baton Rouge: Louisiana State University Press, 1983) and Jean Y. Tussex, ed., *Eugene Debs Speaks* (New York: Pathfinder Press, 1970). Oscar Ameringer's famous autobiography has been reprinted and provides an entertaining and insightful look into life on the road as a turn-of-the-century Socialist. See *If You Don't Weaken: The Autobiography of Oscar Ameringer* (Tulsa: University of Oklahoma Press, 1983).

Why No Socialism in the United States?

Much ink has been spilled on the question of why the United States has not yet given rise to an institutionalized left-leaning political party similar to the social-democratic, socialist, and labor parties of Europe. Eric Foner provides a short and perceptive overview of this debate in "Why is There No Socialism in the United States?" in William Tabb, ed., *The Future of Socialism: Perspectives from the Left* (New York: Monthly Review, 1990).

The 1930s and 1940s

The Communist Party

For years, scholarship on the CPUSA has been clouded by anti-communism, on the one hand, and self-promotion, on the other. With the end of the Cold War and the decline of old partisan battles within the Left, more recent scholarship has begun to reconsider the early CPUSA. Michael Brown, Randy Martin, Frank Rosengarten, and George Snecker have edited a pathbreaking collection of essays that focus on the movement and culture that developed around the CPUSA entitled *New Studies in the Politics and Culture of US Communism* (New York: Monthly Review Press, 1993). See also Fraser M. Ottanelli, *The Communist Party of the United States: From Depression to World War II* (New Brunswick, NJ: Rutgers University Press, 1991).

State and Local Progressive Efforts

Richard Valelly's *Radicalism in the States: The Minnesota Farmer-Labor Party and the American Political Economy* (Chicago: University of Chicago Press, 1989) is a recent interpretation of this effort. The Weinstein book cited above for a general history of socialism also discusses 1920s' Farmer-Labor efforts.

For an excellent short article that points to the forgotten history of independent labor electoral efforts during the Great Depression, see Eric Leif Davin and Staughton Lynd, "Picket Line and Ballot Box: The Forgotten Legacy of the Local Labor Party Movement 1932-1936," in *Radical History Review*, no. 22, winter 1970-80, pp. 43-63.

The Last Crusade—1948

Curtis MacDougall wrote a massive, blow-by-blow, three-volume study of Henry Wallace's 1948 Progressive Party campaign for the presidency. See *Gideon's Army* (New York: Marzani & Munsell, 1965). For a more recent treatment, see Norman Markwitz, *The Rise and Fall of the People's Century: Henry Wallace and American Liberalism 1941-1948* (New York: Free Press, 1973).

Jesse Jackson's Campaign

The best single book on Jackson's campaign was written by Sheila Collins, *The Rainbow Challenge* (New York: Monthly Review, 1986). Collins, a participant herself, most fully captures the sense of Jackson's campaign as a movement. Unfortunately, the book is only about the 1984 effort. Lorenzo Morris, ed., *The Social and Political Implications of the 1984 Jesse Jackson Presidential Campaign* (New York: Praeger, 1990), and Lusius J. Barker and Ronald W. Walters, *Jesse Jackson's 1984 Presidential Campaign* (Chicago: University of Illinois Press, 1989) both provide a wealth of articles on Jackson's 1984 bid. Adolph Reed, Jr. wrote a severe critique of Jackson's 1984 campaign in *The Jesse Jackson Phenomenon: The Crisis of Purpose in Afro-American Politics* (New Haven, CT: Yale University Press, 1986).

Unfortunately, much less has been written on Jackson's 1988 campaign. The Clemente collection cited below provides a brief overview. Charles P. Henry, *Jesse Jackson: The Search for Common Ground* (Oakland, CA: The Black Scholar Press, 1991) looks at both 1984 and 1988 as does James PhilipThompson, *The Impact of the Jesse Jackson Campaigns on Local Black Political Mobilization in New York City, Atlanta, and Oakland* (Ann Arbor: University of Michigan, 1990).

Two collections provide speeches and position papers from Jackson's campaigns. Roger D. Hatch and Frank E. Watkins, eds., *Straight From the Heart* (Philadelphia: Fortress Press, 1987) is from the 1984 campaign. Frank Clemente with Frank Watkins, *Keep Hope Alive* (Boston: South End Press, 1989) is from 1988. Roger Hatch provides an excellent analysis of Jackson's thinking in *Beyond Opportunity: Jesse Jackson's Vision for America* (Philadelphia: Fortress Press, 1988).

Current Political Efforts

Labor and Labor-Community Coalitions

Jeremy Brecher and Tim Costello, eds., *Building Bridges: The Emerging Grassroots Coalitions of Labor and Community* (New York: Monthly Review Press, 1990) provide an inspiring collection of stories and analysis of labor-community coalitions, both electoral and non-electoral. Included is an article on LEAP.

For a short history of the Great Depression and New Deal era with a critical eye to labor's compromise with the Democrats, see David Milton, *The Politics of US Labor: From the Great Depression to the New Deal* (New York: Monthly Review Press, 1982). Kim Moody provides an excellent overview of the history of the labor movement from the New Deal to the 1990s in *An Injury to All: The Decline of American Unionism* (New York: Verso Books, 1988). In particular, Moody profiles conservative "business unionism" while, at the same time, detailing rank-and-file reform efforts.

Labor Research Review is a highly readable, activist-oriented journal-style publication dedicated to profiling innovative ideas and movements within the labor movement. Issue twenty-two, which came out in late 1994, is dedicated to "Labor and Political Action." The issue covers a wide array of examples both inside and outside the Democratic Party, including the Vermont Progressive Coalition, LEAP, the New Party, and the New Democratic Party in Canada. Write to the Midwest Center for Labor Research, 3411 W. Diversey Ave., Room 10, Chicago, IL 60647. Similarly, the monthly magazine *Labor Notes* is dedicated to profiling the thoughts and actions of progressive labor activists. For more information, contact *Labor Notes*, 7435 Michigan Ave., Detroit, MI 48210, 313-842-6262.

Vermont

Burlington

The Soifer book cited in the section on Local Progressive Governing below provides a detailed examination of the policies of the Sanders' administration. Local activist Greg Guma offers his own sympathetic, yet not uncritical view of the Sanders' years in *The People's Republic* (Shelburne, VT: New England Press, 1989). In particular, Guma gives the Greens' side of their falling out with Sanders over the waterfront development and other issues.

Statewide Politics

Ellen David-Friedman, former chair of the Vermont Rainbow Coalition and now co-chair of the Vermont Progressive Coalition, provides a good overview of the progressive movement's growth in two articles: "Bernie Sanders and the Rainbow in Vermont," in Mike Davis, et al., eds, *Fire in the Hearth* (New York: Verso, 1990) looks at the experience of the 1980s, while "Labor, Democrats, and the Third Way," in *Labor Research Review*, no. 22 (cited above) examines more recent experiences. Although difficult to find, Steven Rosenfeld's *Making History in Vermont* (Wakefield, N.H.: Hollowbrook Publications, 1992) provides one man's personal account of Bernie Sanders' winning 1990 campaign.

The New Party

Aside from a few magazine-type articles in publications like the *Progressive* and *Z Magazine*, little has been written about the still young New Party. Joel Rogers has provided major intellectual support to the New Party's conception of politics. His "How Divided Progressives Might Unite," available from the New Party, provided valuable insights as does his comments in "Reviving American Politics: A Debate on the New Party," in the *Boston Review*, vol. XVIII, no. 1, January/February 1993.

The New Party has teamed up with Open Magazine Pamphlet Series (P.O. Box 2726, Westfield, NJ, 07091-2726). The series publishes short pamphlets written by well-known progressive authors examining a wide range of topics. The company has published a series of "New Party Papers" written by activists involved with the New Party. These include Juliet Schor, "A Sustainable Economy for the 21st Century," Elaine Bernard on "Why Unions Matter," Colin Gordon, "Dead on Arrival" on health care, and Tom Frank and Dave Mulcahey, "Solidarity in the Heartland" on the labor battle in Decator, Illinois.

The Greens

In the vastly under-researched area of independent progressive politics, a relatively fair amount has been written about the Green movement generally and Green parties in particular. J. Michael Ochs has compiled a helpful bibliography of books, academic pieces, and magazine articles available in English on the Greens worldwide. His 1989 effort is a seventy-one page comprehensive list. In early 1995, he put together a much shorter list of ninety-five recent and forthcoming material, mostly books. Both are available from him for a quite modest cost. Write to J. Michael Ochs, 1633 Scott Street, Williamsport, PA 17701-4458.

Europe

Dick Richardson and Chris Rootes, eds., provide a recent country-by-country overview of European Green parties in *The Green Challenge: The Development of Green Parties in Europe* (New York: Routledge, 1995). Another edited collection is provided by Sheldon Kamieniecki, *Environmental Politics in the International Arena: Movements, Parties, Organizations and Policy* (Albany: State University of New York, 1993).

Charlene Spretnak and Fritjof Capra, *Green Politics: The Global Promise* (Santa Fe, NM: Bear & Company, 1986) was an early and popular overview of Green politics written by two Green activists that focuses on the German experience. The book also contains a chapter on the Green movement worldwide and two on the United States. In terms of the German debate, Spretnak and Capra come from a perspective closer to the fundamentalists. By contrast, Andrei Markovits and Philip Gorski in *The German Left: Red, Green, and Beyond* (New York: Oxford University Press, 1993) offer a more academic account that clearly sympathizes with the realists. Markovits and Gorski's book is thorough, up-to-date, and informed by their previous work on the German labor movement. At times, however, the authors display little sympathy for the worldview and politics of the fundamentalists, in particular the ideas of German Green intellectual Rudolph Bahro. Another recent, although expensive, study of the German Greens is provided by Thomas Poguntke, *Alternative Politics: The German Green Party* (Edinburgh, Scotland: Edinburgh University Press, 1993). See also Thoman Scharf, *The German Greens: Challenging the Consensus* (New York: Oxford University Press, 1994), and Gene Frankland and Donald Schonmaker, *Between Protest and Power: The Green Party in Germany* (Boulder, CO: Westview Press, 1992).

United States

Aside from numerous magazine articles, little has been published specifically on Green electoral politics. More commonly, a number of Green activists and intellectuals have written book-length overviews of the Green movement and its ideals that often include sections on electoral activism. *Eco-Politics* (New York: Routledge, 1995) is written by Dan Coleman, a Green Party USA activist in Chapel Hill, North Carolina. In contrast, John Resenbrink, a founder of the Green Politics Network, has written *Greens and the Transformation* (San Pedro, CA: R&E Miles, 1992). Brian Tokar's *The Green Alternative* (San Pedro, CA: R&E Miles, 1987) is a classic.

Black Electoral Politics

Clarence Lusane, *African Americans at the Crossroads: The Restructuring of Black Leadership and the 1992 Elections* (Boston: South End Press, 1994) provides an insightful collection of essays that examine the state of black politics from a wide variety of angles, including changes in black leadership, David Duke, the Los Angeles uprising, and the 1992 elections. As with Lusane, James Jennings, *The Politics of Black Empowerment: The Transformation of Black Activism in Urban America* (Detroit, MI: Wayne State University Press, 1992) highlights the current evolution of black politics and the development of a new empowerment activism. Jennings further explores these issues in his forthcoming *Race and Politics in the United States: New Challenges and Reponses for Black Activism* (New York: Verso, forthcoming).

While written in the mid-1980s, Rod Bush, ed., *The New Black Vote: Politics and Power in Four American Cities* (San Francisco, CA: Synthesis Publications, 1984) still provides a useful analysis of political patterns emerging in Boston, Detroit, Chicago, and Oakland. Abdul Alkalimat and Doug Gills extended their analysis of Chicago in a short book that examines Harold Washington's campaign in detail. See *Harold Washington and the Crisis of Black Power in Chicago: Mass Protest* (Chicago, IL: Twenty-first Century Books, 1984). Most of the works that examine Jesse Jackson's campaigns cited above place their discussions in terms of black politics.

Kofi Buenor Hadjor's *Another America: The Politics of Race and Blame* (Boston: South End Press, 1995) provides a recent and powerful examination of how racism is being deployed not only to blame poor black communities for their poverty, but to deflect attention from corporate economic restructuring and build a right-wing coalition among white voters.

Electoral Campaigning

Howard Reiter's *Parties and Elections in Corporate America* (New York: Longman, 1993) provides a textbook style and comprehensive critique of US electoral politics.

An excellent source for the nuts and bolts of electoral campaigning is provided by Dick Simpson in *Winning Elections: A Handbook of Modern Participatory Politics* (New York: Harper Collins, 1996). Although written from the perspective of two party politics, Simpson is dedicated to grassroots, citizen-driven politics. He speaks from his personal experience, including his own bids for office, as well as such progressive Democratic campaigns as those around Paul Wellstone and Carol Moseley-Braun.

Similarly, Charlotte Ryan provides a guide for activists attempting to use the mainstream media to their own advantage in *Prime Time Activism: Media Strategies for Grassroots Organizing* (Boston: South End Press, 1991).

Larry Makinson's *Follow the Money Handbook* (Washington, DC: Center for Responsible Politics, 1994) provides a detailed guide for following the money trail to find out who is giving what to whom. The book includes a detailed listing of corporate and other group contributions from 1990-1991.

Amy Douglas's *Real Choices/New Voices: The Case for Proportional Representation Elections in the United States* (New York: Cambridge University Press, 1993) offers a detailed argument for proportional representation, including a thorough presentation of the specific systems that can be used as alternatives.

Frances Fox Piven and Richard Cloward's *Why Americans Don't Vote* (New York: Pantheon Books, 1988) discusses the history and origins of non-voting, which is so prevalent in the United States today. Piven and Cloward show how non-voting serves elite interests and how progressives might foster greater electoral participation.

Comparisons to Other Countries

European Social Democracy

Several edited works offer recent overviews of social democratic politics. Frances Fox Piven, ed., *Labor Parties in Postindustrial Societies* (New York: Oxford University Press, 1992) spans Europe, the United States, and Canada. Perry Anderson and Patrick Camiller, eds., provide a country-by-country collection of writings on Left party politics in *Mapping the West European Left: Social Democrats, Socialists, Communists, and Post Communists* (New York: Verso, 1994). A short summary of social democracy is provided by Stephen Padgett and William Patterson in *A History of Social Democracy in Postwar Europe* (London: Longman, 1992). By contrast, Donald Sasson's thousand-page *One Hundred Years of Socialism: The West European Left in the Twentieth Century* (London: I.B.Tauris Publishers, 1996) offers a detailed, blow-by-blow account.

Gosta Esping-Anderson's *Politics Against Markets: The Social Democratic Road to Power* (Princeton, NJ: Princeton University Press, 1985) offers a classic analysis of Scandinavian Social Democracy. Esping-Anderson approached this subject as a New Left intellectual sympathetic to revolutionary perspectives critical of social democracy. His political views clearly evolved as a result of his study. Those wishing to examine how progressive governments can make inroads into capitalist investment decision-making should read Jonas Pontusson's *The Limits of Social Democracy: Investment Politics of Sweden* (Ithaca: Cornell University Press, 1992).

Canada

Elaine Bernard's article in the *Labor Research Review,* no. 22 (cited above) provides a brief overview of the New Democratic Party by a Party activist.

For book-length examinations of the NDP, readers will have to turn to Canadian publishers. Ian McLeod is a journalist who has worked for the NDP. In *Under Siege: The Federal NDP in the Nineties* (Toronto: James Lorimer & Company, 1994), he offers a short and highly readable, sympathetic, but not uncritical analysis of the NDP's crisis. While McLeod tends to lean toward the social-democratic, rather than socialist, side of the Party's political spectrum, he conducted a wide range of interviews for the book and tries to faithfully represent all sides of debates. Books on the federal NDP that provide a longer historical view include: Alan Whitehorn, *Canadian Socialism: Essays on the CCF-NDP* (Toronto: Oxford University Press, 1992); Leo Heaps, ed., *Our Canada: The Story of the New Democratic Party Yesterday, Today and Tomorrow* (Toronto: James Lorimer & Company, 1991); John Richards, Robert Cairns, and Larry Pratt, eds., *Social Democracy Without Illusions: Renewal of the Canadian Left* (Toronto: McClelland & Stewart, 1991); Lynn McDonald, *The Party that Changed Canada* (Toronto: Macmillian of Canada, 1987); and Desmond Morton, *The New Democrats 1961-1986* (Toronto: Copp Clark Pitman, 1987).

Several books were written about the Ontario NDP's disaster by writers on the Left. Since the election loss, more will probably follow. Wayne Roberts and George Ehring's *Giving Away A Miracle* (Oakville, Ontario: Mosaic Press, 1993) critiques the Ontario NDP from the perspective of two authors on the Party's dissent Left. Similarly, columnist and economist Thomas Walkom offers a sympathetic, yet ultimately damning account of the New Democratic government in *Rae Days* (Toronto: Key Porter Books, 1994).

Windsor activists Steven Langdon and Victoria Cross have edited an excellent and thought-provoking collection of essays that explore the future of progressive politics in Canada. While concerned with progressive activism generally, *As We Come Marching: People, Power, and Progressive Politics* (Windsor: Windsor Works Publications, 1994) includes material on the NDP—in particular, a direct critique of the experience by the president of the Canadian Auto Workers union.

Brazil's Workers Party

Emir Sader and Ken Silverstein's *Without Fear of Being Happy: Lula, the Workers Party and Brazil* (New York: Verso, 1991) provides an overview of the Party's development up to the 1989 presidential campaign. Sue Branford and Bernardo Kucinski, *Brazil—Carnival of the Oppressed: Lula and the Brazilian Workers' Party* (London: Latin American Bureau Press, 1995) is informed by Lula's loss in 1994. Their book is also generally supportive of the strategy the Party used that year in trying to appeal to more "moderate voters." For a more academic account of the Party, see Margaret Keck, *The Workers' Party and Democratization in Brazil* (New Haven, CT: Yale University Press, 1992).

The Socialist Experience in France

Several accounts were written in the mid-1980s reacting to the dramatic U-turn of the French Socialist government. See, for example, Daniel Singer, *Is Socialism Doomed?* (New York: Verso, 1988); George Ross, Stanley Hoffmann, and Sylvia Lavau, eds., *The Mitterrand Experiment* (Oxford: Oxford University Press, 1987); and Howard Machin and Vincent Wright, eds., *Economic Policy and Policy-Making Under the Mitterrand Presidency, 1981-84* (New York: Pinter, 1985). Anthony Daley has edited a more recent collection that looks at the long-term impact of Mitterrand's change of course for Left politics in France. See *The Mitterrand Era* (New York: New York University Press, 1996).

Local Progressive Governing

Local governance has a whole literature in and of itself. Below we offer a few samples that provide an entry into this topic.

Steven Soifer's *The Socialist Mayor* (New York: Bergen & Garvey, 1991) provides a detailed account of progressive policy during Bernie Sanders' tenure as mayor of Burlington. For a look at progressive policies during Harold Washington's era in Chicago, see Pierre Clavel and Wim Wievel, eds., *Harold Washington and the Neighborhoods: Progressive City Government in Chicago 1983-1987* (New Brunswick, NJ: Rutgers University Press, 1991). Prior to this edited collection, Clavel wrote *The Progressive City: Planning and Participation 1969-1984* (New Brunswick, NJ: Rutgers University Press, 1986), which details examples from Hartford, Cleveland, Berkeley, Santa Monica, and Burlington. Mike Davis, Steven Hiatt, Marie Kennedy, Susan Ruddick, and Michael Sprinker, eds., *Fire in the Hearth: The Radical Politics of Place in America* (New York: Verso, 1990) covers a variety of local progressive efforts. Joan Roelofs examines the worldwide experience in actual working initiatives built around Green values in *Greening Cities: Building Just and Sustainable Communities* (New York: Bootstrap Press, 1996).

Manuel Castells has done now classic work on urban social movements. His *The City and the Grassroots: A Cross-Cultural Theory of Urban Social Movements* (Berkeley: University of California Press, 1983) is one of his much-referenced early works.

Progressive Economic Policy Ideas

Much of the creative grassroots economic thinking exists as living documents not available as formal publications. Several academics with close connections to social movement activism, however, have written sample progressive economic plans that are a good source to start creative thinking. See Sheila Collins, Helen Lachs Ginsberg, and Gertrude Schaffner Goldberg, *Jobs for All: A Plan for the Revitalization of America* (New York: Apex Press, an imprint of Council on International and Public Affairs, 1994) and Juliet Schor, "A Sustainable Economy for the 21st Century," Open Magazine Pamphlet Series, no. 31 (P.O. Box 2726, Westfield, NJ 07091).

Books on the current economic crisis of working Americans abound. In our examination of the evolution of the US economy, we have used the "social structures of accumulation" framework established by Samuel Bowles, David M. Gordon, and Thomas E. Weisskopf. Their *After the Waste Land: A Democratic Economics for the Year 2000* (New York: M.E. Sharpe, Inc., 1990) not only analyzes the roots of the current crisis, but also offers a progressive alternative centered around popular empowerment. French intellectual Andre Gorz provides a detailed theoretical and empirical case for making a reduced workweek a fundamental part of the Left's agenda in *Capitalism, Socialism, and Ecology* (New York: Verso, 1994).

Gosta Esping-Anderson's book, cited above on Scandinavian social democracy, provides helpful ideas on how "social citizenship" can be constructed. As we discussed in Chapter Ten, the Scandinavian experience contrasts sharply with the US welfare state. Jill Quadagno's *The Color of Welfare: How Racism Undermined the War on Poverty* (New York: Oxford University Press, 1994) provides a comprehensive look at the expansion of the US welfare state during the 1960s. She examines a wide range of policies, both enacted and not, including housing, affirmative action, community action, welfare reform, childcare, and Nixon's proposed Family Assistance Plan—all with an eye toward why US policies never developed into the more comprehensive welfare state found in Europe.

In *Democracy at Work: Changing World Markets and the Future of Labor Unions* (Ithaca, NY: Cornell University Press, 1991), Lowell Turner provides an accessible book comparing the changing nature of labor-management relations within industrial firms. Through a detailed comparison of the auto industry in the United States and Germany, Turner shows how politics and government policy made a critical difference in how unions have reacted to the Japanese challenge. While US unions have been put on the defensive, workers in Germany have used legal mechanisms and precedents in the social-democratic system of co-determination of the workplace to generate pro-worker forms of cooperation.

Interview List

In addition to the actual interviews, we personally visited the main cases studied, and, when possible, attended group meetings and participated in local activism. Below, we identify each person's elected office or staff position, when appropriate, and their residence.

Jesse Jackson's Campaign
Teresa Alt (Jackson, Ithaca)
Billie Anderson (Jackson, Binghamton)
Charles Anderson (Jackson, Syracuse)
Louis Antisdel (Jackson, Tioga County)
Andrew Black (Jackson, Binghamton)
Edward Boncek (Dukakis, Binghamton)
Coert Bonethensius (Tompkin-Cortland Labor Coalition, Ithaca)
Lottie Carpenter (Jackson, Ithaca)
Derreck Carr (Jackson, Syracuse)
Mary Clark (Jackson, Binghamton)
Michael Cohen (Jackson, Ithaca)
Gladys Corduaex (Jackson, Binghamton)
Barbara Daley (Jackson, Binghamton)
Al Davidoff (Nichols, Ithaca)
Margaret Dennis (Jackson '84, Ithaca)
Deborah Dietrich (Dukakis, Ithaca)
Linda Donbrau (Dukakis, Syracuse)
Leo Fergesson (Jackson, Binghamton)
Sylvia Grant (Jackson, Binghamton)
Steven Hertzberg (Jackson, Ithaca)
Gloria Hopkins (Jackson, Binghamton)
Janis Kelly (Jackson, Ithaca)
Holly Levine (Jackson, Binghamton)
Nancy McCarthy (Brown '92, Syracuse)
Laberta McGruder(Jackson '84, Ithaca)
James Morran (Jackson, Binghamton)
Benjamin Nichols (Jackson, Ithaca)
Arthur Rhodes (Jackson, Binghamton)
Alan Rosenthaul (Jackson, Syracuse)
Sara Shenk (Rainbow Coalition, Ithaca)
Stewart Stein (Dukakis, Ithaca)
Jim Testani (Dukakis, Binghamton)
George Torres (Brown '92, Ithaca)
Samuel Valazquez (Jackson, Syracuse)
Isabel Walker (Nichols, Ithaca)
Thomas Warzecha (Dukakis, Syracuse)

LEAP
Marc Caplan (staff, North East Action)
George Christie (staff, Dirigo Alliance)
Tom Colapietro (Connecticut state assembly)
Tim Costello (Jobs Coalition, Massachusetts)
Chris Donavan (Connecticut state house)
Lynne Ide (staff, LEAP)
Dona MacDonell
Merrillee Milstein (union 1199)
Richard Sherman (staff, LEAP)

Vermont Progressive Coalition
Gene Bergman (Burlington)

Terry Bouricius (Vermont state house, Burlington)
Dean Corren (Vermont state house, Burlington)
John Gallager (staff, Vermont Progressive Coalition)
William Grover
Tim Kipp (Brattleboro)
Jane Knodell (Burlington)
Phil Philmont (staff, Congressperson Bernie Sanders, Burlington)
John Wagner (Montpelier)

New Party

Milwaukee

Bruce Colburn (secretary treasurer, Milwaukee Labor Council)
Bill Demsey (staff, Sustainable Milwaukee)
John Goldstein (president, Transit Workers Local)
Steve Heinz
Chuck Hoffman (UAW Local 9)
Tammie Johnson (staff, Progressive Milwaukee)
Barbara Minor (Rethinking Schools)
Richard Oulahan (Esperanza Unida)

Madison

Sheila Crowley (co-chair, Progressive Dane)
Doug Kratsch (co-chair, New Progressive Party)
Stephanie Luce
Merrill Miller (city councillor)
Ron Richardson
Carol Wiedel (co-chair, Progressive Dane)

Elsewhere

Dan Cantor (national staff, New Party)
Peter Shapiro (Maryland)

Labor Party Advocates

Bob Kassen (national staff)
Fred Vitale (Detroit)
Various delegates on the convention floor during the 1996 Cleveland convention

Green Party

Tony Affigne (Rhode Island Green Party, Green Politics Network)
Guy Chichester (New Hampshire)
Dan Coleman (North Carolina)
Klara Fuller (co-chair, New Mexico Greens)
Greg Jan (California Green Party)
Dan Solnit (California Green Party)
Jeff Suter (Regeneration, St. Louis)
Betty Wood (clearinghouse, Greens/GPUSA)
Representatives from fall 1995 Green council meeting (GPUSA)

Campaign for a New Tomorrow

Claire Cohen (Pittsburgh)

Coalitions and Other Efforts

Ted Glick (NCIPA)
Linda Martin (Third Parties '96)
Richard Winger (Ballot Access News)

Where to Find the Groups Covered in the Book

Ballot Access News
Box 470296
San Francisco, CA 94147
415-922-9779

Campaign for a New Tomorrow
[Pittsburgh chapter]
P.O. Box 4953
Pittsburgh, PA 15206
(412) 363-3881

California Peace and Freedom Party
P.O. Box 24764
Oakland, CA 94623
213-385-2786

Center for Voting and Democracy
6905 Fifth Street, NW, Suite 200
Washington, DC 20012
202-828-3062

Green Clearinghouse
(Greens/Green Party USA)
P.O. Box 100
Blodgett Mills, NY 13738
607-756-4211
http://www.greens.org

Green Politics Network Information
c/o Karen Mayo
RFD 1, Box 1528
Bowdoinham, ME 04008

Independent Political Action Network
P.O. Box 5294
Pittsburgh, PA 15206
412-784-1332

Labor Party
P.O. Box 53177
Washington, DC 20009-3177
202-319-1932
http://www.igc.apc.org/lap/

LEAP and Northeast Citizen Action
Resource Center

621 Farmington Avenue
Hartford, CT 06105
860-231-2414

National Committee for Independent
Political Action
P.O. Box 170610
Brooklyn, NY 11217
718-643-9603

New Jersey Independents
P.O. Box 86
Hackensack, NJ 07602
201-447-6886

New Party
227 West 40th Street, Suite 1303
New York, NY 10018
212-302-5053
http://www.newparty.org

New Progressive Party of Wisconsin
P.O. Box 1222
Madison, WI 53701

Sustainable Milwaukee
1726 N. First, Suite 202
Milwaukee, WI 53212

Third Parties '96
Linda Martin, Conference Coordinator
4714 Minor Circle
Alexandria, VA 22312

Vermont Progressive Coalition
P.O. Box 281
Montpelier VT 05601
(802) 229-0800

Rep. Bernie Sanders home page:
http://www.house.gov/bernie/
welcome.html

Working Group on Electoral Democracy
70 Washington Street
Brattleboro, VT 05301

Index

About David Reynolds

David Reynolds works with the Labor Studies Center at Wayne State University in Detroit, where he teaches labor education classes to plant workers. He has worked as a labor organizer for the UAW and holds a Ph.D. in Political Science from Cornell University. His writing has been published in *Solidarity, Dollars and Sense, Z Magazine,* and *Nature Society and Thought.*

About South End Press

South End Press is a nonprofit, collectively run book publisher with over 200 titles in print. Since our founding in 1977, we have tried to meet the needs of readers who are exploring, or are already committed to, the politics of radical social change.

Our goal is to publish books that encourage critical thinking and constructive action on the key political, cultural, social, economic, and ecological issues shaping life in the United States and in the world. In this way, we hope to give expression to a wide diversity of democratic social movements and to provide an alternative to the products of corporate publishing.

Through the Institute for Social and Cultural Change, South End Press works with other political media projects—*Z Magazine;* Speak Out!, a speakers bureau; Alternative Radio; and the Publishers Support Project—to expand access to information and critical analysis. If you would like a free catalog of South End Press books or information about our membership program, which offers two free books and a forty percent discount on all titles, please write to us at: South End Press, 116 Saint Botolph Street, Boston, MA 02115.

Visit South End Press, *Z Magazine*, Z Media Institute, Left On-Line University, and the Chomsky Archive on Z Net at http://www.lbbs.org

Other Titles of Interest from South End Press

Keep Hope Alive: Jesse Jackson's 1988 Presidential Campaign
Edited by Frank Clemente, with Frank Watkins

African Americans at the Crossroads:
The Restructuring of Black Leadership and the 1992 Elections
by Clarence Lusane

Beyond Identity Politics:
Emerging Social Justice Movements in Communities of Color
Edited by John Anner